'An incisive biography w
racy. Indira Gandhi may h

'Stunning original material . . . immediately places this biography above others'
Biblio

'Lucid and eminently readable . . . even-handed in acknowledging sterling achievements but . . . unsparing in criticism' ***Indian Express***

'Racy and gripping . . . an unputdownable book . . . highly recommended'
National Herald

'A great labour; in eight trenchant chapters, with the kind of incisive, often coruscating, commentary that marks her journalism . . . [Ghose] updates the leader's life and afterlife for contemporary readers . . . this is neither hagiography nor a muckraker's account' ***Business Standard***

'"The Great Dictator", a chapter that stretches over almost 70 pages . . . is reason enough to pick up this book . . . Drawing from all possible sources, Ghose puts together Indira's life, the events of which would transform this once frail, uncertain woman into the most formidable politician India has seen' **Rediff.com**

'Ghose does a compelling job of building her narrative and weaves in many charming quotes and anecdotes. There is also sharp analysis . . . an engaging critique . . . a creditable book' ***Open***

'Place[s] Indira in the contemporary context, examining her fraught legacy and identifying the lessons she taught Indian politicians . . . makes for riveting reading . . . cannot be accused of hagiography' ***India Today***

'Ghose has put her facts fairly, highlighting Mrs Gandhi's inner strengths as well as her weaknesses . . . peels another layer from one of the most charismatic, intriguing persons of modern times' ***Tribune***

'Would probably find favour with *House of Cards* fans . . . Ghose offers interesting insights' ***Mint***

'There is sufficient objectivity on many issues, such as the Emergency years . . . the book is written very well' ***New Indian Express***

'A no-holds-barred look at the good, bad, and the ugly of . . . [Indira's] life'
Womensweb.in

Reader Reviews on the Juggernaut App

'Spellbinding . . . a masterpiece' **Sahil Pradhan**

'Vivid, absorbing prose. Balanced in approach; doesn't create a hero or villain out of Indira' **Sameer Chopra**

'Unprejudiced and veering away from hagiography' **Sandeep Radhakrishnan**

'Well written. Mrs Gandhi, enigmatic, brave yet fragile, high-handed yet humane' **Dev Raj Gulia**

'Beautifully written' **Amita Thakur**

'Reveals the true . . . Indira' **Hameed Azar**

'My interest in the central character of this book – Indira ji, arguably the greatest Indian PM ever – rose by leaps and bounds' **Aprameya Rao**

'Fantastic' **TG**

'Thorough and insightful, the book sketches . . . [a] layered, inspiring yet controversial personality' **Amit**

'Thanks for taking me through all that tumult through which India and of course Indira lived' **Md Omer Farooq**

'Well written' **Murali Ellanti**

'Great book' **Amit Acharya**

'Wonderful' **Devbani Banerjee**

'Excellent . . . well-paced' **Mangla**

'Excellent, comprehensive' **Ankur Mutreja**

Indira

India's Most Powerful Prime Minister

Sagarika Ghose

JUGGERNAUT BOOKS
KS House, 118 Shahpur Jat, New Delhi 110049, India

First published in hardback by Juggernaut Books 2017
Published in paperback 2018

10 9 8 7 6 5 4 3 2 1

ISBN 9789386228772

Typeset in Adobe Caslon Pro by R. Ajith Kumar, New Delhi

Printed at Manipal Technologies Limited

For my parents,
who grew up in Nehru's India

Contents

Preface

President Pranab Mukherjee once remarked in an informal conversation that only two people would attract instant crowds even in inaccessible parts of the North Pole: the Pope and Indira Gandhi. In January 2006, a nationwide survey conducted by the political science think tank Centre for the Study of Developing Societies (CSDS) ranked Indira Gandhi as the second most recognized Indian, just after Mahatma Gandhi and ahead of her father, Jawaharlal Nehru. The Father of the Nation is still universally revered, his face is embossed on currency notes and he lends his name to at least one major street in almost every Indian city. By contrast the legacy of Indira Gandhi is much more fraught and contested.

Indira Gandhi died in 1984, killed by her own Sikh bodyguards. Like the Mahatma, she too was assassinated, but where the Mahatma's rallying cry for freedom had once united Indians against the British Raj, Indira Gandhi's combative brand of politics is seen as sharply polarizing. She suspended individual rights by declaring an Emergency in 1975, split the Congress, was accused of subverting institutions and giving democratic India its first taste of dictatorship.

And yet, twenty-two years later, in 2006, she was still firmly etched in the popular imagination, admired and reviled in almost equal measure. Even the man whose approval she sought the most, Jawaharlal Nehru, her beloved 'Papu', was ranked behind her in the poll.

What explains the enduring mystique of Indira Gandhi? Why is it that in remote hamlets of north India senior citizens will succumb to a welter of emotions and memories on hearing her name? Why is it that in villages in south India her portrait is still displayed in homes? Why is it that at her memorial museum in her former home, 1 Safdarjung Road in New Delhi, swelling crowds pour in, in far greater numbers than even to Mahatma Gandhi's memorial, the Gandhi Smriti, or even at his cremation site, Rajghat? Why is it that the Congress even two generations later is forced to turn to her as their passport to relevance at the ballot box?

'Indira-amma' to her devoted supporters south of the Vindhyas, 'Indiraji' in the Hindi heartland, venerated as an avatar of Durga but also vilified as the woman who turned politics into family raj, no other Indian politician has attracted such acutely contrasting responses.

Perhaps Prime Minister Narendra Modi could claim to similarly divide public opinion and his style of highly personalized politics certainly draws on the Indira example, but even Modi has not been able to bridge the north–south, urban–rural and rich–poor divide as only Indira Gandhi, India's original mass leader with the famous despotic streak, managed to do.

Which is why the centenary year of Indira Gandhi is an opportune moment to unravel the many layers that defined the former prime minister's personality and create a portrait of her in the context of present-day realities. Who really was this child of privilege and of struggle who spent her early years surrounded by the towering men and women of destiny who won us freedom, but who in her adult life appeared to turn her back on the democratic idealism that had inspired such great sacrifice from so many? Who was this shy, lonely young woman who was never taken seriously by her political peers – or indeed by her husband and father – but who ended up checkmating her rivals and becoming the most powerful prime minister India had ever seen? Daughter of Jawaharlal and Kamala, wife of Feroze, mother to Sanjay and Rajiv, mother-in-law to Sonia and Maneka, grandmother to Priyanka, Rahul, Varun, but above all Mother to a Nation, Indira Gandhi essayed many roles like an accomplished actor for whom India was a stage.

No other Indian prime minister has experienced the kind of highs and lows that she did. Her leadership in the 1971 war against Pakistan is still held up as an example of formidable courage in the face of adversity, of undaunted spirit and unflinching patriotism in taking on the national enemy. Her rousing election slogan of 'Garibi Hatao' is still seen as a template for politicians seeking to sway the voter with populist rhetoric. By mid 1972, her popularity was at its zenith: the Goddess analogy an apt reflection of the near-divine status she had acquired, especially among the multitudes of the Indian poor.

And yet, in 1977, she lost power. She was defeated by the very same voter who once worshipped her. The imposition of the Emergency in 1975 turned the searchlight on her darker side: the imperious, authoritarian figure who would not tolerate dissent and was a prisoner of her suspicions, insecurities and devotion to her son. That she came back to power only three short years later mirrored how her dominating presence dwarfed everyone else at the time, even when she was in the opposition. She was the original political beneficiary of the TINA (there is no alternative) factor, yet she also had an instinctive connect with people that enabled the kind of spectacular comeback that no other politician has been able to achieve within such a short time of a hammering at the polls.

Few politicians have practised realpolitik with greater ruthlessness and a desire for total control: she was, in that sense, India's original high command leader. And yet, the hankering for power, the near-conviction that she alone knew what was best for India, coupled with a deep insecurity about her own future, meant that Indira Gandhi ended up undermining and destroying the very institutions that her father had so painstakingly nurtured. She split and took over the Congress, won several elections, but ended up destroying the party by making the organization subservient to the individual, and bereft of regional political talent. She was guided by powerful bureaucrats but made the bureaucracy committed and servile to the prime minister's office. While she asserted India's status at the global high table, she also pushed Nehruvian non-alignment into the arms of the Soviet Bloc. She spoke of ridding the country of poverty but allowed her socialist zeal to result in the further impoverishment of millions. She was a passionate defender of secularism but chose to compromise with religious extremists to keep her political rivals guessing. And while she claimed to take the moral high ground on corruption, she ended up creating a system that was soaked in venal, manipulative politics.

And yet, she was a tough, courageous patriot, with a firm commitment to the idea of a strong, self-reliant India, someone who never backed down in a crisis or ever lost her nerve. She may have pushed the country into the darkness of the Emergency, but she also let in a ray of sunshine by voluntarily lifting it. She wasn't a natural orator but it didn't stop her from establishing an instant rapport with large crowds: it was almost as if they could identify with her when she claimed to represent their interests against traditional elites.

Is it any wonder then that from Amit Shah and Narendra Modi to Sonia Gandhi and regional bosses, politicians across the spectrum still refer to the Indira Gandhi playbook?

~

Indira's life can be divided into distinct parts: From her birth in 1917 to India's independence in 1947 when she was the young woman who grew up in Anand Bhawan, the Allahabad home that became one of the hubs of the freedom movement, the girl who had an interrupted education studying in Allahabad, Poona, Santiniketan and Oxford but whose emotions and intellect were uniquely – and obsessively – shaped by her father whom she adored but also rebelled against by marrying Feroze Gandhi, the anti-Jawaharlal. From 1947 to Nehru's death in 1964, she was her father's companion and hostess in the prime ministerial home, primarily a mother and wife, yet someone who perhaps secretly knew that politics was her true vocation, into which she made occasional and determined forays like becoming Congress president in 1959.

From 1964 to 1966 she was a member of Lal Bahadur Shastri's ministry, and from 1966, when Shastri died, to 1971 she was the prime minister who decimated her detractors in the Congress, the grandmaster of political chess who split the Congress and created a new party around her own persona. From 1971 to 1977 Indira went from pinnacle to nadir, achieving dizzying heights of power with a spectacular mandate in the elections of 1971. In 1971 she also became the only prime minister to win a decisive military victory against Pakistan in the Bangladesh war. However, triumph sharply descended into loss of momentum and legitimacy, with the lowest point in her public life being the declaration of Emergency and the subsequent defeat in the 1977 polls.

From 1977 to 1980, Indira Gandhi was the outcast, thrown out from the centre of public life, a place she had occupied as Nehru's companion for seventeen years and as prime minister for eleven. These were her years in the wilderness when she was defeated, harassed and humiliated. Then her last phase, from 1980 until her assassination in 1984, when she returned in an electrifying comeback but never seemed to recover her political instincts and shrewdness, a time when she floundered as fires exploded in Assam and Punjab, her last years marked by violence and conflict until she was killed in 1984 by her own Sikh bodyguards.

~

Growing up in the 1970s, I am a child of the Indira age. By examining her life and times, I seek my own answers as a journalist and a citizen to the troubling questions that have confronted many Indians of mine and other generations. The central question is this: would this country have been very different if Indira Gandhi had not presided over its destiny for two decades? This book seeks answers from close friends, associates and observers to recreate a period that continues to flummox and fascinate. Most crucially, it seeks answers from the main character herself. Indira Gandhi may have died in 1984 but her spirit lives on. In a fanciful attempt at a dialogue with her, I interrogate that ghost of Indira, as any citizen of India might want to do, I ask questions that I imagine citizens would want to ask. The questions I pose in my letters to her are questions that I am convinced many readers would like to ask too.

Four 'what-ifs' suggested themselves to me as I examined her life. First, what if Feroze Gandhi had not died as early as he did? Would Indira, as his wife, have been able to give full rein to her political ambitions? Second, what if Lal Bahadur Shastri hadn't died when he did, would she have abandoned politics and departed from India as she confessed to wanting to do in her letters to the American writer Dorothy Norman? Third, what if she had continued the Emergency instead of lifting it, would India have been a one-party dictatorship today? And finally what if she hadn't been assassinated, would the Congress have limped towards an inevitable waning by the end of the 1980s? After all it was her death that gave new life to her party. Rajiv Gandhi's 400-plus seat haul in the 1984 elections was only an accidental result of her assassination. Did her death hold off the Congress's inexorable decline, if only for a while?

There is voluminous biographical literature available on Indira Gandhi – she's been called the sluice gate from which has flowed a flood of writings. There are at least six major biographies and several other books on her life. All told there are over a hundred books on her, many written by those who knew her intimately or observed her closely. I am not a professional historian and this is not a book bringing to light primary archival investigation. Instead mine is a biographical portrait and a journalistic interrogation of Indira the woman and the politician, which seeks to locate Indira Gandhi in today's context. I try to connect her with India's present and seek answers to questions of dynasty, democracy, religious strife, autocratic leadership and gender equations, questions which are of increasing relevance in contemporary India.

Equally, I tried to excavate Indira the woman – not just Indira the power politician – from the history books. I was looking for a flesh-and-blood person, not just the iron lady, and, in the process, I discovered a young girl both protective of her constantly ailing mother and cowed by her accomplished, haughty aunt. I discovered a teenager struggling to keep up with the expectations of her illustrious and demanding father. A woman torn between an unhappy marriage in Lucknow and the thrill of being near the action and her father in New Delhi. A mother compensating her son for her bad marriage by overindulging him, creating a Frankenstein's monster in the process. And finally a paranoid, battle-weary woman whose survival and political instinct were dulled by personal loss.

For this book I have drawn on Indira Gandhi biographies by Pupul Jayakar, Katherine Frank, Inder Malhotra, Usha Bhagat, Mary C. Carras, Dom Moraes and Zareer Masani as well as on her revealing exchange of letters with her American friend Dorothy Norman. All Indira Gandhi's personal papers are still not publicly available but the two volumes of letters between her father and her, edited by Sonia Gandhi, *Freedom's Daughter* (1989) and *Two Alone, Two Together* (1992), throw a lot of light on her early years. I have also drawn on insightful and detailed accounts by Krishna Hutheesing, P.N. Dhar, Bertil Falk (on Feroze Gandhi), Emma Tarlo (on the Emergency), Vinod Mehta (on Sanjay Gandhi), Pranab Mukherjee, H.Y. Sharada Prasad, B.N. Tandon, Uma Vasudev, Anand Mohan, Janardan Thakur, B.K. Nehru, Kuldip Nayar, K.P. Mathur and Nayantara Sahgal and a host of articles and interviews. The Shah Commission Report remains an important record of the Emergency. A stroke of luck for me was being given a copy of her long interview to Emmanuel Pouchpadass, which I found to be a treasure trove of her views since the entire book is in her own words. I also had the privilege of several long conversations with many who knew her closely, such as Natwar Singh, R.K. Dhawan and Manmohan 'Moni' Malhoutra.

~

Initially, when Chiki Sarkar and Nandini Mehta of Juggernaut commissioned me for this book I was a bit daunted. I'm not an academic, only a rather battle-hardened journalist and column writer who has always been fascinated by the Indira persona. History has always been a passion though. My graduate and undergraduate degrees from St Stephen's College, Delhi, and Magdalen College, Oxford, were in history and I have always loved the subject. Researching Indira's life I felt history's rough magic wash over me once again. Indira came alive to me in technicolour, her life and its secrets suddenly an intimate world next to mine. It is quite fitting that in her centenary year we recall and attempt to understand the intriguing, attractive, powerful and paradoxical woman that she was. It has been a joy to rediscover Indira Gandhi and I hope you, dear reader, will share my excitement in this rediscovery.

1

Death of Indira, Birth of a Legend

On 31 October 1984, Prime Minister Indira Gandhi was shot dead by two of her own bodyguards, both Sikhs. The assassination sparked a bloody anti-Sikh pogrom – the 1984 Delhi anti-Sikh riots – that left thousands of Sikhs dead. Her death came at the end of a tumultuous year in which she had ordered the Indian army to storm the holiest Sikh shrine, the Golden Temple in Amritsar.

~

Dear Mrs Gandhi,

I was in college in Delhi University on the day of your assassination. By mid morning it was clear that something terrible had happened to Indira Gandhi. Your death had still not been officially announced but rumours flew. We whispered disbelievingly to each other, 'Mrs Gandhi has been shot at.' We couldn't bring ourselves to think you might be dead.

Could Indira Gandhi ever die? Could the woman who had stamped her presence on our lives so indelibly suddenly cease to exist? It was unthinkable, preposterous. You were larger than life for us children of the 1970s. You were the perennial figurehead at the prow of India's ship, the constant presence in the citadel.

Did you have a premonition of death? Days before your death you told a friend, 'I am just so fed up with it all.' Had you become frightened, haunted by fears of what your enemies were plotting? Perhaps that's why you, daughter of the agnostic Jawaharlal Nehru, had turned to rituals, temples, shamans and superstitions in your later years.

Four days before your death you had travelled to Srinagar on a trip that was like a pilgrimage. You had visited temples, shrines and sages there. Before your Srinagar trip you had left instructions that when you died your ashes should be scattered over the Himalayas.

Your life came to a dramatic, blood-spattered end, a stark contrast to your quiet, timid entry into politics. Yours had been a life of storm and trouble, as your father had predicted it would. Your epic gory death sealed your legend in a way that a lengthy old age petering into irrelevance never could have.

~

She strode out purposefully that morning. It was 31 October 1984. The next day, 1 November, newspaper headlines would read 'Indira Gandhi Shot Dead, Sikh Security Men Pump Bullets in Chest, Abdomen'. The previous evening, she had addressed a rally at Bhubaneswar and yelled to swelling crowds: 'I am here today, I may not be here tomorrow . . . When I die every single drop of my blood will invigorate India and strengthen it.' Wajahat Habibullah, former Indian Administrative Service (IAS) officer, then director in Indira Gandhi's secretariat, having joined her staff in 1982, was with her in Bhubaneswar. 'That speech sounded as if she was bequeathing India to the people. As if she was saying, I have done what I could, it's now up to you.'[1] The holy man Lakshmanjoo, whom she had visited on her last trip to Srinagar, recalled: 'Death was very close to her.' When he asked her to inaugurate a building, she had replied, 'I will come if I am alive.' After her death, a monk at the Ramakrishna Mission at the Belur Math recalled that Indira Gandhi had written him a similar letter about impending death that October.

Death's grasping hands seemed to be closing in, even if the body remained vigorous. The will was ebbing, flowing searchingly towards the unknown.

The 31st dawned cool and sunlit. She had a packed day ahead. In the morning a TV crew led by actor, columnist and broadcaster Peter Ustinov waited to film an interview. In the afternoon she had a meeting with former British prime minister James Callaghan and then a formal dinner with Princess Anne.

'I met her that morning as she was getting ready for the interview while the beauticians were fussing around getting her make-up done,' recalls Dr Krishna Prasad Mathur, her doctor ever since she became prime minister in 1966 and who called on her every morning without fail. She had always been very fit, the doctor recalls, saying he can't remember a time when she was ever ill. 'Her health was so good that we would invariably end up chit-chatting instead of discussing medical problems. That day I mentioned to her that I had read in *Time* magazine that Ronald Reagan had refused to put on make-up for his TV interviews. She strongly contradicted this and said not only did Reagan wear make-up, he even had an earpiece which prompted answers when questioned by journalists.'[2] Mathur believes she had a feeling her end was near. 'She used to tell me, "I will die suddenly, of an accident."'

A little after 9 a.m. she was ready and walked briskly down the winding path from her home, 1 Safdarjung Road, to her office, the adjoining bungalow 1 Akbar Road, where Ustinov's TV crew waited. A police constable held up an umbrella to protect her from the sun. Behind her walked Rajinder Kumar Dhawan, her personal assistant; behind him strolled her valet and the sub-inspector on duty. She was, as always, immaculately groomed. She had always had a slim, well-maintained figure and that day she looked fresh and elegant, radiating good health. She was wearing a saffron-coloured sari with a black border, matched with dainty black sandals and an embroidered red jhola. Mindful to present a photogenic presence on camera, she was not wearing her bulletproof vest. (She had been forced to wear one because of repeated threats to her life.)

Out of the door she came, past the hedgerows, the lily pond and gardens, towards the wicket gate leading to her Akbar Road office. She took this path every day. As she approached the wicket gate, Sub-Inspector Beant Singh loomed into view. Beant Singh had been a member of her bodyguard for nine years and had even been abroad with her, most recently to London. After Operation Blue Star, when he had been taken off her staff because he was a Sikh, she had made sure he was brought back. She greeted him as she always did: namaste. In response Beant Singh raised his revolver. And aimed it at her.

'What are you doing?' she asked.

Indira Gandhi, pragmatic, commonsensical. Not given to flights of fancy. What on earth is Beant Singh doing, she must have thought, on a day when the golden sunlight had driven away all thoughts of death, when a busy day waited to be organized down to the last detail?

A split second's silence hung in the air. Then he fired. Five shots came at her at point-blank range. Across the lawn from Beant, the young constable Satwant Singh, another Sikh, appeared. Twenty-two-year-old Satwant had just returned from long leave in Gurdaspur, breeding ground of Sikh radicalism. Rooted to the spot, Satwant hesitated nervously. Shoot! shouted Beant. Satwant fired twenty-five bullets from his automatic Sten gun. A mini-cyclone of bullets broke over Indira Gandhi, exploding in almost every part of her petite frame.

'I heard 3 single shots,' recalled Peter Ustinov. 'The people in the office said it must be firecrackers. Then a burst of automatic fire as if attackers were making sure of it. I didn't think she had a chance in hell.'[3]

Dhawan stood stock-still, unable to move. 'I go mad when I think about that day,' he recalls. 'I try not to think about it. By the time Satwant began to fire, she was already on the ground.'[4] Dhawan rushed forward. Other security men began to run towards the bleeding heap that was Indira Gandhi. Beant Singh and Satwant Singh, unrepentant, dropped their guns. Beant said in Punjabi: 'I have done what I had to do. Now you do what you have to do.' Within minutes Beant and Satwant were overpowered by the Indo-Tibetan Border Police who were guarding Indira Gandhi's house. Beant was shot dead that day itself in a scuffle with the guards. Satwant and another conspirator, Kehar Singh, were hanged more than four years later.

Three decades after his grandmother's death, Rahul Gandhi recalled his two friends Beant Singh and Satwant Singh. 'They were my friends. Beant taught me how to play badminton. He once asked where my grandmother slept and whether her security was adequate. He told me, if somebody ever throws a grenade, remember you must immediately lie down. I later understood that Satwant and Beant were going to throw a grenade at her during Diwali.'[5]

The Intelligence Bureau (IB) had been alive to the serious threats to Indira Gandhi's life. R.N. Kao, the former head of the Research and Analysis Wing (R&AW), had been called in from retirement to be her security adviser, and had repeatedly sent out warnings about the presence of Sikhs in her bodyguard. Yet the shocking lack of vigilance in her own security was a reminder of the administrative degeneration that her feudal, personalized and centralized style of government had wrought. There were no proper security and intelligence procedures around her. The prime minister's safety was treated with disgraceful and lackadaisical apathy; the fact that Beant Singh was able to appeal to her directly and get his transfer order from the IB chief rescinded showed how gutted administrative decision-making had become. In spite of the IB ruling that two armed Sikhs should never be together in her compound, Satwant had been able to flout this, simply by insisting that he had an upset stomach and needed to be within the residence's premises. She herself seemed to have become uncaring about the lamentable lapses in her protection. 'When they come to kill me, nothing will help,' she had said with almost helpless fatalism.

The driver of the ambulance stationed at the prime minister's house was away for his tea break so there was no ambulance available. She was bundled into a white Ambassador even as Sonia Gandhi came running down the path, shouting, 'Mummy! Oh my god, Mummy!'

Recalls Sonia Gandhi: 'When I heard the noises [of the shots] I thought it was the last of the Diwali patakas. But something was different. I ran out and saw her body riddled with bullets. We were expecting it. My mother-in-law knew. She had spoken to us about it. She had spoken to Rahul in particular. She had given instructions.'[6]

Sonia, Dhawan and another security man, Dinesh Bhatt, all got into the Ambassador, Sonia cradling her mother-in-law in the back seat as they made for the All India Institute of Medical Sciences (AIIMS). It was morning rush hour, traffic was heavy and they could only inch forward. When they arrived at the hospital, junior doctors on duty realized with a shock who the patient was and top surgeons and physicians assembled within minutes. Continuous blood transfusions were started, surgeons operated on her chest and abdomen, even making a public appeal for blood, which almost led to a stampede among the gathering crowd outside rushing to donate.

At approximately twenty minutes past two that afternoon, Indira Gandhi, three weeks short of her sixty-seventh birthday, was declared dead. The BBC had already announced the news several hours earlier. According to constitutional norms when a prime minister dies in office, another has to be sworn in immediately, as the government ceases to exist. So All India Radio (AIR) was allowed to make the announcement only minutes before Rajiv Gandhi was sworn in as prime minister. 'We regret to announce the death of the prime minister Mrs Indira Gandhi,' came the tremulously formal voice on AIR.

It took the son and heir a few hours to reach Delhi. Rajiv Gandhi rushed back from the election campaign in Bengal and President Zail Singh hastened home from Sana'a in Yemen so Rajiv could be hurriedly sworn in. Rajiv had heard the news on BBC Radio. 'Did she deserve all these bullets?' he had asked his companions in anguish.

In her last years, Indira had made sure that only Rajiv could take her place. By now cabinet colleagues, chief ministers and party men had all been so severely cut to size that she, prime minister, Congress president and leader of the party in the Lok Sabha all rolled into one, had no second in command except her son. At 6.45 p.m. on 31 October, nine hours after his mother was assassinated, forty-year-old Rajiv Gandhi was sworn in as prime minister.

~

Dr Mathur reads out a limerick Indira wrote for him:

> We all know a Doc,
> who works around the clock,
> from backaches to colds,
> he cures all ills,
> with ointment, massage or multi-coloured pills.

'The attack on her was so fearsome that when death finally came she was far beyond any cures that I who had looked after her for twenty years could provide,' says Dr Mathur.

Massive crowds filed past her body as it lay in state in Teen Murti House – the house she had lived in for the seventeen years of her father Jawaharlal Nehru's prime ministership. 'Indira Gandhi amar rahen,' they shouted. Among the mourners another blood-curdling shriek was heard: Khoon ka badla khoon (an eye for an eye).

A pogrom tore through Delhi.[7] Vengeance reared a cobra-like head. Attacks on Sikhs began that evening itself. The entire Sikh community became the target of rage. Sikhs were dragged from buses and trains, doused with kerosene and set alight. Others were pulled from their homes and hacked to death. Menacing groups of 'red-eyed young men' in 'half buttoned shirts'[8] armed with bicycle chains and steel rods and knives prowled the streets.

'Are there any Sikhs in this bus?' one such group called up to a bus among whose passengers sat the writer Amitav Ghosh, then employed at Delhi University. 'There was no anger in their voices; that was the most chilling thing of all,' writes Ghosh.[9] The passengers were collectively shielding a Sikh man under the seats. No, no, they replied, shaking their heads, no Sikhs here. 'Eventually the thugs stepped back and waved us through. Nobody said a word as we sped away down the Ring Road.'[10]

Delhi was inflamed. Shops owned by Sikhs were ransacked and buses burnt. In Block 32 of Trilokpuri, the working-class colony now a byword for the Delhi riots, almost all Sikh males were killed, in the 'the largest ever massacre in independent India in a single block in any city'.[11] Two Sikhs were burnt alive at the gates of the Rakab Ganj gurdwara. A forty-five-year-old mother of three boys, Gurdip Kaur, was stripped and raped in front of her teenage sons, and the boys burnt alive in front of their naked mother even as cries of 'Koi bhi Sikh ka bachcha nahin bachega [no Sikh child shall be spared]' rent the air.

In one of the darkest chapters in the history of India's police, law enforcers looked away; in many instances they were complicit in the violence and refused to register complaints. Instead, the few victims who acted in self-defence were arrested. Although the army was deployed by the evening of 1 November till the evening of 2 November, mass killings, rapes and looting went on for three days, until the evening of 3 November. Witnesses identified Congress leaders Sajjan Kumar, Jagdish Tytler, H.K.L. Bhagat and Dharam Dass Shastri leading the mobs.[12]

Columns of smoke from burning bodies, homes, shops and buses rose up, streaking the clear autumn sky with murderous smudges of death. By the end almost 3000 Sikhs lay dead in Delhi and 50,000 had fled the city. 'If the Gujarat riots happened under the nose of a chief minister, the Delhi riots happened under the nose of a prime minister,' says Manoj Mitta, journalist and author of a book on the 1984 riots.[13] A fortnight after the riots, on Indira's birth anniversary, Rajiv was to say at a rally, 'When a mighty tree falls, it is only natural that the earth around it does shake a little.'

Twenty years earlier, over a million had lined Delhi's roads to say goodbye as Jawaharlal Nehru's funeral cortege passed by, the route becoming the most 'overpopulated area on earth'. For Nehru, crowds had stood thirty deep, 'people on every tree and lamp post'. Thousands had even come for Indira's husband Feroze Gandhi's funeral in 1960, lining the route from Teen Murti to Nigambodh Ghat. Silent crowds had lined the roadside after the death of Indira's son Sanjay Gandhi. But on Indira Gandhi's last journey on 3 November from Teen Murti House to the cremation site at Shantivana, on the banks of the Yamuna (today her memorial at the site is named Shakti Sthal – place of power and strength), her flower-bedecked body towed through the streets in a gun carriage with a galaxy of high-profile mourners including Mother Teresa pacing behind, only a sparse, straggling crowd ran alongside. The city was tense and ominously still.

~

Dear Mrs Gandhi,

What would you have made of the savage riots that broke out after your assassination, almost as if they were a blood-swept memorial service, a ghastly death dance around your lifeless body? It was as if the demons of past wrongs had been summoned up and given licence to wreak havoc. Children killed, women raped, men burnt to death, all of one religious community, all in your name? No, this was not the memorial you would have liked, this pogrom against a religious community that besmirched India's secular image of which you were so proud.

Were the riots not a glaring example of your failure in building a secular India? After the Golden Temple had been stormed by the army, when the director of the Intelligence Bureau had forwarded you a proposal saying all Sikhs should be removed from your security guard you had scribbled on the file 'aren't we secular?'

But you had not managed to create a living, breathing secularism among the people. You had muddied the secular waters by your recourse to 'Hindu' rhetoric in your later years. You adopted the practice of bringing religion into the public space in a manner which no prime minister before you, either your father or Shastri, had done. You paid obeisance to a constitutional observance of secularism but allowed religious symbolism to permeate public life and political discourse.

Your confusing mix of religiosity with doctrinal secularism may have been the result of your aristocratic distance from the people, in spite of being the great populist you were. That you did not wear a bulletproof vest or take your security protocol seriously enough suggests you were still trapped in an India of an older era, when the loyalty of household retainers was taken for granted, when the home was protected by the sheer force of personality of the head of the family, when security guards were quasi family members. You felt safe in this sense of entitlement. In the feudal order of your childhood household, everyone knew their place, no one would dream of picking up a gun.

That was the India in which you, Indira Gandhi had learnt your aristocratic secularism, a secularism instituted through hierarchy, a secularism which had to be daily taught to the heaving masses, as an improving lesson imposed from above, even as you dabbled in superstitions and rituals yourself.

Yes, you knew well the urgent daily need for secularism in India. You had witnessed the torments of Partition, Gandhi's agony at communal riots, Nehru's horror at extremism. Yet the squalid outbreak of religious violence at your death was a raucous, mocking laugh at your vain attempts to create a secular spirit in a country you had ruled for almost two decades.

~

The prime minister destroyed the temple and the temple's faithful destroyed the prime minister. After the assassination, martyrdom enveloped the Indira Gandhi persona. She passed into folklore, becoming someone whose life story is still invoked as national mythology.

Revered, feared, adored and loathed, she became the emblem of the supreme sacrifice, she who ruled as a warrior-queen and then gave her life for the cause of the unity of India. Today, 1 Safdarjung Road is the Indira Gandhi Memorial Museum. Crowds pour in as they do to no other politician's memorial, not even to the Gandhi Smriti. To Indira Gandhi's memorial come people from Tamil Nadu, Karnataka and Andhra Pradesh, from Bangladesh, from Kashmir, from Bengal, women, schoolchildren, old and young.

'She was the queen of India, the ruler of India, there can be no one like Indira Gandhi,' says Thyagarajan, a schoolteacher from Tamil Nadu. Queen of India? But wasn't she the prime minister? 'She was the ruler, the ruler, the head.' Not a mere politician, for them Indira was the emblem, the uncrowned monarch, the embodiment of nationhood. 'Nobody can be like Indira Gandhi,' sobs Anuradha Sinha from Kolkata as she watches a short film at the memorial's screening centre. 'There is no one like her nor can there ever be another Indira Gandhi.'

She bequeathed over 400 seats to the Congress with her death. The 1984 general elections gave the Congress its biggest win in independent India. 'I am the issue,' she had said about the 1971 elections. In the 1984 elections her assassination was the issue. In an act of posthumous forgiveness, Indians converted that election into her memorial. The 1984 election was a funeral procession, when people voted in her memory, a democratic wake that became her remembrance ceremony.

Rajiv Gandhi won a thundering victory because he was Indira's grief-stricken son and citizens rallied to his side because they felt his sorrow was theirs too. Love her or hate her, sometimes the intimate enemy, sometimes the remote monarch, her death bereaved almost all Indians.

She left behind an India with a majority government but an

India bristling with restlessness and rage. From Assam to Kashmir to Punjab, communal and religious tensions began to spiral. Communal tensions were on the boil all through the 1980s, spilling into riots, police brutalities and rising deaths. Her assassination had been heralded by a bloody spree of killings, in Moradabad, Assam, Punjab and in the Bombay–Bhiwandi killings. More riots and killings followed in Meerut and Bhagalpur. The 1980s were a decade bathed in blood but an even greater conflagration lay ahead when the destruction of the Babri Masjid in 1992 would lead to some of the worst riots since Partition across north India and Mumbai.

Secularism and harmony between castes were never more in danger. A rising tide of religious sentiment rendered Nehruvian secularism weak and bloodless as religious conflicts built to a fever pitch tipping over with the Shah Bano judgement in which Rajiv Gandhi's government was accused of 'appeasing' Muslim religious extremism. The setting aside of the Shah Bano judgement led, by way of L.K. Advani's Somnath to Ayodhya Rath Yatra, to the rise of angry Hindutva and the growth of the Bharatiya Janata Party (BJP).

Indira thus left behind a democracy assailed by violent fundamentalism of many hues. Had she become too cynical by the end? Had she readily abandoned her father's ideals to score political points through any means? Had political calculation come in the way of striving for the higher ground? With fires flaming on all sides, she seemed to have run out of firefighting skills.

With violent India taking over from Gandhi's India, her governance methods were only causing greater degeneration in administrative institutions. A massive centralization of authority left her government looking helpless and brutal by turn.

Yet, as Jim Morrison sang, 'death makes angels of us all and gives us wings where we had shoulders, smooth as raven's claws'. To the crowds at her memorial, Indira Gandhi is the byword for ruler. They file past her photos marvelling at her forbidding regality, they gaze awestruck at the black-and-white photos of her life that show a woman who was both tomboy and dowager, sari-clad but ducking under a fence, head covered but with a rebellious glare, the woman who lived in darkness and light.

She had made mistakes, they say, but paid for her mistakes with her life. She had sinned, yes, but in their eyes she had achieved sainthood. She had blundered and subverted but somehow the message had been conveyed that she cared. Her turbulent life had played out before the people in a saga of triumph and doom. She had remained the pivot of politics and for better or worse the definer of Indian public life as long as she was alive. For visitors at her memorial, Indira Gandhi's imperfections only make her more heroic.

She wielded absolute power yet was touched by frailty. She was the authoritarian leader who was somehow vulnerable against her opponents. She was a warrior with a soft voice and tiny frame, the gritty fighter with her head draped in a demure pallu, the paradox a perpetual hit with crowds. That she battled personal grief even as she battled for India continues to endear her to her mourners. Nehru's daughter was of a supremely patrician lineage, the princess who mingled with paupers. This combination of aristocrat-as-people's-messiah was a source of her mystique. She was the memsahib who died like a grimy soldier in the battlefield, her elegant sari drenched in blood.

Indira Gandhi ended the Indian citizen's romance with the Indian state. The love affair of the 1950s between the new nation-state and its citizens, exemplified in the movies of Nehru's time, when newly constructed dams and roads were the backdrop to romance and happy endings, was cut short by her. The Indian state was loved in Nehru's time and hated in Indira's. Above all, secular India had been her life's stated mission and secular India was her life's greatest failure.

Whatever her failures, death gave birth to a legend. The leader was sanctified by sacrifice, and her end became her crowning glory. In the eyes of the people Indira Gandhi gained immortality in a way that she surely would never have as a fading senior citizen nodding over the ebbing of her powers. Born in the fires of a nation about to be born, she went out in the fiery blaze of a nation at war with itself.

2

Revolution's Child

Indira Gandhi was born on 19 November 1917 in Allahabad, the only daughter of Jawaharlal and Kamala Nehru and the granddaughter of Motilal Nehru. She was educated in Allahabad, Switzerland, Poona, Santiniketan and Oxford. Through the 1920s and 1930s, her life was turbulent and unsettled, as she witnessed her family plunge deeply into the freedom struggle. She was extremely attached to her mother, Kamala, who died in 1936. She gained admission to Oxford University in 1937, but after a serious bout of illness abandoned her studies and returned to India.

~

Dear Mrs Gandhi,

What did being born a Nehru mean to you? Did your surname and lineage determine your politics? Being a Nehru meant, first of all, a staunch cultural pride in being Kashmiri. Like so many expatriate communities your family clung tenaciously to its Kashmiri identity, stopping short of identifying as natives of Allahabad – the city of your birth, your family's home.

Your family were not only high-caste Kashmiri Pandits but also rich and upper class, many of its members westernized, sophisticated and blessed with the family hallmark of a 'fierce energy'. Your grandfather Motilal was an immensely successful lawyer, your hero-father Jawaharlal was both a revolutionary and an intellectual, his sisters, Vijayalakshmi and Krishna, were accomplished women and your cousin B.K. Nehru would be a future distinguished diplomat. Mahatma Gandhi, Lal Bahadur Shastri, Sir Stafford Cripps, Eve Curie (the scientist Marie Curie's daughter) and others visited and stayed in your home. Your family was the nationalist and the social gold standard. Pride – and even snobbery – in your lineage was an integral part of your personality.

Did being a Nehru mean a constant awareness of being the best of India, as well as being the best in facing dangers, like being born as the captain of the forces? Did it mean an early initiation in cultivating the traits of leadership? The Nehrus led from the front both in social standing and in the fight for liberation. Being a Nehru, did you always feel that your natural place was in the forefront?

~

Indira Gandhi was born on 19 November 1917 in Anand Bhawan in Allahabad. Anand Bhawan was the home of her highly successful lawyer grandfather, Motilal Nehru, the first home in Allahabad to have running water and electricity. The house also had a tennis court, an indoor swimming pool and a riding ring and was set amid vast, tree-dotted gardens. Motilal presided over this splendid forty-two-room home, waited on by liveried servants and decorated with dazzling artefacts like Sevres porcelain and silver cutlery from across Europe. An extended Nehru clan lived in Anand Bhawan, almost like a royal family. When Vijayalakshmi Pandit once asked B.K. Nehru if 'we Nehrus as a family have been a trifle arrogant', B.K. Nehru replied, 'We have much to be arrogant about.'

Motilal earned handsomely and spent lavishly, once even purchasing a set of Bohemian glasses bought by Edward VII, prompting his wife, Swarup Rani, to complain, 'Who in Allahabad is going to appreciate these and why should we be like King Edward?' Fluent in Arabic and Persian, the language of the Mughal court,

Motilal was an amalgam of British, Persian and Hindu, a template of the plural, secular high culture that the Nehru–Gandhis inherited. He was a self-made professional with the airs of a nawab, who rose from the dusty, crowded, old city to live like a 'grand seigneur' in the more fashionable part of Allahabad. A vital, magnetic personality, Motilal gathered around him a circle of the best talents. 'Motilal of all the Nehrus would have been the most outstanding prime minister . . . where he sat became the head of the table.'[1]

But while Motilal wore Savile Row suits, drank Scotch, ate western food, spoke excellent English and hired English tutors and governesses for his children, Swarup Rani remained defiantly traditional. In complete contrast to her husband, she was a pious and traditional Kashmiri whose meals were prepared in her own vegetarian kitchen. Writes Indira's aunt Krishna Hutheesing, 'Six days a week we ate in the western style, wearing our English clothes and sitting on Victorian chairs . . . on the seventh day or on Hindu festivals we ate in the Hindu manner.'[2] East and West coexisted amicably but separately in Anand Bhawan; rarely did the twain meet.

Motilal and Swarup Rani had three children. The eldest, the dashing Jawaharlal, his father's pride, educated at Harrow and Cambridge, who had been called to the bar in England. Next came Vijayalakshmi or Nanni, a pet name shortened by her English governess to Nan, the vivacious elder daughter. And last, the younger daughter Krishna or Betty. Writes Indira's cousin Nayantara Sahgal, 'Motilal lavished extravagant affection on his daughters . . . but his inviolable love was reserved for his son. He [Jawaharlal] was the focus of the entire clan's attention and concern in a way that princes and heirs often are.' The young Jawaharlal was a little prince. B.K. Nehru recalls Jawaharlal hurling a bottle of jam at his faithful retainer, shouting, 'I asked for marmalade not jam!' As the jam bottle was hurled, 'Hari ran for his life and the bottle hit the wall and broke into little pieces.'

In 1912, Jawaharlal returned to India from Cambridge, 'more an Englishman than an Indian' and, in his own words, 'a bit of a prig with little to commend me'.[3] Over the next two decades he would embark on a dramatic transformation, a journey that the historian Sunil Khilnani describes as an act of 'self-making',[4] the process culminating in his book *The Discovery of India* which he would begin writing while in prison a few years before Independence.[5] Making himself into an Indian, Jawaharlal would make a nation for himself in his mind as he wrote the India of his dreams into existence, a book that demonstrated his conviction that the new nation whose birth was awaited had an ancestor to draw on, that the modern India needed only to build upon an older immemorial one, a book that heralded the final flowering of the 'Indian' Jawaharlal.

When his parents decided on an arranged marriage, Jawaharlal protested but not very strongly. 'Unless there is a degree of mutual understanding marriage should not take place. I think it's unjust and cruel that a life should be wasted merely in producing children.' However, Motilal was a conservative Brahmin by instinct, even though flamboyantly modern in his lifestyle, and arranged a match between his adored son and a suitable girl, the 'little beauty' Kamala Kaul, she of the snowy complexion, lustrous hair and brown doe-eyes. Their wedding, on Vasant Panchami day, was a massive affair, almost a royal court, with a huge tented community set up outside the walled city in Delhi announcing 'Nehru Wedding Camp'.

A year later the birth of Jawaharlal's child was looked forward to with much anticipation. On the thundery night of Indira's birth, family and friends awaited the good news in Anand Bhawan, Motilal and his companions drinking Scotch in the library. At around 11 p.m. Indira's grandmother Swarup Rani emerged from the birthing chamber to announce laconically: 'Hua [it's happened].' 'Bachcha hua? [the child's born?]' repeated Motilal, instantly aware from his wife's dull tone that the child was not a boy and rushing to cover any disappointment with ebullient bluster. The Scottish doctor who delivered the baby beamed at Jawaharlal, 'It's a bonny lassie, sir,' but Swarup Rani snapped, 'It should have been a boy.' Even as some of the gathered women 'pulled long faces',[6] and the crowd signalled that it had been let down with a barely audible sigh, the newborn's grandfather quelled any perceptions that he was unhappy. 'Have we made any difference between our son and daughters in their upbringing?' he chided his wife. 'Do you not love them equally? This girl is going to be worth more than a thousand grandsons,' he declared.[7]

The child was named Indira Priyadarshini, born in the same year as the Russian Revolution which would go on to unseat the tsar, a child of revolution born, as her father would say, into a world of 'storm and trouble'. Indira was to write: 'While my family were not orthodox enough to consider the birth of a girl child a misfortune, it did regard the male child a privilege and a necessity.'[8]

As the firstborn of Jawaharlal, golden boy of the Nehru clan, it was, for an early-twentieth-century Indian family, in the fitness of things that this precious child be male. Perhaps she was always conscious of the disappointment she caused. Her mother often dressed her as a boy in adolescence; she was often mistaken for a boy, and signed some of her childhood letters to her father as 'Indu-boy'. Her grandfather, however, never let her feel that she had been a disappointment. Motilal ordered a special perambulator from London for her and held an extravagant naming ceremony. In fact, Motilal's special fondness for his 'little Indu' was a constant of her early childhood. 'When she talked of her grandfather her eyes used to gleam with happiness and affection, I do not recollect her mentioning her father with the same emotion as she did her grandfather,' writes Usha Bhagat, Indira's social secretary for over three decades.

~

She came into the world just as her family was about to be swept up by Gandhi's call for freedom. Gandhi had arrived in India from South Africa in 1915 and had already met and inspired Jawaharlal by the time Indira was born. He entered the Nehru household 'like a hurricane' and became almost a rival father figure to Jawaharlal, putting paid to any dreams Motilal may have had of his son becoming an Indian Civil Service (ICS) officer or a successful lawyer. Gandhian principles such as khadi, satyagraha, boycott of foreign goods now entered Anand Bhawan, a house which glittered with garden parties and glamorous guests.

'So strong was Gandhi's hold over our family that he even decided what sari I would wear at my wedding,' recalled Vijayalakshmi Pandit. 'It couldn't be anything but khadi, much to my mother's anger. Ba [Kasturba, Gandhi's wife] herself spun a fine khadi sari for me which was dyed pink.'[9]

The Nehrus would soon embark on a radically transformed life. In 1919 the Raj's crackdown on widespread Indian protests against the Rowlatt Act (which snatched away civil rights from Indians) had been brutally repressive. Indian leaders of the protests were arrested. An order was issued that Indian men could not walk but had to crawl down a street in Amritsar on which a British woman had been assaulted. On 13 April 1919 British troops fired, without warning, on a peaceful, unarmed crowd which had gathered for a protest meeting and for annual Baisakhi celebrations at Jallianwala Bagh in Amritsar. Jallianwala Bagh was an enclosed garden. Hemmed in on all sides, the crowd could not escape as troops opened fire. Torrents of bullets slammed into trapped men, women and children. Official figures say 379 died and 1200 were wounded.[10] The only reason the troops stopped firing, scoffed General Dyer, the British commanding officer, later, was that he had exhausted his ammunition. He said he had intended on 'producing a moral effect'. The massacre shocked, enraged and electrified Indians. Even those who had been moderate towards the British now plunged full-bloodedly into Gandhi's campaign. The poet Rabindranath Tagore returned his knighthood. Jawaharlal brought back to Anand Bhawan some of the bullets and empty cartridges he had collected from the Jallianwala Bagh ground. Colonialism's brutal injustices were starkly revealed; mild opposition to the Raj was replaced by surging rebelliousness. 'Jallianwala Bagh was a turning point in our history,' Indira would recall, 'hesitation and doubt were swept aside.'

'Something happened which caused great excitement in the family . . . it was a turning point for us,' Indira would say.[11] Plunging into the Gandhian non-cooperation movement, Motilal gave up his legal practice. Satyagraha and swadeshi became the family's crusade. Foreign goods were boycotted, Gandhian protest wholeheartedly embraced. The carpets, carriages and chandeliers of Anand Bhawan vanished. Foreign silks and Savile Row suits were thrown into a giant bonfire. Taunted by a visitor on why she played with a foreign-made doll, the toddler Indira set alight her favourite French-made doll, watching with a mix of grief, horror and patriotic duty as it melted away. 'The doll was my friend, my child . . . to this day I hate striking a match,' she would confess years later.

The child gazed in bewilderment as an opulent mansion turned almost overnight into a revolutionary hub and site for satyagraha. Scores of family members including her parents would henceforth be regularly hauled off to jail. Being a Nehru was no longer about being rich and privileged, it was now also about being a member of a 'rebel family', of starting to endure the physical and mental toil and hardships of the long fight against imperialism. Indira would recall: 'People in the house left early in the morning . . . in different directions. The whole house was in such a state of tension that nobody had a normal life.'[12] The rebellious streak took strong root in the child Indira, defiance against authority and adversity became an integral part of her personality. 'My grandmother was a revolutionary and she remained one all her life,' says Priyanka Gandhi.[13]

Today, the plaque outside Anand Bhawan reads: 'This house is more than a structure of brick and mortar. It is intimately connected with our national struggle for freedom, and within its walls, great decisions were taken and great events happened.' The rooms continue to wear an elegant old-world look. There are upholstered sofas, carved tables, book-lined libraries, monogrammed crockery sets bearing the initials JN in fancy lettering. Its elaborate domed facade with ornate pillars running down open balconies makes the house look like a cross between Rajasthani haveli and Mughal mahal. Today's Anand

Bhawan, however, is not the original. The Nehru family moved to this relatively smaller but still grand structure in 1929, the year Jawaharlal would inherit the Congress presidency from his father and declare the goal of the Congress to be complete independence or Purna Swaraj. The original Anand Bhawan (now renamed Swaraj Bhawan), the mammoth colonial bungalow where Indira was born, adjoins the new one.

Anand Bhawan's transformation from an epicure's palace to a centre of activism was not without some piquant difficulties. The Mahatma's diktats, particularly on total abstinence from alcohol, weren't easy to live up to. B.K. Nehru writes rather hilariously about how Motilal, who had given up drinking during the non-cooperation movement of 1921–22, restarted it in 1925, convinced that the Bengal freedom fighter C.R. Das had died because of the shock his system received on suddenly being deprived of alcohol upon Gandhian command. Motilal said it was Gandhi who 'killed C.R. Das', his close friend, and had he, Motilal, not quickly reverted to drinking whisky he too would probably already have been dead! Motilal would always remain a sort of rival to Gandhi for the affections of Jawaharlal. India's richest lawyer had not joined the freedom struggle so much for Gandhi's sake as for the sake of his son, to be closer to him, march with him and go to prison with him. As Nehru's biographer Stanley Wolpert writes, it was 'because his son had refused to inherit his lucrative legal practice that Motilal had instead taken up his son's profession of politics'.

Soon the family would actively participate in the Gandhian non-cooperation movement and Khilafat agitation of 1921–22, a movement which marked the beginning of Jawaharlal's political career. It was a time when the entire country seemed on the brink of 'an immensely variegated, disorganized but formidable revolt'. In 1921, the British arrested Jawaharlal and sent him to the first of his several spells in jail. (Jawaharlal would be imprisoned nine times during the freedom struggle, spending a total of almost ten years in jail.) The Indian National Congress had been outlawed. Motilal was also arrested in the same year and jailed for six months for organizing a hartal or demonstration against the visit of the Prince of Wales to Allahabad and for being a Congress member. Four-year-old Indira sat upright on her grandfather's lap throughout his trial in Naini Central Jail, staring unblinking and unafraid at the British magistrate. Sitting in the dock with his grandchild on his lap was Motilal's way of thumbing his nose at British authority, of showing that he considered the proceedings a 'farce', to use his word.

Jawaharlal was then a restless young radical bristling to fight for Gandhi's promise of 'swaraj in one year' and would confess to feelings of 'resentment' and 'demoralization' when Gandhi abruptly and unilaterally called off the agitation after it descended into violence when protesters burnt a police station at Chauri Chaura, near Gorakhpur. Subsequently, the national movement almost broke up, split between 'Swarajists' and 'No Changers', that is, those who opted to participate in elections and those who preferred to focus on Gandhian work in villages. The Nehru men differed on which path the Congress should take, with Motilal, never as enthusiastic about Gandhian satyagraha as his son, even setting up the Swaraj Party in 1923 to contest elections. 'Swaraj within the British empire was nothing,' Jawaharlal would insist, 'our great country must be a free country', even as his father mocked his 'raging tearing propaganda in favour of complete independence'. Jawaharlal felt 'mentally deserted' by his father and stayed aloof from the Swaraj Party's ready plunge into British-permitted legislatures which the Congress had boycotted.

With both men actively involved in their differing political careers, meetings and campaigns overwhelmed life at Anand Bhawan. Jawaharlal was now general secretary of the All India Congress Committee (AICC) while Motilal was busy with his own party, and mealtimes at Anand Bhawan were full of tension. The sense of anticlimax that marked the freedom movement after the abrupt termination of the 1921 non-cooperation movement was soon broken, however, when protests erupted over the all-white Simon Commission's visit in 1927, culminating in civil disobedience across India.

Indira grew up acutely conscious of being a member of the freedom struggle's first family. Gandhi was the saint who roused a people but the Nehrus brought prestige and stature to the cause. Growing up with the Mahatma as a frequent guest and almost a family elder in the grand old house, 'Nehru' and 'Gandhi' were equivalent entities in her mind.

Her family did not in any way shield her from their political activities. She was initiated early into rebellion, her grandfather giving her a charkha when she was five years old. She was grabbed by her tiny hands and, rather like a family of expert swimmers might do with their youngest member, thrown into the deep end and expected to master the family vocation.

~

Another important factor shaped the personality of a strong-willed and rebellious Indira. She bore the Nehru name, but she would stand up to those Nehrus who humiliated her beloved mother, Kamala Nehru, née Kaul. She was ferociously protective of the delicate Kamala, and whenever she saw her mother insulted or neglected by her in-laws, she would take up the cudgels on her behalf and stand guard against her father's family. The Indian prime minister who stood for national self-reliance in the face of powerful warring blocs later in life learnt early the virtues and power of defiance.

Kamala came into a smart, English-speaking, westernized household, herself raised in a traditional Kashmiri family from Old Delhi, not fluent in English, speaking only Hindi, unfamiliar with English-style fine dining or the use of cutlery. She was often insulted and ignored for not being sophisticated, or witty and socially adept. Vijayalakshmi and Swarup Rani, both possessively adoring of Jawaharlal, were not kind to Kamala; instead they were openly condescending and rude. Once when plans were being made to watch an English movie, the family did not invite Kamala, commenting loudly that she would not be able to understand English. A frail, young, introverted yet proud and obstinate Kamala was pushed into bewildered misery, left alone to face the insults as her husband remained preoccupied in the Gandhian movement, and her sister-in-law and mother-in-law competed with her for his limited time and attention.

Vijayalakshmi had always shared a special bond with her brother. They went riding together, read poetry to each other, and for Vijayalakshmi, Kamala was an interloper, an unwanted, unsophisticated outsider who had taken her place at her brother's side. Pupul Jayakar, who had been Indira's friend since they were both girls in Allahabad, writes, 'Both Kamala and Indira felt cruelly excluded by the brilliance and good looks that set her father and Vijayalakshmi apart in the admiring glances of people . . . she [Indira] had been driven into herself by feelings of inferiority, feelings which remained with her all her life.'

'It seems fantastically wrong now that just eight months after his wedding Bhai should insist that [he and I ride in the same car],' Vijayalakshmi would write later. 'Perhaps Bhabi had a valid point disliking me – not for anything I had done but for the obvious oneness that existed between Bhai and me.'[14]

'Puphi', Vijayalakshmi, was thus a source of early heartache. Not only did she make her possessive love for her brother and scorn for her brother's wife plain but her destructive and hurtful words changed Indira forever. When Indira was fourteen she overheard her aunt calling her 'ugly and stupid',[15] a cruel assessment which changed a boisterous and naughty child into an introverted and wary adolescent and tormented her youth. 'The remark shattered something within me,' Indira was to later say, and even a fortnight before her death the remark remained fresh in her memory. She never forgot those words, never forgave her aunt and bided her time for revenge. Indira and Vijayalakshmi continued to 'rub each other the wrong way', Nehru noted later. After Indira's assassination Vijayalakshmi rather disingenuously told Stanley Wolpert: 'I don't understand why she hated me so. I always loved her and treated her as my own daughter.'

Indira's hatred never did abate. In 1970 when Prime Minister Indira Gandhi decided to give Anand Bhawan to the Jawaharlal Nehru Trust (a trust formed after Nehru's death), Indira denied her aunt permission to stay at the ancestral home one last time. She also did not invite her aunt to her younger son Sanjay Gandhi's wedding in 1974. Take that, Puphi!

Vindictiveness and ruthlessness were traits Indira Gandhi often displayed, born in many ways from a constant sense of victimhood and persecution. Rather than rise to a higher level of empathy or generosity as her father did, she often responded out of vengeance. Her fierce temper simmered underneath, she bore grudges and never really forgot or forgave.

In the female universe at Anand Bhawan rife with hostility and resentment, while Kamala grieved and fell ill, Indira learnt to survive and fight. While Kamala's emotional anguish began to take a toll on her health, Indira learnt how to score over intimate enemies at home, taking the blows of family jealousies on the chin. She was often angry at her father for neglecting her mother. 'Do you know what happens at home when you are absent?' she would write angrily to Jawaharlal. 'Do you know that when Mummie was in a very bad condition the house was full of people, but not even one of them went to see her or sit a while with her and when she was in agony there was no one to help her . . . there is some danger in Mummie being left to herself.'[16] She never quite forgave Jawaharlal for his treatment of Kamala; the grudge she bore would surface as rebellion against her father when it came to her own decision to marry.

She became determined to avoid the same fate as her mother. 'I saw her being hurt, and I was determined not to be hurt,' she said later. 'I loved her deeply and when I thought she was being wronged, I fought for her and quarrelled with people.'[17] 'My mother had a special role in my life,' she said, 'she had a very strong character and made a very deep impression.'

In her later years it was Kamala Nehru's portrait that hung next to Indira Gandhi's bed, not Jawaharlal's. On one side was her mother, perpetually frail and ill, and on her father's side, the family radiated energy and purpose. The difference between the 'two sides' became etched in her mind. In fact, while a great deal has been written about Indira's relationship with her father, her relationship with her mother is a trifle less explored. Yet at several points in her life, particularly in moments of weakness, Indira invoked the frailty and vulnerability she saw in her mother, the constantly pure but obstinate victim of evil opponents. In times of strength she was a commanding Nehru, but in times of crisis she was Kamala, relying on spiritual guides, reverting to her mother's model of the solitary, suffering, defenceless woman (who was to later become a staunch feminist and freedom fighter), trying to survive against a range of enemies.

The words used to describe Indira when she was growing up were 'docile' and 'good' but few noticed her fiery spirit. Her aunt Krishna Hutheesing claimed Indira once told her, clutching a pillar with one hand, raising the other, with 'her dark eyes burning', 'I'm practising being Joan of Arc, some day I'm going to lead my people to freedom.'[18] She would tell Dom Moraes, 'I have always been quiet and when I was younger people thought there was no fire in me. But this fire has always been there, only nobody saw it except when it flared.'[19]

She may have appeared 'pale, thin and listless' but she was determined to be a Nehru in all her glory one day. 'My favourite game was to collect as many servants as I could, stand on a table and deliver a speech, repeating disjointed phrases I heard from grown up talk.' Dressed in the boys' Congress uniform of khadi kurta-pyjama and Gandhi cap, she was an androgynous young fighter for the cause. 'My shorts have been made . . . for running and gymnastics. From your loving Indu-boy,' she would write to her father at the age of thirteen,[20] the 'boy' who was no less than a girl, who sprinted, climbed trees and did gymnastics to reassure her father of her fitness for the role he wanted her to play.

Her early identity was more boy than girl, she was Jawaharlal's first child, whose sex was irrelevant, a subtle overture that the exceptionality of her birth and family made her more male than female, a beyond-gender exceptionality that would stay with her all her life. She was not the girl Indira, she was the girl-boy, Indu-boy. She often said she had never thought of herself as a girl or a woman and her identity remained defined by lineage, parentage and later by power rather than by gender.

~

'In India today, we are making history,' Nehru would write to her when she was thirteen, 'you and I are fortunate . . . to take part ourselves in this great drama.'[21] She never forgot that she was living and creating history, all her life recording her views and feelings in notes and letters as if leaving behind explanations for posterity. Nehru never allowed her to forget it either. He was a father who expected her to jump through the hoops of future greatness. 'My father believed in physical exercise and in keeping fit, so I had to run every day and not just run but run with style. He said I must be graceful while running. He was very anxious that I should know how to swim; his method of teaching was simply to push me in and then let me try to get on as well as I could.'

Indira had to read H.G. Wells and about Garibaldi, share her father's passion for history, be constantly fit and not behave like a spoilt, indulged girl. Throughout her growing-up years, Nehru was in and out of jail and wrote to her constantly and lovingly, showering intellectual and emotional effort on her mental and physical development, repeatedly exhorting her to do physical exercise. When she began to take part in the activities of the Vanar Sena or Monkey Brigade set up to bring children into Congress activities, Nehru would write from jail: 'Take care of yourself little soldier boy, also try to stand on your head. Nothing like it.'[22] Kamala's ill health had cut her off from the vigorous pace of life in the Nehru household, had become an obstacle in their marriage and a source of fits of depression for her. It was a fate Jawaharlal wished fervently for his daughter to be free of, himself a fit and active man who detested illness and saw it as a sign of weakness of character.

'Be sure you are quite fit,' he advised her in one of his first letters. 'Not to be physically fit seems to me one of the major sins a person can be guilty of.'[23] He continued: 'I wish you would not allow yourself to grow limp and flabby.' When she was in her early teens, Nehru confided in Vijayalakshmi Pandit: 'If there is one type I dislike it's the languishing type which lounges through life . . . expecting everybody to minister to his or her comforts. Indu has already developed many characteristics of this type . . . (she is) self centred, hardly thinks of others.'[24]

When she was studying in Santiniketan he would demand to know: 'What about exercise? You do not mention any. Don't become like the much-too-lady like Bengali girls who are so delicate and willowy and incapable of hard exercise . . . have a run in the morning.'[25] In other letters he instructed her not to become a 'quarrelsome and disgruntled specimen of society',[26] instructing her to wear frocks and not a sari: 'I am glad you have shed most of your hair . . . and you had better stick to frocks . . . the sari is not a worker's dress, it is a lounger's costume.'[27] Nehru as a constantly teaching, instructing father must have been both boon and bane. She was persistently set on the path of self-improvement by her Papu and he was highly sensitive to her weaknesses. When she was fifteen he was to write: 'I know that Indu is fond of me and of Kamala. Yet she ignores us and others completely . . . she lives in a world of dreams and vagaries . . . I feel she requires a course of field or factory work to bring her down from the clouds.'[28]

Affectionate paterfamilias though he was, he was also determined to bring up his daughter as a laboratory specimen of his principles, a daughter of a movement and an ideology, as much as of a family and a privileged social class. In this, Nehru was perhaps more successful in bringing up his offspring according to an ideological blueprint than Gandhi was, whose own experiments with his children's upbringing, at least in the case of his elder son, sparked only lifelong filial insurgence.

Indira's education took place in fits and starts and she never obtained a formal degree. Yet, ranging from Santiniketan to Oxford, her studies made her intellectually curious and an enthusiast of ideas, if not as cerebral or scholarly as her father would have liked. She was instinctive, quick, observant and well read, but not a practitioner of ideas or a lover of concepts like her father. She was artistic and drawn towards literature, less inclined to history and historical analysis. For Jawaharlal, Indira's education had to conform to the needs of nation-building so she could 'play a brave part in putting brick upon brick in the building of the India of our dreams. I want you to train and fit yourself in mind and body for this engrossing task.'[29]

When she was seven, he insisted on withdrawing her from the British-run St Cecilia's School in Allahabad where Motilal had admitted her, arguing that her presence in such a school violated Congress principles of foreign boycott. Indira was withdrawn from school and taught by home tutors on paternal command, a seven-year-old freedom fighter in the making.

~

She played different roles in her parents' lives: her father's protégée and her mother's protector. She was expected to be her father's star pupil, to scale the great heights of his hopes for her. Yet she inhabited the emotionally lonely world of her mother as her care-giver, determined to wage war against their common foes.

In 1924 Kamala's health, both physical and mental, broke down, after the death of a two-day-old baby boy born prematurely. A son would have boosted her standing with her in-laws and given her the sense of self-worth she lacked. But the baby's death denied her this reprieve. She fell gravely ill, diagnosed with pulmonary tuberculosis, the 'death sentence' of the 1920s. She was admitted to a Lucknow hospital but became steadily worse. 'I am a burden to everybody,' a depressed Kamala would write a year later to Syed Mahmud, Nehru's close friend from Cambridge, a nationalist Muslim who would oppose the Muslim League and remain Nehru's loyal friend. Mahmud was also Kamala's Urdu teacher and she shared a close bond with him. 'I wish my end would come soon.'[30] She would write in another letter to Mahmud, 'When I look at my plight, I think small girls ought to be saved from wasting their lives . . . like me.'

In 1926 the family took a trip to Switzerland so Kamala could be treated by tuberculosis specialists. For most of the train journey from Allahabad to Bombay to board the ship, Indira sat on her mother's lap. Motilal, who was accompanying them, wrote to Jawaharlal, 'I noticed Indu frequently kissed Kamala. This should be stopped. If possible they should avoid hugging each other . . . even perspiration carries germs.'[31] Even as an adolescent she had her thin arms firmly around her diseased, grief-stricken mother and through her life she would be drawn to the role and image of protector of the underdog.

In Switzerland she was enrolled by Jawaharlal into different schools, first L'ecole Internationale in Geneva, travelling by herself at the age of eight between the flat she shared with her parents and her school. 'I did not know a word of French and I knew very little English when I arrived [in Geneva]. My father went off [to meetings with writers and political activists] and left me in a flat with my mother who was not well. I had to deal with the maid, order the food and so on . . . I had to go to the market . . . This is how I learnt French . . . it helped me become more independent.' Motilal would write to his son: 'Indu is a wonderful little girl . . . to make her way in a Swiss town. It is a brave thing to do . . . Dear little Indu is a marvel.'[32] However, she soon fell ill and Nehru, fearful that she would inherit her mother's perpetual sickness, sent her away from Geneva to L'ecole Nouvelle in Bex, two hours away from her parents.

Jawaharlal had taken a year off from politics and father and daughter went skiing and had snowball fights. In 1927, on a trip to Paris, she perched on her Papu's shoulder to cheer uproariously among huge crowds as Charles Lindbergh landed in Le Bourget near Paris after his historic non-stop solo flight across the Atlantic.

The bond between father and daughter was particularly close when she was a child, when Nehru played with her, ensured she learnt how to ski and swim and initiated her into the world as the loving guardian he was, before she began to assert herself against his high expectations and controlling paternalism.

~

They returned to India in December 1927, after Kamala's health had improved, Indira now much more grown-up, independent-minded, fluent in French and a proficient skier. The momentum began to build towards the declaration of Purna Swaraj or full independence, In 1928, protests against the Simon Commission (set up to report on political developments in India and recommend constitutional reforms) rocked many Indian cities,[33] Jawaharlal himself being hammered by British lathis during demonstrations. The popular Congress politician Lala Lajpat Rai was hit on the head during a silent protest march in Lahore and later died of these injuries. The Nehru men again clashed over the future of India. Differences between Jawaharlal and Motilal made the atmosphere in Anand Bhawan explosive. While Motilal favoured dominion status for India within the British empire, Jawaharlal had declared he wanted full independence. Motilal grew impatient with his son. He had often despaired of Jawaharlal's inability to manage money and had always been wary of Jawaharlal's Gandhi-inspired radicalism. B.K. Nehru records Motilal saying he would not leave his money to 'that fool' because he would only give it away and instead he would leave all the money either to Kamala or to Indu. Now latent emotional and ideological differences came to a head and 'relations (between father and son) became so bad that discussion on political subjects was avoided'. In 1928, the weakened Kamala, craving a second child, suffered a painful miscarriage and slipped further into sorrow and isolation.

For Indira, though, it was an exciting time. Tossed around in the flux of events, she had begun to grasp that big, important things were happening around her. She was in the presence of the extraordinary and was expected to pull off feats. As an eleven-year-old she journeyed with the family to the Calcutta session of the AICC in 1928. In her excitement, she suddenly devoured half a dozen bananas at breakfast, surprising her family who knew her as a picky eater. Years later a young boy who had been present on that Calcutta trip, Siddhartha Shankar Ray, grandson of Motilal's old friend C.R. Das, would plant a banana tree outside her window in Calcutta in memory of Indira's banana-eating exploit.[34] She later admitted to Ray it was an attempt to impress those who thought that she looked too weak and insignificant for a Nehru.[35]

In December 1929, the Lahore session of the Congress saw the nationalist movement acquire its star, the knight to Gandhi's sage who famously refused to ride in a bullock-drawn carriage, and instead cantered through Lahore's streets on a white horse. 'For Jawahar, Lahore was more than a political triumph . . . it was a coronation,' writes Nehru's biographer Stanley Wolpert.[36] Cometh the hour, cometh the man, and forty-year-old Jawaharlal it was who, as Congress president, inheriting the post, in hoary dynastic tradition, from his father, gave the call for Purna Swaraj: complete independence. India's flag, the tricolour, was hoisted on 31 December 1929 amid euphoria. While drafting the resolution for complete independence, Nehru made Indira read the first typed copy aloud, telling her after she had done so, 'Now that you have read it, you are committed to it.' 'This thing of being completely free made sense to me,' she would say. After Lahore, Nehru became the prince charming of the nationalist movement, so universally worshipped that in an extraordinary piece of self-criticism and reflection, unprecedented for any politician of South Asia, he would write a self-deprecatory essay in 1937 under the pen name 'Chanakya' in the *Modern Review.* Entitled 'The Rashtrapati', it was scathing about this so-called Rashtrapati and how 'the emotion that his mere smile had roused in the multitude were just tricks of the trade to gain the goodwill of the crowds whose darling he had become . . . the carefully thought-out trickery of a public man'.[37] It was a self-mocking, self-critical article, one that Indira Gandhi, a similar darling of the crowds, would never dream of writing even anonymously.

On 6 April 1930 at 6.30 a.m. off the coast of Dandi, the Mahatma waded into the ocean. He scooped up seawater in a pan and let the water evaporate to make salt. Gandhi had just violated the Raj's salt law. A dramatic civil disobedience movement reverberated through India, the Salt March sending powerful waves of political activism throughout the country. Much to Motilal's astonishment, Kamala shunned her sickbed to lead marches, one of them to picket the Ewing Christian College run by the British in Allahabad. The protest was lathi-charged, and in the scorching sun, surrounded by crowds, Kamala fainted. One of the students of the college who so far had been lounging nearby, looking on with amusement at the protesting women, rushed forward to help Kamala. He was an eighteen-year-old named Feroze Gandhi.

A high-spirited youth who had been a mischievous prankster as a child, he was immediately impressed by the delicately beautiful Kamala, now a fervent activist. He dropped out of college and became a Congress volunteer and began to spend his days in Anand Bhawan with other Nehru acolytes, hero-worshipping both the Nehrus. 'Kamala Nehru opened up a completely new world for Feroze,' writes his biographer Bertil Falk.[38] Feroze was the son of a Bombay-based marine engineer but was adopted and raised in Allahabad by his unmarried aunt Dr Shirin Commissariat.[39] Dr Commissariat was a successful surgeon but Feroze's family was of lower social status than the Nehrus, the family was not well known or particularly illustrious, a fact that would give Feroze a lifelong inferiority complex in his unfolding relationship with the Nehru family and Indira.

Indira was by now an energetic member of the Vanar Sena, a child wing of the Congress. She was the general who commanded her team of vanars, often carrying letters, meals and information for Congressmen in hiding. 'When firing broke out in a village not far from our house . . . we had to go ourselves to these wounded young boys [the protesters] . . . this was my introduction to service. I was 13 or 14 at the time.' She was fourteen years old when at a flag hoisting during the salt agitation, the person hoisting the flag was lathi-charged and arrested. As he was being dragged away, he handed her the tricolour, yelling, 'Don't let it fall.' Don't let the flag fall. No, all her life, Indira Gandhi would not let India's flag fall.

The Raj cracked down on the salt satyagrahis; Jawaharlal was charged with sedition in 1930 and slammed into jail again. In Naini Central Jail he began to work on a set of letters to the thirteen-year-old Indira, which would become the passionately written *Glimpses of World History*. *Glimpses* is an extended history lesson, exploring the rise and fall of civilizations and chronicling the lives of figures like Ashoka and Alexander the Great. It shows how keenly Nehru wanted to make his daughter aware of the greats she should try to live up to, creating for himself and her a roadmap of ideas and values for the nation-in-the-making.

While Nehru was in jail, Kamala too was arrested. She by now had been introduced to a new life. The scorned daughter-in-law and neglected wife had taken up the cudgels for liberation, both of herself and of her oppressed countrymen. She knew well the yearning to be free. She had thrown herself into the independence struggle as freedom fighter and organizer and when she was arrested in 1931 it was a triumph for Indira. It marked Kamala's coming of age as her father's comrade, a woman who as the freedom movement progressed became an energetic campaigner. A new respect for Kamala would be born in her in-laws. Krishna Hutheesing writes: 'With unflinching courage Kamala confronted everything smilingly . . . when Jawahar dedicated his life to his country, Kamala did not hesitate to fall in behind him. If India ever had a super-soldier, that soldier was Kamala.'[40] The newly rejuvenated mother would write from jail to her proud daughter a letter that echoed with their tender, mutually protective bond: 'Whenever I go outside the barrack for a stroll I think of you. When I am released we shall go out for walks though that will be six months away, but six months will pass without you or I feeling it.' Kamala would begin her letter with 'Love to Induji',[41] the honorific 'ji' normally reserved for an elder.

'People know my grandfather and father but a more important part was played by my mother,' said Indira; '. . . when my father wanted to join Gandhiji the whole family was against it. It was only my mother's courageous and persistent support which enabled him to take such a big step which made such a difference to the history of India.'

Indira was keen to establish her mother's identity as a freedom fighter in her own right, not just an appendage of her father. 'My mother was a convinced feminist, a position which I didn't understand then because I could do what I liked . . . it didn't make a difference whether I was a boy or a girl . . . My father . . . would receive indignant letters from husbands, saying your wife has been provoking our women.' She would always put her parents on equal terms, as if elevating Kamala to her rightful place in history was her duty. 'I'm the daughter of an extraordinary man and an exceptional woman,' she would say.

~

On 6 February 1931 Motilal Nehru died. His was the first death in Indira's life, one which left her 'stunned'. She lost a champion. Motilal was the kind of robust, large-hearted, masterful man Indira was always instinctively more drawn to than her more refined father. The improving, assessing eyes of Jawaharlal were in contrast to the ready, open, generously pampering love she had received from Motilal.

In May 1931, on the Mahatma's suggestion, Indira was sent away from Allahabad to join the Pupil's Own School in Poona run by the Oxford-educated socialist Jehangir Vakil and his wife, Coonverbai, from where she completed her schooling with mediocre grades. She was unhappy in Poona, haunted by her aunt's devastating remark, worried about her mother left alone amid family strife in Anand Bhawan. Distraught at being torn away from Kamala, she escaped into nature, finding solace in the ancient trees in the school compound. All her life, she would turn to trees and forests to escape her woes. The cathedrals of green drew her in with their whispered wind songs and misty caresses and protected her in their fragrant, abundant shade. 'From childhood I looked upon trees as a life giving refuge,' she said.[42] Jawaharlal would write to her: 'None of us, least of all you, has any business to be depressed and to look it. It is easy enough to smile when everything is right. But when everything is not all right? So, cara mia . . .'[43] After her matriculation she enrolled in Santiniketan in 1934, the unconventional university set up in idyllic surroundings by Rabindranath Tagore. Nehru's letter to the Santiniketan authorities which accompanied Indira's arrival is revealing of the minute care he took over her education: 'Her parents would like her to specialise in some subject . . . which would make her economically independent, not depend for her sustenance on a husband . . . she has a vague desire of doing social or public work . . . but special knowledge is necessary in a special subject . . . absence of physical exercise usually makes her languid and seedy.'[44]

Indira did not complete her studies at Santiniketan, yet Tagore became a seminal influence in her life inasmuch as she had any intellectual influencers apart from her father and later her husband. Tagore's poetry, which often spoke of the soul's yearning for freedom and the divine, appealed to her artistically inclined mind. She thought of 'Gurudev' as the clearest articulation of India's values and culture, proud of being Indian yet the universal man, concerned not just with narrow culture but with freedom and humanism. 'My father expressed the same idea, that no one could be international unless they were intensely national . . . all his [Tagore's] ideas and attempts were to lift the human being to a higher level.' At Santiniketan, she felt that the 'bitterness and hatred I had accumulated was washed out',[45] and she was able to glimpse an entirely new world of artistic and poetic striving and gain a literary and musical enthusiasm that she had missed before.

While Indira was at Santiniketan, Kamala fell ill again and in 1934 she, together with Kamala's cousin and personal physician Dr Madan Atal, accompanied her mother first to a tuberculosis hospital in Bhowali, then in 1935 to a sanatorium in Badenweiler in Germany and finally to the Clinique Sylvana in Lausanne in Switzerland where, on 28 February 1936, Kamala died. Eighteen-year-old Indira was left with a wound that never healed. Kamala, who had become profoundly religious and even taken a vow of celibacy in the last years of her life, remained an embodiment of purity for Indira. '[My mother] was young and pure . . . a beautiful picture of youth and purity.'[46] Kamala's ardent, nun-like purity remained a moral touchstone and an inspiration for Indira's own later religiosity. Although she once referred to her father as a saint, it was Kamala who for her was the epitome of saintliness in a way her father never quite was.

Heartbroken and numb, Indira, for the next five years, 'bent her will and her intellect to living out Jawaharlal's dream'.[47] Even before Kamala's death she had been preparing to take the entrance exams to Oxford University. Four months after her mother's death, she took the demanding seven-hour entrance exams to Somerville College, failing in her first and second attempts but passing in her third, repeatedly thwarted by her lack of proficiency in Latin, a subject she loathed. She had taken admission at Badminton School near Bristol, an academically rigorous British public school for girls, to prepare for the Oxford entrance examinations. Iris Murdoch, the celebrated novelist, also then a student at Badminton, remembers her as unhappy, lonely and uncertain about the future.[48] Her life wasn't entirely unhappy though. Feroze Gandhi, who had faithfully even turned up to visit the Nehrus when Kamala was in the Badenweiler clinic, was studying at the London School of Economics (LSE) at this time and Indira, Feroze and their friend Shanta Gandhi often stepped out into London for concerts and plays, even going in search of paan.

~

Indira joined Somerville College as part of the class of 1937. She would later insist it was her own decision to go to Oxford and not her father's. 'The decision to go to Oxford (and not the Sorbonne) was mine eventually. I don't think my father had much to do with it . . . One reason for choosing Oxford was that Feroze was in England . . . I considered him more as a friend . . . a link with the family and with India. During the whole time I was in Oxford I was intensely involved in everything but my studies.'

By the time she joined Oxford, she had become romantically involved with Feroze. 'I myself was once young and deeply in love,' she would say to Sonia Gandhi years later when meeting her for the first time as Rajiv's fiancée.[49] Although Feroze had proposed to her several times in the past, she finally said yes in Paris. In 1937 on her way to join Somerville, she had met Feroze in Paris and he had proposed to her on the steps of the Sacré-Coeur Basilica in Montmartre. Paris was, in her words, 'bathed in soft sunshine and the heart was young and gay . . . we ourselves were young and in love'.[50]

Feroze had first proposed to Indira when she was only sixteen, but Kamala had insisted that her daughter was too young to marry. For Feroze, Indira was the daughter of his adored Nehrus and he was as drawn to what she represented as much as he was to her. Ironically it would be her family and her life within it that would later become the source of Feroze's emotional troubles.

Feroze's aunt Dr Commissariat had agreed to finance his studies at the LSE only because she thought it would take him away from his obsession with the Nehrus.[51] But Indira and Feroze were never closer than at this time and she was split between two worlds, trying to live out her father's expectations to become an Oxford graduate but becoming drawn more powerfully to the activist life with Feroze in London. With Feroze she became actively involved in the India League, a radical organization agitating for Indian independence in Britain, led by the brilliant, brooding V.K. Krishna Menon, barrister, publisher and public intellectual. Nehru's mind had already been 'captured by Krishna Menon', he was Jawaharlal's 'darker skinned, gaunt, ugly' but fiercely intelligent soulmate. Once when Menon unexpectedly asked her to address a gathering, she acquitted herself so badly that someone in the audience shouted, 'She doesn't speak, she squeaks!'[52] It's a story she often told with a laugh while she was prime minister, by when she could hold a crowd rapt and engaged.

Memories of her from this period are not flattering. Photographs show her as skinny and sallow-complexioned. Her peers remember her as unwell, physically and intellectually nondescript, clinging to Feroze as if he was her lifeline. Her father's friends weren't too impressed either. She was described as 'a mousy, shy little girl who did not seem to have any political ideas', and was 'purely her father's daughter'.[53] However hard she tried, by attending the influential socialist thinker Harold Laski's lectures at the LSE or following the debates at the Oxford Majlis, she simply wasn't as intellectually dazzling as her father would have liked her to be. Nehru's European friends ranged from the French author André Gide, who would go on to win the Nobel Prize, the writer and art theorist André Malraux, the biologist and internationalist Julian Huxley to the social reformer and sociologist Beatrice Webb. When Nehru met and interacted with them, some in Indira's presence, her own lack of brilliance was sadly apparent.

At the end of her first year at Oxford, she failed after two attempts to pass the first year 'Moderations' examinations that she needed to clear to begin the honours degree. She passed all her subjects but each time failed to clear her dreaded Latin, understandably so as she had had no opportunity to master it, unlike other English students who had been studying it for years. She had only one more attempt left; if she failed again she would be faced with the humiliation of being 'sent down', or asked to leave Oxford. She fell ill with a cold, cough and exhaustion. One of her Oxford contemporaries, Nikhil Chakravartty, believed her illnesses in these years were a 'convenient fiction'[54] to avoid being sent down from Oxford. By 1938, she decided not to make another attempt and to abandon Oxford although she evidently didn't yet tell her father, fearing his deep disappointment.

Meanwhile Nehru arrived in Europe, caught in a whirlwind of meetings and lectures, and she set off travelling with him. Before she went, Harold Laski told her, 'If you tag along with your father, you'll just become an appendage . . . so you'd better not go with him. You must strike out on your own.'[55] But she strained to be a part of Europe's political churning and of all the excitement around Nehru who had a hectic schedule meeting politicians and intellectuals as well as attending public meetings and delivering lectures, organized by Krishna Menon. Together father and daughter visited Paris to participate in a world peace conference, where there were protests by Spanish groups, Indira becoming 'excited' and 'involved' when La Pasionaria (or Dolores Ibárruri), the communist heroine of the Spanish Civil War, was not allowed to speak. 'I felt very strongly about the Spanish Civil war,' she would recall in a nostalgic moment about her youthful, radical years.

By the time they arrived in Budapest via Munich and Prague, Indira fell seriously ill with pleurisy and Nehru urged her to return to India with him, which she did. Back in India in November 1938, having just turned twenty-one, she joined the Indian National Congress as she had been longing to for a while. It was as if Oxford was behind her already, and her path ahead was clear. She wasn't cut out for long hours of study in ivory towers; radical campaigning excited her more. She didn't want to battle to learn Latin, she wanted to battle for different causes. In her mind the choice was clear: goodbye Oxford, hello political activism. She pined for the heady, politically charged days in London and for Feroze. She was a young radical, madly in love, and restless to be a greater part of the youthful ferment among Indian students in England. Her health remained fragile all the while she was in academic surroundings, but later when she joined politics she would become robust and sturdy; a wilting flower would suddenly spring to new life when she found the terrain in which she really belonged.

Feroze was still in London and she desperately wanted to be back with him. She argued with her father that she needed to be back in Oxford when in fact she had no intention of rejoining Somerville. She prevailed over Nehru, who was worried about her health and impending war in Europe, and insisted on returning to England, arriving back in London in summer 1939 and renting a room near Feroze, who had by now dropped out of LSE and was working in various activist groups.

In London she got drawn even deeper into the activities of the India League and became closer to Krishna Menon. By now she had also formed friendships and associations with Feroze Gandhi's circle of Leftist friends like Mohan Kumaramangalam, P.N. Haksar, Nikhil Chakravartty and Mulk Raj Anand, who were all Menon's acolytes. Kumaramangalam would be a future minister in her cabinet. Haksar was destined to be her crucial ally.

By September 1939 war broke out across Europe and Indira's health broke down too. Family and friends decided that she should be moved out of London and by late 1939 she was admitted, on the Mahatma's advice, to Les Frênes sanatorium in Leysin, in Switzerland. After a long stay in Leysin, she travelled back to London in 1941 through war-torn Europe to stay with Feroze. 'Arrived last night,' she cabled Nehru. 'Well. Plans uncertain.'[56] In fact, her plans were definitely not uncertain. By now Feroze and she had been secretly engaged for four years and they now decided to return to India and marry. In March 1941, they sailed for home.

Unable to gain an Oxford degree, Indira was engulfed by embarrassment, shame and feelings of inadequacy. She would explain her stint at Oxford thus: 'With everyone at prison and so on, my heart was not in my studies at all.'

~

Dear Mrs Gandhi,

Were you embarrassed and ashamed about your failure to gain a degree at Oxford? You chose to study your father's favourite subject, modern history, but you had not really developed an interest in any subject and lacked academic direction. Santiniketan was the only academic institution where you had flowered, where your 'mind and soul unfolded',[57] where you were free to pursue more artistic inclinations, where the subjects you chose were less demanding than the challenging Oxford course.

How did your failure at Oxford affect your relationship with your father? Were you painfully aware that you had failed to live up to his dreams? One of your rather endearing letters to Nehru from Somerville shows how desperate you were for his approval. 'Darling Papu, I am afraid I am acquiring some of your bad habits . . . I had to go out in the morning, then at two there was a Labour study group, at seven I was having supper with The Darb [Helen Darbyshire, head of Somerville], at 8.30 I had to go for a Majlis meeting for Krishna Menon was speaking . . . my essay on the Evolution of Parliament had to be read in class at 10 am . . . I read until twelve forty-five and then wrote until three fifteen . . . I got Very Good for my essay!'[58] When you fell ill your father had been a trifle flippant: 'health is very much a mental affair . . . put worry and nerves on the shelf', he would write[59] while you were in the Leysin sanatorium, advising you not to have an 'obsession about a return to India'. 'I want your love,' he wrote, 'not your duty or a feeling of responsibility which becomes a burden to you or me.'

Nehru clearly wanted you to spread your own wings, not rush

to be back in his universe or under his wing. Did you feel your father's regard for you had dipped after Oxford? Your decision to marry Feroze, immediately after abandoning Oxford, was a bid to create a life for yourself away from your father's expectations. Were your later attempts to cultivate intellectuals and thinkers an attempt to compensate for your lack of academic achievement? You were quick-witted, sensitive, 'an amazingly rapid and voracious reader' but the Oxford experience left you with a lifelong lack of self-confidence and an insecurity around those more academically talented than yourself. Did your truncated stint at Oxford make you long to prove yourself in your father's eyes?

~

3

From Woman-in-Waiting to Nehru's Heir

Indira Nehru married Feroze Gandhi in 1942, with whom she had two children, Rajiv and Sanjay. When Jawaharlal Nehru became prime minister in 1947 she moved into her father's home as his official hostess. In 1959 she became Congress president. After Nehru died in 1964 she joined Lal Bahadur Shastri's government as information and broadcasting minister and her political ambition came to the fore.

Indira's romance with and marriage to Feroze Gandhi was a natural progression of his closeness to her mother and to her family; theirs was a bond which grew by the bedside of Kamala Nehru as they both kept vigil over the dying woman they adored. As we have seen, when Kamala was being treated in the Badenweiler sanatorium, Feroze had arrived to keep Indira company. As her friend Shanta Gandhi put it, 'The memory of Kamala was a bond between Indira and Feroze . . . they were resentful of Vijayalakshmi's influence over Nehru. They shared the feeling that Jawaharlal and his family had not understood Kamala's innocence and simplicity.'[1]

Her decision to marry was also a rebellious assertion of will against her father. Feroze Gandhi was a boisterous, loud and gregarious man, who loved eating and leading the good life, the opposite of the polished, cultivated Jawaharlal. He was not the scion of an upper-class family and, in spite of his aunt Dr Commissariat's qualifications, Feroze's family did not match the pedigree of the patrician Nehrus. In his youth Feroze had been a devoted Nehru follower, becoming captivated by Kamala on first seeing her. There was even some talk of an affair between Kamala and Feroze, which Feroze's biographer dismisses saying even Nehru heard these rumours, brushed them off and did not stop Feroze from coming to Anand Bhawan.[2] But there was much gossip about their relationship and suggestive posters had even appeared in Allahabad. In an amusing exchange, Jawaharlal had once asked then fellow Congress member and his friend Minoo Masani (who would later go on to form the Swatantra Party), 'Minoo, can you imagine anyone falling in love with my wife?' Masani had chivalrously responded that he himself could fall for Kamala, at which point Nehru glared angrily at him. Masani later noted: 'Feroze had calf-love for Kamala.'[3] However, a Kamala–Feroze affair is highly unlikely given how deeply attached Kamala was to her husband and family, the very public life at Anand Bhawan and the fact that the youthful, idealistic Feroze regarded both Kamala and Jawaharlal as his mentors.

Feroze was a great source of solace and stability for Indira when Kamala lay dying in Badenweiler. After her mother's death, when Indira felt 'left all alone', he was by her side. 'Feroze was always there for me,' Indira would say. He was already at the LSE when Indira joined Oxford and throughout her time there she remained engaged to him.

In 1941, an academically talented, radical young Kashmiri from Allahabad, Parmeshwar Narayan Haksar, was training to be a barrister in London. He was an expert cook and was often invited to prepare his signature Kashmiri dishes for his homesick Indian friends. He recalls cooking for Feroze and Indira in Feroze's flat. Indira was thin and pale, having returned from the Les Frênes sanatorium, where she had been treated for her persistent ailments.

But Haksar remembered her as being radiant in Feroze's company and the couple made 'no pretence of what the sleeping arrangements were in Feroze's tiny book-filled flat'.[4]

Earlier, in 1937, while still an Oxford undergraduate and under Feroze's influence caught up in the radicalism of the India League, she had been led into her first open bitter disagreement with Nehru when he wrote to her of his decision to stay at the house of Philip Henry Kerr, the Marquess of Lothian, on Nehru's forthcoming visit to England. Lothian, former private secretary to British Prime Minister Lloyd George, was known for being one of Hitler's 'appeasers' and Indira had raged at her father for accepting an invitation to visit Lothian's home, a visit the more consensus-minded Nehru defended on the grounds that he, Nehru, was a prominent leader who had a 'special place' in India.[5] Nehru's reply was a subtle put-down of his daughter, and this was the first recorded instance of the daughter strongly challenging her father and vociferously disagreeing with his views. Soon she would challenge him even more obstinately.

Feroze and Indira came back to India via Durban in April 1941. In apartheid-ridden South Africa Indira had a first-hand taste of racial discrimination. When the Indian community invited her to a function she made her first impassioned political speech about the meek way Indians accepted apartheid and white rule, shocking her audience. She landed in India, fired up and eager to launch a determined battle against Jawaharlal on her decision to get married.

First she went to meet the Mahatma. At Gandhi's ashram, seeing that she was wearing silk and lipstick, she was told to change into khadi and wash her face. Indira was put off by the ashram. 'The atmosphere at Sevagram was one of petty quarrels: who would take (Gandhiji's) food in, who would carry his papers . . .' She was not a Gandhian by instinct, even though she admired how the Mahatma would rejoice in discussion and challenge. 'How many times have I not argued with him . . . he regarded no honest opinion as trivial and always found time for those who dissented from him . . .' She was one of those dissenters, a critic of what she called the 'hypocrisies of Gandhianism'.[6] In later life, however, she was to admit that what she perceived as his anti-intellectualism was a great strength: 'He had to take the masses with him, and he had to put everything in an idiom they could understand.' Yet Gandhi's ideas were too abstract for her liking and the Mahatma did not hold the blueprint for the new country. The blueprint copyright belonged entirely to her Papu.

For now though Papu had to be fought. If the young England-returned revolutionary was disenchanted with the Gandhian ashram, an even greater gap of understanding yawned between Indira and her father over Feroze. Nehru was bitterly opposed to the match, not because of differences in caste or community but simply because Feroze was not of the same social class as Indira. Nehru's sisters, Vijayalakshmi Pandit and Krishna Hutheesing, had also married outside the Kashmiri Pandit caste and community but their husbands, Ranjit Pandit and Gunottam (Raja) Hutheesing, were highly educated and scholarly, both from renowned families, both a part of the interconnected world of India's elite, a community of the great and the good which Nehru greatly valued. Feroze was not a part of this world and did not even have – like Indira – a university degree. Pride in the family was integral to Jawaharlal and he feared she was turning her back on what he called her 'great inheritance'. 'There is an element of the absurd in your returning from Europe in frail health and suddenly marrying,' he would write to her in distress.[7]

Indira's biographer Katherine Frank believes Nehru's objections could also have stemmed from a conversation in the presence of their family friend A.C.N. Nambiar in which Kamala told Nehru that Indira should not marry Feroze as he was 'unstable' and it would be the 'mistake of her life'. Proffering rather un-aunt-like advice, Vijayalakshmi Pandit suggested that instead of marriage Indira have an affair with Feroze, an insulting comment that angered Indira and made her stubbornly resistant to family pressure.

However, the Mahatma intervened and gave his consent, saying the couple's personal decision had to be respected. Wrote Gandhi about Feroze and Indira's wedding: 'He [Feroze] nursed Kamala

Nehru in her sickness. He was like a son to her. During Indira's illness in Europe, he was a great help to her . . . a natural intimacy grew up between them which ripened into mutual attraction . . . it would have been cruelty to refuse consent . . . As time advances such unions are bound to multiply with benefit to society.'[8]

The young couple were delighted to receive Gandhi's blessings, even though they strongly resisted the Mahatma's subsequent suggestion of marital celibacy. Nehru could no longer hold out and in this first serious contest of wills between father and daughter, the daughter won. If Indira's personality had been split between being her father's protégée and her mother's guardian, clearly Kamala's side prevailed over Jawaharlal's in the choice of her husband. Marrying Feroze, who had been almost as devoted to Kamala as Indira, was not just a demonstration of loyalty to her mother, it was also a signal to her father about her own autonomy of thought and action. 'Papu understood concepts: it was a long time before he could understand relationships,' she would say.[9] Later in life, in her letters and words Indira spoke of her father with admiration and protective-ness but never with much ready emotion, almost as if her hurts and insecurities were too mixed up in her feelings for him. Indira and Nehru shared a very close, fond but not really a warm relationship, however devoted she was to him and constantly at his beck and call.

Feroze Gandhi and Indira Nehru were married on 26 March 1942, Ram Navami day, the year Gandhi gave the call to the British to 'Quit India'.[10] The bride wore a sari made from the thread spun by her father in prison, the groom wore the white khadi of the Congress and the ceremony took place outdoors in the back verandah of Anand Bhawan. Indira looked beautiful, willowy and delicate, her fine-featured face glowing and fresh, yet somehow pensive.

'In marrying Feroze, I was breaking age old traditions . . . and it did "raise a storm" . . . there is no doubt that many people in my own family were very upset.' Asserting herself against patriarchal disapproval would remain a dominant theme in her life where she would reveal a stubbornness that belied her outwardly docile appearance, a sudden revealing of her real self under the mask of what was only a strategic timidity. She was to say with a touch of pride at her own rebellion, 'the whole nation was against my wedding'. She had waged her own freedom struggle against her father and was very pleased at her victory. Soon, however, her England-returned romanticism would be engulfed by ennui.

~

Dear Mrs Gandhi,

Your marriage to Feroze was not a success and brought both of you a great deal of unhappiness and loneliness. You would write to Dorothy Norman in 1955, after thirteen years of marriage: 'I have been and am deeply unhappy in my domestic life. Now the hurt and unpleasantness don't seem to matter so much. I am sorry though to have missed the most wonderful thing in life, having a complete and perfect relationship with another human being; for only thus I feel can one's personality fully develop and blossom.'[11]

What went wrong between you and Feroze? Did he begin to seriously resent the fact that you were the prime minister's daughter, that, for example, you sat by your father's side at official banquets whereas he, only a son-in-law and later a member of Parliament (MP), was always seated far down the line with lesser mortals?

When Nehru asked you to move into his prime ministerial residence, you agreed to do so and virtually abandoned the home in Lucknow that you had created with your husband. You were always Nehru's daughter before you were Feroze's wife, not content to be a Lucknow housewife when a much grander and more exciting life unfolded before you in Teen Murti House, the life you felt you were destined to lead. Feroze offered you a humdrum life as wife and mother in Lucknow, but you always believed you were meant for higher things and that you must take your place in the national firmament. Asked about why you moved back with your father, you would say: 'Obviously I had to do it because my father was doing more important work than my husband.'[12] You made moving back into your father's home akin to patriotic duty, telling a friend: 'It was . . . important for the country that someone look after him. And there was no one else but me.'[13] You fought your father to marry Feroze, but in the choice between Nehru and Feroze, did you finally choose Nehru and then resign yourself to the consequences of that choice? It was your life's most crucial personal decision, one that would have a negative impact on your relationship with your husband and sons.

~

Six months after their marriage, Feroze and Indira found themselves in prison, having passionately participated in the Quit India movement. Indira was locked up in Naini jail and Feroze in Faizabad prison. She was released after less than a year, but going to jail was an important rite of passage. Having seen her father and so many relatives repeatedly imprisoned, she believed it was her baptism into her family's way of life. 'Prison was a special sort of experience for me . . .' she would say, 'dozens of my relatives both on mother's and father's side had spent long years in prison . . . I do not know of any family which was so involved in the freedom struggle and its hardships . . . herded together like animals, devoid of dignity . . . when I fell ill I was prescribed Ovaltine. The Superintendent tore up [the prescription] and said if you think you are getting any of this you are mistaken . . . my months in prison were a very important part of my life.'

Once she and Feroze were released they began to live in Anand Bhawan, both taking pride in the house which had been at the centre of their shared history. Feroze worked in the garden and Indira set out to repaint the grand old house and restore its rooms to some of their past glory.

She was soon pregnant and her first child, Rajiv Ratna Birjees Nehru Gandhi, was born on 20 August 1944 in Bombay, the name chosen for him establishing that he was as much Nehru's grandson as Feroze Gandhi's son. 'What about adding Nehru as an additional name,' her Papu wrote to her from prison, 'not Nehru Gandhi, that sounds silly, but Nehru as an additional name.'[14] After the baby's birth, Indira's worries about money began to grow as Feroze, then working in the Congress's legal aid committee, was not earning much and the family of three had to depend on her father for money. 'It is rather silly of you to go on worrying about money matters . . . do not hesitate to draw upon my account whenever Feroze thinks it necessary,'[15] wrote Nehru. It was an ignominious situation for Indira and she escaped her worries for a while by taking a holiday in the 'lovely pine-laden air' of Kashmir with the newborn Rajiv, staying in the luxurious bungalows of her relatives, away from an increasingly fretful existence with Feroze.

She was always happiest to visit Kashmir, was supremely proud of her Kashmiri ancestry and all her life would keep returning to Kashmir. She may have been born in Allahabad but called herself a 'daughter of the mountains' and always proudly spoke of her family as 'we Kashmiris'. Recalls Bhagat, 'She would say, "we" don't cook like this, or "we" don't put certain spices. The "we" referred to the Kashmiris.' Pictures of Kashmir's mountains and trees hung in her bedroom all her life and she regularly celebrated Navreh, the Kashmiri new year. Kashmir was her ancestral home, her life's anchor, her idealized homeland. Kashmir was India's crown, lofty, sparkling, elevated and Himalayan, in a higher realm from the jostling, sweltering provinces down below. The chinar trees of Kashmir would become a source of strength, symbols of an unchanging India.

While she was in Kashmir news came that Nehru had been released after his longest and most gruelling spell in a British jail. She knew at once she had to be by her father's side. 'I was nothing but a wife and mother [at this time] . . . [but] the moment when I heard my father was released . . . at that moment, I forgot the baby. When the family wondered how I could help by going, I said "I don't know but I just have to go. I returned to Allahabad."' 'I just have to go' is what she would later signal to her husband, when Nehru asked her to move in with him into the prime minister's home as his hostess and housekeeper. Even if she was a self-confessed 'wife and mother', for her the most valuable work was always at her father's side – husband and children only came second.

On 15 June 1945 Jawaharlal Nehru was finally released from his last prison term. Nehru emerged from prison a colossus, his spirit unbroken, the object of adoration of a vast swathe of humanity. Fifty-six-year-old Panditji had trudged through the cyclone. In the torturous struggle for liberation by Gandhi's side, he had been beaten, battered and betrayed, yet had refused to let his idealism about a future India be extinguished. In jail for these crucial last years before Independence, he was as yet unaware of the machinations of the Muslim League and plans afoot for the division of India, emerging from prison 'blinking in the sunlight'.[16] Yet it was a grand homecoming. '*Hum laye hain toofan se kashti nikaal ke*', we've steered the boat through the storm, went a popular Hindi film song in the 1950s and it aptly described the odyssey of independent India's founders, journeying to the eye of the storm to bring out from its howling depths the little sailboat of independent India.

In the general elections of 1945, the last conducted in British India for 102 seats, the Congress emerged as the single largest party with fifty-nine seats but Jinnah's Muslim League swept the Muslim constituencies. When an interim government of India was sworn in with Nehru at the helm, Indira wrote to 'Darling Papu': 'How I long to be in Delhi to witness this triumph for you personally but even more for the great organisation you represent.'[17]

By early 1946 Indira was pregnant again. By now Feroze had got a job as director of the *National Herald*, a newspaper founded by Nehru, in Lucknow and they rented a bungalow in the Hazratganj area. Feroze was an expert gardener and carpenter and together with Indira's homemaking skills they created a little family nest. But she wasn't happy and would write to her father: 'What a peculiar deadness there is in our provincial towns . . . what makes the atmosphere sickening is the corruption and the slackness . . . the smugness of some, the malice of others . . . life here has nothing to offer . . . it's not surprising that the superficial trappings of fascism attract them in their tens and thousands . . . The RSS [Rashtriya Swayamsevak Sangh] are gaining strength rapidly, following the German model. Most Congressmen and government servants approve of these tendencies.'[18] The Hindu right would remain her lifelong enemy even though she would later often try to outsmart them at their own game.

A happy family life was not in their stars. Infidelity haunted their relationship. The extroverted Feroze, whom Dorothy Norman disliked intensely and described as 'crude',[19] was a faithless husband, Indira always well aware of her husband's roving eye. Feroze's friend Nikhil Chakravartty believed Feroze was 'loose with women, had a girlfriend in England even when he visited Indira every weekend, had many affairs and could not resist relationships, which Indira knew about'.[20] The *Herald* soon ran into financial troubles and Feroze was accused of mishandling the newspaper's money, causing Indira much agitation. To make matters worse, he fell in love with the 'strikingly beautiful' wife of Ali Zaheer, a Lucknow politician, while Indira was pregnant with Sanjay and was even said to be 'too fond' of Indira's younger cousin Chandralekha Pandit.[21] Bertil Falk quotes one of Feroze's friends saying, 'Romantic by nature he was a quick and easy victim of Cupid's darts.'[22] Feroze's affair with Mrs Zaheer became so serious that Nehru had to send his friend Rafi Ahmed Kidwai to sort out the matter and persuade Feroze to give up the affair.

On 14 December 1946, a second boy, Sanjay, was born in Nehru's home in York Road (today's Motilal Nehru Marg) in Delhi after a very difficult labour in which Indira haemorrhaged badly and almost died. 'We were really hoping for a daughter. In fact, we had kept only girls' names ready,' Indira recalled. The child was named Sanjay after the Mahabharata's Sanjaya who described the scene of the battle of Kurukshetra to the blind king Dhritarashtra. The choice of name was intriguingly apt. In his time Sanjay would convert his mother into a blind parent, making her suffer from what can be called the 'Dhritarashtra syndrome' or the parent blinded by love to their child's follies.

At the time of Sanjay's birth, Nehru's home was overcrowded with guests and Feroze was forced to sleep in a tent pitched in the garden in the chilly Delhi December. The not-so-exalted, unsung son-in-law awaiting the birth of his own child in a version of an outhouse must have been an embarrassing memory. When the boys grew up, they were to 'resent their grandfather's antipathy to Feroze' and feel Indira neglected their father.[23] But the boys misjudged their nana. Nehru, contrary to some accusations that he contributed to the breakdown in his daughter's marriage by asking her to live with him, instead fervently wished Indira and Feroze would be happy. 'I want very much for Indu to settle down. Feroze must carry on with the Herald and Indu should live there for a good part of the year,'[24] he would write to Vijayalakshmi Pandit.

At a minute before midnight on 14 August 1947, Nehru rose in India's Constituent Assembly in Delhi to tell the world about India's tryst with destiny. Indira was in the audience listening, transported to another world. 'It was one of the proudest and most exciting moments of my life . . . the culmination which so many people had fought for.' Nehru was sworn in as prime minister on 15 August 1947 by Lord Louis Mountbatten, now Governor General of India. Afterwards, at the sumptuous banquet presided over by the Mountbattens, Indira sat near her father while Feroze was placed far down the table with Mountbatten's press attaché. The Mountbattens thought of Feroze as a 'nonentity'. It was clear that 'she was being dragged in two directions' and that there was 'trouble in the marriage'.[25]

Indira longed to answer the call of destiny, her ambition and spirit leaping towards new beginnings. Feroze recoiled in irritation, as she leaned more and more towards her father. He whiled his time away in Lucknow, visiting the Lucknow coffee house every morning to discuss politics with his friends, while she was in a Delhi state of mind. She was already in awakened mode after the exhilarating midnight hour, her indomitable courage at the ready. At Independence the bliss of freedom gave way to the barbaric communal riots of Partition in which at least a million lives were lost and some 17 million displaced from their homes. Britain's retreat from the Indian empire reeked of mass murder. Hindus, Muslims and Sikhs butchered each other as communities struggled to migrate to either India or Pakistan. Entire trainloads were massacred. Railway stations ran with blood.

'I could not conceive of the gross brutality and sadistic cruelty that people have indulged in,' wrote a horrified Nehru after Partition. 'There is a limit to brutality and that limit has been passed during these days in North India . . . little children are butchered in the streets . . . it's more than I can bear.'[26] He would later say, 'As long as I am alive India will not become a Hindu State. The very idea of a theocratic state is not only medieval but also stupid . . . one can either follow the lead given by Mahatma Gandhi or oppose it. There is no third way open . . . India is getting a bad name in countries abroad.'[27]

Nehru's resolve to preserve Indian secularism led him to 'save' his homeland Kashmir from the grasp of the 'tottering state' Pakistan. In October 1947 Pashtun tribesmen from Pakistan's North-West Frontier Province were sent hurtling across the border from Pakistan into Kashmir, looting, killing and raping as they went, in an effort to forcibly secure Kashmir. Maharaja Hari Singh of Kashmir fled to Jammu where he signed on the dotted line of Kashmir's accession to India even as Indian troops landed in Srinagar on the morning of 27 October and secured the capital.[28] Alas, today Nehru's hope of Kashmir being an integral part of India's secular union of people looks tattered. Instead, Jinnah's two-nation theory looks dominant as we can see in the unending bloody protests in the Valley and the bitter divide between a 'Hindu' Jammu and a 'Muslim' Kashmir, something Nehru tried so hard to prevent.[29]

Amid the bloodshed of Partition, Indira, on a train back from Mussoorie to Delhi, saw two old Muslim men being attacked by a mob at Shahdara station. She immediately jumped out of the train, 'merely dressed in a towel', confronted the mob and managed to rescue one old man. In a conflict, her first reaction was always to wade in and take charge, not shy away. She never lost her nerve in a tense situation, as if programmed since childhood to cope efficiently in any kind of calamity. In another incident during the riots she angrily faced and stared down a mob, telling them, 'I am saving this man's life, you can kill him only after you have killed me.'

The Mahatma was impressed with her pluck. He asked her to start work in Delhi's refugee camps. She plunged in, gaining admiration for her efforts, a crisis as always bringing out the best in her. It was at the refugee camps, she would later say, that 'my feud with the RSS began. Some innocent looking people walked around with swords hidden in their sticks so if they hit someone with them, their heads would split open.' The feud dogged her entire political life. In the 1970s, the RSS would mainstream itself by participating in the anti-Indira movement led by Jayaprakash Narayan. She would return the favour by banning them during the Emergency.[30]

On a cold evening in January 1948, religious hatred claimed the life of a pleader for love. On 30 January, the assassin Nathuram Godse pumped three fatal bullets into Gandhi as the Mahatma walked towards a prayer meeting at Birla House in New Delhi. The hate he had battled all his life proved too powerful for even a Mahatma. Indira was shaken. Gandhi had been a rock-like presence in her life since her birth. She rushed to Birla House as soon as she heard the news, later taking armfuls of flowers to deck the body. The mood in Birla House was numb and tremulously silent, the deep shock of Bapu's murder hanging in the air. In the hushed room, when the *Life* magazine photographer Margaret Bourke-White suddenly came 'tick tocking into the room' on impossibly high-heeled shoes, Feroze, who was present, jumped up, snatched away her camera and led her from the room, as if she had defiled a place of homage, prayer and terrible grief.[31] 'With his frail two hands, Gandhiji lifted up a people,'[32] Indira would say. Nehru addressed India: 'The light has gone out of our lives and there is darkness everywhere . . . a madman has put an end to Bapu's life . . . we must face this poison . . . we must root out this poison.'

Nehru's security now became a serious consideration and it was decided he should move into what had been the British commander-in-chief's residence or Teen Murti House. So far Nehru had had no personal security guards. Anyone could walk into the prime minister's office or residence. But Nehru now needed police protection. With Nehru's move to Teen Murti, Indira and the boys more or less moved in with him, Indira at this point 'neither married nor separated'.[33] 'My father would feel hurt if I didn't come, it was very difficult to say no. It was a real problem because naturally Feroze didn't always appreciate my going away.' Did Nehru ask her to stay with him for his sake or hers? In all probability, both. Writes Sahgal, 'It was painful for her father to see the loneliness and heartbreak her troubles with Feroze consigned her to.'[34]

Her decision to leave her husband's home and instead go to her father's was a crucial life choice, one that convinced Feroze of his secondary status in her life. At a Congress meeting when Nehru scolded Congressmen for bringing their wives and children, with Indira ironically seated by his side, Feroze burst out, 'It wasn't I who brought my wife here!'[35]

The boys joined a nursery school in Delhi and Indira busied herself in managing the challenging household of Teen Murti, organizing formal meals and events to graceful and quiet perfection. In 1949 Indira suffered a miscarriage and without a new baby to reignite marital bonds her marriage too suffered an abortion. Instead doors opened to a new world with her father. Not only did she manage the high-powered life of Teen Murti House, she travelled with Nehru to America and later other countries. After her miscarriage, doctors had advised her to cancel her US trip, but she was determined to go and had her way. Feroze was left behind as she took off away from him.

In America, Vijayalakshmi Pandit, then ambassador to the United States, pointedly left Indira out of all official functions. Sensing her exclusion, the physicist Homi Bhabha, founder of the Tata Institute of Fundamental Research and of the Atomic Energy Commission of India, took her out to lunches and dinners. On this trip she also met the writer and photographer Dorothy Norman, soon to become her close friend, who introduced her to authors, painters, thinkers and musicians; she visited the theatre, opera and art galleries and came back to India with a sense of having discovered a new way of being. Indira later recalled those times: '[there was] continuous contact with a wide cross-section of leaders . . . I went with my father on some of the trips. Sukarno, Hatta and others had stayed with us . . . In China I met Mao-Tse Tung and Chou En-Lai . . . in Switzerland Charlie Chaplin came to meet us.'

She was in her element now, not in the dreary world of Lucknow. She insisted that she was initially reluctant to enter the high life. 'I resisted every inch of the way about becoming a hostess. I was terrified of so-called social duties . . . we always had guests.' Whatever her nervousness, she was in her natural habitat, at the centre of things, determined to make a success of her new task. She was keenly interested in menus, table plants, flowers, linen and service and was a sensitive and thoughtful hostess. She would recall her initial concerns about Teen Murti thus: 'Such enormous rooms, such long corridors! Could this ever be made livable? Could it ever have a semblance of a home?' She set herself high standards and lived up to them, checking every minute detail of household organization herself, her excellent organizational skills to the fore, living by the dictum 'If one has to do a thing one might as well do it well, so I grew into it'.[36]

She continued to have an expert eye for household management even when she became prime minister. During a stop at an inspection bungalow on a tour of West Bengal, a then young district commissioner recalls her telling him, 'Mr District Commissioner, I appreciate the work you've done in putting in new towels for me in the bathroom. But next time you buy new towels, make sure you wash them once before putting them out for use by guests. New towels don't dry up wetness unless they've been washed once.'[37]

As prime minister she retained her inclination to look for style even in gritty surroundings. On the same West Bengal trip, riding in an open jeep flanked by waving crowds, she spotted a beauty amid the throng. It was Ruma Pal, née Ghose, a junior lawyer who would go on to become a well-known Supreme Court judge, who was visiting her brother Bhaskar Ghose, then a district officer, and had gone that day to see Indira's rally. Looking at her, Indira posed a challenging question to the IB director Gopal Dutt seated behind her. 'Tell me, Mr Dutt,' she asked while continually waving and smiling, 'what sort of sari do you think that young girl there is wearing?' 'Looks like a silk sari, ma'am,' fumbled the IB official. 'It's not silk, Mr Dutt,' retorted Indira. 'It's a handloom from Coimbatore. You better stick to gathering intelligence.'[38] When Ghose later asked Pal whether her sari was indeed a Coimbatore handloom, Pal confirmed it was. Indira Gandhi's expert eye and innate aesthetic sense – she had a natural feel for fabrics and textures – would spot colour and design where others wouldn't and infuse her surroundings with touches of art.

~

In the prime ministerial home, she began to take tentative steps into the prime minister's work and into politics. In 1949 she wrote to her father about the rot in Uttar Pradesh politics and how the then chief minister G.B. Pant was interfering with the editorial policy of the *National Herald*. 'If you don't call Pantji to order . . . then please in future stop talking about democracy and freedom of the press in India,' she would write to Nehru. When she became the authoritarian prime minister two decades later those words would be revealed as laughably ironic. Nehru brushed her off but was later impressed at the energetic manner in which she campaigned in the 1952 elections for both men in her life, for Feroze in Raebareli and for Nehru in Phulpur. He wrote to Edwina Mountbatten saying how surprised he was at the fine work done by Indira,[39] and to Vijayalakshmi Pandit saying, 'Indu had indeed grown and matured very greatly during the last year and especially these elections. She worked with effect all over India . . . like a general preparing for battle . . . She is quite a heroine in Allahabad now.'[40] It was almost as if he was pleasantly surprised, not having expected her to really excel at anything.

In Raebareli, residents remember Indira campaigning for Feroze in a tonga. 'There were no AC cars or jeeps in those days, she rode a tonga or went on foot,' recalls O.P. Srivastava, a veteran advocate based in Raebareli. 'She campaigned as a bahu, very respectful to the elders in the constituency, she never took anyone's name, it was always Thakur Sahab or Panditji. Her head was always covered.'[41] Feroze, known for his fearlessness during the freedom struggle, having stoutly stood up to British beatings several times in spite of his weak heart, was an effortless politician. He spoke fluent Hindi as well as several Allahabadi dialects, and showed an 'enormous ability to work with people'. Gandhi once said of Feroze, 'If I could get seven boys like Feroze to work for me, I will get swaraj in 7 days.'[42] Feroze won an overwhelming victory from Raebareli, awakening in Indira a barely conscious longing to be part of the election excitement. Her attraction to politics was obvious. She was more enthusiastic about public life than she cared to admit, even to herself. Outwardly she was in denial, inwardly she yearned to do more.

Although they were estranged, her strenuous campaigning for Feroze in 1952 showed that beyond the personal there remained a political comradeship between them. They had forged their bonds during political ferment, they had been partners in the ideological commitments of their university days, they had unfurled the tricolour in their youth and their lives had revolved around the thrilling spirit of Anand Bhawan.

However, professional competitiveness would creep into their relationship as Feroze's political career took off. The role of hostess and supportive actor would become irksome for Indira as Feroze's parliamentary performance began to become noteworthy. She had the advantage of birth but the talented Feroze fought his way up by winning twice from Raebareli, emerging as a fiery speaker in Parliament and tenaciously exposing corruption scandals.

Although a silent backbencher at first, Feroze soon became a stellar parliamentarian. He remained a left-winger within the Congress, as Nehru had been in the 1930s and 1940s. In 1955 Feroze forced the nationalization of life insurance in India after his exposé of the illegal dealings of businesses and insurance companies. A vociferous defender of the freedom of the press, he also piloted a law allowing the Indian press to report on parliamentary proceedings, a law Indira Gandhi would repeal during the Emergency.

In spite of these successes or perhaps because of them, and Feroze's arrival in Delhi, their relationship did not improve. He was suffocated by Nehru's presence and found living in Teen Murti House intolerable. 'Although he genuinely admired his father-in-law, he thought there was something counterfeit in the cult developing around Nehru . . . and intensely disliked being called "the Prime Minister's son-in-law".'[43] Rumours flew about Feroze's peccadilloes and affairs. He would even publicly show off his friendships with the glamorous members of Parliament Tarakeshwari Sinha, Mahmuna Sultan and Subhadra Joshi[44] as if to thumb his nose at his illustrious in-laws and delight in embarrassing them. Tarakeshwari Sinha, however, denied any such affair, saying, 'If a man and woman have lunch together immediately there are rumours of an affair . . . I once asked Indira Gandhi if she believed all the rumours, that I was also a married woman and had a family and reputation to guard, she said she did not believe the rumours.'[45]

Whether Feroze's love affairs were just romantic enthusiasms or full-blown lusty liaisons, they were still talked about breathlessly, and most people were certain there would be a divorce because of Feroze's affairs or because Indira wasn't a devoted enough wife. There were also rumours of Indira's own affair with M.O. Mathai, Nehru's secretary, the aggressive, short-statured factotum, who was Nehru's shadow for thirteen years from 1946 to 1959. Mathai, also called 'Mac', was a lively, interesting personality, with a gift for languages and the art of witty conversation. He was an energetic workaholic and an efficient, frank and fearless man who Nehru relied on completely and whose intimacy with Nehru Indira resented, just as she had been uncomfortable with Nehru's closeness to Vijayalakshmi and even to Edwina Mountbatten. Yet, however much she may have been resentful of Mathai, she was also allegedly his lover.

In Mathai's autobiography, *Reminiscences of the Nehru Age*, he allegedly wrote a chapter entitled 'She' which describes a 'passionate' Indira with whom he apparently had a twelve-year-long affair. The version of the alleged chapter widely available online on various right-wing websites has lines such as 'she has Cleopatra's nose, Pauline Bonaparte's eyes and the breasts of Venus'. The chapter says her 'cold and forbidding' reputation was only a measure of 'feminine self-protection'; she was 'exceptionally good in bed'; 'in the sex act she had all the artfulness of French women and Kerala Nair women combined'; she loved 'prolonged kissing'; and she became pregnant by the author and had to have an abortion. The unverified online version quotes Indira as saying she could not bear to ever be married to a Hindu, and once said, 'I like the Queen Bee. I would like to make love high up in the air.' At the end of the chapter is the line 'I had fallen deeply in love with her.'

'She', containing highly explicit details of an apparently intensely physical relationship, was never published. Frank, however, believes Mathai did write it and that Maneka Gandhi circulated this same chapter (which is now available online) after she fell out with her mother-in-law. The publisher of Mathai's book, Narendra Kumar of Har-Anand Publishers, says that he cannot verify if Mathai wrote 'She' as the publishers did not receive the chapter with the original manuscript.

Indira's relationship with Mathai has never been clarified. Nehru's biographer Sarvepalli Gopal says Indira and Mathai 'enjoyed baiting one another' and describes the relationship as one where 'Indira encouraged him [Mathai] beyond normal limits'.[46] Frank writes that in her interview with B.K. Nehru, who had no reason to bad-mouth

Indira, he suggested that there might have been some sort of affair between Indira and Mathai and that the 'She' chapter contains 'more fact than fiction'.

'Mathai did a lot of damage to Nehru,' says Natwar Singh, close associate of the Nehru–Gandhis, former Congress politician and bureaucrat in Indira's secretariat from 1966 to 1971.[47] 'He was close to the CIA [Central Intelligence Agency]. Between 1946 and 1959 every single paper that passed Nehru's desk went to the CIA. As for the affair, he spread all these tales for his own reasons.' Mathai would quit Nehru's service in disgrace in 1959, after Feroze Gandhi's friend Nikhil Chakravartty exposed his various shady dealings in property and cash stashed abroad. His writings on Indira thus could well have been the vengeful outpourings of an embittered individual.

In 1958, two years before Feroze's death, when Jayakar informed Indira about rumours that she was having affairs with other men to take revenge on Feroze, she became furious and said, 'Before you hear it from Delhi gossip circles, let me tell you that I am divorcing Feroze.'[48] Feroze for his part would growl at his friend Inder Malhotra: 'Look here, before you hear a doctored version of it, let me tell you I've stopped going to the Prime Minister's House completely.' He now started to refer to Indira as 'Shrimati Indira Gandhi' not 'Indu' or 'my wife' as he had done until now. It would become clear later that neither of them had any intention of a formal separation and even attempted a sort of reconciliation months before his death.

As Feroze blazed a trail in Parliament, Indira sought to create more room for herself politically, becoming a member of the Congress Working Committee in 1955. It was from this time onward, writes Nehru's biographer Marie Seton, that she ceased to be 'her father's hostess and a nice girl ... Attitudes changed overnight towards her and she was instantly reclassified as a politician.'[49] She was also elected to the Congress Central Election Committee in 1955, and became president of the All India Youth Congress and the Allahabad Congress Committee in 1956. After campaigning hard in the 1957 elections, she became member of the powerful Central Parliamentary Board of Congress in 1958. She still outwardly kept up a disingenuous disinterest in public life. '. . . I still haven't gotten used to being on the Working Committee . . . Can you imagine me as an elder statesman?'[50]

She made it a point to repeatedly say how ill-disposed she was towards politics. 'When Gandhiji was still alive Govind Ballabh Pant had asked me to join the UP Assembly. I had said no categorically to which Pantji had complained to Gandhiji "look at this slip of a girl who thinks she's much clever than I am" . . . I didn't think I was cut out for that work, besides my children were too small.'

She was the reluctant eager beaver, the disingenuous naysayer; the more strongly she denied that she wanted to plunge in, the clearer it was that the opposite was true. Wrote the American journalist Welles Hangen, 'No public figure disclaims political ambition so insistently and none is more disbelieved.'[51] This would be the pattern all through her life and political career. She would keep accumulating more and more power and as she did so, also keep outwardly professing she didn't want any of it and in fact wanted to be rid of it.

In the 1957 elections Feroze was re-elected from Raebareli. She campaigned as hard as she had in 1952 but this time more energetically for Nehru than for Feroze. Once again Feroze dominated Parliament, 'red, rotund and Pickwickian, enlivening Central Hall with his sense of humour, his designated corner now named "Feroze's corner"'.[52] He shot into the limelight when through a careful investigation he revealed on the floor of the House how the Life Insurance Company of India had bailed out a private businessman through a loan. The 'Mundhra Scandal' rocked Parliament and the finance minister, Nehru's close associate T.T. Krishnamachari (TTK), was forced to resign. Feroze, now dubbed 'giant killer', was at the peak of his parliamentary fame.

Yet he remained frustrated and angry at the decline of his marriage and in 1958 moved out of Teen Murti House and into his own MP's flat, the once-ebullient, high-living jokester now lonely and depressed, seeking comfort in excessive drinking and smoking. The mark he made in Parliament was tinged by an edge of bitterness towards Indira and Nehru. When Feroze did visit Indira at Teen Murti, he was morose and uncommunicative, hardly speaking even at the dinner table. 'Always welcome at Teen Murti, he chose to treat himself as an outsider and behaved with scant courtesy when he came to a meal or to spend time with his sons,'[53] and in response Indira, now the First Lady of India, was disdainful and contemptuous. Feroze's mood only changed when he was in the boys' room, when father and sons, both fascinated with mechanical equipment, would be engrossed for hours building various objects. When a friend once asked why Feroze taught his sons so much mechanical work, he muttered cynically, 'My sons have a rich mother but a very poor father. And I'm making sure they don't starve.'[54]

In contrast to her husband's sullen choler, Indira Gandhi was in excellent spirits and health. She was miraculously free of the ailments of her student days. She was now practising yoga daily, under the tutelage of none other than the handsome and muscular Dhirendra Brahmachari who had been introduced to Nehru.[55] With her children away at boarding school, she was casting around for a way forward and a role that went beyond heading safe, non-controversial welfare bodies. She had campaigned during elections, helped with candidate selection, served in the Congress party in various capacities but so far had coyly maintained that only 'mischievous people' had been talking about her contesting elections. While campaigning in the 1957 elections, however, she confessed she had found the experience 'exhilarating' and she wrote to Padmaja Naidu: 'I had 100,000 people in Rohtak just for me . . . imagine that!'[56] There was little doubt where her heart lay. She was like a child gingerly tasting a sweet, afraid that she would like it too much. She dipped her toes into political waters only cautiously as if she knew its seductive thrill could sweep her away in a jiffy.

~

In 1959 Indira allowed herself to be persuaded to become Congress president at the age of forty-one, largely on the urgings of the then Congress president, U.N. Dhebar, and home minister G.B. Pant. When these senior Congressmen urged Indira to take up the mantle, Nehru merely said, 'It must be your decision, I'm not going to enter into it.'[57] He was clearly not very keen and made his coolness to the idea known. He would say, 'Normally speaking, it is not a good thing for my daughter to come in as Congress President when I am Prime Minister.'[58] Whether Nehru asked her to come and live with him in Delhi out of fatherly sympathy for her floundering marriage or because he genuinely wanted her by his side as his hostess is unclear but it is evident that the democrat in Jawaharlal did not want to create a dynasty in his name and he was irritated and uncomfortable with her eager entry into the political world.

'It never crossed Nehru's mind that she would ever succeed him as prime minister,' says Ramachandra Guha. 'He knew she would play a political role of some kind, but a minor political role. What eventually happened did so purely by accident.' Nehru indulged his family but only up to a point. After the resignation of TTK, when some suggested that Vijayalakshmi Pandit join his cabinet, Nehru had made it clear that while he was prime minister neither his sister nor his daughter would ever join the council of ministers. For Indira, the desire to assert her identity spurred her on to seek greater political space and her family's vocation drew her like a magnet. An ageing prime minister needed his daughter by his side; Indira used the situation to her advantage. In spite of his bids to resign, Nehru 'clung to his throne with tiger-like tenacity', his continuous and long tenure greatly benefiting Indira, who used the latter years of her Papu's prime ministership to create room for herself in the highest echelons of politics.

And why not? The freedom movement had boosted women's emancipation with Sarojini Naidu and Vijayalakshmi Pandit making a powerful mark and parliamentarians like Subhadra Joshi and Shivrajvati Nehru strongly raising women's rights during debates over the Hindu Code Bills. Indira may not have ever identified as a feminist but she refused to dampen her ambition for the sake of her marriage or her father's reservations. The spirit of the ambitious Motilal lived on in his granddaughter. Trying to make her marriage work or being her father's hostess were inadequate goals compared to the larger role she wanted to play.

This is evident from her keenness to visit the United States with Nehru in 1949 in spite of ill health, her ready plunge into the Congress by taking up various party posts, her hectic campaigning in elections and her determination to fight for Nehru politically first as his eyes and ears and then as his understudy. She would never have been content growing roses in a Lucknow garden, however hard she may have tried to project that image. 'I hear these stories that my marriage collapsed and I left my husband . . . both of us were so headstrong . . . I wouldn't have gone into public life if he had said no. But when I went into public life, he liked it, yet didn't like it. Other people were the worst. They would say, "How does it feel to be so-and-so's husband?" . . . To hurt the male ego is the biggest sin in marriage.'[59] For Feroze, Indira's political emergence was a mark of her move away from him, away from her role as a wife and rather chauvinistically he saw it as a final repudiation of their relationship. But quietly ignoring male disapproval in the family, she eagerly plunged in.

She would later say about her decision to take up the post of Congress chief: 'Then Congress president, U.N. Dhebar said to me: Rather than criticising things from the outside, you should come in and do the job . . . when the Congress is under attack do [others in the Congress] come forward to defend it? Do they speak out boldly? . . . Nobody does anything. I am sorry I didn't take an active part much earlier, because I could probably have saved my father much unhappiness.' She would insist to her biographer Dom Moraes that she had never wanted to be Congress president and her father didn't want her to be either, but the Party Elders 'bullied' them both into it.[60]

On 2 February 1959, the day of her inauguration as Congress president, amid seasoned veterans, dressed in a plain white khadi sari and a white knitted blouse, with her fine features and downcast gaze, she looked like a delicate lamb. 'Youngest Woman to be Party Chief,' gushed the *Statesman*. In her inauguration speech, however, she belied any impression of weakness when she quoted from a song in the 1957 film *Rani Rupmati*: 'Hum Bharat ki nari hain, komal komal phool nahin, Hum jwala ki chingari hain [We Indian women are not soft flowers, we are sparks of fire].' When Indira demonstrated her fire as president her husband soon became her political adversary.

Her time as president was impactful. The Bombay State was divided after linguistic agitations and Maharashtra and Gujarat came into existence in May 1960. Nehru had deep reservations about linguistic states but political calculations trumping all else in major executive decisions was Indira's forte, established even at this early stage. She would say: 'I was positive we would lose the elections in Gujarat and Maharashtra and parties who were committed to separation would come in and vote for separation. What would we have gained?'

In 1957, a decade into his prime ministership, Nehru faced his first challenge when the communists won the elections and came to power in Kerala. The win stunned the country: it was the first time in India that the Communist Party of India (CPI) had come to power through an election, joining the democratic mainstream rather than being confined to the realm of revolutionary insurrection. The Congress was upstaged and insecurities mounted about the growing challenge to the Congress vote bank, as photos of Marx and Stalin replaced Gandhi's in Kerala school classrooms. The Congress had vowed never to ally with religion-based parties like the Muslim League but political calculation won over ideology. Indira Gandhi as the Congress president now showed that she was not shy of making common cause with non-secular outfits if a political opponent had to be defeated. In Kerala, the Congress decided to support protests by the Christian Church, the Muslim League and the Nair Service Society against Chief Minister E.M.S. Namboodiripad's new education bill. Protests spiralled and, as Congress president, Indira lent her weight to arguments that Nehru must dismiss the Namboodiripad government on the grounds that the education bill was hurting the interests of Muslim and Christian communities. According to Falk, 'she orchestrated the unrest from New Delhi through her loyal AICC workers in the state hand in hand with communal Hindus in the state and with the Muslim League . . . she showed that she could be a stiff and authoritarian leader and it paid off.'[61] In 1959 the communist government in Kerala was dismissed to vociferous outrage, notably from Feroze himself.

The dismissal of the Kerala government has been seen as the first unveiling of the Indira style of decisive, authoritarian action, without pause for institutional propriety, stamping over Nehru's more tentative, constitutionally correct methods. Her perfectionist homemaker's obsession with an orderly household overrode any intellectual anxieties over democratic norms. When the Congress won the subsequent elections in Kerala, defeating the communists, Indira was jubilant, even though a democratically elected state government had been brought down.

The question arises, as the foremost proponent of institutional integrity, why did Nehru give in to Indira on Kerala? Perhaps Nehru too was worried about the Congress's future and felt that the communist challenge had to be nipped in the bud. Ideologically, Nehru himself was becoming increasingly disapproving of communism and a critic of communist methods in Yugoslavia and Hungary. He also seemed to genuinely believe that the protests against EMS were a 'mass upsurge' and an expression of real public grievance against a government which by now was arresting and lathi-charging thousands of protesters regularly, once even opening fire and killing twenty. On a visit to Kerala, Nehru witnessed 'hysteria' and 'thick walls of group hatred' on the streets[62] and became convinced that communism was creating violence and lawlessness. Nehru did ask Namboodiripad to call for fresh elections but EMS refused, leading to his dismissal. But the daughter was to sense her father's serious unease about the decision.

Indira later denied having played a major role in the Kerala government's dismissal. 'The Marxists are always accusing me of having brought down their government . . . but it could never have been done had the central government not been willing . . . My opinion would not have changed things. My father and Feroze were not happy about it but Mr Pant, the then home minister, was determined it should happen. My part was not as important as it was made out to be.' Historians believe she wasn't responsible because as Congress president she could argue her case, but in the end it was Nehru who finally wielded the axe on EMS, in a decision which Sarvepalli Gopal says 'tarnished Nehru's reputation and weakened his position'.[63] In any event, whether she was directly responsible or not, Kerala became a source of intense marital strife between Indira and Feroze.

Feroze had become intensely agitated about Kerala, relentlessly lobbying ministers against the 'folly' of dismissing the Kerala ministry, his 'defeat' making him embittered about what he perceived was his wife's anti-democratic role. Falk narrates a story reported to him by the journalist Janardan Thakur. One morning the Kerala issue came up at the Nehru–Gandhi breakfast table with Feroze telling Indira, 'It's just not right. You are bullying people. You are a fascist.' Indira had flown into a rage and walked out of the room saying, 'You are calling me a fascist, I can't take that.'[64]

Kerala brought the differences between husband and wife into the open. Indira's friend, Mary Shelvankar, a committed Marxist, clearly unhappy about the dismissal of a communist government, believed that although both Feroze and Indira were socialists and nationalists, Feroze was a federalist and Indira was authoritarian.

'She wanted all the power in her hands. She was against a federal India. In her opinion India was not enough developed to be a federal state.'[65] She was the imperious Nehru, with a queenly resolve to call her subjects to order when they became unruly. He was always the radical activist, happiest fighting for a cause.

In 1959 Indira would write to Dorothy Norman: 'A veritable sea of trouble is engulfing me. Feroze has always resented my very existence but since I have become President he exudes such hostility that it seems to poison the air . . . just to make things difficult for me, he is leaning more and more towards the communists and sabotaging my efforts to strengthen the Congress.'[66]

Indira subsequently resigned as Congress president – before completing even a year – telling her father that she felt she had paid off her debts. On the wintry night of 30 October 1959, after tossing and turning in bed for hours, she rose at 3.45 a.m. to write to her Papu: 'These last eight years, I have worked harder and harder, feeling I could never do enough . . . last year came a moment of lightness, as if the last of the debts had been paid off . . . I have felt like a bird in a very small cage.'[67] Her tone is somehow unconvincing. She knew she was turning her back on her destiny and became acutely despondent about the decision later. She was proud of what she had achieved as party president and felt unhappy at having given it up, which she did more in deference to her father's and husband's unstated wishes than because she really wanted to.

She looked back on her time as president with nostalgia. 'I used to go to office absolutely on the dot, at nine in the morning . . . we innovated in that for the first time the Congress office was open to all . . . I travelled extensively . . . I organised seminars . . . I undertook padyatras . . . I put the finances right and arranged an entirely new younger set up . . . unfortunately the Congress party refused to climb the slope with me.' Writes H.Y. Sharada Prasad, Indira Gandhi's media adviser from 1966 to 1977, 'As Congress president she did not have the smoothest of relations with her father. They differed over

Kerala. That and Feroze Gandhi's health were responsible for her abrupt relinquishment of office.' A decade later she would make a Congress party in her own image, with no father or husband looking over her shoulder.

Did she then give up the presidentship as a last-ditch attempt to devote herself to her marriage? Feroze had in a way been her political guru; as students in England, it was he who had encouraged her to take an interest in Labour Party politics and anti-fascist movements. Feroze had even introduced her to western classical music. She would say: 'the Nehrus were very unmusical people. It was Feroze who introduced us to the joys of western classical music.' Above all it was Feroze who had helped devotedly nurse her mother. Such a partner was not just a husband, but a comrade-in-arms, a companion through an arduous journey, a protective ally and guide.

In June 1960 Feroze, Indira and the boys went for a holiday to Kashmir and stayed in a houseboat on the Dal Lake. It was at this point, she would say afterwards, that she had decided that after her father died she 'would commit herself totally to him [Feroze]'.[68] Her resolve was never tested. On 8 September 1960 Feroze died of a heart attack, leaving her in a state where 'my whole mental and physical life changed suddenly . . . I was physically ill . . . cut in two'.[69]

Bhagat remembers that of the deaths of Nehru, Feroze and Sanjay, she was most devastated by Feroze's, perhaps because 'there was so much that was left unresolved and unfulfilled'. Perhaps she understood his humiliations and heartsickness at being married to Nehru's daughter and somewhere deep down even forgave him for his playboy antics and mutinous behaviour. Their relationship was complex and multilayered and Feroze was more a part of her than may have been readily apparent, almost a family member rather than a husband. 'We quarrelled a lot yes, we were two equally strong types, equally pig-headed – neither of us wanted to give in. And I like to think that those quarrels enlivened our life, because without them we would have had a normal life but banal and boring. We didn't deserve a normal banal and boring life.'[70] They were more alike than different: strong, rugged individualists each with an urge to dominate the other.

'She was shattered by his death,' recalls Natwar Singh. 'It was the only time I had seen her cry. His body was brought to Teen Murti. When Panditji saw the number of poor people who thronged to pay their respects he said, "I didn't know Feroze was so popular." Indira Gandhi was in tears the whole time.' Writes Anand Mohan, 'Indira didn't like Feroze, but she loved him.'[71]

Indira would laugh with genuine affection every time she told a funny story about Feroze, recalls Dr Mathur. One of her favourite stories was about how he fell off a horse. There was another about how Shankar made a cartoon of him sleeping because he had forgotten an appointment and instead slept through it. 'She narrated these stories while laughing throughout,' recalls Dr Mathur.[72]

After Feroze's death she threw herself into political work. In 1961 she was elected to the Congress Working Committee, became a member of the Central Election Committee and vigorously campaigned, setting aside her grief for Feroze, for the 1962 general elections.

Within four years of Feroze's passing, Nehru too would be dead. In the absence of the two most important men in her life, another Indira would emerge.

~

In October 1962 the Chinese army came marching across the McMahon Line, the effective border between India and China, and captured Indian territory. Tensions with the Chinese had been rising: the Chinese were building a road, parts of which had encroached into the Indian Aksai Chin area. China was also incensed that the Dalai Lama, the leader of Tibet, had been given asylum when he fled to India.

The Chinese assault was massive and unexpected and Indian forces fell back. An unprepared and ill-equipped Indian army was no match for the invaders. In some valiant instances like in the battle of Rezang La, Indian soldiers laid down their lives defending Indian posts. Nehru had boldly extended a hand of friendship to China. In 1954 India and China had signed a peaceful coexistence treaty based on the five principles of the Panchsheel and the slogan 'Hindi Chini bhai bhai' had sweetened the Asian air. Now Nehru, who had initially downplayed the Chinese incursions as 'petty conflicts between patrols', was caught completely by surprise. Distraught at the Chinese betrayal of the 'bhai-bhai' spirit, his voice kept breaking in an AIR broadcast a few days into the war. 'The Chinese government has returned evil for good,' he almost whispered.

But Indira Gandhi gathered herself together energetically and rushed to the war front to ensure proper distribution of relief supplies. Almost in a protective gesture towards her father, perhaps knowing that he would not be able to take the shock of the Chinese aggression, she charged off to do her bit, journeying to Tezpur in Assam, once again fearless, efficient and thriving in a crisis, to show that at least this member of the Nehru family had her wits about her and was ready to meet the challenge head-on.

Off she went by army plane to Tezpur, heeding no warnings about danger, striding through heavy rain and visiting terrified locals. 'The Chinese were only 20 or 30 miles from Tezpur and were expected to reach by dawn . . . it was an unprotected town, deserted by troops and police . . . her visit was a great morale booster . . . she was brave.'[73] Daring came to her naturally; when there was a larger battle to be fought, her personal safety simply didn't matter. 'Do not go gentle into that good night,' she seemed to be signalling to Nehru, 'rage, rage against the dying of the light.' In a crisis her courage and resoluteness were always tremendous.

During and after the 1962 war, Indira showed a combative nationalism and an exceptional courage. She also showed her trademark ruthlessness in telling her father, 'if people do not function, they should go', referring to calls for Defence Minister

V.K. Krishna Menon's head even as Nehru dithered about sacking his long-time friend and colleague. Menon had failed to take the Chinese threat seriously. Convinced that the real threat came from Pakistan and not China, he had stalled the upgradation of India's weaponry and meddled in army appointments, which had led to a resignation threat from the then army chief, General K.S. Thimayya. As a result of Menon's indecisiveness, Indian troops were tragically unprepared.

The 1962 war destroyed India's first prime minister and he was never again able to recover his old physical strength, intellectual prowess and moral glow. Exhausted and disillusioned, his shoulders drooped and a blank drowsiness came into his eyes. Nehru had already made three attempts to resign. At one point Indira had encouraged him to do so, writing to him, 'so much is rotten in our politics . . . people are unable to understand nobility and greatness'.[74] Now after the Chinese war, he sorrowfully admitted India had been living in a 'make believe world' all this time. Even President Radhakrishnan openly criticized Nehru, accusing him of 'credulity' and 'negligence'. In the 1962 polls the Congress had won convincingly but the party's vote share had dipped slightly. The Bharatiya Jana Sangh and Swatantra Party had won fourteen and eighteen seats respectively. Nehru was no longer completely unassailable. By 1963, in Parliament, J.B. Kripalani, Minoo Masani and Ram Manohar Lohia began to attack Nehru relentlessly, thumping the table and shouting, 'Quit, Nehru, quit!', a chant echoed by thousands of opposition supporters gathered outside the Parliament building.

Indira sprang into protective mode. As she said, 'I was looking after myself from the time I was three or four, and . . . I was always looking after my parents.' Now, just as she had once defended Kamala, she stood guard over Nehru as even close colleagues turned on the fatally weakened titan. Krishna Menon was hounded out of office. A post-Nehru power centre – the Syndicate of state leaders – began to emerge in the party.

In 1963 Indira wrote to Dorothy Norman that she wanted to leave

India and settle down in a small house in England. 'My need for privacy and anonymity has been growing steadily these last years,' she wrote, mentioning a house in London which she was keen to buy but which she subsequently heard had been bought by someone else.[75] In April 1964 she journeyed to America to deliver a letter from Nehru to President Lyndon Johnson, who was charmed by her. (He would later be even more bedazzled.) At a 'Meet the Press' programme, when asked if she would refuse to serve as Nehru's successor, she said, '90 per cent, I would refuse'.[76] It was in the unstated, barely realized 10 per cent realm that the dreams of Indira Gandhi lay, even if she had written to Norman trying to convey the impression that she wanted to bow out.

In January 1964, while addressing a Congress session in Bhubaneswar, Nehru suddenly collapsed. It was a stroke which left him paralysed on the left side. Sensing Nehru's vulnerability, his opponents closed in. 'The campaign against Papu is studied and well organised,' Indira wrote to B.K. Nehru in May 1964. 'Every effort is being made to weaken, and if possible, dislodge him. He is no longer his old self. One after the other old colleagues have gone . . . he is surrounded by people of small stature.' The extent of her power was feverishly speculated on in Delhi's durbars at this time and she was not at all unhappy at being perceived as the 'power behind the throne'. However, she still practised the fine art of dissembling. She would again write to Norman: 'The desire to be out of India and the malice, jealousy and envy is overwhelming.'[77]

On 27 May 1964 Jawaharlal Nehru died. Ashen and dry-eyed, bereft of that all-encompassing umbrella that had sheltered her, Indira Gandhi now drew towards herself his legacy and name as her shield. She saw to the funeral arrangements with meticulous care, not letting personal sorrow overwhelm her, even making sure that the household staff looked well turned out, firmly instructing them not to be slovenly given how much Nehru always insisted on neatness.

She determinedly took charge of her father's funeral – as

efficiently as she would take charge of his legacy – seeing that huge blocks of ice kept the body from decomposition in the midsummer heat, that adequate amounts of lilies, marigolds and roses were brought in to decorate the body, that kirtans were sung in the way Nehru would have liked. In a spotless cotton sari and long-sleeved blouse she sat ramrod straight as thousands of mourners filed past the body of one of the twentieth century's greatest statesmen, one who had dared to dream that the newborn Indian nation state would be equal to the highest democratic standards in the world. A sea of humanity lined the route taken by the special train carrying his ashes to Allahabad. 'There were people on platforms, showering petals, on the ground, on pillars, on roof girders, on top of stalls, on home tops, on trees . . . just no end to the crowds.'[78] Such was the popularity of the 'buoyant, charming, majestic' Jawaharlal, the man who wouldn't be king.

The humble and unassuming Lal Bahadur Shastri was already the de facto successor. He was the independence-era activist who had functioned as Nehru's deputy, the target of some snarky comments from Indira. In 1956 when Shastri resigned after a railway accident, winning praise for his renunciation of office from Nehru and others, she would sarcastically point to his more strategic motives. 'Everybody thought he had resigned his ministership because of the accident, but it may have had something to do with the elections,' she said, referring to the upcoming 1957 general elections.

Now after her father's death, the deputy reached out to the daughter. 'I didn't want to be a minister at all,' she would say. 'Mr Shastri came to me and said he must have a Nehru in the Cabinet to maintain stability, I had not said yes. I was very reluctant. But the announcement was made on AIR that I was going to be sworn in with the others. That's how I became Minister . . . while I say I didn't want political leadership . . . it's not possible for me to be away from problems . . .' Her political instincts were sharply awakened. She had already confided to Pupul Jayakar that 'they will not let me survive when Papu is no more', as if to justify the battle she had already set upon waging.

Indira Gandhi readied to accede to her father's martyrdom. She regularly insisted she didn't want power, but she had always made it clear that she could not stay away if her father's legacy was in danger of being overthrown. Then naturally she would have to do everything in her power to see that India remained safely in the Nehruvian mould. That was her duty as Nehru's daughter.

~

Dear Mrs Gandhi,

You were a political animal from the start, however much you tried to convince people you weren't. When exactly was your political ambition whetted? Was it when Feroze won from Raebareli and began to shine in Parliament? Was it when you campaigned for the 1952 and 1957 elections and confessed to feelings of exhilaration? Your clear political inclinations were certainly to the fore when you became Congress president and took quick decisions. After your father's death you felt that there would be no turning back for you if you wanted to remain the sentinel of the Nehruvian legacy. At the time of your marriage, you had told your father you wanted anonymity, a life free from turmoil, that you wanted to look after your husband and children and have a home filled with books, music and friends. But anonymity was the last thing you wanted.

You said, 'It is absolutely untrue to say my father groomed me to be head of Government because if he had he would have taken me into confidence about his decisions and so on. He didn't.' You used to badger Nehru with questions at mealtimes, but he always stayed silent. Did you almost resent your father for not grooming you? Was that why later in life you were to so diligently groom your own son because you nursed a grievance that your father had not launched you well enough? Did you rebel against his fondly paternalistic view that saw you as only good enough to be hostess and housekeeper? Nehru, kindly patriarch that he was, after all never thought you as intelligent enough or visionary enough for greatness. From Gandhi to Patel, India's freedom fighters pushed their children offstage and Nehru was no exception.

Did Nehru's death in a way liberate you from the shadows and free you to express your true self, not the shy girl but the alpha female that you really were? Once your father had passed from the scene were you at last able to reveal yourself not just as Nehru's daughter but also as Motilal's granddaughter, the kingly natural leader who never did accept any challenge to his authority? You were ready for battle, for a life that would go well beyond what your Papu could ever have imagined for you.

4

From Goongi Gudiya to Goddess

After Nehru's death in 1964, Lal Bahadur Shastri became prime minister. Indira Gandhi became information and broadcasting minister in Shastri's cabinet. When Shastri died in 1966, she became prime minister, remaining at the post until 1977. From 1966 to 1971 she rose to the zenith of power, splitting the Congress party in 1969, securing a massive election victory with her slogan 'Garibi Hatao' in 1971 and leading India to a military victory against Pakistan in the 1971 Bangladesh war. In these years she was hailed as the 'Empress of India'.

~

Dear Mrs Gandhi,

Did you secretly always want to succeed your father as India's prime minister? Did you always believe that only you could create and preserve the India of your Papu's dreams? You felt slighted when Nehru turned for counsel to colleagues like Morarji Desai or K. Kamaraj while you remained consigned to the hostess role. You told your friends that you wished your father would confide in you more.

Your early years as prime minister were difficult. Your opponents called you a 'goongi gudiya' or dumb doll. Did you feel misjudged, that your detractors failed to notice the steel within? You had cleverly hidden away your strengths to seem appealing and you must have had a quiet laugh at those who did not know about the 'atomic energy',[1] which you once said lurked within you. You were drawn to politics with an almost irresistible force. 'When I see things that are not being done, I feel a strong need to do them. This is my attitude. If this room is dirty I will sweep it.'

The truth is, you were never a goongi gudiya, and escaping politics was only your favourite fantasy. In those shadowed yet penetrating eyes burned the spark of an unshakeable belief in your own exceptionalism. It was not the others of 'small stature', as you called them, but you who would be your father's worthiest successor. Even if he himself may not have wanted it.

B.K. Nehru recalls your hard, disapproving stare when he tried to help in collecting Nehru's ashes after his funeral as Rajiv and Sanjay were doing. 'The look on Indira's face convinced me that she highly disapproved of my being there . . . She was giving a clear and unambiguous signal that the successor to power would be her, and after her, her sons; no other Nehru had better attempt to claim the Nehru mantle.'

~

Indira Gandhi's rise to become supreme leader of the Congress party, through a bruising battle of wits and nerves against a phalanx of implacably hostile veteran party bosses and jeering rivals in Parliament, was a triumph of willpower against serious odds. It was the ruthlessly determined ascent of a woman who was not only constantly conscious of her manifest destiny but for whom understanding and wielding power was almost second nature. She was the child of revolution and she rode the turbulent seas of politics with the naturalness of a political athlete. 'She had it much tougher than her father,' says Natwar Singh. 'Nehru never faced the difficulties she did, he never had any competition. In his time there was no opposition. Nehru's first ten years were a completely smooth run. Hers were not. But she had a fine political brain.'

Nehru may not have had a serious political rival but his tenure was not exactly a smooth run and he faced his own set of grave challenges from the economy to growing corruption, to language agitations in states, to violent opposition from the Hindu right as well as from the communists. He had been deeply worried about the principle of linguistic reorganization of states,[2] saying after the formation of Andhra Pradesh, 'we have disturbed a hornets' nest and I believe most of us are likely to be badly stung'.[3] When Nehru's government passed the Hindu Code Bills boosting inheritance and marriage rights for women, the RSS marched on the streets shouting 'May Pandit Nehru perish.'[4] He faced communist upheaval in Andhra Pradesh during the Telangana revolt,[5] there was severe criticism of the Second Five Year Plan and his valued colleague C. Rajagopalachari left the Congress in 1957 to form, at the age of eighty, the Swatantra Party in 1959 in protest against Nehru's socialist stand. He was disturbed about the future of India as a secular state, alarmed by the steady stream of Muslims leaving India for Pakistan, writing agitatedly to the chief ministers in 1953, 'ultimately it is up to us to create an atmosphere in which our minorities can live with assurance of full and equal treatment. If we do not succeed in doing this, we fail.'[6] When his friend André Malraux asked him what his greatest challenge had been since Independence, Nehru replied, 'Creating a secular state in a religious country.'

Nehru strained every nerve and sinew to establish independent India as a successfully functioning constitutional secular democracy, almost as if to repudiate all those who hadn't given the fledgling India a chance, as if to prove a point to his own domineering father who had once mocked his son's 'raging tearing' agitation for a free country. Whatever his myriad problems, abiding by constitutional discipline, Nehru remained temperamentally inclined to dialogue and accommodation. His daughter was not. 'My father was a saint who strayed into politics,' she would say, 'but I am a tough politician.' As the Red Queen said in a movie version of Lewis Carroll's *Through the Looking-Glass, and What Alice Found There*: 'I am many things, darling, but pure of heart is not one of them.'

She could not afford to be consensual given the trenchant opposition she faced from the old guard. The male hostility to her was unbound and brazen, and she was often isolated. In the drive for survival and then supremacy, her politics was rougher and more brusque than Nehru's needed to be. Nehru could be languidly grand but she was always on guard, always ready with swift feints and guerrilla tactics, 'the people' her perennial weapon of destruction against the phallocrats. She fought powerful men at every turn, anxiously sought approval from the men she loved and used feminine unpredictability to stymie the men who plotted against her. Magnanimity was a luxury she felt she couldn't afford.

As mentioned earlier, there is no evidence to suggest that Nehru was grooming his daughter to succeed him as prime minister. When Morarji Desai, the puritanical veteran who believed he was Nehru's natural successor, had hinted that Nehru wanted to push for Indira as prime minister, Nehru had said, 'this showed . . . the most fantastic kind of motive hunting . . . dynastic concept of succession is altogether foreign to a parliamentary democracy, besides being repulsive to my own mind'.[7] Indira said almost regretfully, 'My father never spoke to me about government matters. Never. I never asked him and he never volunteered any information.'

Even before Nehru's death, it was widely believed that the diminutive, mild-mannered and respected Lal Bahadur Shastri would be prime minister. Nehru had made his approval of Shastri quite clear. For Nehru, Shastri was a trusted colleague, one to whom he seemed to be getting ready to cede greater powers. In 1956, when Shastri, then railway minister, resigned after a train accident, Nehru wrote to Vijayalakshmi Pandit, 'There has been a cry of regret all over the country . . . this shows how popular Lal Bahadur is . . . it pleases me to see how he has grown with additional responsibilities.'[8] Six months before his death, Nehru had delegated most of his responsibilities to Shastri, who had suddenly been brought back into the cabinet, after he had resigned as part of the Kamaraj Plan.

As twilight began to close in around Nehru and his health and mental energy began to fade after the 1962 Sino-Indian war, the Congress party had come up with a strategy by 1963. Known as the Kamaraj Plan, this was a strategy ostensibly designed to re-establish the Congress's links with the people. It was felt that those continuously holding high office had become distanced from the grassroots. According to the plan, senior Congressmen, whether they were chief ministers or cabinet ministers, would resign from their posts and plunge into party work. To be 'Kamarajed' meant being relieved of office and sent to work for the party in the field. Some accounts suggest that the Kamaraj Plan was a Machiavellian design by Indira, a 'shrewd scheme to eliminate potential rivals in Nehru's last days'.[9] Indira, however, professed to have no inkling of it. 'I was in Pahalgam with my father . . . Mr Biju Patnaik put this proposal to me. I didn't know that it was Mr Kamaraj's idea, I asked "how will they take it?" "I can convince them," he replied. Much later we heard it was really Mr Kamaraj's idea.' Yet the decisiveness of the plan and the lightning speed with which it was executed does suggest Indira's imprimatur, her clear preference for the centralization of her own authority much in evidence, her political brain revealed in the shrewd laying out of a level playing field between the top leadership so that no single person could put himself forward as Nehru's successor. Nehru himself quite approved of the plan – some accounts even suggesting it was his idea – and said it was an 'idea taking hold of the mind and growing by itself'.[10]

As part of the plan, six cabinet ministers and six of the strongest chief ministers resigned. Thus Morarji Desai, Lal Bahadur Shastri, Jagjivan Ram, Kamaraj himself, Biju Patnaik and S.K. Patil, among others, gave up their posts and went back to work for the party, thereby creating a level playing field between Morarji and the others. The plan was named after Kumaraswami Kamaraj, the burly, moustachioed chief minister of Tamil Nadu, the Congress's famous 'kingmaker' who would become Congress president in 1963. Kamaraj, along with other seasoned veterans, formed what was called the 'Syndicate'.

The Syndicate were battle-hardened, doughty fighters, the Congress's powerful regional satraps. Among them, Atulya Ghosh, formidable organization man from West Bengal; Siddavanahalli Nijalingappa, bespectacled strongman of the Mysore State (later Karnataka); N. Sanjiva Reddy, tough independence movement activist and first chief minister of Andhra Pradesh; and Sadashiv Kanoji (S.K.) Patil, scholar, fiery orator and 'uncrowned king of Bombay'. Nehru believed federalism was key to the parliamentary system although he was not able to institutionalize the federal structure as well as he would have liked. Yet he had worked with mutual respect with these regional chieftains, believing that political and cultural heterogeneity generated India's strength. Unable to conceive of laying their allegiance at the feet of any successor to Nehru, the regional overlords believed that after his death the party as a collective would reign supreme. Soon after Nehru's death Kamaraj declared: 'No person would be able to fill the void left by Jawaharlal's disappearance from the scene. The party would therefore have to function on the basis of collective leadership, collective responsibility and collective approach.'[11]

The Syndicate became the power centre of the Congress, the men of the moment, when Nehru died. They were influential but their outlook was hemmed in by their provinciality. 'The Syndicate were provincial satraps who did not possess the stamp of greatness of Nehru, Patel or Azad . . . they were unable to grasp that it was contrary to the spirit of parliamentary democracy for a Prime Minister to be subordinate to any group,' writes Sharada Prasad.

By the time of Nehru's death the Congress's lustre had begun to fade. The assertion of regional and linguistic identities had led to the linguistic reorganization of states in the 1950s; now dominant castes were being challenged by backward castes, and the 'Congress system'[12] of remaining in power through the 'patronage chains of big men',[13] – or relying on regional strongmen to deliver votes – began to look shaky. The communists entered the political scene and began to wean away sections of the rural poor from Congress patronage.

The Congress with its broad centre-left secular identity had an acute threat perception from the communists on one side; it was also intensely threatened by the stirrings of Hindu politics, by forces represented by the Jana Sangh, the latter increasingly the choice of conservative Hindus within the Congress who, disenchanted with Nehru's socialism, were leaving the party. Communal tensions had begun to grow dangerously; riots were breaking out with increasing frequency, such as the serious communal outbreak in Jabalpur in 1961, with slogans like 'Pakistan ya Kabristan' (Go to Pakistan, else we will send you to the grave) entering the lexicon of Hindu religious rage. Just when the Congress began to face new and varied threats, it lost its giant.

When Nehru passed away, the Syndicate threw its weight behind Shastri in deference to the wishes of the dead first prime minister. The highly capable Morarji Desai, all were agreed, had to be kept out. Desai, almost seventy years old, and former home minister in Nehru's cabinet, was a rigid loner, a 'seasoned administrator'[14] who the Syndicate feared would strip them of their power and reign supreme. Desai, a moral puritan who was fanatical about the prohibition of liquor, and who had famously outlawed any depictions of kissing in films, had never been at ease in the byzantine politics of the Congress's Delhi durbar. Indira feared and hated Morarji, always suspicious of his right-wing leanings. The idealism of the Nehruvian 1950s was slowly giving way to the growing compromises the party was willing to make to retain power in the 1960s. Morarji, the stern, old-style Gandhian, discomfited and unnerved the post-Nehru Congress leadership and they were determined to keep him at bay. Lal Bahadur Shastri was duly sworn in as prime minister on 9 June 1964, leaving Morarji chafing at the bit and the Syndicate triumphant.

Shastri included Indira Gandhi in his cabinet because she was Nehru's daughter and would be a vital link between the new government and the aura of Nehru and the freedom movement. He offered her the relatively low-profile portfolio of information and broadcasting, worried that she had the potential to outdo him.[15] Shastri's biographer C.P. Srivastava writes that three days after Nehru's death, Shastri called on Indira to say, 'Ab aap mulk ko sambhal lijiye [now you must take charge of the country]' but she refused,[16] later saying she had no choice in the matter and was forced to join Shastri's ministry.

Her professed 'reluctance' was what Welles Hangen called her regular pattern of disclaiming political ambition in spite of an instinctive desire to be close to power. If she really was oh-so-reluctant why did she agree to join the government, particularly just a year after she had written to Dorothy Norman that she wanted to leave India for good? Indira Gandhi was a creature of the limelight. She had occupied centre stage all her life and was not about to slip unnoticed into the wings. After being sworn in as minister, in August 1964 she was elected to the Rajya Sabha from Uttar Pradesh, for now choosing not to contest the Lok Sabha by-poll from Nehru's seat, Phulpur.

From the start she was restive at being consigned to the information and broadcasting ministry, often feeling slighted and marginalized and that she was not being given her due. When Bhaskar Ghose joined the ministry as undersecretary, on transfer from north Bengal, the first question she asked him was, 'How is our party being managed in north Bengal and how are the local MLAs doing?' Her interests were squarely on the political fortunes of the Congress, almost as if she was unsure of the present leadership, and worried that Shastri was simply not up to the job.

She said later, 'Whether Shastri really was or not I don't know but he always said that after Panditji he was a small man. This gave the people a feeling of insecurity. Whoever is leading, must be sure he is the leader . . . in the beginning although people admired his modesty, they wondered if it was conducive to strength.' She had no time for Shastri, and thought him weak and incapable of living up to the post he occupied. In fact, she would repeatedly demonstrate her contempt for his government.

As information and broadcasting minister she was allotted a new home, a charming Lutyens-style house surrounded by trees and gardens. 1 Safdarjung Road was a relatively small bungalow but it would be her home throughout her public life. It was here that she started her morning 'durbars' of meeting people, her way of slowly staking claim to her father's inheritance. Her oft-demonstrated connect with people would be crucial to Indira Gandhi's bid for power in the coming months and these daily durbars were her version of democracy in action. 'To me this is how democracy should work. A cross-section of people come to see me, middle class, poor, industrialists, professionals, I take feedback from them.'[17]

It wasn't a time of peace. In 1965, language riots broke out in Madras. Protesters publicly immolated themselves at the prospect of Hindi replacing English as India's official language. It was a movement that would eventually lead to the rise of the Dravidian parties in Tamil Nadu. As she had dashed to Tezpur during the China war, Indira now once again rushed to the scene of the action, catching the first available flight to Madras and making contact with the protesters to try to calm the situation even as the prime minister remained meekly in Delhi. She exceeded her brief as information and broadcasting minister and acted as if she was the one in charge. When Inder Malhotra suggested that she had jumped over the prime minister's head she 'flared up' and said she wasn't a 'mere Information and Broadcasting Minister' but 'I am one of the leaders of the country. Do you think this government can survive if I resign today? I'm telling you it won't. Yes I have jumped over the Prime Minister's head and would do it again if the need arises.'[18]

Nehru's daughter would not rest easy until the job of setting the country in order – her version of order – had been embarked upon. Her conviction that it was her destiny – and only hers – to sort things out in the manner in which her father would have wanted far overrode any smaller considerations about the exact limits of her role in the cabinet. Shastri sensed her rivalry and blocked her access to the upper echelons of government. But she upstaged him repeatedly by her trump card of oneness with 'the people'.

The need for Nehru's daughter to storm into action soon arose again. In August the same year a crisis erupted in Kashmir, when rumours began to circulate that Pakistani army infiltrators had sneaked into Srinagar and were about to overthrow the civilian government. Indira Gandhi happened to be on holiday in Srinagar at this time. As India launched a full-scale military attack on Pakistan in retaliation for Pakistani infiltration into Jammu and Kashmir, and the hostilities of the 1965 war broke out, unmindful of warnings of danger, she stayed on in Kashmir.

She even jumped on to a helicopter to fly to the front to galvanize the soldiers' morale, visiting military camps and hospitals. She flew to the Haji Pir Pass, a strategic outpost India wrested from Pakistan after heavy casualties. Surprised soldiers cheered when she unexpectedly arrived. The capture of Haji Pir had been led by Major Ranjit Singh Dyal, who as general would go on to draw up plans for Operation Blue Star in the Golden Temple in Amritsar in 1984. Indira revelled in being among the troops – men at war were an echo of her own gallant and belligerent defence of India. 'After the Chinese war, I was continuously visiting the front line and I had established a special rapport with the armed forces . . . I told the cheering soldiers we would not give up Haji Pir.'

'The only man in a cabinet of old women' is not exactly a feminist compliment but that's how Indira was described at this time. She was the 'chokri' who showed what tough manliness meant in a war. When she returned to Delhi, she made sure to instruct Shastri on how the war must be directed, much to his discomfiture. She even wrote a paper on strategies for the war and presented it to Shastri. The nonplussed Shastri reportedly held the paper like one would hold a dead rat by the tail and asked, 'Iska kya karein? [what should one do with this?]'[19]

But Shastri would soon emerge as a hero and Nehru's daughter would find herself relegated to the back row. Pakistani attacks were strongly countered by Indian forces, and in September the United Nations called for an unconditional ceasefire and the war ended. India had halted Pakistan's attempted seizure of Kashmir and matched the Pakistani army battle for battle. Compared to 1962, 1965 was a proud moment and the 'little man' Shastri now looked ten feet tall, his slogan 'Jai Jawan, Jai Kisan' on every lip. Shastri journeyed to Tashkent for peace talks with Pakistan's Ayub Khan mediated by the Soviet Union. Indira Gandhi became furious at Shastri's success. 'Shastri was weak but we have made him a national hero,' she wrote to her son Sanjay, already it seems a political confidant.[20] She gathered together a close circle of advisers, among them Dinesh Singh, deputy minister for foreign affairs; Ashoka Mehta, deputy chairman of the Planning Commission; Inder Kumar Gujral, then a Rajya Sabha MP; and the journalist Romesh Thapar, who urged her to claim her rightful place in the political sun.

After the 1965 war, her political ambitions, always latent and under the surface, now began to dominate her actions. She readied for more confrontation with Shastri. Of course, in characteristic fashion she would deny this. She wrote to Vijayalakshmi Pandit in 1965: 'It may seem strange that a person in politics should be wholly without political ambition but I am afraid I am that sort of freak.'[21]

She was the freak who knew politics was her true calling, but still kept disingenuously denying it. Instead she continued to insist that Shastri was just not up to the job of filling her father's shoes. 'Mr Shastri was surrounded by people who are biased in favour of the western bloc. For instance when the Russians suggested the Tashkent meeting, Mr Shastri asked if the Americans would mind. I remember I was most distressed by this attitude for I felt we should not encourage any country to interfere in our affairs . . . I remember warning against the Congress sliding away from the socialist path . . . conservative groups had come very much to the fore after my father's death.' Socialists and conservatives would be euphemisms for pro-Indira and anti-Indira forces respectively in her dictionary. Those who were on her side were progressive and socialist, those against her, pro-American right-wing stooges. Had Shastri lived and prospered as prime minister, Indira Gandhi might well have seen his tenure as a diversion from the Nehruvian path. She would say disapprovingly, 'Shastriji seemed soft towards the Jana Sangh . . . his nature was gentle and some people take civilised and gentlemanly behaviour to mean weakness.'

As it turned out, in an accident of history – and history is littered with such accidents that favour those destined to stamp their presence on it (would Nehru, for example, have ruled unrivalled if Sardar Patel had not died in 1950?) – on 11 January 1966, a day after the Tashkent Agreement between India and Pakistan was signed, sixty-one-year-old Lal Bahadur Shastri, prime minister for only nineteen months, died in Tashkent.

~

The Congress found itself in a quandary. The Syndicate tried hard to persuade Kamaraj to take Shastri's place. Kamaraj is supposed to have replied, 'No English, no Hindi – how?' Once again the Syndicate united in common cause: Morarji had to be stopped. Domineering as he was, they were fearful he would unflinchingly chart his own course and grow too big for them.

The eye of the Syndicate fell on Nehru's daughter. The general elections of 1967 were only thirteen months away. She was a national figure, not identified with a group or region, she was a link to Nehru and would be more of a vote catcher than any of them. She was forty-eight, relatively young, her hands shook violently when she answered questions in Parliament,[22] suffering as she did from painful nervousness while making public speeches. Her natural place, they thus assumed, was the background. She was soft-spoken, reticent, hardly a threat. Her gender became her advantage too. 'If I had been a son, I could not have helped him [Nehru] in the way I have . . . the political world would have been much more sensitive to the situation and wary of it,'[23] Indira would say. Gender was both her asset and her liability. The chauvinistic Syndicate thought her harmless enough for their patronage. Once elevated, she would, they expected, be a mere figurehead, 'a lump of clay to mould and re-mould'.[24] She would, like the Queen of England, be a pretty figurehead, while they ruled from behind. B.K. Nehru noted: 'To them Indira was a chit of a girl whom they thought they could manipulate . . . How wrong the Syndicate were in judging that chit of a girl they were soon to discover to their cost.' 'It is always a great advantage to be underrated,' writes Sharada Prasad, '. . . she very soon demonstrated to the country what a grandmaster she was at political chess.'

As we have seen in the previous chapter, a year before her father's death, Indira Gandhi had written to Dorothy Norman about wanting to leave India. If Shastri hadn't died, if she had continued only as a junior minister, it is possible that she may have eventually left India. As it turned out, Shastri's death cleared her way. Poised at the pinnacle of power she would write to her son Rajiv these lines from Robert Frost: 'How Hard Is It To Keep From Being King, When It's In You And The Situation . . .' When Pupul Jayakar visited her after Shastri's death, she found Indira 'holding her excitement in check, outwardly calm but bursting out, "No one can be Prime Minister without my support."'

She played her cards with quiet skill. While Desai openly declared his intentions, she stayed coyly and strategically reticent, only venturing to say she would be 'guided by the wishes of the Congress and its president, Kamaraj'. Morarji demanded an open election between himself and Indira with all Congress MPs voting. In the leadership contest on 19 January 1966 by secret ballot, she won 355 votes to his 169.

On 24 January Indira Gandhi was sworn in as prime minister for the first time. She was to admit: 'There was a very strong feeling against Morarji Desai. I think at that point, they were not so much for me as against him.' Morarji, lacking in the communication and strategic skills to win people over, lost out to both Shastri and Indira.

Indira made sure that everyone registered that she was about to take her place, watched over by the exalted spirit of the national struggle. On the day of her election, she had entered Parliament with a rose pinned to her shawl, just as Nehru had worn a rose on his sherwani. When she took the oath of office, she used the words 'solemnly affirm' rather than 'I swear in the name of God'. She was Nehru's proxy in power; above the daughter's head floated the holy ghost of the first prime minister.

She would remain prime minister for the next eleven years, essaying what many have called an epic transformation – from shy novice to domineering matriarch. It was less a transformation and more a revelation of her real nature. It was an evolution of characteristics she already possessed and a flowering of dormant seeds. The curtains would part to reveal what had always existed. The tomboyish child may have become a trembling young adult but those were only the natural nerves at the rehearsal. When it came to opening night, the performance revealed a talent that had germinated for long.

'She was at sea in the beginning,' recalls Mark Tully.[25] 'At a press conference in 1966 she just sat there looking shell-shocked while being attacked by journalists from all sides.' Wrote another journalist, 'She doesn't have a style of her own . . . the style is phony . . . her every gesture seems modelled on the late Jawaharlal Nehru . . . a trifle parodied, a trifle grotesque as it evokes nostalgic memories of the original.'[26]

But she soon did acquire a distinctive style. 'Just five years later when I met her before the Bangladesh war, she had become a completely different person, very determined, someone you couldn't break in an interview,' says Tully. Her slight frame belied her capabilities. 'When you first saw her and saw how small and how slight she was, the first reaction invariably was gosh, is this the woman who's trying to run the country? My god, how does she do it,' recalls former bureaucrat Manmohan 'Moni' Malhoutra, who joined her secretariat in 1966.[27]

India got its first woman prime minister, who refused to be cast as a woman. The women's movement was flowering in the West but she refused to box herself into any kind of alternate corner, to be anything other than strongly mainstream. 'I do not see myself as a woman in regard to this task . . . if a woman has necessary qualifications for whatever profession she should be allowed to work in that profession. I'm no feminist, I'm a human being. I don't see myself as a woman when I do my job. I am just an Indian citizen and the first servant of this country, desh sevika.'

It was an ordeal at first. Inexperienced and hopelessly intimidated by her rivals, she was tongue-tied and inarticulate in Parliament. Nineteen sixty-six was an 'annus horribilis'.[28] Indira came to power in an India where the rains had failed two years in a row, an India besieged by drought, food shortages and rice riots. There was an insurgency in Nagaland, demands for a separate state by Mizo tribes and a growing, openly communal demand for the Punjabi suba or a Sikh state. The economy was faltering badly. It was reported that with an imports bill of Rs 2194 crore and an exports bill of Rs 1264 crore, India's trade deficit stood at a whopping Rs 930 crore.[29] During the 1965 war, the United States had suspended aid to both India and Pakistan and the food distribution system of transferring grain from food surplus zones to deficit zones had broken down.

In that winter of discontent, there was growing anger against the government for giving away the Haji Pir Pass to Pakistan under the Tashkent Agreement. Indira was subject to mocking and bitter diatribes in Parliament. 'She's nothing but a goongi gudiya,' jeered Ram Manohar Lohia, socialist leader and lifelong baiter of the Nehru family, in a sexist attack. 'They were very rough with her in Parliament,' recalls Natwar Singh. 'Minoo Masani, Nath Pai, Hiren Mukherjee, Lohia, they gave her a terrible time.' The jaunty, liberal Masani, LSE graduate and barrister; the eloquent orator and passionate socialist Nath Pai; the scholarly and articulate Lohia; and the communist, Oxford-returned barrister Hiren Mukherjee – Nehru's favourite parliamentarian who spoke such impeccable Oxonian English that even Nehru sat spellbound during his speeches[30] – were some of the formidable, swashbuckling parliamentary talents Indira was up against in her early years. These were men who openly scoffed at her and delighted in cheerfully reminding her of her inadequacies. In a recent interview Sonia Gandhi recalled how badly Indira was ridiculed. 'In the early days, she used to get stomach upsets because she was so nervous,' recalls Dr Mathur. 'Even later in 1969 when she had to present the budget she was so nervous that she lost her voice. I suggested gargling and sprays but nothing helped . . . the malady was in her mind.' It was an initiation by fire she would never forget and led her in later years to downgrade and scorn Parliament rather than rejoice in its debates as Nehru had done. 'You can't really compare them,' insists Natwar Singh. 'Every time Nehru rose to speak in the House everyone would automatically sit down and listen quietly. She certainly didn't get the same respect.'

In 1966 Indira Gandhi knew that the most urgent task ahead of her was to secure adequate supplies of grain. Food stocks were running out and there was little foreign exchange to import food. The threat of starvation deaths loomed. In late March 1966 she journeyed to America to persuade President Lyndon Johnson to give India food and foreign exchange 'without asking for them',[31] even though when she arrived in the US, some US newspapers ran the headline 'New Indian Leader Comes Begging'.[32]

The tall Texan was charmed by the elegant, young prime minister from India, superbly stylish with a fashionable bouffant hairstyle, beautifully chosen saris and charming manners. 'She was very elegantly dressed abroad, hair perfectly coiffeured, high-heeled shoes, she looked like a queen. She stood out,' recalls Natwar Singh. Johnson was bowled over and said he wanted to see that 'no harm comes to this girl'. Recalled Indira later, 'The papers said no President had gone out of his way for a guest as President Johnson had for me . . . he came for a dinner and wouldn't leave.' Her visit for the moment was a great success.

In the romance of her presence, Johnson promised three million tonnes of food and $9 million as aid. In return, however, India would have to begin economic reforms that the World Bank, the International Monetary Fund (IMF) and the US administration had been demanding, namely, higher priority to agriculture, more measures to spur private investment and private foreign investment, downgrading public sector undertakings (PSUs) and, most important, substantially devaluing the Indian rupee.

~

Perhaps because she did not fully understand the repercussions of the decision, perhaps because the adage good economics is bad politics was not familiar to her just then, or perhaps because she was overwhelmed by the warmth she received in the United States and the highly positive tone of her meetings with President Johnson, she took a bold decision just four months after becoming prime minister. Ignoring growing rumblings of protest about her US trip, Indira Gandhi devalued the Indian rupee. Reporting on the famous decision taken on 6 June 1966, the *Times of India* ran a banner headline: 'Rupee devalued by 36.5 per cent'.

Famine was averted. India staved off bankruptcy. By fiercely stepping up domestic production the trade deficit came down.[33] But politically, all hell broke loose. Food aid from America was humiliating enough but devaluing the Indian rupee as a result of US pressure became politically explosive. Socialist India, proud leader of the Non-Aligned Movement, now with a begging bowl in hand meekly subjecting herself to Uncle Sam's diktats? Devaluation made Indira Gandhi universally unpopular. Even the Congress Working Committee passed a resolution condemning it. Her old associate Krishna Menon led a fierce attack on her. Her left-leaning friends and advisers, members of her 'kitchen cabinet' – such as the young Nandini Satpathy, author and MP, her close colleague who would go on to be chief minister of Orissa; Uma Shankar Dikshit; D.P. Mishra, chief minister of Madhya Pradesh; and I.K. Gujral – urged a speedy return to the socialist nationalist line to recoup the loss in public confidence and fight the charge that Indira had become an American stooge.

Shocked and caught completely off guard by the attacks on her, she moved fast to re-establish her left-secular credentials. She condemned American bombing and 'imperialist aggression' in Vietnam. Any further liberal reforms such as removal of control on capital inflow were immediately halted. In November 1966 Hindu groups in their thousands, among them trishul-brandishing naga sadhus, attempted to storm Parliament demanding an immediate ban on cow slaughter. The crowd became violent, and the police opened fire. Some protesters were killed, sparking more disturbances, shops and buildings were torched and by nightfall the army was out on the streets for the first time since 1947.[34] Indira Gandhi attempted to bolster her secular credentials by declaring that she had no intention of being 'cowed down by cow savers'. Nehru had rejected all demands for a ban on cow slaughter saying he would rather resign than give in to this 'futile, silly, and ridiculous' demand. Nehru's daughter similarly stared down the mutinous holy men and firmly, even brutally, put down the cow agitation. She also took this opportunity to force the resignation of the home minister, Gulzari Lal Nanda, whom she had never liked and who was a devout Hindu committed to cow protection.

A sudden return to America-bashing leftism naturally did not go down well in the United States. Johnson, who had been so enchanted by Indira, was now enraged at her denunciation of America. The friendship established in the United States was shattered. Food shipments were delayed. Already American aid had been erratic and slow to appear. Burdened with the charge of a 'sellout' from both left and right, and not even any fulsome supplies of grain to show for it, she became politically isolated.

She seemed at this stage not to quite understand the political process, or the need to do the homework to find a political consensus before announcing policies. In the absence of such understanding she got carried away by her belief in her own connect with the people. In a highly telling statement about her brand of politics, even as she weathered criticism from her own party, she declared, 'Here is a question of whom the party wants and who the people want.

My position among the people is uncontested.'[35] 'She very much regretted the devaluation decision. The decision had been sold to her by rightists like B.K. Nehru [then Indian ambassador to the US] and L.K. Jha [then her principal secretary]. She thought afterwards that she had made a big mistake,' says Natwar Singh.

The Syndicate blustered openly. Did this creature, obligated to them for her position and survival, an unelected nominee, now dare to think and act autonomously? That she had not even consulted Kamaraj before devaluation opened up a crater of misunderstanding between her and her erstwhile benefactors. Devaluation marked a fundamental parting of ways between Indira Gandhi and Kamaraj: the Syndicate wanted the party to be all-powerful in decision-making while Indira, quite contrary to their early assessment of her, was now insisting on asserting her supremacy as prime minister. 'A big man's daughter, small man's mistake,' muttered an angry Kamaraj.

On AIR on 12 June 1966, Indira Gandhi took the country into confidence: 'Let me be frank with you. The decision to devalue the rupee was not an easy one . . . there are times in the history of every nation when its will is tested and its future depends on its capacity for resolute action and bold decisions.'[36] American aid and American pressure to devalue may have become political dynamite in 1966 but ironically, just three years later an American, who had first come to India in Nehru's time, would come to India's rescue. By the 1970s what is called the Green Revolution would make India self-sufficient in wheat, maize and rice, the foundations of the Green Revolution laid by Lal Bahadur Shastri and his agriculture minister C. Subramaniam.[37] The 'father' of that revolution was Norman Borlaug from Iowa, the Nobel Prize–winning American who decades later an Indian government would honour with a Padma Vibhushan.

~

Dear Mrs Gandhi,

Was the devaluation of the rupee the first show of your hand to the Syndicate? Was this the first glimpse you gave them of your resolve to act autonomously? It was the first sign that, however much you may have been their appointed goongi gudiya, in the exercise of prime ministerial authority you would act on your own without deferring to party strongmen. You were in the chair where you rightly belonged and you would govern in what you thought was the best interests of the country. You knew that to function as prime minister and to create the India of Nehru's dreams you would need more autonomy than they would ever be willing to concede.

You hated the control that party bosses thought they had over you. Kamaraj wanted power to be shared not only with the party leadership but also with state chief ministers, a power-sharing which would have made you a non-functioning prime minister and made governance impossible. Nehru did not need to share power because his stature was unchallenged. But your supporters believed you needed to strike out against the party bosses, while your detractors argued that you were unable to rule by consensus and wanted sole decision-making rights.

Had you realized by now that the doyens of your party were becoming acutely uncomfortable with you and there would be no easy coexistence between you and them? Had the storm over devaluation convinced you that from now on every decision would have to be measured by its populism and 'the support of the people', because your rivals were waiting to strike?

~

Nineteen sixty-seven, the twentieth anniversary of Independence, was the year Indira would turn fifty. She was, by her own admission, 'very fit' and kept up her daily regimen of yoga. Her stamina was tested that year. In February general elections were held as scheduled. More sexist remarks were hurled at her. Ram Manohar Lohia exhorted the public to throw out the Congress so that this 'pretty woman' did not have to 'suffer pain and trouble beyond her endurance'.

Indira plunged into the election campaign with gusto, even breaking her nose at a rally in Bhubaneswar when a stone was thrown at her full in the face. Undaunted, yelling 'what insolence is this!' at the stone-pelting crowd, her fighting spirit at the ready, she charged on to rally after rally, a bandage covering half her face, making her look, she said, 'like Batman'. After her broken nose she would even contemplate a nose job, writing to Dorothy Norman: 'Ever since plastic surgery was heard of, I have been wanting to get something done to my nose . . . I thought the only way it could be done without the usual hoo-haa was first to have some slight accident which would enable me to have it put right.' But she never did find the time for this cosmetic surgery and all her life remained painfully conscious of her long nose.

She was the refined memsahib, the object of awe and adoration for India's public, which still admired memsahibs in the 1960s. At the same time she conveyed a wholesome maternal good sense with which the Indian housewife could identify. As one of her biographers writes, this subtle synthesis of aristocracy and populism was to be the secret of her political success.

Hemmed in by the Syndicate, she fought the 1967 campaign like a lone virangana, calling all Indians her family in a tone so many politicians emulate today. The 'little woman', the 'mere chokri', reached out and embraced voters, saying 'you are my family . . . crores of my family members who I have to look after'.[38] She knew the language of 'family' was a resource they could never have. Could Kamaraj sail into crowds and be welcomed every time with open arms? Could Morarji?

The faltering, weak-voiced girl was now gone. Shuffling movements were replaced by determined, quick strides. Her voice, still thin, rang with new energy. Her normally shy, retiring expression changed: now her chin tilted upwards aggressively, her smile changed from lopsided, shaky grin to a bright-eyed beaming. She contested elections for the first time from Feroze Gandhi's constituency of Raebareli as if to lay claim to his pro-poor leftist radicalism. Old-timers in Raebareli still remember her campaign. 'She came here as a bahu,' recalls Deen Dayal Shastri, who was then a young member of the Congress's grassroots organization, Seva Dal, 'the pallu never left her head and she waded deep into the crowds. We knew her well since the time she had campaigned for Feroze Gandhi.'[39]

She rallied to muster pro-poor sentiment and win back the common people. Out of the churn of politics rose a new deity – Indira Gandhi, champion of common people. She attracted gargantuan crowds, speaking the language of hope for the poor, as if hers was the voice that would represent the dispossessed and downtrodden. Ideology became the accessory of politics, not the other way around. Ideology for Indira Gandhi was not steeped in conviction but an instrument to seize power. Ideology made sense only when it would lead to power; it was not a commitment for its own sake as it had been for Feroze Gandhi or for Nehru.

This was the lesson of the rupee devaluation fiasco. Economic decisions must always be tested on their politics. If the political fallout was guaranteed to be positive then that's where the economics had to go. She did not have the insight to realize that it is incumbent upon leaders to create a conducive political environment for the economic policies (such as devaluation) that they want to pursue. Instead of moving to create a policy consensus, hers was the politics of smash and bludgeon. Populist economics and an emotional bond with the people were and would always be Indira Gandhi's weapons against her rivals.

Yet her first test as a vote catcher didn't quite go according to plan. In 1967 the Congress's vote share plummeted steeply. The Syndicate were decimated, felled in their bastions. Kamaraj in a 'fantastic fall' lost to a twenty-eight-year-old student leader of the Dravida Munnetra Kazhagam (DMK). S.K. Patil's Goliath crumbled to George Fernandes's David in Bombay, giving Fernandes the epithet 'George the giantkiller', and Atulya Ghosh and Biju Patnaik were vanquished in Bengal and Orissa respectively.

The Syndicate lost but Indira Gandhi won, romping to a win in Raebareli with a large majority. No wonder after her thumping electoral debut, Pupul Jayakar found her friend in a 'sparkling mood', saying that it was clear the older leaders of the Congress had lost touch with the people. With the Syndicate cut to size she would now be left to fend for herself, a situation that, in the years to come, would bring out the best and the worst in her.

The general elections of 1967 came as a shock for the Congress. As the political scientist Rajni Kothari puts it, it was a 'watershed in Indian politics'. For the first time in independent India, Congress dominance was seriously challenged. The Congress only managed a perilously thin majority of 283 seats, and across India there were gains for the Swatantra Party and the Bharatiya Jana Sangh, parties that Indira held were 'diametrically opposed to our secularism, our socialism and our foreign policy'. The Swatantra Party or right-wing party was the gainer with as many as forty-four seats; the Hindu revivalist Jana Sangh won thirty-five seats.

In state elections in the same year the grand old party was bundled out in several states. The Congress collapsed in the crucial Hindi heartland states of Uttar Pradesh and Bihar, as it did in Kerala, Punjab, Orissa, West Bengal, Rajasthan and Tamil Nadu with parties opposing the Congress like the communists, Akalis, DMK and the Samyukta Vidhayak Dal (SVD) coalitions (rather ragtag alliances) taking charge. The Congress had never faced such a nationwide challenge before, the brutal suppression of the sadhus' cow agitation partly blamed by many observers for the rout. Indira Gandhi would react with what would become her customary brahmastra (supreme weapon): the imposition of a Pax Indira.

If Pax Britannica or British Peace in the nineteenth and early twentieth centuries created relative order in the world because of the hegemony of the British empire, a Pax Indira was Indira Gandhi's very own imperially imposed order based on the hegemony of Indira Gandhi, of Indira Regina. She imposed the Pax Indira whenever she was faced with what she deemed was 'disorder'. By

1969 President's Rule would be in place in West Bengal, Uttar Pradesh, Bihar and Punjab.

In a badly damaged party, Indira Gandhi and the Syndicate could no longer cohabit amicably and a do-or-die face-off looked inevitable. She would have to destroy the Syndicate or they would destroy her. For the moment though, with a big victory under her belt, the annihilated Syndicate could not stop Indira Gandhi from taking the top job.

On 13 March 1967 Indira Gandhi was sworn in for the second time as prime minister. Now she was no longer nominated by the bosses – she was an elected leader with the force of the people behind her, although she had to compromise with Kamaraj and accept Morarji Desai, who had also won, as deputy prime minister and finance minister. To demonstrate her autonomy and executive authority she kept loyalists like Y.B. Chavan as home minister and appointed Jagjivan Ram to the key ministry of agriculture without consulting Kamaraj or Desai. She was faced with a twofold challenge: to establish her own set of policies and assert her pre-eminence in the cabinet. This was not easy. Morarji went out of his way to slight her in public, sneering at a meeting of the Planning Commission: 'Indira-ben you don't understand this matter. Let me deal with it.'[40] She was enraged. The uneasy equilibrium seethed with tension.

However, by now she had an able adviser by her side, someone who would guide her sure-footed through the political labyrinth. Lessons learnt from the rupee devaluation brought this important person to Indira's side. He would be the man behind the glory years of Indira Gandhi, her Chanakya and strategist. By the time his tenure ended he was referred to as a 'legend', the man behind the successful woman.

After the shrill accusations of a surrender to America, and a quasi defeat at the polls, Indira lurched to the left and towards extreme populism. On her return to power in 1967 she eased out the brains behind the devaluation, her advisers Ashoka Mehta and C. Subramaniam, and also removed L.K. Jha, her principal secretary, who had been in favour of the move. She replaced Jha with Parmeshwar Narayan Haksar.

In 1967, fifty-four-year-old P.N. Haksar, or 'Babboo' Haksar, who would soon be called 'the country's most powerful civil servant',[41] became Indira Gandhi's principal secretary, remaining in that post until 1973.[42] Handsome, erudite, a Kashmiri Pandit, Feroze Gandhi's friend, bar-at-law, LSE graduate and former diplomat, P.N. Haksar was a 'force of nature'.[43] Many years ago in London he had cooked delicious Kashmiri dishes for his friends Indira and Feroze. Now as her most trusted mandarin, he would stir up even more potent fare than Kashmiri goshtaba. 'Warm-hearted, generous, a vibrant intellectual, it was Haksar who was behind many of her triumphs,' says Malhoutra. 'He played a key role in bank nationalization, in coining the slogan "Garibi Hatao" and in the 1971 war.' Haksar was committed to secular values but recited Sanskrit shlokas and Persian verses with equal ease and his arguments were peppered with quotations from Valmiki to Voltaire. Haksar's leftism was hard-headed. 'Haksar tempered the leftism of her other friends like Romesh Thapar and moderated their inputs for her. It was because of Haksar that she often did not go as far left as they might have wanted her to,' says Wajahat Habibullah. For example, as she pressed ahead with her socialist agenda, she would nationalize banks but not foreign trade, nor withdraw all concessions to foreign investors. Haksar's leftism did not altogether blunt his pragmatism.

'She had an outstanding person in Haksar,' says Natwar Singh. 'Someone who would not hesitate to tell her if he thought something was wrong: Indiraji, yeh nahin hoga, iske baare mein sochiye [this can't be done, please rethink this], he would say. He was the man behind the 1971 war. In fact, he was the brains behind it, not her.'

Others are not so laudatory about Haksar's role. Inder Malhotra believed Haksar pulled her firmly down the leftist ideological road and weakened the administrative ethos by his partiality to 'the committed civil servant' (an officer who was ideologically aligned rather than a neutral executive). The politicized bureaucrat was a constitutional aberration.

'Indira herself was neither leftist nor rightist,' says R.K. Dhawan. 'It was Haksar who converted her into leftist mode. That was Haksar's big mistake.' The early years of Indira Gandhi thus became Haksar's regime. The left-wing devotee of Nehru was passionate about the transformation of India in Nehru's image. It was a mission that led to a search for the like-minded at all levels of government, blurring the lines between ideology and impartial administration. Under Haksar, the prime minister's secretariat became a well-organized leviathan, towering over even the cabinet secretary, who in normal circumstances is the head of the bureaucracy. P.N. Dhar, who succeeded Haksar to the principal secretary's post, calls Haksar an 'activist', keen to make his boss a successful prime minister. Before appointing anyone to the prime minister's secretariat, he would make sure the person was loyal to Indira and it was under Haksar that Indira established her political identity as one based on economic radicalism and an anti-American slant.

Haksar and his merry men – diplomats T.N. Kaul and D.P. Dhar, economist P.N. Dhar and security adviser R.N. Kao, a clutch of highly competent Kashmiri Pandit bureaucrats seen as Indira's chosen knights in shining armour – were committed to making India in a 'progressive' image. The larger institutional implications of the ideologizing of administration and creating a looming prime minister's office were lost in the passion to transform India in the 'correct' and 'progressive' way. In the end Haksar fell afoul of his boss. In a precipitous fall from grace he became persona non grata when he crossed someone more dear to her than anyone else could ever be: her younger son, Sanjay Gandhi.

~

In 1967, a new battle between Indira and the party opened on who should be the Republic of India's third President. President

S. Radhakrishnan's term was coming to an end. A well-disposed President was of utmost importance for Indira, given the hostility of the party and ever-present danger of being removed from office. Dr Radhakrishnan treated Indira as a protégée; his attitude to her in the paternalist tradition was affectionate and non-serious.[44] Rather than listening, he would lecture her on what to do. Getting a less superior president was key to handling the building tensions with her party and she managed to get her nominee Dr Zakir Husain to become rashtrapati in the face of the Syndicate's determination to push a second term for Dr Radhakrishnan.

She scored over her opponents by asking a question that appealed to the then sacred secular identity of the Congress in need of reiteration given the renewed intensity of communal conflicts at this time. 'When people want to know why Zakir Husain was bypassed, what answer will you give?' she taunted the Syndicate, saying 'a lot of people didn't like a Muslim becoming president'. Indira was very proud of this 'secular' achievement. 'When I was Congress president and even earlier, many people felt how can a minority person be a Chief Minister because the majority is another religion and they won't stand for it. So I worked for it without any fanfare or slogan mongering and I was able to change the atmosphere, so now we've had Muslims in the highest possible places like the President of India,'[45] she would boast. Alas, it would become apparent in the future that her way of practising secularism always remained more symbolic than substantive.

Zakir Husain duly became president in May 1967. In the same year Indira also announced a socialist ten-point programme. By 1968 the first gains of the Green Revolution began to appear. District collectors, who had at first been unable to convince many farmers to buy Borlaug's high-yielding seeds, now watched in wonder as the seeds became so popular that they were even sold in the black market. While India's tall, wispy local rice plants collapsed in heavy rain, there through floods and storms stood Borlaug's squat, sturdy new plants, delivering bumper crops.[46] With the dismissal of state governments in Bihar, Uttar Pradesh, West Bengal and Punjab, Indira was by now a formidable adversary and her success was becoming intolerable for her detractors. By late 1968, Desai and Kamaraj became determined to oust Indira.

They still did not know what they were up against though. Soon Indira Gandhi would move to pre-empt her rivals by launching an offensive that literally bankrupted them. After the 1967 election setback, younger members of the Congress had been urging a return to the pro-poor, socialist, pro-Scheduled Caste–minorities–downtrodden plank. The rightward turn of devaluation and ties with the United States were seen as responsible for the disaster of 1967. The Syndicate was painted as a bunch of reactionary right-wing old gents, and she was seen as the head of the Young Turks, the bright-eyed socialist hope that would now recapture the Congress's past glory. 'She slowly began to gather around her all the younger people in the Congress. She brought together all the socialist and progressive-minded people, and the Syndicate got isolated,' recalled Vasant Sathe, Congressman and Indira loyalist.[47] In the gathering clamour for another leftward lurch, Indira Gandhi turned a political conflict into an ideological war. With the shrewd Haksar by her side, she scarcely put a foot wrong.

When Zakir Husain suddenly died on 3 May 1969, another contest of wills began. The Syndicate was once again determined to install their candidate, N. Sanjiva Reddy. Forcing a presidential candidate on a prime minister, Indira Gandhi told the press, amounted to an assault on her office. Instead of accepting Sanjiva Reddy, she pushed for her own nominee, V.V. Giri. In the looming war with her rivals, Indira Gandhi was observant, astute and sure-footed, 'a remarkable and brilliant politician', notes Natwar Singh.

Indira was convinced that the reason the Syndicate was pushing Sanjiva Reddy to become president was to relieve her of her prime ministership and install Morarji in her place. On 16 July 1969, in a 'lightning strike' advised by Haksar she suddenly stripped Morarji Desai of the finance portfolio, telling the media that she was being held back from implementing her 'progressive' economic agenda with him as finance minister. Even though he was not removed from the post of deputy prime minister, Desai, taken aback by Indira's move, promptly resigned just as Indira and Haksar had expected him to.

Within days, in another 'sensational move', on 19 July, Indira Gandhi nationalized fourteen of the largest private commercial banks by presidential ordinance as a 'personal act' of the prime minister. These banks were, in the government's view, only working for the rich and not providing credit to the poor. 'Mother Indira', whose heart bled for her less privileged children, announced on All India Radio: 'I complained that I had no shoes, when I met a man who had no feet.' The business community, hereditary princes and others denounced the move, saying Indira was trying to create a communist state in India, but she justified her action thus: 'Bank nationalisation was inevitable if Communism had to be stopped. The business community don't understand that there is no alternative, the extreme Right position has just no place in India. The whole mood of the country is Centre Left.'[48] Bank nationalization was aimed at winning the hearts of the poor and holding the Syndicate and the Opposition at bay. The politics was bold, calculated and strategic, designed for a capture of the political centre stage, even though the economics was to take a toll on India's emergence as a liberal economy. 'There is no doubt in hindsight,' says Moni Malhoutra, 'that many of her economic decisions were mistakes.' Bank nationalization was a powerful political bludgeon for the Syndicate but without accompanying measures to kick-start growth it became, as many feared it would, only a descent into even greater populism. Guha writes that bank nationalization as a policy appealed to Haksar because his socialism had a strong moral core; for Indira though it was primarily a pragmatic means of distinguishing herself from the Congress old guard.[49]

The journalist Swaminathan Aiyar points out that before 1969 banks were fiefdoms of big business, and that Indira Gandhi nationalized them to make them fiefdoms of politicians. If her aim was to help the poor then she could easily have ordered banks to lend to them. Instead, her motives in the bank takeover were to bankrupt the opposition and cut off the money supply to the Swatantra Party, the main opposition after the 1967, led as it was by businessmen and maharajas. As a result, 'the Swatantra Party collapsed, and businessmen crawled . . . The poverty ratio did not fall at all after 1947 till 1983 . . . [which] exposes the fraudulent intent and outcome of Indira's Garibi Hatao policies, spearheaded by bank nationalization.'[50,51]

Fraudulent or not, the main aim of bank nationalization was to checkmate the Syndicate, a 'masterstroke', according to some.[52] The move rallied public opinion firmly behind her. If the Syndicate had entertained any hopes of dismissing her, the tide of public approval now stood like a protective wall around Indira Gandhi.

'Bank nationalization was one of the best-kept secrets of the government of India,' recalls Natwar Singh. 'Nobody knew about it except four or five people. That's what made it such a potent weapon against her opponents, they were caught by surprise by the suddenness of it. In those days the secretariat didn't leak!' Prime Minister Narendra Modi's November 2016 demonetization announcement similarly caught the country by surprise and turned out to be politically almost as profitable, although the jury is still out on its impact on the economy.

Inder Malhotra went to report on the bank nationalization fallout among cheering crowds on Delhi's streets. 'Sir, have you ever visited a bank?' Malhotra asked rickshaw-wallahs and other poor who were dancing on the streets. 'No, we haven't,' they responded. 'Are you likely to visit a bank?' asked Malhotra. 'No,' came their answer. 'Then why are you jubilant?' probed Malhotra. 'Don't you understand?' the crowd shouted, 'because at last something has been done for the poor and the rich have been taught a lesson!'[53]

Indira Gandhi, the people's prime minister, bore down on the Syndicate from the high perch of popular adulation. The old guard was demonized as a set of crusty, conservative geriatrics out of touch with the surging energies of new India and a new socialist pro-poor movement. The mood on the street was exultant and Indira Gandhi was the bold young woman of the masses.

To crown her triumph, Indira Gandhi's nominee V.V. Giri won the presidential election in a down-to-the-wire battle. Indira handled the face-off with her customary poker-faced calm. On the evening before the results were to be announced Pupul Jayakar found Indira eating an omelette and listening to Beethoven. 'Don't be low, Pupul. It will be a tough fight but I am ready for it.' Giri became President on 24 August 1969, defeating the Syndicate's candidate Sanjiva Reddy. Once Giri's win was announced, a full-blown crisis began in the Congress and Indira Gandhi's clash with the Syndicate reached fever-pitch. The Congress was heading for an irrevocable parting of ways.

~

Siddavanahalli Nijalingappa, stalwart of the Syndicate, had replaced Kamaraj as Congress president in 1968. In October 1969, he wrote an open letter to Indira Gandhi accusing her of creating a 'personality cult', pointing out that the 'handful of people' she blamed for arrogating undue powers to themselves were the very people who had made her prime minister. In what would turn out to be an accurate prediction, he accused her of making 'personal loyalty to you the test of loyalty to the Congress and the country'.[54] Nijalingappa, writes Sharada Prasad, was a good man but out of his depth as a national leader. He was up against a formidable practitioner of the art of combative politics and he was no match for her.

On 1 November 1969, astoundingly, two parallel Congress Working Committee meetings were held, one at the Congress headquarters on Jantar Mantar Road, convened by the old guard, the other at the prime minister's residence at 1 Safdarjung Road. After the meeting, Indira Gandhi wrote to Congressmen: 'This is not a mere clash of personalities . . . it's a conflict between those who are for socialism, for change . . . and those who are for status quo and conformism.'[55] A flustered and weakened Nijalingappa expelled her from primary membership of the Congress in an announcement that read 'the Congress is regrettably obliged to remove Mrs Gandhi from the primary membership of the Congress'. Indira Gandhi shot back furiously: 'It is presumptuous on the part of this handful of men to take disciplinary action against the democratically elected leader of the people. Are we to submit to them or clean the organisation of these undemocratic and Fascist persons?'

Amid hectic political activity, the inevitable happened at last. The 'Great Split' took place. Congressmen were asked to make a choice. Out of a total of 429 Congress MPs in both Houses of Parliament 310 opted for Indira Gandhi. Indira became the leader of the new Congress(R) (Requisitionist) and the Syndicate formed the Congress(O) (Organisation). She lost her majority in both Houses but luckily the communists and regional parties were at hand to provide support, and the no-confidence motion brought by the Congress(O) was defeated. Indira Gandhi was now the supreme leader of the new Congress, with its members wedded to her ideology of socialism and secularism. She had outmanoeuvred the Syndicate repeatedly. Her aim had not been to split the Congress but to take it over. As if to bury the Mahatma's politics of high idealism, the Congress split took place in Gandhiji's centenary year.[56]

'The Congress split was the beginning of the end of democracy in the party,' says Mark Tully. 'She destroyed inner-party democracy by making herself the supreme leader of the Congress. She really came into her own when she broke the party but it was the end of the Congress, the beginning of autocracy. The split laid the ground for the consequent establishment of dynastic rule.' The single-leader-ruled party began to 'deinstitutionalize' the Congress: Indira sought absolute control over party organs such as the working committee and the parliamentary board. For the rest of her life, party elections were never held in the Congress faction she controlled. Loyalty to Indira now became the new examination all Congressmen had to take. Over time, all chief ministers who had not supported her against the Syndicate would slowly be eased out and 'nominated' chief ministers appointed in their place. Indira would not allow another Syndicate of regional powers to emerge. Her act of splitting the Congress was described as that of a 'political gangster', someone whose personal dominance was now seen as 'menacing' and 'dangerous'.

It was the end of Nehru's Congress. Indira's notion of political power was fundamentally different from Nehru's. He believed that true power came from nurturing a situation where power would not have to be overtly displayed. She often sought to overcompensate for her own credibility gap in her opponents' eyes by demonstrations of muscle-flexing. Perhaps she thought Nehru had it wrong, that power had not only to be wielded, but had to be seen wielded. She once told a friend that her father was too gentle with those who had crossed him and if it were within her power she would unhesitatingly dismiss such people.[57] Indeed when she was in a position to do so, she would frequently deploy the Queen of Hearts' famous retribution, 'Off With His Head'. When it came to understanding power and using power, Indira Gandhi left her Papu far behind.

She once sent Sharada Prasad a poem that especially resonated with her.

I would have gone to my Lord in his need,
Have galloped there all the way,
But this is a matter concerns the State;
And I, being a woman, must stay.
I may walk in the garden and gather
Lilies of mother-of-pearl.
I had a plan would have saved the State
But mine are the thoughts of a girl.
The Elder Statesmen sit on the mats
And wrangle through half the day;

A hundred plans they have
Drafted
And dropped,
And mine was the only way.

~

Dear Mrs Gandhi,

Did you ever regret breaking up the Congress party? The Congress had been the historic force, the movement to which your family had been dedicated, the party for which your grandfather, father and husband toiled, the party that even your mother had slaved for. And yet you went ahead and broke this party apart. When it came to your own survival did democracy within the party simply not matter to you? If you had handled the situation better and attempted greater dialogue and consultation perhaps your conflict with the Syndicate would not have become so big and taken the heavy toll it ultimately did. But splitting the Congress was the only way to ensure not only your own survival but also your supremacy.

Did you ever ponder on the dangers of personal rule where a once-great Congress would be reduced to a cluster around a personality? No, these considerations did not trouble you. You acted in the way you did because of your hatred for the Syndicate and because of the way your Papu had been treated in his later years. You were convinced that your father's goodness had made him weak, his idealistic nature had made him incapable of tough action against his detractors.

'During this period some people started measuring my actions by my father's standards,' you said in an interview. 'I don't like these comparisons . . . *A qui venge son pere, il nest rien d'ímpossible.* (For he who avenges his father, nothing is impossible.) Something of that spirit (of revenge) was there, in the beginning at least, because I did feel I had to vindicate his stand and politics.' But in the attempt to avenge your father, did you only end up hastening the decline of his party?

~

For Indira Gandhi, once she had acquired it, the leadership of the nation became her right, her drive for power a sacred duty, a duty that honoured her family and the memory of the freedom struggle. Without her there was no India, there was no link to the independence era, there was no Nehru–Gandhi legacy. Her triumph was India's triumph, her fall was India's defeat.

Pro-poor activism had now been established as the device to shore up power. The newly crowned radical princess now had to continue her energetic socialist agenda as part of the rise of a new, invigorated Congress-of-the-people. After bank nationalization, Indira Gandhi's government moved to discontinue special privileges for India's hereditary princes by abolishing privy purses, or payments that hereditary princes received from the government, through a Constitution amendment bill brought before Parliament in September 1970. What could be a more striking example of the battle against elite privileges than a battle against the feudal maharajas with their inherited riches, a move that brought over 6 million dollars to the exchequer?[58,59] She would say: 'What irritated people most was not the privy purses but the rest of it, the fact that princes didn't pay water and electricity rates. The poor man had to pay but the prince did not . . . these privileges were an irritant to the common man.'

When the bill was defeated in the Rajya Sabha, Indira Gandhi obtained a presidential proclamation to make it a law but it was challenged by the princes in the Supreme Court, which struck down the proclamation. Already the apex court had struck down compensation provisions for nationalized banks although it had upheld Parliament's right to nationalize banks and other industries. The radical government's agenda would need a bigger mandate, to keep its 'pledges to the people' and bring about 'social and economic changes through democratic means'; a bigger mandate was needed to amend the Constitution. So on Haksar's advice she called a mid-term poll in 1971.

With banks nationalized, an assault against privy purses launched and the Congress split, Indira Gandhi went into the mid-term polls of 1971 with the powerful slogan 'Garibi Hatao'. She struck the moral high note while her opponents persisted with a petty, resentful wail, 'Indira Hatao'. 'Garibi Hatao was Haksar's idea,' says Moni Malhoutra, 'and it was another masterstroke.'

Residents of Raebareli recall how in rallies she would mock the Opposition Grand Alliance (comprising the Jana Sangh, the Swatantra Party, the Congress[O], socialists and others), which in response to 'Garibi Hatao' was campaigning on the slogan 'Indira Hatao'. 'Woh kehte hain Indira hatao, main kehti hoon garibi hatao,' she yelled aggressively. When a *Newsweek* reporter asked her what the main issues were in the 1971 election, she beamed, 'I am the issue.'[60] The fumbling apprentice politician was gone; in her place stood an impassioned orator, the 'heroic crusader against reaction'. In forty-three days she travelled over 36,000 miles, addressed over 300 meetings and was heard or seen by an estimated 20 million people. Her ferocious energy paid off. In 1971 the new Congress(R) won a two-thirds majority with 352 seats. The losses of 1967 were reversed. Indira Gandhi streaked to the zenith of power. On 18 March 1971, she was sworn in as prime minister for the third time.

The scale of the 1971 election victory now convinced Congress radicals that it was their socialist agenda which had been endorsed by the people. The victory of progressive forces, the vanquishing of the old feudal order, the creation of laws that would make this 'social and economic transformation' a reality, these were now the declared motives of the Indira revolution, and the period began when Indira Gandhi, in Frank's words, began to 'see red'. The colour red would soon suffuse her own vision and thoughts, as war broke out and crimson waves came flooding into her brain.[61] The revolutionary leader's personality cult was about to be massively enhanced.

To her pro-poor radical stance would be added the halo of war heroine.

~

In December 1971 the Indian army 'liberated' East Pakistan after a short and decisive war. Bangladesh was created and Indira Gandhi became the first Indian prime minister to win a decisive military victory. After the Bangladesh war, her popularity knew no bounds.

~

Dear Mrs Gandhi,

Was the Bangladesh war for you a settling of scores with history? Was it a settling of scores with Pakistan, with the United States for supporting Pakistan, an opportunity to expose the hollowness of the two-nation theory[62] so bitterly opposed by Gandhi and your father? The 1971 war cancelled out the humiliation your father suffered in 1962. Nehru had inherited an India of enormous prestige in the world, an India of Mahatma Gandhi.

But you inherited an India humiliated by China, an India seemingly at the mercy of Pakistan, an India which had signed away the hard-won Haji Pir Pass at the Tashkent talks. India's greatness was in need of reiteration.

As a fanciful aside: were the Bengalis of East Pakistan rather special for you because of your long association with Bengal? Tagore's 'Ekla Chalo Re' was one of your favourite songs. You had studied at Santiniketan in Bengal, it was the place where your spirit had flowered more than even at Oxford and you idolized Rabindranath Tagore. On the eve of the Bangladesh war you told a public meeting in Calcutta, 'Ami bangla bujhte pari, bolte pari na [I can understand Bengali but can't speak it].' So just as the Bangladeshis have a special place for you reserved in their heart, perhaps there was a place in your heart reserved for Bengal too.

The Bangladesh war carved a distinct identity for you on the world stage. Your father had led the Non-Aligned Movement to become a global leader; now, you showed the world that Nehru's daughter had well and truly arrived. You were sending a tough message to Islamabad and Washington by changing the geography of the subcontinent and splitting Pakistan. After the 1971 war you were Indira Gandhi, India's most powerful prime minister, who would act aggressively in her nation's self-interest and according to her own moral values. The sheer guts and defiance you showed in standing up to a hostile America established you, at this time, as India's superwoman. No world power would dare push you or India around.

~

Separated by over a thousand miles of Indian territory, split into a West and East wing, Pakistan had been schizophrenic since birth. The fair-skinned Punjabis and Pathans of West Pakistan dominated government, the darker-complexioned, Bengali-speaking Pakistanis of the East had no place in administration or in the Pakistani 'Establishment'. The Bengalis of East Pakistan were passionately attached to the Bengali language and opposed to Urdu being declared as Pakistan's official language. Students killed in the 1952 anti-Urdu riots are revered as martyrs to this day in Bangladesh. In Pakistan's first general elections of December 1970, Sheikh Mujibur Rahman's Awami League won an overwhelming victory,[63] one that entitled the pipe-smoking Awami League leader Sheikh Mujib, whom Indira described as 'a sentimental, warm-hearted person, a father-figure', to become prime minister of Pakistan. But Zulfikar Ali Bhutto, leader of the Pakistan Peoples Party, which had emerged as the single largest party in West Pakistan, and Pakistan's military ruler General Yahya Khan refused to accept the Awami League's victory, suspicious that Mujib wanted to secede from Pakistan. Bhutto was hostile to Mujib and found the idea of him as Pakistan's prime minister insupportable. Yahya Khan indefinitely postponed Pakistan's National Assembly, to keep Sheikh Mujib out. Yahya reportedly told his officers, 'There can be no settlement with the "Bingos" until they are sorted out good and proper.'[64] When it looked as if the Awami League would be denied its place in the National Assembly, a powerful civil disobedience movement broke out in East Pakistan. While Yahya Khan and his team negotiated with the Awami League and Sheikh Mujib, there was an army build-up by West Pakistan in the East.

As massive protests raged through East Pakistan, Yahya responded with brute, merciless force, unleashing wave upon wave of slaughter, rapes, looting and burning by the Pakistani army. Thousands of innocents, professors, intellectuals and students were murdered – according to independent researchers 300,000 were killed and as many as 400,000 women were raped and children's eyes were gouged out and their limbs roughly hacked off. Women's breasts were torn out with specially designed knives.[65] 'Kill three million of them,' Yahya said, 'and the rest will eat out of our hands.'[66] The so-called democratic Bhutto apparently approved of this massacre, publicly thanking the army for saving Pakistan. Mujib was spirited away to jail in West Pakistan. Ravaged, frantic refugees from East Pakistan poured into India, reaching ten million at the height of the crisis, stretching India's resources to breaking point. Washington stayed deplorably silent. In fact America silenced officials who dared to speak up about the genocide, and even supplied weapons to Islamabad. As Gary J. Bass writes in his chilling book *The Blood Telegram*, it was a scandalous chapter for American diplomacy because of the way Washington allowed a bloodbath to unfold.[67]

'What was claimed to be an internal problem in Pakistan had also become an internal problem in India,'[68] Indira was to say. For a while Indira Gandhi was inactive and activists like Jayaprakash Narayan, who had organized a world conference on the genocide in East Pakistan, burst out, 'Does Indira think she can ignore me? I have seen her as a child in frocks.'[69] JP impetuously called on Indira to immediately attack Pakistan.

But Indira Gandhi bided her time. At the end of May 1971 she visited the refugee camps in West Bengal, Assam and Tripura.

P.N. Dhar, who accompanied her, writes: 'What we saw defied description . . . their physical and mental state . . . their terror stricken faces and individual tragedies, assaulted our moral sensibility.' Hordes of refugees waited for her to talk to them but, 'the PM was so overwhelmed by the scale of human misery, she could hardly speak'. Regiments of the Bangladesh army which had rebelled against West Pakistan were part of the exodus. They would become the Mukti Bahini, the guerrilla army for Bangladeshi liberation, receiving advice and training from the Indian army. 'The world must know what is happening here,' said Indira, 'we cannot let Pakistan continue this holocaust.'[70]

Indira Gandhi sallied forth. She would warn the international community about Pakistan's reign of terror in the East, she would, as she said, 'waken the conscience of the world', bring the ghastly sufferings of the East Pakistanis to the world's attention. Why was nothing being done to stop Pakistan? Diplomatic preparations made ahead of the war were careful and systematic.

On 7 July 1971, US National Security Adviser Henry Kissinger visited India. Soon after he left, India learnt that Kissinger had only stopped in Delhi on his way to China to prepare the ground for a dramatic détente. Coincidentally while Kissinger was in Delhi the Indian government had thrown a sumptuous Chinese banquet for him, the aptness of the cuisine later remarked on by Haksar. From Delhi, Kissinger flew to Pakistan from where Yahya Khan enabled him to fly to Beijing on a Pakistani military plane.

Within days, after a Sino-US estrangement of over two decades, Nixon announced he would visit China, which he did on 21 February 1972. While in India, Kissinger had indicated that, in the event of a war with Pakistan, India could not count on the United States to play any part against China's friend Pakistan. In fact, much of the groundwork for Nixon's China visit was done by Yahya Khan by opening secret talks with Pakistan's friend Chou En-lai. The United States leaned heavily in favour of Pakistan, against India.

India needed friends. Indira and Haksar now took up the offer of a friendship treaty extended three years earlier by Leonid Brezhnev with a clause which committed both countries 'to abstain from providing any assistance to any third party that engages in conflict with the other party'. Indira's close confidant D.P. Dhar, then ambassador to the Soviet Union, carried out negotiations in Moscow. The Indo-Soviet Treaty of Peace, Friendship and Cooperation was signed in Delhi on 9 August 1971 when Soviet Foreign Minister Andrei Gromyko visited India. With this treaty sewn up, Indira Gandhi, accompanied by Haksar and others, took off first to the Soviet Union to hold talks with Soviet leaders Brezhnev and Kosygin and ensure Soviet aid in the event of a military conflict. She then flew off on a twenty-one-day tour of Europe and America, addressing audiences in London and Washington to build opinion among intellectuals and in the media. In a BBC interview, asked why India should not show more restraint on Bangladesh, with eyes flashing (Jayakar saw in Indira 'Motilal's pugnacious jaw'), Indira snapped, 'When Hitler was on the rampage why didn't you say let's keep quiet, let's have peace with Germany and let the Jews die?' She went on to assert in biting tones: 'I don't think we can shut our eyes to the situation in a neighbouring country . . . we are threatened by the military regime of Pakistan, there has been a situation of indirect aggression . . . Pakistan as it existed can never be the same again.' 'That woman will not cow me down,' fulminated Yahya Khan in an apparently drunken outburst. 'I am not concerned with the remark,' retorted Indira in response, 'it shows the mentality of the person.'

On the way to America, Moni Malhoutra recalls her warning him about the conservative Nixon, known for his administration's face-off with student protesters. 'I had long hair at that time and I remember her telling me, "Moni, I think you better cut your hair. I hear Nixon is allergic to young men with long hair." It turned out both Indira and President Nixon were allergic to each other. She had flown to meet the American president in a last-ditch attempt to get the Americans to put pressure on Yahya Khan. But the tough lady from Delhi and the ruthless Republican from California who had no time for India disliked each other from the start. Nixon, according to Bass, found Indians repellent, deceitful and pro-Soviet, snarled that Indira was 'the old bitch', said, 'I don't know why the hell anybody would reproduce in that damn country but they do', and even said, 'Indians are such bastards. They need a mass famine.'

He was rude and the American journalist Seymour M. Hersh reported that he kept her waiting for forty-five minutes. Bass quotes Kissinger to say she treated Nixon with the elegant condescension of a 'professor praising a slightly backward student', which Nixon found intolerable and his comments about her were 'not always printable', as Kissinger wrote later. 'We really slobbered over the old witch,' Nixon told Kissinger later after the two leaders had sparred fiercely. The summit between Indira and Nixon, says Bass, was a 'cathartic brawl'. 'The talks went very badly,' says Moni Malhoutra. 'Kissinger was grateful to Yahya and had always had an awkward relationship with India. Nixon hated her and was horrible to her. There were reports that Nixon had told Kissinger, why is she allowing Bangladeshi refugees to come into India, she should shoot them at the border. That's the kind of mindset she was up against.'

Malhoutra recalls a telling incident, highly revealing of how Indira Gandhi dealt with hostile situations. At the state dinner that Nixon gave for her, she sat at the head of the U-shaped table next to the president, keeping her eyes completely closed through the dinner and refusing to speak. As she sat with her eyes closed, Nixon became more and more nervous. If he asked her a question, her answer would be laconic. She sat stock-still in front of all the guests with her eyes firmly closed all through a formal banquet. It was Indira's version of a classy but deadly snub. When Malhoutra asked her afterwards why she had done that, she responded airily that she had had a terrible headache. 'Of course, the headache was a complete lie,' says Malhoutra. 'She was a real player.' Insulted by the US president, Indira Gandhi had delivered a public retort to Nixon in style.

Nor did the urgency of war interfere with her penchant for the accessories of elegant dining. On the way back from the United States, at a stopover in Brussels, Malhoutra recalls how she pulled out a stylish pair of lorgnettes to read the menu at a restaurant. With war clouds gathering around her, she still took time off to attend a concert of the New York Philharmonic Orchestra in New York, watched Igor Stravinsky's ballet *Rites of Spring*, starring the great Soviet dancer Rudolf Nureyev, at the Royal Ballet in London and also watched Beethoven's opera *Fidelio* in Vienna. Europe was the playground of her youth: she had lived here in stimulating if war-torn times, when she had discovered new vistas in political thought and the arts, first with Nehru, then Feroze. A taste in the high culture of Europe and America was part of her self-image of an inheritor of classical traditions, both Indian and western. Without the pressure of the media trailing her every footstep, an Indian premier in the early 1970s could partake of a bit of leisure even with war looming ahead and genocide on the borders. Ballet and hostilities with Pakistan, strategic diplomacy and Beethoven, all were part of the Indira persona, hers was an assertion of a world identity for herself and for all Indians. She was the internationalist-patriot who emphasized not only India's moral leadership but also its cultural leadership in the world. Work and leisure for her were never compartmentalized, but flowed into each other. Later that year, rushing back from Calcutta on the eve of the Bangladesh war, she was calmly immersed in the Norwegian adventurer Thor Heyerdahl's book on his transatlantic voyage on a boat built of papyrus, and everyone around her was struck at the composure with which she was handling the crisis.

After her US trip, it was clear that Nixon would do nothing to help and India was on its own. The presence of the refugees and the Bangladesh government-in-exile led by Tajuddin Ahmed made it imperative for New Delhi to act. Indira didn't want India to be seen as the aggressor, but Pakistan played into her hands. On 3 December 1971 the Pakistanis launched Operation Chengiz Khan against India. The Pakistani Air Force bombed Indian airbases in the western sector and there were artillery attacks in Kashmir. The attack was called Pakistan's 'unlucky strike', an allusion to the famous cigarette brand at this time, Lucky Strike. Indira was addressing a meeting in Calcutta when she heard the news. 'Thank God they've attacked us,' she said. India was now handed a reason to go to war. And once Indira decided to hit, she always brought down a sledgehammer. With Generals S.H.F.J. 'Sam' Manekshaw, then army chief, and Jagjit Singh Aurora, Commander-in-Chief, Eastern Command, leading her armies, Indira Gandhi invaded East Pakistan.

In her now-famous open letter to Nixon, which was drafted by Haksar while the war was on, she didn't hesitate to sound angry and belligerent, directly accusing America of not doing enough. '. . . lip service was paid to the need for a political solution but not a single step was taken to bring this about . . . we seek nothing for ourselves . . . we are deeply hurt by the innuendoes and insinuations that it was we who precipitated a crisis.'[71]

Nixon was furious and denounced India's 'aggression'. A task force of the US Seventh Fleet, led by the nuclear warship *Enterprise*, was dispatched and began to steam towards the Bay of Bengal. But Indira was defiant. On 12 December, at a public rally in Ram Lila Maidan, Delhi, as news of the Seventh Fleet's advance on India exploded in the press and Indian fighter jets circled overhead to protect the gathering, she thundered, 'We will *not* retreat. Not by a single step will we move back.' 'We shall always defend our freedom,' she would later say, 'if need be with our bare fists. We must have arms to defend our country . . . conviction in our ideals.'

B.K. Nehru, whose 'pro-Americanism' was destroyed by America's attitude to the war, writes, 'This crude attempt at terrorizing India was given the contemptuous response it deserved by Indira Gandhi whose courage at this time even her greatest detractors have never questioned.' Guha, however, points out that the American threat to India was an idle one. Already bogged down in Vietnam, America could hardly afford another war, particularly not with an Indo-Soviet treaty in the mix. But Indira's impressive stoicism won universal admiration. She was, like Motilal, as hard as a rock.

The war was over in fourteen days. Before the Seventh Fleet reached the Bay of Bengal, Pakistan surrendered and the Indian army liberated Dhaka. Indira Gandhi had outwitted Nixon and Kissinger at a time when any loss of nerve could have meant all-out war on India. In sharp contrast with the savagery of the West Pakistan forces, the Indian army maintained an exemplary code of conduct. Wrote a British journalist: 'The Indian army's performance as a temporary occupation force has surpassed its performance on the battle field.'[72]

On 16 December 1971, the defeated Pakistani army surrendered unconditionally to India in the largest surrender since the Second World War. Over 93,000 officers and men laid down their weapons. Bangladesh was born. That same day Indira Gandhi announced in Parliament: 'The West Pakistan forces have unconditionally surrendered in Bangladesh . . . the instrument of surrender was signed by Lt. Gen. A.A.K. Niazi on behalf of the Pakistan Eastern Command. Lt. Gen. Jagjit Singh Aurora . . . accepted the surrender . . . Dhaka is now the free capital of a free country . . . we are proud of our Army, Navy, Air Force and the Border Security Force . . . the people of the new nation of Bangladesh have our good wishes.'

The House rose in standing ovation. Uproarious cheering and celebrations erupted in Parliament and across the country. Some leaders hailed her as Goddess Durga. Jana Sangh leader Atal Bihari Vajpayee reportedly called her 'Abhinav Chandi Durga', although he later denied this.[73] Opposition MPs lauded her, the public was jubilant, a nation humbled by the Chinese just a decade earlier bounded to its feet, its nationalism and its moral purpose flying high.

~

Indira Gandhi had taken direct responsibility for the war, along with a small group of officers – Haksar; 'spymaster' R.N. Kao, special secretary external intelligence; D.P. Dhar, ambassador to the Soviet Union; and T.N. Kaul, foreign secretary, her Kashmiri knights, branded the 'Kashmiri mafia' – a high-risk strategy that meant failure could have become her Waterloo. She would confidently say: 'I had not the slightest doubt that the Bangladeshis would win their freedom . . . and we couldn't afford to be on the wrong side . . . What I am most proud of is that the war was so neatly done . . . due to the leadership in the army and the excellent rapport between me and the armed forces. I kept in constant touch with them.'

Mark Tully believes the role of the army was crucial. 'The fundamental people in 1971 were the army. She had wanted to do it very quickly. But Manekshaw, under the advice of the Eastern Command, refused. He told her that it could not be done until proper preparations were made and the monsoon was over,' says Tully. However, military historian Srinath Raghavan argues that in the early period of the Bangladesh crisis India was circumspect about plans to attack East Pakistan anyway so the story of the delay advised by Manekshaw may be somewhat apocryphal.[74]

The ceasefire on the western front that she immediately announced, again reportedly at the behest of Haksar, was praised for its statesmanship. The knock-out punch that wrestled Pakistan to the ground but retreated almost immediately into the velvet glove would not have been quite so effective had hostilities continued messily and needlessly in the west. In victory, Indira was graceful and restrained. In later months, the act of sending back the ten million Bangladeshi refugees with remarkable speed and efficiency sealed her Bangladesh triumph.

She had become the first and only Indian prime minister who rose to the level of de facto commander-in-chief of the nation, winner of a decisive military victory against the perpetual enemy, Pakistan, liberator of the helpless Bangladeshis, woman with courage unbound yet for her it was all in a day's work. What if the United States had come to Pakistan's aid? What if China had acted against India? What if the Indo-Soviet Peace Treaty had not been honoured? None of these possibilities apparently fazed her.

When Dr Mathur visited her home the day the Indian army attacked, he found her changing the cover of her divan, and Bhagat recalls that even as the war raged she made it a point to rearrange the flowers in the vase at home before leaving for office. Natwar Singh reiterates the reason why she was so calm, why her leadership remained serene in the face of war, was that 1971 was almost entirely handled by Haksar. 'He was the brain behind her prime ministership. He was the man who executed the 1971 exercise, along with other brilliant minds like D.P. Dhar, T.N. Kaul, [defence secretary] K.B. Lall and of course General Manekshaw and others on the military side,' says Singh.

At the peace talks in Simla in June 1972, which followed Pakistan's defeat, Indira was keen to show that India did not want Pakistan to be made to eat humble pie. When she arrived at Himachal Bhawan, where Bhutto would be staying, she found the arrangements were shoddy, the colours of the upholstery did not match, the furniture had been clumsily placed and the curtains ended a foot above the floor. So she took it upon herself to decorate and arrange Bhutto's living quarters even as the gathered staff looked on, whispering about the prime minister's 'international standards'. A marathon session of rearrangement followed, writes Bhagat. 'We went to the chief minister's house and got a few things from there including his bed. We went to Raj Bhavan and picked up a deep-red raw silk bedspread, we wrote to Rashtrapati Bhavan asking them to send silver writing sets and stationery . . . I wonder if Mr Bhutto and his daughter realised the effort put in personally by Mrs Gandhi to make their place of stay somewhat better.' Indira enjoyed these designing exercises and often talked about her love for interior design, even mentioned her desire to be an interior designer. Interior design and fighting wars, doing crossword puzzles and outmanoeuvring a phalanx of crafty politicians, Indira Gandhi lived in many worlds.

But if only arriving at a durable Indo-Pakistan peace was as easy as redecorating a room. The Indian and Pakistani delegations were uncomfortable in each other's company, and the Simla talks almost failed, only to be rescued at the last minute by a one-on-one between Indira and Bhutto. The Simla Agreement committed India and

Pakistan to negotiate over Kashmir bilaterally and the December 1971 ceasefire line was renamed the Line of Control (LoC) – with the implicit hope on the Indian side it would develop into an international boundary, thus settling Kashmir's status – which both countries agreed would be 'respected by both sides without prejudice to the recognised position of either side'.

But the Simla Agreement was fatally flawed; not only was it not legally binding but it was 'dependent upon a continued occupation of their positions of power by the two leaders who had signed it'.[75] Bhutto reneged on the agreement within a month when he announced in Pakistan's National Assembly that far from respecting any international border he would continue the struggle for the self-determination of the people of Jammu and Kashmir. The return of Pakistani and Bangladeshi prisoners of war also continued to be delayed as Pakistan denied recognition to Bangladesh. The return of PoWs was only completed after protracted negotiations by 1974. Today the Simla Agreement is honoured more in the breach – Pakistan has often tried to internationalize the Kashmir dispute and the Kargil war and cross-border attacks and raids cast into grave doubt any respect for the LoC.

Indira was to admit later to a sense of disappointment over the Simla talks. She believed she had been overgenerous with Bhutto, and he for his part had not shown a commitment towards friendship with India. Bhutto was too much in the grip of the army, she believed, to be a peacemaker with India. 'When he started to compromise with the Military, that was bound to give the edge to the Military,' she would say.

Yet the Bangladesh war consolidated Indira Gandhi's image as leader in perpetuity, as the woman who humbled and dismembered Pakistan the way no other leader could possibly have done. India was isolated yet victorious and India was embodied in the courage of a woman. She was awarded the Bharat Ratna by the president she had chosen, V.V. Giri, and the Congress swept the 1972 assembly elections in thirteen states after fresh elections were called in the flush of military victory. Thousands of female babies were named Indira. Durga incarnate now stood in the place of the goongi gudiya who only five years ago had been heckled and humiliated in Parliament. She was worshipped as an incarnation of Shakti. *The Economist* called her the Empress of India.

The 1971 elections witnessed the emergence of a kind of mass leader India had not seen before. And the Bangladesh war revealed a prime minister who would remain boldly resolute even when almost the entire world turned away from her. Indira's role in the world was like her role in India: defiant, self-righteous, driven by a robust pursuit of what she perceived as the 'national honour'. She would say: 'Open frank honest colonialism has given way to veiled neo-colonialism . . . to face them we need more than mere idealism or mere sentimentalism, we need very clear thinking and hard-headed analysis.' Her insistence on autonomy in the world mirrored her insistence on her freedom of action vis-à-vis the Syndicate, vis-à-vis her father and her husband.

Non-alignment was not just a conviction but also a means of assertion of identity. India was isolated in the world before the Bangladesh war, with no country except the Soviet Union by its side, yet Indira had not just prosecuted the war but insisted on convincing the world on the justness of her cause. Writes the journalist Inderjit Badhwar, 'By the time of her death, she was able to establish an Indian world identity – that this was no banana republic and would tenaciously assert its rights to speak on its national interest.'[76]

Indira Gandhi guarded India like a lioness, with a possessive, maternal protectiveness that was anything but democratic. Soon democracy itself would be suffocated by maternal control. Democratic India's darkest hour was ahead when Nehru's daughter would destroy Nehru's dream.

5

The Great Dictator: Downhill towards the Emergency, 1972–77

Within four years of the triumph of the Bangladesh war, Indira Gandhi imposed the Emergency. For twenty-one months India ceased to be a democracy. Civil rights were suspended, thousands were jailed, slum clearance and mass sterilization drives were launched and the media was heavily censored. But unexpectedly in 1977 she announced general elections, which brought the Emergency to an end. Indira Gandhi and the Congress were routed in the 1977 elections, and the Janata Party came to power, ending eleven years of Mrs Gandhi's prime ministership.

~

Dear Mrs Gandhi,

The one question which every Indian citizen would like to ask you is, why did you impose the Emergency? Why did you snatch away democratic liberties from the same citizens who gave you a massive mandate in 1971, citizens for whose rights your grandfather, father and Mahatma Gandhi devoted their lives? What they wrested from the Raj, you in turn took away. For twenty-one months Indian citizens were almost as subjugated as they had been under the imperialist jackboot.

An Allahabad High Court judgement declared invalid your election win from the Raebareli seat in the 1971 general elections. By court order, you could no longer remain prime minister. What would Nehru have done? He would have immediately resigned, shown the idealist's disdain for the throne and returned to power, morally vindicated.

In one of his letters to chief ministers, Nehru wrote: 'We must remember that what our governments are doing today will set the tone for future administrations. The very powers that may be exercised, perhaps for adequate reasons today, may be exercised later for totally inadequate and perhaps even for objectionable reasons. It is always unsafe to weaken on principle.'[1]

You weakened on principle. You imposed the Emergency. You staved off the immediate challenge to your rule but did you ever stop to think about the long-term effects of such a move?

No story of the Emergency is complete without the story of your relationship with your younger son, Sanjay, your 'emotional blind spot'. You knew Sanjay better than anyone else; as a child it was Sanjay who always worried you, you felt he needed more care than your older son Rajiv. Why then did you turn almost your entire government, indeed the reins of the country, over to him?

Sanjay's urgings, however, were not the only reason why you imposed the Emergency. Instead you did it because of that constant factor of your political life – the belief in your own indispensability. You, in your own mind, exemplified the good and the right, whatever you did was sanctified by birth and lineage. Only you could rule India, the country simply could not be trusted to others because your enemies were India's enemies. An India pushed out of the Nehruvian universe was an unimaginable prospect and your proprietorial instincts were at the fore. As you said after the Allahabad High Court judgement, there was 'no one else around who could cope with the grave threat . . . it was my duty to stay [as prime minister] even though I didn't want to'.[2]

On the eve of declaring the Emergency you said to your old friend and West Bengal Chief Minister Siddhartha Shankar Ray, 'I feel that India is like a baby and just as one would sometimes take a child and shake it, I feel we have to shake India.'[3] When an entire country is your baby, then the ruling principle becomes mummy knows best.

~

In 1971–72, Indira Gandhi was at the pinnacle of power, the embodiment of the word 'Leader'. So much so that today even her implacable ideological opponents, the RSS and the BJP, look on her as a model of strong leadership, however zealously the then Jana Sangh had sought her downfall. The BJP, RSS and Sangh Parivar may vociferously attack the Gandhi family and Jawaharlal Nehru but only rarely do they train their guns on Indira Gandhi.[4]

She was a master tactician in politics, a natural. 'From the time she was three or four, Indira heard nothing but talk of politics,' recalls Krishna Hutheesing.[5] Remembers her cousin Nayantara Sahgal, 'Those for whom politics is merely a chosen profession do not have what Indira had – a feel for the territory, an instinctive sleepwalker's acquaintance with the terrain.' Supreme in her party, her personal popularity outstripping that of the entire Congress, described as the first woman monarch of India since the thirteenth-century reign of Raziya Sultana, she was even called India's 'mon general' by her critics.

As the road curves into her constituency in Raebareli, at the entry point stands a statue of Jhalkari Bai. According to many historical accounts, it was Jhalkari Bai, the Dalit warrior and virangana, who often fought disguised as the celebrated Rani of Jhansi in the 1857 rebellion.

The statue shows a woman soldier astride a charging warhorse, her sword held aloft, her face set in fierce resolve to fight to her death. The lone warlike woman in fighting mode, fighting for her own and her nation's survival was the imagined iconography of the Indira persona. In the popular imagination she was and remains an amalgam of India's fighter queens from Durga to Raziya Sultana to remembered viranganas, someone who blurred the lines between myth and reality. 'Hone de dihon, mukuraj na dihon',[6] whatever happens, I will not surrender the kingdom, was Jhalkari Bai's legendary war cry. It could have been Indira's too.

Yet the avenging heroine failed to grow out of her politician's clothes and don the robes of a humane visionary leader. In her obsession with winning a maze of little fights and personal skirmishes, she lost the big picture. She didn't seem to grasp that, as a leader of such tremendous standing, an immediate outwitting of the opponent was too inadequate a goal. If her father was the idealist, she remained the calculating realist. A sympathetic argument would be that the opposition to her was just so fierce that she had to weaken institutions not only to rule, but just to survive.

'The prime minister had become very very arrogant,' Indira's private secretary N.K. Seshan recalled.[7] 'She loved being called Durga. The Bangladesh victory was a turning point. Sanjay was the only person who had a total hold on her. She had no tolerance for any other person . . . she lost her balance after Bangladesh. Sanjay took complete control. She would have been a great Prime Minister if Sanjay had not been there.' The enormous power she wielded after the 1971 general election victory and the Bangladesh war went to her head. The magnitude of the Bangladesh achievement made her fearful, and comparisons to Durga led to insecurities about her own inadequacies. This insecurity led to an astonishingly rapid descent into suspicion and paranoia after such grand success. After the zenith of 1971, she slipped precipitously towards the nadir in 1975, in just four short years. Surrounded by sycophants she shut out independent-minded competent advisers, listening only to lesser minds.

Dangerous delusions of invincibility began to grow within her. Reflecting on the role of charisma in a democracy, the *Statesman* wrote about the 1971 election: 'Whether . . . charisma exploited by ruthless determination is compatible with a democratic system is something on which thought is overdue.'[8] Is an excess of charisma sometimes a bad thing in a democracy?

'There are some people who can't cope with failure, but there are those who can't cope with success,' recalls Moni Malhoutra. 'She belonged to the latter category. The mass adulation, the sweeping victory – coping with that kind of success was a problem and resulted in hubris. Her success became overwhelming and she went off the rails a bit. The darker side of her character began to surface. Then of course her son made her go completely off the rails.' The contrast to Nehru was sharp: if she couldn't cope with success, Nehru couldn't cope with failure. The China war, corruption scandals in his time and the impasse on Kashmir[9] broke Nehru's spirit, the leader whose steady moral compass even his harshest critics couldn't help but recognize.

Indira Gandhi's rise to authoritarianism is also the story of the ascent of her younger son, Sanjay Gandhi. It is a story that shows how a leader turned her back on party and movement and turned instead to family and bloodline. Nehru, the disciplined Congress soldier, regarded the party as bigger than himself, part of a far greater freedom movement; the party was an entity to which he felt he owed a great debt. But Indira Gandhi had created a new Congress to enable her political emergence and supremacy, a Congress reliant entirely on herself, a party in which careers depended not on political talent but on loyalty. She was comforted by the mediocre and threatened by exceptional talent, particularly ill at ease with autonomous stature that grew from the ground: 'any show of political virility alerted her to danger'.[10]

Nehru remained unthreatened by accomplishment in and disagreement from others, including in his first ministry diverse ideologies such as those represented by Shyama Prasad Mukherjee (later founder of the Jana Sangh) and B.R. Ambedkar; in fact, his own stature grew because of the stalwarts that surrounded him, his letters to chief ministers revealing how invested he was in creating bonds with colleagues. But perhaps Nehru could do this because of his clear dominance in the party. Indira, by contrast, struggling up as she did through ferocious rivalries with heavyweights, would brook no competition. 'On power she was always very clear. She could not tolerate any rivals,' believes the BJP leader Subramanian Swamy.[11] With an accelerated personalization of politics and sidelining of the party, it was inevitable that she would turn, in the resulting vacuum, to the ties of blood.

Indira had destroyed the democratic, multilateral Congress by splitting it. After the Bangladesh war, she moved to a unilateral, monarchical style. India's Constitution had created a nuanced balance of power, vesting the sovereignty of the people in the equipoise of institutions, where judiciary, legislature and executive and a free press together held up democracy by functioning as checks on each other. Indira drove a coach and horses through that balance. This was no open army coup; instead hers was the coup from within, regular corrosive jabs at the carefully constructed machinery of party and government so meticulously maintained by Nehru. When the once-mighty Congress accepted without protest the overlordship of Indira's completely inexperienced son, it showed how badly the party had been eviscerated.

~

Let us now turn to Sanjay Gandhi, the son who many believe was his mother's nemesis. Indira Gandhi's younger son returned to India from England in 1967, a good-looking, rather supercilious twenty-one-year-old. He had no inclination towards history and philosophy like his maternal grandfather or towards the arts like his mother. Instead, like his father, he was fascinated with cars, aeroplanes and all things mechanical, growing up playing Meccano with Feroze Gandhi. He had dropped out of Doon School, completing his school education from St Columba's in Delhi. Uninterested in college, he had been sent on a five-year apprenticeship to the Rolls-Royce factory in Crewe, England. He dropped out after three years, getting instead a reputation for being a rather spoilt delinquent, and was arrested for violating speed limits and driving without a licence while in England.[12] 'Sanjay was wild and wayward,' remembers Jayakar, 'often in scrapes, fiddling with cars, attracting questionable friends.' Born and reared only in prime ministerial homes, first Nehru's and then Indira's, Sanjay took the 'power-soaked' and entitled environment for granted, with the pampered child's proclivity to taking the short cut. Yet he was a quirkily gifted, dynamic youth. He wanted to find his own way, perhaps always oppressed by the pantheon of greatness he had to live up to and as conscious of being 'handcuffed to history' as his mother always was. Sanjay would insist his mother become his helpmate as he struggled to find his place in the family sun.

He returned to India from England, fired by the dream of creating an entirely indigenously produced Indian car, the Maruti, named after the son of the wind god, Vayu. Maruti, son of a god, may have been a figure Sanjay identified with. The offspring of awe-inspiring parents whom he had the potential to outstrip. Maruti is also sometimes a name given to the Ramayana's Hanuman, who could fly as fast as the wind. Sanjay, the high-flyer, Sanjay Maruti Gandhi.

Yet Sanjay would soon become someone whose shadow loomed over India, more sprite than God, his very name evoking sinister machinations and flaunting of brute state power, of public resources being channelled to private vanity and profit by a fawning government.

Sanjay was adored by his mother and his young wife, Maneka. 'The contrast between Sanjay and Rajiv couldn't be greater,' recalled Maneka. 'Rajiv and Sonia were very western. They had western friends. They went out a lot, knew the fashions in Europe and America. Their holidays were always abroad. Their acquisitions were always "acquisitions". Sanjay was completely Indian. He was more comfortable speaking Hindi, wore kurta-pyjama, we didn't socialize or have well-off friends. And we owned nothing. Once when I bought a sari, he asked me, do you really need this? Have you used up all your other saris? I ended up returning the sari.'[13] Wajahat Habibullah went to Doon School with Rajiv and Sanjay. 'The mother seemed much closer to Sanjay than to Rajiv. Sanjay was lively and gregarious, always playing pranks. Rajiv was more sober,' Habibullah recalls.

Just a year after Sanjay's return to India it was announced in the Lok Sabha in November 1968 that, along with other car manufacturers, Sanjay Gandhi had applied for a licence to produce an affordable, indigenously manufactured car for the nation, which would cost Rs 6000. It was to be India's first self-made car. Lo and behold, two years later, bypassing all other established and reputed claimants like Citroen, Renault and Toyota,[14] this licence to produce – for these were days when industry needed special licences to set up businesses – 50,000 cars per year using only Indian materials was duly granted to the twenty-two-year-old greenhorn Sanjay at a cabinet discussion presided over by Sanjay's mother. It was reported that both the then minister for industrial development, Fakhruddin Ali Ahmed – later to be Indira's loyal President who signed her Emergency proclamation – and his deputy had 'leaned heavily' on the right quarters to issue the letter of intent to Sanjay.[15] The opposition howled 'nepotism' and 'disgrace'. Indira is practising 'nepotism of the worst type', the socialist MP George Fernandes raged. This is 'corruption unlimited', roared Atal Bihari Vajpayee. With no qualifications or expertise in business, he would benefit massively from the largesse of his mother's government, 'suddenly heading a huge car manufacturing industrial complex involving an investment of ten million dollars when his declared income for the year 1969–70 was Rs 748'.[16] Indira Gandhi's blind support of Sanjay's car project, brooking no words of criticism about him, again echoes the words of the Queen of Hearts from Lewis Carroll's *Alice's Adventures in Wonderland*: 'I rule Wonderland alone. Your interference will not be tolerated.'

With the benefit of hindsight, we now see that Sanjay, though only after his death, went on to become the accidental father of India's Maruti revolution. But at the time the Maruti project became his mother's Achilles heel. She had always inspired intense hatred among her opponents and for them the Maruti project became Indira's uncovered flank, open for easy – and justifiable – attack.

Today the Maruti Suzuki car is a piece of history. For generations of cyclists and scooterists of the 1980s, the Maruti 800 was the stepping stone to driving on the road to social mobility, to becoming proud owners of automobiles, a symbol of social ascent in socialist India. If the Ambassador exemplified India of the 1950s, the Maruti was India's chariot of the late 1980s and early 1990s, the first set of four wheels millions of families ever owned.

Sanjay dreamed of creating the desi Volkswagen and his mother was determined to make this dream come true. The Maruti project became an instant entry point for Sanjay into the world of high politics and big business, and as his activities became more controversial, he was drawn towards acquiring political power. Maruti Motors Limited was incorporated in 1971 with Sanjay as managing director. He had reportedly designed the chassis in his workshop in Gulabi Bagh in Old Delhi earlier, with parts sourced from the Jama Masjid area and powered by a Triumph motorcycle engine.[17] The process is reminiscent of how across north India even today rural, often illiterate, mechanics use the 'jugaad' method to create vehicles. Sanjay's was more high-quality jugaad – he was creating a handcrafted objet d'art rather than an assembly line for mass consumption.

The Indira establishment rushed to help Sanjay. Recently nationalized banks granted him unsecured loans totalling approximately Rs 7.5 million. When the chairman of the Central Bank, Dharam Vir Taneja, was compelled to tell Sanjay that he could not release any more money, Taneja was summoned to 1 Safdarjung Road where Sanjay reportedly threatened him with dismissal. Taneja refused to give in and his chairmanship of the Central Bank was not renewed.[18]

The Haryana chief minister Bansi Lal threw rules and regulations to the wind and sold Sanjay 400 acres of agricultural land close to an ammunition dump – defence rules prohibited the setting up of a factory close to an ammunition pit – at a throwaway price. The land was reportedly sold to Sanjay at Rs 10,000 an acre while the price for the adjoining land was Rs 35,000 per acre.[19] In 1973, when B.G. Verghese, editor of the *Hindustan Times*, published critical articles on Sanjay Gandhi's company, he was summarily sacked. (*Hindustan Times*'s proprietor, K.K. Birla, was an investor in Maruti.)

The wheels of government and business seemed to turn to Sanjay's beck and call. When Dhawan telephoned industrialists from the prime minister's house, they would naturally be only too willing to oblige, assuming that Indira herself was taking a personal interest in the project. But in spite of all this heavy-lifting, Sanjay failed to produce the Maruti.

In May 1973 when journalist Uma Vasudev was taken on a test drive of the Maruti with Sanjay, she realized that the car, which leaked oil and became overheated, was a 'disaster'. 'He drove me around the factory campus in a Maruti 800 at the speed of 80 kilometres per hour. I was terrified,' recalled Vasudev.[20] Instead of being a mass-produced product for the general public, it was a designer, custom-made vehicle that simply didn't work.[21] Evidently, Sanjay's Maruti was quite unlike the jugaad vehicles of the rural countryside, which efficiently transport rural denizens to their destinations, snorting and coughing as they do so!

Maruti became a symbol of the ills of the licence-permit raj, a glaring example that Indira was suffering from the 'Dhritarashtra syndrome' of Indian politics or the parent blinded to the child's ambitious folly.[22] She even held up Maruti as an inspiring example of home-grown Indian enterprise for youth to emulate,[23] apparently unaware of what Maruti was doing to her government's reputation. Sunil Sethi, then a journalist with *India Today* magazine, summed it up thus: 'Maruti Ltd. turned out to be a huge land grab and financial scam . . . a sycophantic loan mela by nationalised banks, extortion and blackmail to squeeze funds from business groups and traders. Bankers, cabinet ministers and captains of industry who opposed or resisted Sanjay's muscle-flexing were . . . sent packing.'[24]

Maruti was consigned to the back burner during the Emergency when Sanjay had bigger fish to fry. The Janata government liquidated it in 1977 and a committee appointed to investigate it produced a highly critical report.[25] When Indira Gandhi returned to power in 1980, and after Sanjay's death, she attempted to resurrect her son's dream. In 1981 Maruti Udyog was incorporated as a government company and it entered into a joint venture with Suzuki of Japan. Sanjay had failed to produce a car, and a professional car manufacturer was needed to breathe life into the scrap heap. Suzuki stepped up and, in place of the leaking, overheating non-starter that Sanjay had produced, built the Maruti Suzuki, tough little road roller for India's potholed, narrow lanes.[26] The vehicle of the upwardly mobile aam aadmi was born. Sanjay didn't manage to create India's Volkswagen, yet he did dream an impossible dream which was fulfilled, although only because it was powered by foreign technology and state patronage.[27]

Throughout his Maruti experiment and the heavy toll it was to take on Indira Gandhi's prime ministership, Sanjay had been subject to withering attacks from both the Opposition and the press. Indira appeared uncomprehending and outraged at the attacks, referring to an East European priest who had built a plane in a Bombay garage, and exclaiming, 'If he could build a plane, why can't Sanjay build a car?' She would repeatedly say that her son was being unfairly targeted and maligned, saying in interviews that 'my son is not in politics at all'.

She fervently, almost desperately, wanted him to succeed, as if she owed it to him, as if it was her duty to help him. Whether she actually expected him to deliver the Maruti or she just wanted to keep him gainfully occupied, it seems as if she was not able to deny him anything. She was proud too. The prospect of India's first entirely Indian-made car quickened her nationalism; that her own son was trying to undertake this made-in-India car project made him in her eyes a fitting scion of the patriotic Nehrus.

During the Bangladesh war Sanjay had remained on the sidelines of Indira's work. The magnitude of the crisis demanded those with proven competence and Indira was forced to defer to men of wisdom and experience like Haksar and Manekshaw. After the war, as Sanjay began to grow larger than life, he ran into conflict, almost inevitably, with the man in charge of his mother's regime. Sharada Prasad confirms, 'There was growing friction between sovereign and chamberlain over the doings of the prince.' Haksar and Sanjay had disliked each other from the start. Haksar at one point had even warned Indira that awarding Sanjay the Maruti contract would leave her politically exposed.

He also raised questions about the Haryana land deal with Bansi Lal and advised Indira Gandhi to send Sanjay away from Delhi to allow the scandals surrounding Maruti to die down. 'Haksar had very frankly told her,' says Natwar Singh 'that you will have to choose whether you want to be prime minister of India or Sanjay's mother.' 'Haksar warned her about the young man and his activities, but his warnings did not go down well,' recalled Vasant Sathe.

Sanjay for his part attempted to turn his mother against Haksar. Mysterious rumours began that Haksar was taking the credit for the Bangladesh victory, that he was granting too many favours, behaving like a power centre in his own right, stealing Indira's authority. The protective mother and paranoid prime minister moved to axe her son's bête noire. The marginalization of Haksar began. 'The distance began to widen for a number of reasons, one of which was the praise heaped upon him by his admirers,' notes Sharada Prasad. In 1973, when Haksar's term as principal secretary came up for renewal, Indira Gandhi dismissed him. He was later given a sinecure as deputy chairman of the Planning Commission. In 1975, after the Emergency had been proclaimed, a well-known textile store in Delhi, Pandit Brothers, owned by Haksar's relatives, would be raided and Haksar's octogenarian uncle would be arrested on Sanjay's orders, so badly had relations soured by then. Indira reportedly did not know about the arrest when it happened and when she found out she did intervene to have the senior citizen released immediately. Almost as if to make amends, when Haksar's mother died in 1979, as well mannered as she was, in spite of everything, she made sure to visit him and convey her condolences.

With the departure of Haksar, Indira lost her most fearless adviser. P.N. Dhar, another Kashmiri Pandit and a wise and accomplished economist, replaced him, staying in the post for the next four years, but Dhar was unable to stand up to her in the way Haksar could and Haksar called Dhar 'spineless'[28] if he found himself in conflict with the prime minister.

Parmeshwar Narayan Haksar, the super-mandarin who guided Indira through the nationalization of banks, the Congress split, the abolition of privy purses, and the Bangladesh war, was now forced to leave a post which had become synonymous with him, because of Sanjay Gandhi. His departure would cost Indira dear.

With Sanjay's rise, others came into prominence, such as the chain-smoking, workaholic Rajinder Kumar Dhawan. Dhawan was a former employee of All India Radio and was brought into Indira Gandhi's staff in 1962 by his cousin Yashpal Kapoor, then part of Jawaharlal Nehru's staff. The rise of R.K. Dhawan presaged the rise of the all-important personal assistant (PA) in India's government apparatus. Right-hand man of the power centre, the PA installs his own people with a range of VIPs, increasing his circle of power and information, becoming indispensable to his boss and a power broker in his own right. If M.O. Mathai, Nehru's private secretary, was India's first power-broker PA, then the second position could be claimed by R.K. Dhawan. The power of the PA is of course dependent on the power of the individual he serves and if his master is a supremo then the PA rules supreme too. Before Dhawan there was Mathai, afterwards came Vincent George, reportedly the winner of a fastest typist in Kerala award,[29] who first joined Indira Gandhi's staff, then became Rajiv and Sonia Gandhi's PA. The importance of Dhawan and George showed that power in the Congress increasingly came not from popularity on the ground, but from those who controlled access to the all-powerful first family. If after Nehru's death the second most important people in India were the veterans of the Syndicate, after Indira's death the second most important person was R.K. Dhawan, a revealing transition showing how the centralization of power led to access brokers assuming overweening influence.

Dhawan's name became a byword for the unseen goings-on of the Emergency; he was Indira's constant, unbreachable shadow. Over time he and Sanjay Gandhi became the gatekeepers of the prime minister's home. 'Whatever tasks we did, our interest was always Indira first,' says Dhawan. 'My loyalty to her was total, I never did anything to harm her in my entire working life with her. I worked for her twenty-four hours a day, seven days a week, for twenty-two years from 1962 onwards. No off days, no holidays. I refused to depose against her in the Shah Commission [the commission of enquiry set up by the Janata government in 1977 to look into the excesses of the Emergency] and was jailed for my loyalty. Would I ever do anything to harm her or Sanjay's interests? My only aim was to see that nothing goes wrong.' Unfortunately, everything did begin to go wrong.

~

Indira Gandhi and Sanjay's was a mutually protective, secretive, powerful bond that did not yield to any form of parental disciplining nor any filial deference. The mother seemed powerless in the face of the son's suzerainty, meekly laying her empire at his feet. She had declared motherhood to be 'a woman's highest fulfilment', yet interpreted motherhood as a sharing of the spoils of power. 'Because my childhood was so insecure and so lonely, I was determined to devote full time to my children . . . a child's need of his mother's love and care is as urgent and fundamental as that of a plant for sunshine and water. To a mother, her children must always come first. Once another lady had said I could not be spending much time with my sons. This hurt Sanjay and he rushed to my rescue with the words:

"My mother does lots of important work, yet she plays with me more than you do with your little boy."'

Sanjay, his mother's rescuer, and she, the mother who, once she had the power, would do everything she could to see that he received her full love and care. Nehru, as we have seen, lavished intellectual and emotional attention on Indira and she showered the same abundance of parental care on Sanjay, but in a completely contrasting way, bestowing material rather than intellectual gain. Indira Gandhi failed both as mother and prime minister when she made available the prime minister's office as a plaything for her child.

Parenthood is often seasoned by guilt and Indira observers from the time say that it is possible Indira was always a little guilty about her difficult marriage and the sharply contrasting lifestyles between her and Feroze. As her boys grew up they may have felt that their father was treated unfairly given the power and influence Indira commanded as Nehru's daughter and the ordinary, modest circumstances in which Feroze lived.

Unconsciously guilty about being the mother who had chosen Nehru over Feroze, who had relegated his father to second place in her life, she was acutely conscious that Sanjay perhaps even secretly blamed her for his father's death. Leveraging parental guilt is often a child's way of securing a blank cheque and Sanjay clearly played to Indira's vulnerabilities. Rebelling against her own father's refusal to dream of greatness for her, she by contrast did as much as she could to propel her son to the pinnacle.

Indira had been the powerful mother ensconced in her father's home. Feroze Gandhi was the talented father from the unremarkable background whom Sanjay had idolized. There was an emotional schizophrenia in Sanjay's childhood by which he held his mother duty-bound to support him, perhaps as an unconscious act of vengeance for the humiliations Feroze endured.

Protective and demanding by turn, Sanjay would make sure Indira met his demands. His household manners were princely. He was particular about his breakfasts, sticking to an unchanging menu of boiled eggs and porridge with cream. Once when Sonia Gandhi, in charge of the household when the family had shifted out of the prime ministerial house after Indira lost power in 1977, failed to cook his eggs exactly the way he liked them, he hurled his plate across the table. B.K. and his wife Fori Nehru looked on in shock, while his mother watched in silence, not daring to utter a word in reprimand, but looking embarrassed.[30] During the Emergency when a new signature tune was being chosen for AIR, Sanjay accompanied Indira when she came to listen and approve of the tune composed by Ravi Shankar. But instead of Indira it was Sanjay who began to give his opinions and comments on the music, while Indira listened silently and let him do all the talking.

In the adoring yet fearful dependence of the mother on the son germinated the seeds of the misjudgements that led first to delusions of grandeur, then to paranoia and isolation, and then to the assumption of authoritarian power. He convinced her that it was the two of them against the world. 'There is no doubt that they had a very deep relationship,' says Mark Tully. He recalls how once, while he waited to interview Indira on the campaign trail, just as she was walking towards him she received word that Sanjay was on the phone. 'She literally skipped and ran to the phone as if a phone call from him brought enormous happiness. No doubt he meant a huge amount to her.' There were all kinds of bizarre rumours about their relationship, some even suggesting an unnatural bond. The journalist Ian Jack in his collection of essays, *Mofussil Junction*, confesses that he was ashamed to have written during the Emergency that the hold Sanjay had over his mother could be because of blackmail and even incest. Jack said these claims were totally ludicrous.[31] She clearly drew a great deal of strength from him, he was a personification of masculine power that Indira in a way had aspired to, another 'Indu-boy' come to new life.

~

Let us now turn to the events that led to the declaration of Emergency on 25 June 1975. They tumbled upon each other, like a set of collapsing dominoes. The wave of jubilation that rose to great heights after the Bangladesh war almost immediately crashed on to jagged rocks of biting economic hardship and political conflict. It seemed as if the gods themselves became jealous of the goddess who ruled India.

Immediately after the Bangladesh victory came a series of disasters. Ten million refugees from Bangladesh had placed a huge burden on India. Added to this, in 1972, 1973 and 1974, for three years in a row, the rains failed. Grain production plummeted by 8 per cent and food prices soared. On its heels came the first 'oil shock' of 1973 when the Organization of Petroleum Exporting Countries (OPEC), for the first time, pushed a steep fourfold rise in oil prices overnight, and therefore the prices of all commodities shot upwards. By 1974 inflation was almost 30 per cent. High prices and shortages raged through the country. India faced a full-blown economic crisis.

Chaos ensued. Protests, gheraos and strikes began to erupt in every part of the country. There were food riots in Bombay, Mysore, Nagpur and parts of Kerala. More than 12,000 strikes took place in Bombay alone during 1972 and 1973. Factories closed down and unemployment spread like an epidemic. Desperate young men lounged on sun-scorched street corners, spoiling for a fight. The economic situation in the western world too took a turn for the worse, ultimately leading in the 1980s to the rise of leaders like Margaret Thatcher and Ronald Reagan and radical new economic policies. For Indira Gandhi, however, most of this was nothing but the Opposition at work: 'Anti-Congress parties were obstructing development . . . there were frequent calls to stop work. Farmers were asked not to sell their produce, non-payment of taxes was preached . . . their aim was to paralyse the government and walk to power over the body of the nation.'

After the Bangladesh victory, Indira had acquired the power to create a genuine transformation. But she failed to make the best use of this power. She had always been conscious of being a participant in history-in-the-making but somehow did not trust herself to fashion a new narrative of history. Victory in Bangladesh had given the country mental renewal and optimism, a sense of hope that could have been channelled into creating a new kind of politics and for the start of an era of reconciliation by a leader who should have had the confidence to attempt a consensus with her detractors.

However, instead of focusing on the need to create a larger political understanding in order to move towards garibi hatao, instead of recognizing the signs of a sharp decline in the economy in the widespread labour and rural unrest and growing frustrations of youth, Indira Gandhi became immersed in petty politics. She retreated into suspicion and wariness and saw every protest or criticism as an attempt to obstruct her forward march as head of the metaphorical Indian army. She looked backwards instead of forward, lacking the skill to create new institutions and ideas relevant for the future. Intent on outscoring rivals and staying ahead politically, she did not allow herself to provide India a fresh intellectual direction. That she did not inherit nor possess this capacity to create a new way forward was a tragedy, given the mandate she had.

The political calculations of those waiting in the wings mixed explosively with the plummeting conditions of daily life. The Opposition had been wiped out in 1971, its Indira Hatao campaign blasted out of the water. Now it looked for opportunities to make a re-entry into politics. The realization began to slowly dawn on her enemies that, given the fragmentation of vote shares, the best chance to defeat Indira was a united front against her, what today is called a mahagathbandhan. An anti-Indira coalition began to take shape,[32] even as Indira Gandhi turned to political control to stem the discontent rolling through the country. Faced with rising social restlessness, she imposed her trademark: Pax Indira, or imperial control foisted from above with lightning speed. The process of appointing Congress chief ministers from Delhi had begun in earnest. Nominees of Indira Gandhi took charge in the states, while not-so-loyal leaders were dismissed.[33] States were administered from Delhi by imposing President's Rule and legislatures kept in suspended animation so the Opposition was blocked from challenging the ruling party. Cabinet and party were by now almost entirely under Indira's thumb.

Economic policy was confused even in the face of a crisis. It oscillated between the immediate needs of the hour and inarticulate populist socialism. She accepted an IMF loan and swallowed its tough conditions, yet at the same time rushed to contradict a press report that she was inviting multinational corporations into the Indian market. The lessons of devaluation were still fresh in her mind. Due to the pressure from the leftists in her own party the crisis could not be converted into an opportunity for more basic reform of the economy. She often said she preferred the pragmatism of a mixed economy and had no fixed ideology on economic issues. She was devoid of strong convictions either way. In an interview in 1970 she said, 'We have been committed to the concept of a mixed economy . . . we remain centrists but left of centre . . . mixed economy is a viable concept and a means of attaining a socialistic society.'[34]

In a later interview she would say: 'We have the significant problem of poverty. We can't just leave it to market forces and big business to do what they like. We call ourselves socialist but it's not the socialism of the Soviet Union or the communist countries. We're trying to find our own path.'[35]

She could not find that path, cut off as she was from genuine feedback from political and economic actors. The licence-permit raj stamped out freedom in the economy and political control silenced voices of criticism in politics. Reliant only on the feedback of sycophants, how could she build a new way? No wonder she failed to properly define and implement this mixed economy or clarify what 'our own path' was.

Instead, she remained a prisoner of short-term measures. Conditions were so disastrous that, socialist or not, private big business had to be permitted to expand production and demand had to be restricted. At one point, the government tried to lower demand by freezing wages, a move which was assailed as 'anti-working class'. Ideological commitments made about expanding the public sector, strictly regulating the private sector and becoming less dependent on foreign aid had to be put on hold in the face of mounting shortages and spiralling protests.

Policy and ideological confusion was illustrated in the manner in which the government in 1973 took over the wholesale trade in foodgrains and then hastily abandoned the utterly misconceived decision when the takeover ran into problems. Food stocks disappeared when the decision to nationalize the grain trade was announced. Consumers panicked at the prospect of no wheat or rice being available. Food trucks were looted in Kerala. Shortages resulted, leading to the need to import massive quantities of grain, dragging India back into the food imports trap. The attempted nationalization of the grain trade showed how, in the face of hard economic realities, Indira still remained saddled with far too much ideological baggage.

When the rains failed for the third time in 1974, there was no option but to prioritize the economy over politics. In 1974, she introduced an anti-inflation package and backed her team of liberal economic advisers led by Manmohan Singh. There was also no option but an IMF loan. As mentioned earlier, this came with the usual conditions on rolling back populist schemes and expenditures.

In a surge of pragmatism she accepted the IMF's conditions but it was too late. Manmohan Singh was to say later that he was impressed at the courage with which she at this time accepted the need for a potentially politically unpopular anti-inflationary policy package. But short-term firefighting could not be a substitute for the need to systematically hack away at the tentacles of an economy that had become a predator on India's citizens, as Manmohan Singh was to do almost two decades later. In 1974, the economy called for policies that would bring a dramatic overhaul. But Indira took only half-hearted knee-jerk measures and the slogan 'Garibi Hatao' began to sound like a cruel joke.

~

The goddess thought she had the divine right to rule but her subjects had begun to rebel violently, among them the influential legal community. Indira and the judiciary collided head-on.

The Indira revolution based on enacting 'progressive legislation' needed a cooperative judiciary. Many of her policies had already been thwarted by the courts. As mentioned earlier, the Supreme Court had struck down the presidential proclamation on abolition of privy purses and compensation provisions in bank nationalization had also been legally challenged and been overturned by the Supreme Court.

Congress radicals began to mutter that the judiciary (like the bureaucracy) had to be 'committed' to the larger goal of bringing in the colossal social and economic change so vehemently promised by the Indira revolution. One of the most vocal advocates of a 'committed judiciary' was Mohan Kumaramangalam, the Eton- and Cambridge-educated socialist, Indira's close associate, Feroze Gandhi's friend, as well as minister in the Indira cabinet. An exemplar of India's patrician left, his group, the Congress Forum for Socialist Action, had come to the fore in 1971. They were restless for transformation and chafed at the roadblocks created by the judiciary. In the Golak Nath case in 1967, the Supreme Court had held that the legislature or government could not tamper with fundamental rights. Fundamental rights could not be amended by ordinary amending processes.

But now in the flush of the mighty 1971 victory in the name of the poor, politics spilled over into an interference in the judiciary and radicals asserted Parliament's rights to change the Constitution and alter fundamental rights. Who were mere judges to hold back the Indira-led brave new era?

And so the 24th, 25th and 26th amendments to the Constitution were passed in quick succession in one year between 1971 and 1972, upholding bank nationalization and the abolition of privy purses, and asserting Parliament's right (as the representative of the people, who were sovereign) to dilute fundamental rights. Repeated tampering with the Constitution set a terrible precedent. It meant that in the future even the less enlightened could – and would – feel empowered to roll back certain individual rights for the greater 'good of the community'.

These amendments were challenged. In April 1973 in the famous Kesavananda Bharati case, described as the case that saved Indian democracy,[36] seven judges on a thirteen-judge bench (a wafer-thin majority), while excluding the right to property from the 'basic structure' of the Constitution, agreed that Parliament did not have unlimited powers to amend the Constitution and changes Parliament made to the basic structure or essential features of the Constitution could be struck down by the courts.[37]

The Kesavananda Bharati judgement, broadly reiterating the principles of the Golak Nath judgement, was seen by the Indira government as a serious setback. The day after the judgement, the Chief Justice of India, S.M. Sikri, retired. In the appointment of the next Chief Justice, Indira Gandhi dramatically bypassed three senior judges and appointed A.N. Ray, a judge who had ruled in favour of the government,[38] as Chief Justice of India.

The appointment of A.N. Ray hit the country like a thunderclap and created a furore. The three superseded judges resigned. Cries of 'suborning' the judiciary rose. Jurists signed a statement decrying the government's attempt to undermine the independence of the courts. But this was increasingly her style when responding to any obstacle in her path. Pax Indira would be imposed here again and like a one-eyed Cyclops playing whack-a-mole, the Indira government would quell any dissenting voices and opinions when and where they popped up.

Former chief justice M. Hidayatullah remarked that the government's action was an attempt 'not to create forward-looking judges but an attempt to create judges looking forward to the plumes of the office of Chief Justice'. The supreme ruler started to make people supremely angry.

~

In May 1973 Uttar Pradesh's Provincial Armed Constabulary (PAC) rose in revolt against shortages of basic commodities and demanded better pay and working conditions. They seized armouries, attacked government property and refused to obey orders.[39] The army was called out to crush the PAC mutiny, thirty rebellious policemen were shot dead and the Uttar Pradesh chief minister, Kamalapati Tripathi, resigned.

In January 1974 students took to the streets in Gujarat to protest against high prices. The protests soon snowballed into the Nav Nirman movement, or movement for political regeneration, which questioned the raison d'être of Indira's government and called for the resignation of the Gujarat chief minister, Chimanbhai Patel. Enraged students rampaged across the state. Buses were burnt, shops were looted, near-anarchic conditions prevailed. In one month alone, over a hundred were killed in riots, 300 were injured and 8000 were arrested. President's Rule was imposed in Gujarat in February 1974, even though it was the Congress's own government. Through it all, Indira remained convinced that a political conspiracy masterminded by the CIA had been launched against her. Her government struck back with ferocity. In Gujarat, the unprecedented use of force on the part of protesters and the government was a turning point in the history of the government's response to dissent in India.

Fierce protest and a merciless state response was seen in West Bengal as well. From the late 1960s onward, Naxalites had begun to gain support in rural Bengal and among Calcutta's urban youth. In 1971, the Naxal leader Charu Majumdar declared the 'annihilation line', that is, those who were the class enemy should be killed. The violent Naxal movement in Bengal was systematically crushed by the West Bengal police. Siddhartha Shankar Ray, then Union education minister (Ray, a close childhood friend and associate of Indira, would become West Bengal chief minister in 1972), and the Congress leader Priya Ranjan Dasmunsi were accused of being complicit in the so-called elimination of scores of Naxals. President's Rule was repeatedly imposed in West Bengal between 1968 and 1971.

As protests and strikes continued, it was an important organizational moment for 'Hindu' forces. The suffocating dominance of the Congress at this stage gave the Opposition a David vs Goliath quality in the struggle against Indira, and they were seen as heroes against a titanic state machinery. The Jana Sangh had already begun to build its own students' movement, the Akhil Bharatiya Vidyarthi Parishad (ABVP), a Hindu youth outfit to combat left student groups. The ABVP played an important role in the Nav Nirman movement and took the initiative along with other students to launch the 'Bihar movement' later. The Jana Sangh had always had a visceral dislike of the Nehrus because of the powerful secular challenge they offered to the Hindu majoritarian world view, and they saw this as their opportunity. Ideological or not, all those opposed to Indira began to leverage whatever opening they could find to beat her. Indira's contempt and paranoia about her opponents created a confrontational atmosphere, leaving no room for negotiation.

Instead of attempting a reconciliation or trying to build bridges with dissenters, Indira Gandhi turned her back on normal democratic processes. Wrote the CPI leader Hiren Mukherjee in 1973: 'Unlike her father who rejoiced in Parliament . . . Mrs Gandhi has an allergy to it . . . Parliament is representative of the people's soured mood and the Prime Minister must come to terms and make friends with it . . . but she is keeping away even when most needed in Parliament sessions. One wonders if she prefers the Presidential form of government but meanwhile the business of the country suffers.'[40] Politics was bitterly divided and India slid into near anarchy.

Into the chaos of early 1974, claiming leadership of the anti-

Indira movement, and saying that he could no longer be a 'silent spectator to misgovernment', stepped the seventy-two-year-old Jayaprakash Narayan. Freedom fighter, described as 'a strange mix of Marxism and Gandhism', born in mofussil India, educated at US universities, Jayaprakash Narayan had once been an admirer and friend of Nehru and his wife Prabhavati Devi had been a close friend of Kamala Nehru. Born in Sitab Diara in Bihar in a rustic lower-middle-class home, he was at the opposite end of the social spectrum from the privileged, westernized Indira. For youthful protesters, he was the grizzled subaltern to her high-and-mighty Marie Antoinette. JP, as he was called, had retired from mainstream politics after Independence, choosing to live an austere life devoted to social reform. In fact, the left wing of the Congress had been bitterly disappointed when JP made his reluctance to succeed Nehru as prime minister plain.

Now on the rising tide of discontent across India, he gave a call that questioned the current complexion of parliamentary democracy itself. JP's stature as a freedom hero and his long years away from power and pelf made him a moral rallying point around whom clustered all anti-Indira forces from left to right – from Jana Sangh and RSS to socialists and CPI(Marxist–Leninist), all united under JP's banner, to press for the overthrow of Indira. This coalition was a sort of grander ancestor of the 'moral coalition' of the anti-corruption movement around Anna Hazare in 2011.

JP did, however, attract the robust distrust of some. B.K. Nehru recalls how when Jawaharlal, unhappy about the lack of an Opposition in Parliament, had 'begged, cajoled, asked and tried to persuade' JP to come to Parliament and take on this role, JP's answer to Nehru had been a steadfast no. Writes B.K. Nehru: 'The man was totally negative, not positive. He was totally destructive, not constructive. He would criticise, he would agitate, he would even encourage violence, but he would not suggest any positive, constructive way to achieve what he thought required to be done. He did not, in fact, know what should in positive terms be done.'

Whatever the criticism of him, JP was the messiah of the moment. The 'Bihar movement' began under JP in early 1974, with student processions, marches and a gherao of the Bihar assembly. As in Gujarat, the goal was to oust the chief minister. JP's stature and appeal united varied groups. Lalu Prasad Yadav, then in Patna University, became president of the Bihar Chhatra Sangharsh Samiti; among its members were Sushil Modi and Ram Vilas Paswan.

~

The Hydra-headed monster of corruption reared up in these turbulent times. With laws such as the Monopolies and Restrictive Trade Practices Act 1969 and the Foreign Exchange Regulation Act 1973, the government's control over business had become a stranglehold. Too much control inevitably breeds corruption. Those who controlled permissions, licences, permits and clearances enjoyed enormous discretionary powers. 'Lalit Narayan Mishra, who held various government portfolios, was well known to be the fund collector of the Congress,' says Mark Tully. As minister, he reportedly presided over a system where huge sums of money were allegedly paid to the Congress party by those wanting licences for businesses. There was much gossip about the wheeling and dealing of Dhawan and Yashpal Kapoor, but nothing was ever proven.

If we rewind a little to 1971, we see that underneath the gloss of socialism unseen forces were already afoot. The Nagarwala incident of 1971 revealed the fantastical forms extortion rackets arising from access and proximity to the powerful could take.

In May 1971, before the Bangladesh war, Ved Prakash Malhotra, chief cashier at the State Bank of India, received a phone call from someone who claimed to be the prime minister and mimicked her voice. This person persuaded Malhotra to withdraw Rs 60 lakh in 100-rupee notes and deliver them to a 'Bangladesh ka babu', who turned out to be the former army officer Rustom Sohrab

Nagarwala who, some believed, worked for R&AW.[41] The prime minister's office was apparently shocked when Malhotra informed them of this and Haksar, then still at the helm of affairs, advised Malhotra to immediately go to the police. Nagarwala was arrested and confessed to impersonating Indira Gandhi. After an unusual high-speed three-day trial, Nagarwala was sent to jail, where he subsequently retracted his confession and died of heart failure in 1972, before his retraction could be investigated. Coincidentally, the police officer investigating the case was killed in a car accident, Malhotra was sacked from the State Bank and the mysterious case was closed, even though 'the Nagarwala Affair' had become a cause célèbre in the press.

No one ever got to know on whose behalf Nagarwala had acted, whether he was a crank, or an operative of the CIA trying to embarrass Indira Gandhi, as was later alleged,[42] or indeed an agent of the prime minister. Would Nagarwala have dared to imitate the prime minister's voice if he didn't have powerful protection either at home or abroad? Was it Indira Gandhi herself who was Nagarwala's hidden protector and who then had him eliminated? Why would Malhotra withdraw a huge amount of money just on the basis of a phone call? Questions and speculations swirled in the shadowy corners of the opaque Indira regime.

'Nehru had never dirtied his hands with money collection. He had left it to others like S.K. Patil, the Congress stalwart in Mumbai,' said Inder Malhotra. However, Indira, unable to trust anyone else, kept a tight control herself on the collection and disbursement of party funds. Since she controlled the party's money flow, 'rumours began to spread that suitcases of money were being taken to the PM's house'.[43] In a move now seen to have bolstered political corruption, Indira had banned corporate donations to political parties in 1969, fearing that companies would donate only to the right-wing Swatantra Party. Since legal contributions were now banned, underhand deals were struck between politicians and industrialists. Business–politician dealings, instead of being open and transparent, were driven underground. Shady alliances developed under the stifling hypocrisy of disallowing parties to honestly raise money.

~

Between 1972 and the declaration of Emergency in 1975, mayhem ruled in India; it was the most harrowing period in the governance of India so far, with gheraos, bandhs, calls for revolt and revolution, agitations and strikes. The most formidable protest was the nationwide railway strike which began on 8 May 1974 when 1.4 million railway workers demanded an eight-hour day and a 75 per cent increase in wages.

Indira Gandhi declared the strike illegal and arrested the railway trade union leader, the firebrand socialist George Fernandes. The militant Fernandes had taken over the leadership of the railway workers' strike from more moderate leaders, declaring that his aim was to bring down the Indira Gandhi government and force railway transport to a dead stop. Dhar later wrote, 'He was a political adventurer who was in need of a constituency and two million restive workers suited him admirably.'

With Fernandes's arrest, a million railway workers stopped work, bringing upon themselves a heartless retribution from the government. Thousands – some accounts say forty thousand – railway workers were arrested and thrown into jail. Their families were evicted from their homes and many became destitute. Scores were wounded in the violence. The government showed a merciless brutality never before witnessed in India. Indira Gandhi's pitiless suppression of the railway strike won praise from the middle classes delighted that trains began to run on time but it marked the beginning of the Opposition's determination to create an anti-Indira wave. The strike was smashed but sent out ripples of resentment and unease about a Mother Indira who had turned into a cruel stepmother.

Why did she put down the strike in so heavy-handed a manner, when she was the self-appointed guardian of the poor? Convinced that railway workers were against her, she was unable, even in the initial stages, to extend any gesture of genuine sympathy. She would say: 'The railway strike at a time when movement of food was of paramount importance showed how little the opposition cared for the true interests of the people. They tried to persuade workers not to work but to agitate. This is not the kind of climate in which any nation can prosper or survive.' It was a weak defence of a hard-hearted act that only created more suffering. She never answered why the Opposition was so successful in mobilizing workers even after being trounced in elections. Why did she, with her famed connect with the people, fail to win over railway workers?

In the midst of strife, the nation achieved a milestone. The railway strike began on 8 May 1974; just ten days later, by interesting coincidence, on 18 May 1974 the Buddha smiled. India went nuclear after testing a nuclear device in the deserts of Pokaran, Rajasthan. The 'peaceful nuclear explosion' was the culmination of India's nuclear programme started by nuclear physicist Homi J. Bhabha in the 1950s. Attacked by China in 1962 and by Pakistan in 1965, the Indian leadership had been under domestic pressure to take up an aggressive nuclear policy, although Shastri, believer in Gandhian non-violence and morally opposed to nuclear weapons, had announced that India would pursue the development of only peaceful nuclear explosives. Once Indira Gandhi was prime minister, she made her own moral opposition to nuclear weapons publicly evident, but after the Bangladesh war, with India emerging as the dominant power in the subcontinent and the experience of American strong-arm tactics, she gave her support for testing a nuclear device.

On the morning of 18 May, the earth under the Thar rumbled with deadly intent. In a grim irony that linked the Buddha to a nuclear bomb, the test was conducted on Buddha Jayanti, earning it the sobriquet 'the smiling Buddha'. Had the Buddha always been scheduled to smile in that burning summer of 1974 or had he been asked to smile on command as a show of strength and a face-saver for a prime minister who faced grave threats across the country? Only the Buddha knows the answer to that question!

Dr Mathur visited Indira Gandhi that day to find her 'fidgety and ill at ease'. He was surprised to find her formally dressed even at that early hour and repeatedly picking up the phone and putting it down again. On her bedside table he noticed an open notebook in which the Gayatri Mantra was inscribed in long hand. 'I heard her mutter in my direction, go, in the name of god, go! I was very upset and left immediately.'

The doctor then visited P.N. Dhar, who looked equally tense and ill at ease. He realized what the matter was when Sharada Prasad phoned him later in the day to say, 'India exploded an atom bomb! PM made the announcement in Parliament this afternoon. The explosion occurred at 8 am. PM received a code message – Buddha is smiling.' Says Mathur, 'I realized then why she had been so tense and nervous that morning.'

~

'The smiling Buddha' brought no peace to the land. Wave upon wave of violent protests were shaking India. Describing JP's movement, Sham Lal wrote in the *Times of India*, 'JP is creating a political climate propitious not for a revolution but for anarchy.'[44] Asked *The Hindu*: 'Should JP exploit his public standing and usher in disrespect for law and order and the democratic set up as a whole?'[45]

To youth looking for a leader, JP was a legend who had stepped through the mists of history to lend his presence to their cause; he was a bridge between them and the freedom struggle which they adopted as the precursor of their movement, a Gandhi come to life. Realizing that only a united Opposition could defeat Indira, JP, Morarji, now chief of the Congress(O), the Jana Sangh and the socialists formed the Janata Morcha or Janata Front against Indira

Gandhi. This front would be the precursor to the Janata Party which would go on to fight Indira Gandhi at the hustings. Early straws in the electoral wind revealed that the public responded readily to a united Janata. In by-elections in Jabalpur, a Congress stronghold for half a century, the Janata Front candidate vanquished a once unshakeable Congress. It was, wrote the *Times of India*, 'a veritable tornado' against the Congress.[46] The winner of the Jabalpur by-election in 1974 was an unknown engineering student who became the youngest member of Parliament: Sharad Yadav. More wins in by-elections would follow for the Janata Front. Meanwhile, protests in Bihar built to a crescendo. The central government bore down forcefully. Protesting crowds were lathi-charged and tear-gassed. Unbowed, at a rally in Gandhi Maidan in Patna on 5 June 1974, JP called for 'sampurna kranti' – total revolution.

Indira refused to make any attempt to reach out to the leaders of the Bihar movement even though Congress members such as Mohan Dharia, the steadfast opponent of the Emergency in the Congress, urged her to do so. Through this period Indira Gandhi remained fixated on the conspiracy theory of the 'foreign hand' trying to destabilize her. 'The movement [of the early 1970s] was supported from outside, it was not only internal . . . We have to look at the doings of international agencies and who was in India and at what time.'[47] She was to repeat: 'Our aim was the eradication of poverty. But as soon as we bend to this task . . . the full weight of money, economic power, the press, industry, local and foreign, combine to obstruct us.'

She refused to believe there were legitimate grievances or grounds for discontent. 'In a situation of extreme economic difficulty, the Opposition wanted to bring down the government by entirely unconstitutional, undemocratic means. They were not prepared to wait for elections. They were not prepared for peaceful demonstrations. Students were on the street, they were setting fire to libraries and breaking up scientific equipment. The government machinery was becoming irresponsible. At all times you would see government functionaries playing cards on the roundabouts of Delhi. There was a danger of the whole thing cracking up.'[48]

Congress radicals like Dharia, Krishan Kant and the former student leader Chandra Shekhar urged Indira to read the lessons of the Janata Front's electoral advances and renewed their calls for political reconciliation. There must be an all-party united initiative to tackle the economic and social crisis, they argued. Indira would have none of it. Instead she wrote to Dharia saying, 'It is not proper for you to continue in the Council of Ministers since your views are not in conformity with the thinking of the Congress party.' Dharia resigned from the Indira government in 1975 and would quit the Congress once the Emergency was declared. 'Mrs Gandhi was not prepared for a dialogue with JP at all! She thought he wanted to dislodge her and become Prime Minister. But JP was not interested in doing that. If demanding a dialogue was considered a crime, then I was prepared to commit that crime a thousand times,' Dharia would say later in an interview.[49]

~

The goddess was embattled at home but pulled off another Durga-like act abroad. She demonstrated that, besieged or not, there would be no insubordination in the neighbourhood while Pax Indira prevailed. When the hereditary ruler of Sikkim, then an Indian protectorate, with India looking after its defence, the Chogyal, and his American wife, Hope Cook, began to make moves towards a more autonomous Sikkim, Indira Gandhi struck.

There had been a long-standing demand in Sikkim for a more democratic government and Indira believed it was her duty to stand by as liberator of the Sikkimese people and sternly put down any attempt by the Chogyal to chart his own course and possibly move closer to China. There was a pro-democracy movement in Sikkim with several pro-India parties in the fray as well as others like the Sikkim National Congress. In 1974, elections were held in Sikkim.

After the elections threw up a pro-democracy, anti-Chogyal verdict, a chief minister took charge and the Chogyal became a constitutional monarch. In Parliament a constitutional amendment bill was moved to make Sikkim into an associate state of India. A panic-stricken Chogyal flew to Delhi to try to save his position only to be met by a curt and aloof Indira. India's interests were at stake and Indira Gandhi was in no mood to deal with Sikkimese angst about autonomy. It was also likely that amid political turbulence Indira grasped any opportunity she could get for a demonstration of power.

On 8 April 1975 the Indian army marched into Gangtok. The Chogyal's palace was surrounded and he was put under house arrest. A referendum was arranged. The Chogyal and the 300-odd-year-old rule of his dynasty came to an end. Sikkim became India's twenty-second state. At the time of the merger of Sikkim, Indira Gandhi was under siege. The JP movement was at its height; the economic crisis had India in its grip. Yet Indira-led India absorbed Sikkim with supreme self-confidence even as Morarji Desai protested at this forcible 'annexation'.

~

Pax Indira was upheld in the neighbourhood but was being battered from within. Her enemies had her in their chakravyuh. Like Karna, the mythological hero whose chariot failed him in a crucial battle, her much-vaunted political instincts deserted her when she most needed them. Well-wishers on both sides of the divide pressed on for a reconciliation between Indira Gandhi and JP and a meeting finally took place in November 1974. But Indira Gandhi had scant respect for JP. At his death, in 1979, she would write: 'Poor old JP! What a confused mind he had, leading to such a frustrated life! He was a sufferer of what I can only call Gandhian hypocrisy . . . jealousy of my father conditioned his life.'[50]

The septuagenarian crusader and the all-powerful prime minister were old family associates. When they met, through the fog of mistrust, recalling the old ties between the families, the older man reached out to the woman he had known as a girl. JP handed Indira a collection of Kamala's letters to Prabhavati Devi which Indira gratefully received. But the meeting proved futile and turned out to be an angry confrontation. Indira accused JP of being a CIA agent; he regarded her as a nonentity with no real right to be where she was and accused her of trying to establish a Soviet-style dictatorship in India. She had no time for JP and what she described as his 'woolly and irresponsible ideas', calling him 'a theoretician of chaos'. For JP, Indira's personality cult and her supreme power were an outrage. The meeting ended on an acrimonious note.

Visiting India from the United Kingdom, where he was high commissioner, towards the end of 1974, B.K. Nehru discovered a central government frozen in fear of Indira. Bringing with him a message that Lord Mountbatten was aggrieved that his portrait no longer hung in Rashtrapati Bhavan, Nehru met President Fakhruddin Ali Ahmed. Ahmed agreed that Mountbatten was right to feel hurt but confessed he could do nothing about it. 'Zara aap unse kah dijiye [maybe you should tell her],' was all he said, the 'unse' clearly meaning Indira Gandhi. 'I learnt later by accident that the Prime Minister so dominated the President that the "official portion" of Rashtrapati Bhavan was under her control.' Months later, Fakhruddin Ali Ahmed would indeed prove himself as Indira's faithful loyalist when under her instructions he signed the order proclaiming the Emergency, prompting popular cartoons eluding to presidential indignity by showing him signing the Emergency proclamation while sitting in his bathtub.[51]

~

In January 1975, Lalit Narayan Mishra, Indira's railway minister and the main Congress party fund collector, died in a bomb blast in Samastipur railway station, an act Indira Gandhi said was only a 'dress rehearsal' for her own planned assassination. 'Mishra's killing played on her mind badly,' recalled Vasant Sathe. 'She yielded more and more to suspicions that her life was in danger from her enemies.' A group of Anand Margis, a secretive Hindu sect, then accused of plotting to bring down Indira Gandhi, was convicted for Mishra's murder.[52]

Her own political 'assassination' seemed at hand. In February, JP exhorted the army and police not to 'obey orders that are illegal and unjust', a call he would renew at the famous Ram Lila Maidan rally in Delhi on the eve of the declaration of Emergency. In March, JP led a march to Parliament, a gigantic procession winding through the streets of Old and New Delhi, calling for Indira Gandhi's resignation at a rally afterwards, in a voice ringing with emotion.

In Gujarat, on 12 March 1975 the seventy-nine-year-old Morarji Desai went on an indefinite hunger strike in support of the Nav Nirman movement and demanded announcement of elections in the state. This was the start of 'the battle with Indira Gandhi I had been dreaming of since 1969', Desai admitted to the journalist Oriana Fallaci.[53] Confronted with the possible death of her long-time bête noire, Indira Gandhi agreed to fresh elections in Gujarat in June 1975, in which the Congress was trounced by the Janata Front.

~

A day after the Janata's victory in Gujarat came the lowest moment of Indira Gandhi's political life. On 12 June, Justice Jagmohan Lal Sinha of the Allahabad High Court delivered a judgement holding Indira Gandhi guilty of electoral malpractice. The case had been filed by Raj Narain, known as the 'Clown Prince of India', the buffoon-like bandana-sporting socialist leader she had defeated in Raebareli in 1971 who had coined the term 'Indira Hatao'.

The Allahabad High Court now declared Indira Gandhi's election to the Lok Sabha from Raebareli invalid, and she was barred from contesting elections or holding elective office for six years. The court found that her private secretary Yashpal Kapoor had worked as her agent during the elections, before he had resigned from government service.[54] It also found that Indira Gandhi had used the help of Uttar Pradesh government officials to build rostrums and supply electricity for loudspeakers during her 1971 rallies.

The implication of the judgement was immediately obvious: she would have to resign. Yet the charges were so trivial that *The Times*, London, wrote, 'it was like dismissing a prime minister for a traffic offence'. In comparison with the charges politicians face today and the brazen use of government machinery for electioneering, the dismissal of a prime minister on the grounds of using local loudspeakers and rostrums was hardly a case of the punishment fitting the crime. The charges were undoubtedly trivial but the moral responsibility on Indira Gandhi loomed large. On the same day as the Allahabad High Court judgement, news came in that in the Gujarat assembly elections the Janata Front had defeated the Congress; 12 June 1975 was not a good day for Indira Gandhi.

'She was very shocked when she heard the judgement,' says Dr Mathur, 'as she didn't realize the case was going against her. She had been summoned once to the court and been questioned by Shanti Bhushan, Raj Narain's lawyer.'[55] In fact, she was the first prime minister summoned to appear and testify in court in a case of this kind. 'When she came to the court she was very gracious and composed at first, but later became a bit disconcerted and flustered at the cross-questioning,' recalls senior lawyer Prashant Bhushan, Shanti Bhushan's son who has written a book on the case.[56] Bhushan says that the cross-questioning was tough though gentlemanly and by the end Indira seemed satisfied that the questioning had been fair.[57]

Trivial charges or not, what would her father have done? Stickler for nurturing institutions, Nehru would in all probability have immediately resigned in the face of such a judgement. As we have seen, Nehru had been ready to resign three times during his prime ministership on far less personal charges. But Indira, in pursuit of self-preservation against her enemies, whom she also cast as India's enemies, was already on her way to creating a political culture that scorned institutions, a culture so prevalent today where personalized rule means a disdain not just for laws but also for moral norms.

The Allahabad High Court judgement gave a massive impetus to the anti-Indira movement. They now felt she had no option but to quit forthwith. While her opponents wanted her to depart without delay, she remained convinced of her popularity. Crises and difficulties had always strengthened her and now the more they pushed for her resignation, the more defensive and abrasive her speeches became. Within a fortnight India's goddess would summon up such a powerful counter-attack that her rivals would be flummoxed into submission and wonder what exactly had hit them. Durga would unleash her wrath in a sensational and completely unexpected manner.

Immediately after the judgement though, there was shock and disorientation that midsummer afternoon. Reports began to come in that Anand Margis, already under suspicion for the murder of L.N. Mishra, were behind it.[58] Siddhartha Shankar Ray had written in January that year that lists of Anand Margis and RSS members should be prepared by every state as he feared that they were behind the attempts to destabilize Indira.[59] The prime minister's house became a hive of activity. Ray, Indira's old friend, a strapping, cricket and tennis playing barrister and West Bengal chief minister, rushed to Delhi on her request. Her advisers clustered around offering advice. Indira Gandhi's motivations at this time in not resigning have been interpreted in various ways. Had she wanted to resign or hadn't she?

Former joint secretary in the prime minister's secretariat, B.N. Tandon notes in his diary: 'It [soon] became clear that the PM never intended to resign nor was she going to . . . I felt she would not hesitate to use any means to remain in power . . . she seems to have convinced herself that the judgement is not against her but against the people of the country . . . in the PM's thinking every possible means is justified if it helps in remaining in power.'[60]

Ray later recalled that her first instinct was to resign. Recalls Bhaskar Ghose, then secretary to Ray: 'Ray said Indira was determined to go. She had made up her mind. She changed it only after veteran Congress leader Jagjivan Ram said, madam please don't resign, but if you do, please leave your choice of successor to us. As soon as he said that, she stiffened and realized what their game was. A hard glint came into her eyes. She felt that if she resigned she would lose power for good.' In fact Jagjivan Ram, the diehard Congress stalwart who would later desert Indira, had made it clear that his loyalty was reserved only for Indira; if it came to any other successor, he had signalled that he had the 'superior' claim.

Jayakar believes that at this point Sanjay's wishes were uppermost. On the day of the judgement, when Sanjay returned home from his car factory, he had angrily insisted that there was no question of his mother resigning. All those who were swearing allegiance would only stab her in the back and take over power, he had asserted.

Maneka Gandhi's interpretation is different. 'Sanjay was not the architect of the Emergency as is said. It was Siddhartha Shankar Ray, D.K. Barooah [then Congress president], [Congressman] K.C. Pant, a small leftist ginger group, who pushed her and pushed her and pushed her. Her first instinct was to make Babu Jagjivan Ram the prime minister and wait until her case was sorted out. But they instilled terror in her saying once you give up the prime ministership you will never get it back. He'll finish you off. That's why she stayed on. If there was one quality my mother-in-law had to the nth degree it was the quality of self-preservation.' She may also have been afraid that whoever came to office after her would use the skeletons in Sanjay's cupboard to keep her out for good.

'She was a hundred per cent democrat,' says Dhawan, 'and she kept offering to resign. But all the others, Barooah, Jagjivan Ram, they all said she shouldn't. They kept pressing her. They even gave a statement, a loyalty pledge that was drafted by P.N. Haksar [now marginalized in the Planning Commission] and signed by her ministers.' To demonstrate his loyalty, D.K. Barooah at this time cried out dramatically, 'Indira is India and India is Indira, the two are inseparable.'

She would insist that staying on was nothing but a call of the conscience, a discharging of her duty to the people and resistance to foreign conspirators. She would often say she didn't stay on for the sake of mere office but because the charges were trivial and she had miles to go before she could sleep. 'If I (only) wanted to remain prime minister all I would have had to do was listen to the party bosses. They would not have wanted me out at all. I could have been prime minister for life.'[61]

In the context of the JP movement and the surrounding clamour against her, the Allahabad High Court judgement was a debilitating lightning strike in an already storm-swept night. The son now stepped forward as his mother's protector.

'Sanjay had been apolitical all this time. But when the JP movement took off and the judgement came in, that's when he stepped in,' recalled Maneka. The boy became the mother's guardian. Trusting nobody, ringed in by potential back-stabbers, she clutched her ruggedly loyal wild child close to her, his words worth more than any other advice. Her behaviour at this time was another contrast with Nehru, who had hardly ever turned to his daughter for counsel even in his weakest moments. However, she, quite unlike her father, in a moment of supreme political crisis found herself unable to trust anyone except her own younger son. He, for his part, violently disliked all his mother's colleagues who he felt were not on his side and had not supported Maruti strongly enough. Knowing that he and his Maruti project would get into serious political trouble with another political dispensation, he needed his mother in government to protect him. She in turn drew him closer to her as one would a warm blanket on a cold shivery night. Protecting each other, mother and son faced the gathering darkness together.

B.N. Tandon notes that whatever the legalities, 'no one seemed to have the courage to examine the moral basis of the judgement . . . thanks to the PM during these last five years moral values and yardsticks have been totally devalued'.[62]

Justice Sinha of the Allahabad High Court had in his original ruling of 12 June granted a twenty-day stay on the judgement in order to enable the government to find a successor to Indira. On 23 June Indira appealed in the Supreme Court asking for an unconditional and absolute stay of the Allahabad High Court judgement. On 24 June Justice V.R. Krishna Iyer of the Supreme Court granted only a 'conditional stay': she could remain in office but not vote in Parliament until her appeal was settled. This reduced her to a non-functioning figurehead prime minister, a lame duck.

The Opposition in any case was not willing to let the case make its way through the courts. There was no holding them back now. JP's army wanted Indira out, and they wanted her out now. Said Morarji Desai to Oriana Fallaci on the eve of their planned 25 June rally at Delhi's Ram Lila Maidan: 'We'll camp there [at her house] day and night. We intend to overthrow her, to force her to resign. For good. The lady won't survive this movement of ours.'[63]

Before the Supreme Court judgement came in, Sanjay and Dhawan had been organizing pro-Indira demonstrations around her house and the Congress held a series of rallies in support of her, all overseen by Sanjay. The largest and most impressive of these was held at Delhi's Boat Club, where a massive crowd had cheered her on. B.N. Tandon notes in his diary: 'I learnt from I.K. Gujral [then information and broadcasting minister] today that Sanjay had given him a severe dressing down because yesterday's [pro-Indira] rally was not properly publicised. He is annoyed that the campaign that is underway in support of the PM is not getting proper publicity.'[64] Bhagat was witness to a 'disgusting scene' where Sanjay humiliatingly shouted at Gujral: 'Sanjay was angry and shouted at Gujral for poor coverage of the rallies. Gujral looked embarrassed but did not utter a word. After Sanjay left, we exchanged glances and with folded hands I looked heavenwards.' After the Emergency was declared, Indira sacked I.K. Gujral as information and broadcasting minister at Sanjay's behest and replaced him with Vidya Charan Shukla, the man described as Indira's Goebbels, the Nazi propaganda minister.

On the morning of 25 June, Indira Gandhi told Ray: 'Siddhartha, we're in serious trouble. The Gujarat assembly is dissolved. Bihar is dissolved. There will be no end. Democracy will come to a grinding halt. Some drastic emergent action is needed.'

She may not yet have known about Article 352 but 'emergent' action for her meant immediate action to save democracy. Democracy-in-danger was her oft-used line to justify the Emergency. From her point of view, she protected India's democracy by taking democracy away. Ray then explained to her that Article 352 of the Constitution allowed the government to impose a state of national Emergency in the face of external aggression or internal disturbance.

The Opposition's Ram Lila Maidan rally provided Indira Gandhi the trigger she needed. It had already been reported to her by intelligence officials that at the Ram Lila Maidan in Delhi that evening JP would give a call for the army and police to mutiny, which he did. An enormous crowd gathered at the Ram Lila Maidan on the evening of 25 June. Cheers and applause broke out when JP recited Ramdhari Singh Dinkar's poem, *'Singhasan khaali karo, ki janta aati hai* [Vacate the throne, the people are coming].' JP gave the call he had in the past: police and armed forces must not obey 'illegal and unconstitutional orders'. As JP called for Indira to immediately relinquish office, the crowd roared its support.

Indira would say, 'They attempted to undermine the loyalty of the police and military . . . would any country tolerate a call to the armed forces to revolt?' Indira Gandhi was clear: JP's call was internal aggression against the government's sovereignty; India's sovereignty was being threatened by an internal war. Coomi Kapoor points out that while JP's words were later quoted repeatedly by Mrs Gandhi to justify the Emergency, in fact, preparations for the Emergency were being made for many months before.[65]

That Emergency-like actions may have been thought of for almost a year is revealed in an interview given by Siddhartha Shankar Ray. He said as far back as August 1974 he had written to Indira Gandhi saying he was taking action against antisocials, even though he knew this 'may create difficulties'.[66] Ray was referring to the kind of harsh and brutal line his government had taken against Naxals in the early 1970s, when he had been accused of large-scale human rights violations.

On the evening of 25 June 1975, Indira Gandhi and Siddhartha Shankar Ray went to meet President Fakhruddin Ali Ahmed in Rashtrapati Bhavan. They told the president that an internal Emergency had become necessary given that the country's sovereignty was being directly threatened. Later that night the 'Emergency Order Proclamation' was sent to Rashtrapati Bhavan for the president to sign. Just a few minutes before midnight of 25 June the president signed the proclamation order. The Republic of India passed into a state of Emergency.

~

The Emergency was justifiably pilloried but questions were raised about the JP movement too. Is the concept of 'satyagraha' against an elected government by definition invalid? Guha quotes a letter to JP from a former ICS officer which said, 'By demanding the dismissal of an elected assembly, the Bihar agitation is both unconstitutional and anti-democratic.' After all, satyagraha was the Gandhian instrument against imperialist rule not intended to be used against a democratic dispensation elected by the people. Is a government confronted by strikes, satyagrahas, mass civil unrest and calls for civil disobedience of the police not duty-bound to act to enforce its authority? Did Indira Gandhi have no alternative but to impose what she described as only a temporary suspension of democracy? 'I described the Emergency as a medicine,' she said later. 'If a person is ill you have to give a medicine which the person may not like but is essential for him.'[67]

When JP declared that an elected government had lost its moral right to govern, was he not sowing the seeds of a sinister trend by which elected governments could be overthrown simply by a hysterically whipped-up popular demand of the moment, rather than by the verdict of the ballot box?

Yet even if we accept that the JP-led movement was not a democratic one, Indira for her part remained obtuse about exactly why the opposition to her had become quite so fierce. She confused an assertion of power with a maintaining of authority, but she had allowed her moral authority to become steadily and disastrously eroded by Sanjay's activities, by her open protection of Sanjay and by her refusal to meet the protesters even short of halfway or show that she was attempting to understand their grievances. 'The Emergency was resorted to because governments have really no answer to satyagraha,' writes Sharada Prasad, 'she was only too aware of its [satyagraha's] power . . . governments response to satyagraha is use of force.' Emergency powers are also resorted to when governments have no other idea on how to restore their moral legitimacy. For Indira's side, the JP movement lacked grassroots support; it was a campaign launched by the RSS and Jana Sangh, which fizzled out as quickly as it had begun. In the end the Janata revolution devoured its leaders and proved to be only a flash in the pan and Indira Gandhi would be revealed as only a 'half-hearted dictator'. This half-heartedness on both sides was a saving grace. Unimaginable strife may have befallen India if 'people power' had overthrown an elected prime minister or if Indira had stamped out democracy for good. The Emergency was an original sin, but those who tried to bring down an elected government through sheer public pressure weren't exactly democracy's ministering angels.

~

It was said that Indira Gandhi's habit of using 'a hundred units of force where ten would do . . . led to the Emergency'.[68] Indira herself gave several justifications for the Emergency when questioned about it later and for the first months remained convinced that it was highly beneficial. She wrote, 'no civil war has been declared. It is true I have imposed Emergency and a number of Opposition leaders have been arrested including Jayaprakash Narayan and Morarji Desai. Jayaprakash addressed a meeting at Ram Lila Maidan where he appealed to the army and police not to obey the orders of the government. No government can tolerate this.'[69]

Indira's close friend Jayakar was very critical of the Emergency, particularly press censorship, and asked her, 'How could you, the daughter of Jawaharlal Nehru permit this?' 'You do not know of the plots against me,' Indira replied. 'Jayaprakash and Morarjibhai have always hated me. They were determined to see that I was destroyed.'[70] She consistently maintained that it was the protesters who were jeopardizing democracy, not she, and that she had in fact acted in defence of democracy. She would say: 'On the night of June 27 in a broadcast to the nation, I gave the reason for proclaiming the state of Emergency: a climate of violence and hatred had been created . . . One of them [the Opposition leaders] went to the extent of saying that armed forces should not carry out orders which they consider wrong . . . since the proclamation of Emergency, the whole country has gone back to normal . . . violent action and senseless satyagrahas will pull down the whole edifice which has been built over the years with such labour and hope . . . I trust it will be possible to lift the Emergency soon . . . You know I have always believed in the freedom of the press and I still do, but like all freedoms it has to be exercised with responsibility and restraint.'

She would go on to say: 'Suppose we hadn't been able to reach food to the people. They would have said the system doesn't work, so let it go. This is how democratic systems have been removed earlier . . . so we actually saved democracy.'[71]

Those close to her believe, however, that though she stoutly defended it from the beginning, Indira had not been fully convinced of the decision. Bhagat writes, 'Mrs Gandhi could be a ditherer and procrastinate but she was an astute and experienced person . . . and sometimes it's best to dither than to take quick cut-and-dry decisions . . . perhaps in the two most tragic decisions of her political career – the Emergency and Operation Blue Star Mrs Gandhi was not allowed to take decisions in her own style.'

~

Dear Mrs Gandhi,

Was there no alternative to declaring the Emergency? No, once you decided not to resign, there was no other alternative. But with your long experience in politics could you not predict what suspending the Constitution would do to India? Your open championing of your son Sanjay took a tragic toll on your moral authority in the public's eyes. Yet with royal confidence you expected people to dumbly accept the follies of mother and son. Did you think 'the people' would accept whatever you did simply because you were Indira Gandhi? When your colleagues urged you to restrain the use of force and reach out for a dialogue with your opponents, you did not try this route even once, convinced they had no grounds for protest.

Instead you invoked sinister powers, rather like calling up ghouls from a medieval past when despots ruled through fear. Erstwhile political colleagues were thrown into often filthy, overcrowded prison cells. You were to say that 'people arrested for ordinary crimes pretended they were political prisoners',[72] but was there any reason to imprison L.K. Advani, Atal Bihari Vajpayee, Vijaya Raje Scindia other than that they were leaders of the Jana Sangh and your political opponents?

If your instinct was to resign, why did you let yourself be talked out of your gut feel? You were clearly trying to camouflage and protect Sanjay's activities, keenly aware of what a new government would make of his doings. You were simply determined to prevent the Opposition from coming to power, convinced they would destroy both India and Sanjay. Did you fear that the House of Nehru would be destroyed forever if you left office?

~

The story of the Emergency has been told often and in deservedly lurid shades. The jailing of dissenters, muzzling of the press, forced sterilization campaigns and slum-clearance drives remain etched in India's post-Independence history. The Emergency's stark images are an 'I told you so' moment for those who had argued that India could never survive as a democracy and was unsuited for the Westminster style of government. The Mahatma had awakened a people into a quest for individual freedom. Nehru, with his intellectual centre in Cambridge and Harrow, had dreamt that India could be a version of English democracy. Ambedkar had drafted the republic's Constitution with progressive social change at its heart. Patel had unified the geography of India, bringing hereditary princes under the sovereignty of the people.

Yet that courageously bold sketch of India at Independence, those confident brushstrokes of progress drawn on a chaotic, teeming map of conflicts, unresolved identities and wildly differing levels of awareness needed fresh coats of paint and doses of strong idealism for the portrait to retain its identity, freshness and appeal. Indira Gandhi's India had replaced that audaciously confident painting with a series of petty doodles of power and intrigue and the Emergency finally tore through that bravely painted canvas, leaving it flapping in a dirt storm.

Where Mahatma Gandhi exhorted his followers to be their best selves, to rise to the highest personal standards of truth and non-violence, Indira Gandhi set the stage for a pulverizing populism, for an appeal to the lowest self where simplistic messages about the end of poverty obliterated the higher calling that Gandhi had held out as the mark of Indian democracy. The freedom struggle had created an enormous pool of political talent, as the educated came forward to test their ideas among those less fortunate, but Indira Gandhi's distrust of free thought and speech became a disincentive for high achievers to find their calling in the Congress, as so many had done during the Nehru era. During the Emergency scores of India's brightest political minds found themselves behind bars. Politics as the vocation of the educated and talented soon became closed to those who were unable to accept craven loyalty as the only qualification of public life.

She had a golden opportunity in 1971 when with a thumping mandate she could have begun the politics of generosity. But believing that the mandate and the military victory were hers alone, that she was India's only hope, she failed to renew the reconciling politics of her father or usher in an era that would have been a worthy successor to Nehru's valiant constitutionalism. As Mountbatten – peeved with her move to abolish privy purses and later the jailing of Maharani Gayatri Devi – noted in his diary: 'She has of course not been corrupt in the ordinary sense of the word but has certainly grown too big for her boots and is being tough and difficult with everybody.'[73]

However, after declaring the Emergency, she got support from an unusual quarter. Even though she banned the RSS during the Emergency, a book by a former director of the Intelligence Bureau, T.V. Rajeswar, says that the RSS chief Balasaheb Deoras[74] was a strong supporter of her attempts to enforce order in the country and Sanjay Gandhi's later drive for family planning, particularly among Muslims. Deoras was reportedly very keen to meet Indira but she declined because she did not want to be seen as an 'RSS sympathiser'.[75]

For now she was hardly anyone's sympathizer. Sanjay Gandhi and Om Mehta, Sanjay's crony and minister of state for home affairs, had drawn up lists of the names of Opposition members to be arrested. The arrests began late from the night of 25 June itself. Jayaprakash Narayan and Morarji Desai were woken up and informed that they were under arrest. Congress members Chandra Shekhar and Mohan Dharia, known to be sympathetic to JP, were also jailed, as were most Opposition leaders. As the arrests began, the power supply to Delhi's Bahadur Shah Zafar Marg or 'Fleet Street' was suddenly turned off. Darkness descended on newspaper offices so only a couple of broadsheets – *Hindustan Times* and *Statesman*, whose offices were not located on Bahadur Shah Zafar Marg – were available in Delhi to report the Emergency proclamation. 'President Proclaims National Emergency, Preventive Arrests: Press Censorship Imposed' read the headline of *The Hindu*.

Indira Gandhi had reportedly not given permission to cut off electricity to newspapers but Sanjay and his associates went above her head. On 25 June she had apparently assured Ray: 'Siddhartha, it's alright; there will be electricity.'[76] As it turned out, electricity was cut anyway. Shah Commission witnesses said that it was on Sanjay's orders that power to newspaper offices was cut. When Ray had expressed his serious discomfort at the decision, saying the 'whole thing was absurd', Sanjay had told Ray: 'You people do not know how to run the country.'

Indira had disdainfully bypassed her cabinet in the decision to impose the Emergency. The cabinet was told of it only early the next morning when only one minister, Sardar Swaran Singh, dared to ask why an Emergency was needed when an external Emergency was already in place. Swaran Singh later told his friends, 'Yeh thanedari nahin chalegi [these strong-arm tactics won't do].' For his pains he would soon be dropped from the cabinet, and replaced with Sanjay's crony Bansi Lal, the Haryana chief minister who was such a dedicated supporter of the Maruti project.

Across India, fundamental rights were suspended, strikes and unions were banned and there was a crackdown on protesters. The notorious law MISA, or Maintenance of Internal Security Act, enacted in 1971, was used to jail activists, protesters and almost anyone who questioned Indira. Under MISA, detainees could be held for two years without trial. Twenty-six anti-Congress outfits were

Wikimedia Commons

The Times of India Group. © BCCL. All rights reserved

Sputnik Images

Clockwise from top left: Jawaharlal, Kamala and Indira Nehru at Anand Bhawan in Allahabad (1931). Anand Bhawan was shorn of its silks and European artefacts and became the hub of the national movement shortly after the Jallianwala Bagh massacre in 1919.

Indira (*left*) with her aunt Krishna Nehru, later Hutheesing, in Bombay in 1930. Indira and her mother both had a prickly relationship with Jawaharlal's other sister, Vijayalakshmi Pandit. Such was the rancour that Pandit would not be invited to Indira's son Sanjay's wedding several decades later.

Indira with her father, reading his autobiography (1937). Nehru was obsessed with improving his daughter and spent much time and energy on her intellectual and physical development. Among other things he would tell her not to wear a sari, 'a lounger's costume', and to stand on her head.

Bettmann, Getty Images

Wikimedia Commons

Top: Indira and Feroze Gandhi's wedding in Anand Bhawan in 1942. Seated on the extreme right is Vijayalakshmi Pandit. Nehru was at first opposed to the match and relented only after Mahatma Gandhi intervened. Indira wore a sari woven of thread spun by Nehru.

Bottom: Indira and Feroze Gandhi. The Gandhis had an unhappy marriage. Feroze was openly unfaithful to Indira and they were soon estranged and lived separately.

Wikimedia Commons

Top: Baby Rajiv with his parents, Feroze and Indira, and grandfather Jawaharlal in Anand Bhawan in 1945. Jawaharlal wanted Indira to add 'Nehru' to Rajiv's name.

Bottom: A devastated Indira sitting with Rajiv and other mourners after her estranged husband Feroze's death at Teen Murti House on 8 September 1960. They had just, in June, been on a holiday to Kashmir together, where Indira decided that after Nehru died she would 'commit herself totally' to Feroze.

Hulton Archive, Getty Images

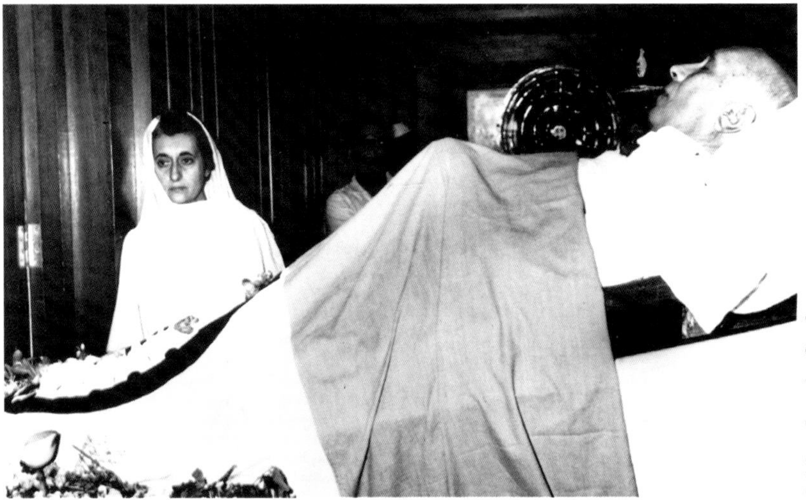

Rolls Press, Popperfoto, Getty Images

Top: American President John F. Kennedy and his wife, Jackie, with Nehru and Indira in Washington in 1960. Indira often accompanied her father on official trips abroad. The sari–fur combination became her signature look.

Bottom: Indira with Nehru's lifeless body in May 1964. Nehru's successor, Prime Minister Lal Bahadur Shastri, apparently insisted that Indira join his cabinet. An announcement to this effect was made on the radio, presenting Indira with a fait accompli.

Bettmann, Getty Images

Everett Collection, Alamy

Top: Indira Gandhi on a visit to the US in March 1966, a few weeks after becoming prime minister for the first time. After this visit Indira would devalue the rupee in return for aid from America, a politically unpopular move that brought her into confrontation with a group of veteran Congress leaders.

Bottom: President Radhakrishnan and Prime Minister Indira with her face heavily bandaged after she was hit with a stone at a rally in Bhubaneswar before the 1967 general election. Indira remarked that she looked 'like Batman'.

Paul Popper, Popperfoto, Getty Images

Keystone Pictures USA, Alamy

Top: President Radhakrishnan administering the oath of office of prime minister to Indira Gandhi for a second time, after the 1967 general election.

Bottom: Prime Minister Indira with senior party leaders K. Kamaraj (*centre*) and Morarji Desai in March 1967. Desai, then deputy prime minister and finance minister, would often slight Indira in public. Indira split the Congress in 1969 and formed the Congress (R), of which she was the undisputed boss.

Agence France Presse, Getty Images

Bettmann, Getty Images

Top: Indira shakes hands with Pakistani president Zulfikar Ali Bhutto as Benazir Bhutto looks on in June 1972. The two leaders met in Shimla to negotiate the terms of peace after India won the 1971 Bangladesh war. The US tried its best to intimidate India during the war, including by sending a nuclear warship to the Bay of Bengal. But Indira didn't blink.

Bottom: A beaming Indira with her son Sanjay after the 1980 election results, the Congress's big political comeback after being routed in the post-Emergency 1977 election. In 1977 Indira and Sanjay both lost their Lok Sabha seats.

The India Today Group, Getty Images

Gery Gerard, Getty Images

Top: Indira with Sanjay's lifeless body (23 June 1980). Sanjay died in a plane crash. Indira visited the site of the wreckage twice, inspecting the debris as if looking for bits of her son.

Bottom: Indira with her grandchildren Rahul (*left*) and Priyanka (March 1975). She loved spending time with her grandchildren, playing with her many dogs, and doing crosswords.

banned, including the RSS, the CPM and the CPML, although the CPI remained a staunch Indira and Emergency supporter. A pall of silence descended as no one, not even senior politicians, spoke out. An eerie hush enveloped the normally cacophonous Indian subcontinent. Authoritarianism gave birth to obsequious art: the artist M.F. Husain created murals of a triumphant Indira, seated Durga-like, on a rampaging tiger, which were sent across the country for public viewing.

Not only were newspapers censored but guidelines were issued that 'positive' news was to be emphasized. Giant billboards of Indira appeared on streets with slogans such as 'The Leader's Right, The Future's Bright'. Foreign journalists, including the BBC's Mark Tully, were told to leave India. Censorship regulations were laid down for foreign correspondents if they wanted to report from India. 'There were weeks of negotiations between foreign correspondents and the government,' recalls Tully, 'about whether we would sign the new censorship regulations. The BBC refused to sign, along with many others. I received a call one evening telling me apologetically that I should leave in twenty-four hours or face arrest.' A total of 253 journalists were imprisoned, among them the Indira-baiter Kuldip Nayar of the *Indian Express*. 'We had been good friends,' recalled Nayar, 'she used to love dirty jokes and used to urge me to tell her more.'[77] However friendly they once might have been, Nayar's candidly critical articles directed at her clearly did not go down as well as his ribald jokes.

In the first few months of the Emergency, the urban middle class welcomed the restoration of order, the freedom from endless strikes and hartals and the slow recovery of the economy. With most of the Opposition in jail, the Emergency was easily ratified in Parliament. The first few months of the Emergency were calm and tranquil. Guha quotes a *Time* magazine reporter who visited India in October 1975 and reported that press freedom and the like were of no great interest to the majority of India's 600 million people who were more concerned with the rate of inflation (down 31 per cent in the past year). Most of the urban middle class welcomed the Emergency and breathed a sigh of relief, some even asking if India really needed to be a democracy.

But at a time when Indira Gandhi should have taken the bull by the horns and pushed for a thoroughgoing transformation of the economy, she failed to do so. Hard economic decisions are often not taken by democratic governments for fear of a political fallout. Without the inconvenience of democratic clamour, with no opponents to block her path, the Emergency could have been an opportunity to put India on the path to steady growth by doing away with ideological baggage. Instead numerous obstacles remained for setting up businesses. Indians had no access to foreign exchange so Indian companies could not go beyond the country's borders. Controls and licences made the Indian state a feared shadow in citizens' lives. Any attempt at change was met by cries of burying the Nehruvian legacy, not only from her communist allies but from within the Congress. At a time when Indira Gandhi could have mobilized politics to give shape to real change, she failed to do so. She had always chafed at not having enough power to implement policies; indeed her quarrel with the Syndicate had been a power struggle for her own autonomy. Yet once she acquired all the power she needed, she remained curiously helpless and frozen in stasis, reacting only to the crises of the moment. The truth was that she simply did not have any clear insights or a social and economic scheme in her head to push for a growth-oriented economic structure, her vision for India's future curiously limited only to the medium term.

Instead of embracing economic liberalism, Indira Gandhi turned towards assuming overweening political control. A series of bills were passed arrogating supreme powers to Parliament. The notorious 42nd Amendment, derisively dubbed 'the constitution of Indira', was enacted, giving Parliament the power to amend the basic structure of the Constitution. The terms of the Lok Sabha and state assemblies were extended to six years and the central government was given the power to send in armed forces into whichever state it deemed was facing a breakdown in law and order. The Preamble to the Constitution was changed. From 'sovereign democratic republic', India became a 'sovereign, socialist, secular democratic republic'. Feroze Gandhi, champion of the free press and once the editor of the *National Herald*, had as an MP in 1956 introduced a law giving legal protection to journalists while reporting parliamentary debates. This law was repealed. Speeches of MPs now could not be published in any manner or form. 'Newspapers were part of a force that was trying to obstruct the social and economic changes we are trying to bring about,' said Indira Gandhi later about censorship, although she was embarrassed enough to admit, 'Censorship was not properly managed. We had thought a code of conduct could be worked out.'[78] On 10 August 1975 the 39th Amendment was enacted, placing the election of president, vice-president and prime minister beyond the scrutiny of law courts. Indira Gandhi's 1971 win was declared valid by the Supreme Court.

Two months after the Emergency was imposed, on 15 August 1975, Sheikh Mujibur Rahman, President of Bangladesh, and his family were savagely assassinated. Even his ten-year-old son was gunned down in cold blood in the family home. Indira's paranoia that her enemies were similarly plotting her murder began to grow. To the quest for absolute power was added the fear that any criticism could snowball into a potential threat to her life. Indira's and Mujib's rise and fall had been similar: both reached the pinnacle of political authority before suddenly experiencing a precipitous collapse in legitimacy. Three years after the birth of Bangladesh, Mujib had turned his back on democracy and assumed emergency powers, suspending civil liberties and turning Bangladesh into a one-party state.

Indira Gandhi's fury against her opponents swept through the land like an aandhi (dust storm), to quote the name of the popular film allegedly based on her life. According to Amnesty International, more than 110,000 were arrested and detained without trial in the first year of the Emergency. Twenty-two Emergency prisoners died in prison. Apparently personal enmities, and feminine rivalries, played their part too. Two maharanis, Gayatri Devi of Jaipur, regarded as one of the most beautiful women in the world, and Vijaya Raje Scindia, Rajmata of Gwalior, both of whom were politically opposed to Indira, were thrown into jail with thieves and criminals. Writes Dr Mathur, 'for PM's adversaries like Tarakeshwari Sinha [rumoured to have once been Feroze Gandhi's lover], jealousy was the cause of arrest of these two ladies as also the maltreatment and humiliation meted out to them'.[79] George Fernandes had gone underground and started to organize a series of bomb blasts, blowing up bridges and derailing trains. 'Fernandes intends to blow me up,' Indira told Fori Nehru. Fernandes was finally arrested but not before his brother Lawrence was caught and viciously tortured by the police.

Out of the ashes of democratic functioning, phoenix-like rose Sanjay Gandhi and his cabal, soon dubbed 'the Emergency caucus', of Bansi Lal, R.K. Dhawan, Om Mehta, V.C. Shukla and others. Sanjay's hold over his mother was now total. Rumours about the mother–son equation flew about. A foreign correspondent quoted an anonymous dinner guest at the Gandhi household to report that Sanjay had once slapped his mother across the face six times and 'she just stood there and took it. She's scared to death of him.' However, the slapping story was emphatically denied by Maneka Gandhi and the writer Ved Mehta quoted a family friend as saying, 'not even God could slap Mrs Gandhi across the face six times'.[80]

These bizarre rumours only reflected the anomaly of Sanjay's position. He was not in politics or government, not even a member of the Congress party, but dominated decision-making and seemingly dictated Indira Gandhi's moves. 'She herself was a victim of Sanjay,' says Dr Mathur, 'she was a victim of the tyranny of the excessive love she had for her younger son.' Inder Malhotra recalled that K.D. Malviya, minister in both Nehru and Indira cabinets, told him that Indira remained convinced that, in her darkest hour after the Allahabad High Court judgement, it was Sanjay alone who not only saved her from being politically destroyed but also protected her from being murdered.

Indira Gandhi announced a twenty-point programme aimed at national regeneration during the Emergency, including cancelling debts of the rural poor and making bonded labour illegal. Shop windows were required to display her picture prominently and pledge their support to the programme. Sanjay Gandhi introduced his five-point programme, which enthused the public more. His aims were adult literacy (with the slogan 'Each One, Teach One'), abolition of dowry, abolition of the caste system, beautifying the environment (by clearing slums and planting trees) and, most controversially, a radical programme of family planning. Perverse yet futuristic, ruthless, impractical, lumbered with a complete lack of understanding of the social processes that enable real change, Sanjay managed to captivate many with his new way and a new coterie gathered around Sanjay, of bureaucrat Naveen Chawla, police officer P.S. Bhinder, politician Ambika Soni, socialite Rukhsana Sultana, Dhawan and Dhirendra Brahmachari. In Delhi's durbar, a city where ambition always trumps moral values, many bowed before the new regime. 'I was upset . . . at the dreadful manner in which men and women denigrated themselves for fear of jail or losing their jobs . . . my own self-respect demanded that I should protest,' Vijayalakshmi Pandit told her daughter Nayantara.[81]

Sanjay's famous slogan 'Talk Less, Work More' was illustrative of his harsh, let's-clean-up-the-mess approach, of a man in a hurry, contemptuous at one level of slothful India, the 'doer' who would show his 'Mummy' how to get the job done. He believed shock treatment and dictatorial methods were needed to lick into shape the dreadful mass of humanity for whom he had scant respect, indeed to pulverize people into consenting to the leaders' wishes. The Emergency was Sanjay's political coming-of-age moment; he was its face. He even put his mother in the shade at this time and his power, influence and confidence surged. He was twenty-nine years old when the Emergency was declared, a young man now convinced that his inheritance, India, was finally, and rightfully, his. He could set it right as he pleased because he was his mother's son and this was a country his family ruled by birthright. Sanjay Gandhi set about creating the reign of Sanjay. In 2013 when Rahul Gandhi famously scorned a United Progressive Alliance ordinance as 'nonsense', demonstrating in public his scorn for the government, he was imitating the entitled, princely style of his flamboyant uncle.

A revealing incident in August 1975 shows how fearful Indira Gandhi was of Sanjay and how little she could do to control him. In a no-holds-barred interview, Sanjay, who had always hated his mother's left-leaning friends and advisers, told Uma Vasudev of *Surge* magazine that the socialist economy was all wrong for India. He poured scorn on communists, said that as far as the communist bigwigs were concerned, 'I don't think you'd find a richer or more corrupt people anywhere,'[82] and said the public sector should be allowed to die a natural death. He said all economic controls should go, praised big business and MNCs and suggested that the entire structure of the Nehruvian economy which his mother was protecting needed to be destroyed. It was even reported that he had called his mother's cabinet a bunch of 'ignorant buffoons'.

When news of the interview came out in the agencies Indira Gandhi flew into a panic. Her very own son pouring public scorn on the socialist inheritance of Nehru and on her leftist allies was political dynamite. 'Sanjay has made an exceedingly stupid statement about the Communists . . . what are we to do? I am terribly worried . . . I am really upset. What excuse do we find or concoct? I am frantic,' she wrote in a hastily scribbled handwritten plea to Dhar. She requested Dhar and the information and broadcasting minister, V.C. Shukla, to help her withdraw copies before the magazine reached the public. The interview was withdrawn and Sanjay issued a half-hearted clarification. But the CPI was outraged and the Soviets expressed their displeasure. The *Surge* interview was a massive embarrassment to Indira Gandhi, a daring bid by Sanjay to override the prime minister, a supremely confident oration by a putative prince who believed he towered over a bunch of pygmies and a dithering mother, and that he alone possessed the panacea for India's ills. Rather than Sanjay being scared of his mother's wrath, it was she who scurried around trying to do damage control as if she was afraid of angering him. Indira Gandhi's inability to stop Sanjay from doing and saying exactly what he wanted was a reflection of the sickness of the Emergency. This fearful mother was the insecure wielder of overwhelming power.

During the Emergency, the Youth Congress became Sanjay's chosen platform for political action. At the December 1975 Chandigarh (at Komagata Maru Nagar) session of the Congress, Sanjay officially became a politician, for the first time appearing on stage at a Congress session. Thunderous cheers and applause established him as his mother's successor. Sanjay began to work on re-energizing the so far moribund Youth Congress and make it a rival power centre vis-à-vis the Congress. Thirty-five-year-old Ambika Soni, a Sanjay acolyte and wife of a diplomat who had been brought into politics by Indira, became president of the Youth Congress. 'Sanjay was just beginning to come into public life,' recalls Soni, 'he never took a position and was more interested in meeting people. People have extreme opinions of Sanjay, but when he used to meet us often and come to our Youth Congress office to chat with us, he never tried to throw his weight around. There was an aura about him.'[83] 'Sanjay's basically not interested in politics . . . but there's criticism and a tremendous attack on him . . . he wanted to stand for Parliament because he felt it was the only way he could reply to the false allegations,' Indira would tell Mary Carras in 1978.[84]

The Emergency brought good days for the Youth Congress. Young bloods whom Sanjay recruited toured the countryside in his shadow, not on a mission to humbly discover India like Gandhi and Nehru had once done but to stride around and issue commands, basking in the reflected power of the omnipotent Gandhi son. The Youth Congress consisted of some dynamic political talents, many of whom were Sanjay's chosen commandos in politics, but the outfit also sheltered some who were seen as thuggish, known for extorting money from shopkeepers and generally using muscle power. Indira Gandhi looked on, seemingly deeply impressed by Sanjay's organizational skills, calling him a 'doer not a thinker'. The November 1976 Guwahati Congress session established Sanjay as the supreme leader of the Youth Congress and he was seen to have replaced the Congress president in importance and clout. Indira Gandhi declared with maternal pride, 'our thunder has been stolen'. That someone who had witnessed the evolution of the Congress from the days of Motilal to Jawaharlal was now gasping in admiration at Sanjay's helmsmanship says a great deal indeed of the transition Indira had made over the years. There should be another explanation for her admiration. It was almost as if she saw in Sanjay and his cohorts shades of the 1930s young radical student gang in England of which she herself had been such an ardent part. Perhaps the revolutionary she had once been warmed to a disruptive son, seeing him as the forceful challenger of the old established order, as she had once hoped to be.

Sanjay and the Youth Congress would destroy an entire generation of the Congress, already emasculated by Indira's personality cult even though many of Sanjay's young recruits have today gone on to become powerful Congress leaders, showing that Gandhi junior was not too bad a judge of political talent. Party stalwarts Ambika Soni, Kamal Nath and Anand Sharma initially started out in the Sanjay Gandhi–led Youth Congress and were once Sanjay's foot soldiers.

A parallel government rose at the PMH, or the prime minister's house, to rival the PMS, or the prime minister's secretariat. Sanjay's associates Om Mehta and Bansi Lal were already installed as ministers in the home and defence ministries. The PMH came into repeated conflict with the PMS because Sanjay and his men demanded a controlling say in appointments, often marginalizing veteran officers.[85] 'It was a time when the centre of gravity shifted to her residence. To comfort themselves people in South Block would say this [her office] is the water works, that [her residence] is the sewage works,' recalls Moni Malhoutra. Despondent and frustrated, Dhar wanted to resign but was dissuaded by Haksar. 'We must stay in the system to prevent its further degeneration. Outside the system you will count for nothing,' Haksar advised.

In late 1975, on a visit to India, B.K. Nehru, now a Bheeshma Pitamaha in Indira's court, confided to P.N. Haksar that he wanted to speak to Indira Gandhi and tell her that it was 'highly dangerous and highly objectionable that the rule of law was being replaced by the rule of Sanjay Gandhi, when he had no official position of any kind either in the party or in the government. The sole basis of his authority was that he was his mother's darling boy.'

However, Haksar advised him not to say a word to Indira because she regarded Sanjay with a 'curious mixture of awe, admiration, respect', she regarded him as perfect, and in her eyes he could do no wrong. The slightest expression of doubt about Sanjay was resented. Haksar told him if he said anything at all to Indira, his access to her would be barred. 'Babboobhai [Haksar] could speak with experience because the reason for his [own] dismissal was . . . Sanjay.'

~

The high noon of Sanjayism, of brute state power to bludgeon citizens into falling in line with official policy was seen in the remorseless clearance of slums at Delhi's Turkman Gate and forced sterilization drives.

In April 1976 slum clearance drives were in progress in Delhi. On an inspection tour near Turkman Gate, standing at the gate, Sanjay made an announcement to Jagmohan, his steadfast loyalist and vice chairman of the Delhi Development Authority: I want to see Jama Masjid from Turkman Gate. Once the royal edict was issued, the loyalists rushed to obey. Turkman Gate had to be cleared forthwith. Jagmohan would later make a transition from diehard

Sanjay loyalist to BJP member, an example of how in personality-oriented Indian politics, loyalties are always personal rather than ideological.

The Turkman Gate area was then a teeming sea of shops, jhuggis, slum colonies and markets, home to thousands of people. In mid April 1976 the glamorous jewellery designer Rukhsana Sultana set up the Dujana House Sterilisation Centre in the area to encourage Muslims to get sterilized as part of the government's family planning drive. On 13 April the first bulldozers began to arrive at Turkman Gate, demolishing walls and roofs of homes. As residents sought Sultana's help she in return asked them to help her to meet the target of 300 sterilization cases a week.[86] Between the sterilization camp and the bulldozers, tensions began to build dangerously at Turkman Gate until on 19 April protests began at the Dujana House Sterilisation Centre after a van full of potential sterilization patients arrived. The Central Reserve Police Force (CRPF) rushed in and tried to calm the situation by using teargas. But tempers were running high and crowds began to hurl bricks, soda bottles and acid bulbs. The CRPF opened fire, 'resorting to 14 rounds of firing'.[87] Estimates of the dead vary. Official reports maintained that eight died but unofficial figures say over a hundred lost their lives and many more were injured. Among those killed was a thirteen-year-old boy who was only a bystander. Twenty-four-hour curfew was imposed on Turkman Gate until mid May so that demolitions could continue. By the end of the Turkman Gate 'slum clearance' exercise, one and a half lakh jhuggis and shops had been demolished in a streak of relentless destruction,[88] and 70,000 inhabitants had been pushed into vans and forcibly resettled on the banks of the Yamuna on small wire-fenced plots.

The harshness of the Turkman Gate slum clearance was a stark reminder that India had ceased to be a democracy. Instead it was now a country where homes could be destroyed and even lives snuffed out in the pursuit of state diktat. Other cities too fell victim to Emergency-style beautification drives. Varanasi's ancient havelis were sliced in half to widen roads, making the historic Vishwanath Gali look as if it had been 'bombed'. Sanjay's methods were a far cry from the tentative and nuanced steps that a democratic process has now forced on governments when it comes to land acquisition and resettlement.

More brutal than beautification drives was Sanjay Gandhi's other brainchild, the forcible sterilization campaign. India's exploding population had long been regarded by many as the main reason for its poverty. Policy measures such as the distribution of condoms had failed. Sanjay now decided that India's population had to be immediately and efficiently reduced. Indira Gandhi started out as an enthusiastic supporter of the family planning programme and would hear no criticism of it.

Maneka Gandhi explains Sanjay's motivations for the family planning programme: 'Sanjay was not politically sensible enough, he was unpolitical, and he didn't realize that you cannot mix a programme like the Emergency with a family planning programme. The family planning programme was on the anvil from much before. But by hideous coincidence, they both intersected and he got the flak for both . . . He was twenty-seven years old [sic]. We never forgave him for any of his shortcomings. We didn't forgive him anything. We expected him to have the wisdom of a hundred-year-old.' She hastened to add, 'This is not an apology of him. There is no doubt that strange things did happen in his name.' The question arises, by what right was Sanjay deciding and executing policy anyway? By birthright, of course, granted by a mother who had paradoxically sought to end the inherited privileges of hereditary princes.

In 1976, the government started a National Population Policy to 'mount a direct assault on the problem of numbers' and lower the annual birth rate from 35 to 25 per 1000 persons by 1984. Mass vasectomy – or male sterilization – the chilling 'nasbandi' programme, was to be the way to achieve this. This 'terrifying new policy' was designed to free India once and for all from the debilitating grip of its teeming millions. Vasectomy clinics were set up in Delhi and other north Indian towns and sterilization vans criss-crossed the rural countryside. Each person who opted for vasectomy was awarded a transistor, some cooking oil and Rs 120. Emma Tarlo in her book includes pictures of nervously smiling sterilized men receiving ghee and clocks as a reward for undergoing vasectomy.[89]

Government employees such as policemen, doctors and teachers were set targets: they would be paid their salaries only after they had 'motivated' a certain number to undergo vasectomy. Inevitably, the government machinery ran amok and turned on the vulnerable to fulfil sterilization targets. The poor became the victims. Millions were lured, persuaded and forced to undergo sterilization. Rumours of ever harsher sterilization measures spread like wildfire, resulting in fear and panic after a few incidents were reported that men had been dragged out of cinema halls and bus queues and carted off to forced sterilizations.

By the time the campaign of forced sterilization ended, it had overshot its target of 230 lakh in three years, with 37 lakh sterilized only in the first few months. The number of sterilizations shot up from 9.4 lakh in 1973–74 to 82.6 lakhs in 1976–77. The brunt of the programme had been borne by Indira's most loyal constituency, the poor, lower castes and Muslims. 'There was a lot of fear about nasbandi even here in Raebareli,' says O.P. Srivastava. 'The karamcharis were most upset with it because they were given targets to fulfil and were penalized when they couldn't. That's why even they went against her in the 1977 elections.' 'The Emergency was perfect,' Siddhartha Shankar Ray would say decades later, 'but the excesses were bad and nobody could stop it.'[90]

Indira had been enthusiastic about sterilization at first. But she started to develop reservations when the facts about the coercive measures began to sink in, even though her 'blind spot' for Sanjay still stopped her from calling a quick halt. Initially whenever she was sent reports about forced sterilization her normal response was that these were baseless allegations and nothing but anti-Sanjay propaganda. Once when Fori Nehru reported to Indira that men were being forcibly sterilized in Chandigarh, she apparently broke down and wailed, 'Main kya karoon, main kya karoon [what am I to do, what am I to do], they tell me nothing,' although she later calmed down to assert that these allegations were lies.[91] Dr Mathur recalls that in the early days of the Emergency people were happy that trains were running on time and the public distribution system and other services were better. 'But then with the sterilization things began to go wrong. The PM used to be upset when B.K. Nehru used to talk to her about Sanjay. Once I saw her sitting at her office table virtually in tears after something Mr Biju Nehru told her in strong words.' B.K. Nehru had obviously not heeded Haksar's advice and had conveyed his views on Sanjay's 'ham-handed and tyrannical' methods of population control.

Sanjay himself did not seem to be troubled by self-doubt. A propaganda campaign orchestrated by V.C. Shukla pumped out adulatory and eulogistic news reports about Sanjay, which were eagerly lapped up by the press. 'An incredibly handsome young man,' gushed Khushwant Singh in an interview in the *Illustrated Weekly of India*, 'with fiercely honest and intense eyes.'[92] Singh in fact became Sanjay's great champion, lauding his 'determination, sense of justice, a spirit of adventure and a total lack of fear'. After the Emergency, the new information and broadcasting minister, L.K. Advani, was to describe the behaviour of India's press thus: 'You were only asked to bend, but you chose to crawl.' In a piquant twist of history, journalists now defer to Advani's party and its leaders even more reverentially than perhaps they did to the Congress during Indira's time.

With the press spookily silent, unseen goings-on would be chronicled only later. Emma Tarlo shows how after the Emergency was lifted a rash of new books suddenly burst into publication with dramatic titles and explosive headlines, 'as if to compensate for the burden of censorship'. One of these books on its back cover provided an entire potted history of the Emergency in the following sensational bullet points: 'Political leaders and workers, intellectuals and journalists nabbed in midnight swoop and jailed! Press gagged and emasculated! Prisoners subject to torture and unheard of brutality!

Houses and bazaars bulldozed into rubble! Men and women driven like cattle into FP camps! The "caucus" striking terror, unhindered by law! Sycophants and hangers on calling the tune!'

Added to that list of the Emergency's sensational headlines was another initiative that mercifully did not come to fruition: the dream of ruling in perpetuity. Armed with a prime ministerial carte blanche, Sanjay's cronies began to dream of perpetual power and a one-party state. Bansi Lal had even come up with the idea of a new constituent assembly to produce a new constitution, a constituent assembly which would declare Indira Gandhi president for life. 'Arre Nehru saheb, yeh sab election phelection ko khatam kar dijiye. Behanji ko president for life bana dijiye [Mr Nehru, forget elections, let's make Indira president for life],' Bansi Lal told B.K. Nehru at this time. The Punjab, Haryana and Uttar Pradesh assemblies even passed resolutions for convening a constituent assembly but thankfully Indira distanced herself from these moves. In fact, contrary to the general belief that Indira wanted to remain a dictator, she clearly did not. Even in the daze of absolute power, Nehru's daughter had not forgotten him completely. In fact, she increasingly seemed to have moments of self-doubt and anxiety about how the Emergency was progressing.

Towards the end of those surreal twenty-one months, when an ever-growing number of reports began to come in of forcible sterilization, of how village schoolteachers had been coerced into fulfilling their sterilization quotas, she asked Dhar in a 'tired low voice' if he thought the Emergency should continue. She sent out a strict message to chief ministers saying: 'Anyone engaged in harassment while propagating family planning measures will be punished.' But by now it was too late.

'For the first six months she thought she had done the right thing by bringing in the Emergency,' says Subramanian Swamy.[93] 'But later I remember she developed a great deal of depression on that. The philosopher Jiddu Krishnamurti used to give her solace and she used to break down crying before him.'

In a 1976 meeting with Krishnamurti, she had dissolved into tears. 'Right action is necessary,' he had advised.[94] Observers say she knew more about the Emergency than she admitted, perhaps even to herself. By the end, she was acutely uncomfortable and wanted to get out of the Emergency, 'somehow, anyhow'.

But even if she had wanted to end the Emergency sooner than she eventually did, Sanjay's strong disapproval may have prevented her from doing so. 'She knew exactly what was going on, there's no question about that. She just chose to look the other way because of Sanjay,' believes Natwar Singh.

In the end, Indira Gandhi did prevail over her demons. Her better self won over her worst self. In moments of solitude, Jawaharlal's presence seemed to appear and linger. His photos gazed down on her as if in remonstrance, his voice reached her ears, memories of the way he had practised his politics and her long years by his side flashed into her mind. She had already once postponed general elections due in 1976. She who had always rejoiced in election campaigns felt a second postponement would send the wrong signal. She became nostalgic about 1971, missing the cheering of mammoth crowds, the exhilaration she always experienced among an adoring throng.

In a move that shocked everyone in its suddenness, that electrified the country and became a bombshell of a newspaper headline, on 18 January 1977 she unexpectedly and matter-of-factly announced that the fifth Lok Sabha was dissolved and elections would be held two months later.

'Every election is an act of faith,' said Indira Gandhi in her broadcast announcement of the 1977 polls. 'It is an opportunity to cleanse public life of confusion. So let us go to the polls with the resolve to affirm the power of the people.'

In a later interview, she expressed herself with typical plain-speaking pragmatism: 'The reason for the Emergency and the postponement of elections was instability and indiscipline in the country. We got over that position so I thought it was time to have the election . . . it was a purely democratic action.'

The announcement took her opponents as much by surprise as the imposition of the Emergency had done and she had clearly made it in the teeth of opposition from Sanjay, who was 'dead against' elections and had told her 'you are committing a horrible mistake'. That she defied Sanjay revealed that she wasn't as completely dependent on him for her politics and decisions as it appeared though it seemed so because of the many extra miles she went to indulge him. Her unending indulgence of him looked as if he controlled her, but like a watchful lioness padding silently after a daring, noisy and adventurous cub, in fact she never quite lost the upper hand.

She would say, 'I declared the Emergency and I revoked it . . . We had taken Parliament's permission and postponed elections by an entire year. After that I thought the country is sound, the economy is stable and there's no reason not to have elections.'[95]

The Emergency had brought relative economic stability, there had been two good harvests and prices had stabilized. One of her calculations in postponing elections was that the 'gains' of the Emergency needed to be consolidated. She said: 'The decision I took [to impose the Emergency] was ratified by the cabinet and by the parliament. It was not only accepted, it was applauded by the entire nation. Had we held elections in 1976, we would have won hands down. We didn't hold elections because we wanted to stabilize the economy.'[96] She could well have calculated that elections a year later would bring even better results.

There was another reason why she ended her own dictatorship. The opprobrium of many international friends such as Dorothy Norman in the United States and John Grigg in the United Kingdom, who had been bitterly critical and even organized protests against the Emergency, had been particularly difficult for her to bear. *The Times*, London, had run advertisements saying 'Don't Let the Light Go Out on India's Democracy', and leading lights like the actress Glenda Jackson and the historian A.J.P. Taylor had made their disapproval known. In a self-mocking, embarrassed note to Norman in September 1975, she wrote, 'If you can bear to accept a gift from the "Great Dictator" here is something which I had kept for you some years ago.'[97] 'An important reason for calling elections could indeed have been disapproval of the international opinion,' says Tully. 'She liked to think of herself as a stalwart of the international community.'

'I remember taking Margaret Thatcher to meet her once,' recalls Moni Malhoutra. 'Mrs Thatcher was like a kitten in front of her. After the meeting, she said, the trouble with Maggie is that she's so predictable. She thought of that as a weakness. To her it was good to be unpredictable and good to keep people guessing.'

An unlikely champion lauded her call for polls. 'Indira has shown much courage. It is a great step for her to take,' said Jayaprakash Narayan.

~

Dear Mrs Gandhi,

When you finally decided to call for elections after twenty-one months of the Emergency, had you been troubled by guilt? Did you wonder what your father and even mother would have made of all that had happened during the Emergency? Just a few weeks after the Emergency was declared you had developed a twitch in your left eye, a sign of inner tumult tightly controlled. The twitching got so bad that J. Krishnamurti even offered to help you with it.

You did express as much remorse as could be expected from a queen. 'We've expressed deep regrets if any hardships were caused. People at different levels misused their authority . . . some things did go wrong. Even in hospitals with the best of care, things do go wrong.'[98]

Did your famous political instinct finally awaken and make you realize how unpopular your government, you and Sanjay had become? Isolated, with the flow of information turned off, the enveloping silence sent you an alarming message. There was a menace in the quietude, waves of unease in the stillness. Distant cries came to your ears, you heard stories, you saw the glum expressions of P.N. Dhar, B.K. and Fori Nehru and Pupul Jayakar. In shadowed glances and whispered tones, you sensed an absence, the lack of something vital, a vacuum. But once again your belief in your own indispensability was to the fore, and you hoped against hope that 'the people' would understand your good intentions, that they would always be on your side and give you the benefit of the doubt. After all, you were Indira Gandhi, born to rule. You had not yet grasped that India was changing faster than you, still a prisoner of an age-old family legacy, would or could ever admit to yourself.

~

Once elections were announced, most political prisoners were released, censorship rolled back and Mark Tully and other foreign correspondents arrived back in India. 'The important thing to note is that she called elections,' says Tully. 'She didn't formally lift the Emergency. That means that if she had won, the Emergency may just have continued. The Emergency was only formally lifted after the elections.'

Even after calling fresh elections, Indira continued to defend her decision to impose the Emergency: 'They were the ones destroying democracy. They said they could not win in an election so they said we must take the battle to the streets. Morarji Desai is on record to say we will surround the PM's house and Parliament. Another Opposition leader said if we can't win by the ballot we will win by the bullet. They incited the police and army and created extreme indiscipline in the country. If we had not stopped them, India would not have survived.'[99] She went to the people determined to convince them that the Emergency had been a signal service to India, almost certain that 'my people' would understand.

With polls just two months away Indira plunged into the campaign, Sanjay contesting for the first time from Amethi. The campaign was a shock. After being closeted away in her fortress, she faced the full blast of public disapproval. Anxiety took its toll. 'She made forceful speeches but the attendance at rallies was thin. Just at this time she had a severe attack of herpes zoster across her face and must have been in great pain but continued campaigning,' recalls Dr Mathur.

Women turned their backs on her at rallies, speaking out angrily against the sterilization campaigns and how their men had been rendered weak and impotent. Nasbandi had become a chilling metaphor: the perceived weakening of men a symbol of the emasculation of the nation as a whole. 'There was a dead quality to the crowds,' recalls Tully, who covered the campaign. 'They seemed unresponsive to her, which made her nervous. At a Ram Lila Maidan rally, she tried to climb down and go towards them, but was held back by security.' During the campaign, an angry Indira even barked at her rivals, 'Jahannam mein jao [Go to hell].'

A seasoned veteran sensed the changed direction of the winds, realizing that the person who had been the Congress's greatest asset was in this election its biggest liability. Jagjivan Ram, Congress heavyweight, member of Nehru's cabinet, once Indira's trusted ally, resigned and formed his own party, which joined the Janata coalition. His departure created shockwaves. The Opposition seemed to steam ahead of Indira, rushing past her on strongly gathering tailwinds.

In March 1977, the unthinkable happened. Indira Gandhi and the Congress were routed. Indira and Sanjay were also thrown out in their constituencies of Raebareli and Amethi, Indira defeated by her old adversary Raj Narain, who became the only politician to ever defeat Indira Gandhi. In its worst performance since Independence till then, the Congress crashed to 153 seats, failing to win a single seat in Uttar Pradesh, Bihar, Punjab, Haryana and Delhi. The party was driven out of north India, winning just two seats, although it did remain dominant in the south.[100] Indira's opponents triumphed. The Janata Party won an absolute majority, with a 40 per cent vote share, racing to power with 298 seats.

For the first time since Independence, the Congress lost control of the gaddi of Delhi. The woman synonymous with India, and with unquestioned power, was vanquished. She had sought to negate the power of the vote, but now she submitted to the power of the vote. In her downfall, she paradoxically reaffirmed faith in democracy, in defeat she still paid obeisance at a shrine she had defiled.

Indira Gandhi lost but democracy won. That she called elections and accepted the verdict when she lost redeemed her somewhat; she became at that time perhaps the world's only dictator to voluntarily give up power. Her defeat allowed the first constitutional transition from one regime to another in independent India, thus paradoxically strengthening the foundations of Indian democracy in a way that none of the actors in the drama could have predicted.

In the 1977 elections, not only did Indians realize the power of the vote but political leaders across the board realized the pitfalls of seeking and exercising absolute power. Writes Sharada Prasad, 'One thing that Indira Gandhi achieved by the Emergency: she ensured that no future prime minister would be tempted to resort to it.'

Pupul Jayakar met Indira Gandhi on the night of 20 March 1977. 'Pupul,' she said, 'I have lost.' Her voice was quiet, numbed. 'I will never forgive Sanjay for having brought Mummy to this position. He is responsible,' muttered Rajiv Gandhi, who had always been openly critical of the Emergency. Later, reiterating the same sentiments Rajiv told his mother, 'You have been brought to this pass by Sanjay and Dhawan.' Indira said nothing, but looked 'forlorn'.

~

Dear Mrs Gandhi,

What lessons did you learn from your defeat? Today the Emergency lives on, its bitter ghosts still circling in our lives. What advice would you pass on to those in office today if you could? Would you say, respect the orders of a judge, however unacceptable? Trust the civil servant even if he or she doesn't make a fetish of loyalty? Learn to respect talent in political colleagues? Don't allow family members to intrude into political life?

If you had witnessed the scenario today, when a politician disregards a court judgement, when honest bureaucrats are transferred on political whim, when parties are made subordinate to a supreme personality cult, when families are indulged by politicians, when Parliament is disrespected, you would certainly have felt a little guilty. The Emergency showed that absolute power corrupts absolutely. Not corruption just as a matter of thirty pieces of silver; instead the Emergency accelerated a corrosion of India's ethical core, a moral and intellectual corruption that cracked apart the institutions on which the daily well-being of Indians was crucially dependent.

If you had still been alive and seen what the Emergency led to more than four decades later, would you have led a JP-like satyagraha movement against the political culture of today?

~

By the imposition of the Emergency, judges were intimidated, bureaucrats lived in fear, the press crawled, state assemblies lost their autonomy and the party bent to the government's will: in short India's precious organs of state so lovingly built by the Constitution-drafters collapsed. In place of citizens, Indira created legions of sycophants, the scourge of feudal societies. The intellectual distance between Nehru and his daughter had never been greater. Today when a gargantuan executive in the form of a supreme leader looms threateningly over both judiciary and legislature, we can say, thank you, Mrs Gandhi.

The intoxication of riding roughshod over institutions continues to hold sway and India remains institutionally fragile and weak. Many politicians are convinced that efficient governance requires accumulating absolute power, stamping on civil rights and crushing dissent. Indira was the parent and original of the 'supremo' cult by which towering personalities seek complete control over the system and the elimination of their rivals.

One of the Emergency's legacies was the hostility Indira unleashed on the media, failing to understand that in a democracy the media needs to always preserve an adversarial relationship with those in power. However, at least in her time, she took press conferences and gave interviews. Today's leaders seek control over information with government handouts and scripted interactions. Most leaders after Indira have not been able to create a 'normal' relationship with the press. Her son Rajiv Gandhi attempted to bring in the anti-defamation bill,[101] her family members Sonia and Rahul Gandhi shun the press and generally refuse full-length interviews.

She refused to accept, as leaders do today, the importance of adversarial journalists as part of the constitutional balance of power. 'To have had to impose regulation on newspapers does not make me happy, but some journals had shed all objectivity and independence and allied themselves totally with the opposition front and done everything to spread doom and defeatism . . . the press was very much against us even before.' Is the press against me or for me was her outlook, a way of thinking that has shaped mindsets of generations of politicians since her prime ministership.

'Imposing an Emergency won't be easy but the Emergency mindset hasn't gone away,' said L.K. Advani in 2015 on the fortieth anniversary of the fateful day. Perhaps Indira's one-time rival Advani was obliquely referring to Prime Minister Narendra Modi, whose critics have often accused him of authoritarian tendencies. Perhaps he was hinting at several chief ministers who run their state governments like mini-despots.

Or maybe he was simply acknowledging that Indira Gandhi is still held up as a role model on the dark arts of wielding power by India's politicians. The darkness of the Emergency years has somewhat lifted. But we still await the full glow of sunlight in which all politicians recognize the true spirit of democracy. Like Jawaharlal Nehru did, but Indira, tragically, failed to imbibe.

6

Resurrection: 1977–80

After her defeat in 1977, in just three short years, Indira Gandhi staged a spectacular comeback. She even overcame another split in the party in 1978 when the Congress(I) was born. In the same year she won the Chikmagalur by-election by a big margin and re-entered Parliament. The Janata government collapsed in 1979. In 1980 Indira won the general elections and was sworn in as prime minister for the fourth time on 14 January 1980.

~

Dear Mrs Gandhi,

Nineteen seventy-seven was a debacle. The country you called your baby was jubilant at your fall. When the results were declared, people set off fireworks and beat drums late into that March night. The Emergency which you had always insisted you imposed for the people's sake was rejected by the people. They roared out their disapproval of what you were trying to do in their name. Sanjay Gandhi's ascendancy, forced sterilization, beautification drives which left thousands homeless and the Emergency's economic programmes became a bonfire of your vanities.

Did you contemplate giving it all up? You were almost sixty years old, the Emergency had been a shameful descent into arrogance, and you had been punished by the voters. You told friends that you wanted to retire to the hills, to a 'sylvan spot' in the Himalayas. Karan Singh, former governor of Kashmir and minister for health and family planning during the Emergency, even offered you a cottage in the Jammu hills. But others said you were determined to force the Janata out of office. Feeling the pressure of the many legal charges that the Janata Party brought against you, you said you had no option but to carry on fighting. 'I fight best when my back is against the wall,' you were to say.

Seclusion was not your style. You were too powerful a personality, a creature of the hurly-burly, accustomed to sitting in the front row. You were far too keen on realizing your destiny as Nehru's daughter to ride into the sunset. When Ambika Soni asked why you didn't take a break, you replied, 'One just can't afford to go into the wings, Ambika. One must always stay centre stage.'

After your defeat you made it a point to attend every high-powered function you were invited to. At one such gathering hosted by the British high commissioner to celebrate the Queen's birthday, as soon as the new prime minister arrived, everyone rushed towards him and ignored you. But you stayed on, refusing to leave. You even tried to make your peace with India's new rulers. Wrote a visiting journalist in the *Guardian*: 'She is resigned and wary, like a broken boxer hoping for a miracle.'[1] The thought of your presence fading away from public memory frightened you. You were not ready to accept the overlordship of the 'men of small stature' who had toppled you.

When the veteran freedom struggle activist and family friend Aruna Asaf Ali assured you that you would return, you had shot back impatiently, 'When, after I'm dead?'[2] No, you were not going to wait that long. Your fightback began only a few months after you were thrown out. You rushed towards the crowd that had defeated you, as if daring them, tell me you really don't want me. Obstacles and hindrances had in any case always strengthened your fighting spirit.

Among your collection of toys displayed at your memorial museum, among plastic vegetables and fruit, is a rather unlikely toy for a fastidious lady like you: a plastic life-size cockroach, sitting between two brilliantly coloured butterflies. The cockroach, the only living thing expected to survive the nuclear holocaust.

~

Indira Gandhi resigned as prime minister in March 1977, declaring that 'the collective judgement of the electorate must be respected' and saying in a public statement: 'As I take leave of you as Prime Minister I should like to express my deep gratitude . . . since childhood my aim has been to serve the people to the limit of my endurance. This I shall continue to do.'[3]

The service of the country as a blood-and-guts physical odyssey would surface often in her speeches from now on. She would speak of how a frail woman was being hunted, how she would live and die with her people, how her blood would energize India. The election results were not just a political and emotional assault, they were almost a physical wound, and she would often describe the fate that befell her as bodily injuries, a spilling of blood. Kamala Nehru, whose physical pain mirrored her emotional one, now became her template. In flashes of intense vulnerability, Kamala's daughter seemed to take the place of Nehru's daughter. In Indira's bedroom in Anand Bhawan, there are photos of Ramakrishna Paramahamsa, Anandamayi Ma and rudraksha beads by her bedside: her mother's spiritual anchors over time had become hers too.

Slowly all the trappings of prime ministership melted away. The house, personal staff, even the party faithful. In 1970 she had given up family ownership of Anand Bhawan and the Nehru ancestral home had been turned into a museum open to the public. She did not have a house of her own to live in. Yet she had become accustomed to living with ease and grace, surrounded by artefacts and paintings, her furniture collection including an Eames lounge chair and a Le Corbusier chaise. Her style was elegantly austere; anything obtrusive or showy had always been for her a sign of tastelessness.

In May 1977 she moved out of the prime minister's residence at 1 Safdarjung Road, where she had first moved in thirteen years ago as information and broadcasting minister. On the day of the move Bhagat recalls her urge to clean up. 'When a chest was lifted from her bedroom, she noticed that dust had collected behind it. She remarked on the inadequacy of the way the cleaning was done and asked for a broom and herself started sweeping.'

She and her family moved into her friend Mohammad Yunus's bungalow, 12 Willingdon Crescent, which he vacated for her. There, in a much smaller, cramped house with files, books and trunks piled up on all sides, she took up residence with her family and five dogs – the fallen dictator, the almost universally shunned former supremo, with practically no one around her except old friends like Pupul Jayakar and faithfuls like R.K. Dhawan and Dr Mathur.

She began her post-defeat life somewhat marooned and keeping a low profile at first. 'She was living in isolation with her two sons and their wives who were certainly not on the best of terms,' recalls B.K. Nehru. 'Stupid and ill-informed people said Indira Gandhi made a lot of money during her term of office as Prime Minister. I can say with absolute certainty that when she was thrown out of 1 Safdarjung Road she had no roof to cover her head . . . she lived most frugally.' In 1959 Feroze Gandhi had bought some land in Mehrauli and Rajiv had started construction on a family home but it was incomplete and not fit to live in. However embroiled the Congress party may have become in underhand moneymaking, Indira Gandhi's personal wealth showed no sign of enhancement. Stopping by for dinner, Pupul Jayakar was sometimes served a meal of only a boiled egg, boiled potatoes and a mango. 'Can any politician today ever think of giving away a vast property like Anand Bhawan, spread over 6 acres as she did?' asks Pramod Pandey, former director of Anand Bhawan. 'It would be unthinkable today.'

She lived, some accounts say, on money from loyal businessmen and industrialists based abroad. One of them, Swaraj Paul, whom Indira had helped when his daughter was suffering from leukaemia, had reportedly telephoned her to say after her defeat, 'Indiraji, as long as I have something to eat, you will eat first.'[4] Her main source of income, however, through the 1960s and 1970s was from the royalties she received for her father's books, almost one lakh a year, money which went a long way in her time.

'For the first couple of months after the defeat, my mother-in-law was very shell-shocked,' recalled Maneka Gandhi. 'She would hardly come out of her room, she did a lot of thinking. There was a lot of upheaval in the house with people going away and nobody talking. And then she realized that there was lots of love to be had at home and it wasn't the end of the world. She would play badminton. There would be long walks. The family became very tightly knit because the whole Congress party disappeared. There was very little money. We didn't even have a cook.'

Dr Mathur remembers Indira Gandhi feeling 'lonely and abandoned by everyone except the immediate family'. She had no visitors and nothing to do. Dr Mathur says she would go from room to room rearranging furniture and curtains as if to evoke memories. 'Her adversaries spread rumours that she had lost her mental balance and walked around the house aimlessly with eyes and mouth wide open.' Visiting a colleague in hospital, she once sat next to Dr Mathur in the front seat of his self-driven Fiat because she had no car of her own. While today's former prime ministers are allotted government bungalows and security protection is provided even to their children, Indira Gandhi was suddenly cast out of the comfortably secure official cocoon she had inhabited for almost three decades, first as prime minister's daughter, then as prime minister. Natwar Singh recalls visiting his former boss. 'She was all alone. There was nobody there.

Of course the IB chaps took down my number when I went to see her. But she had the stamina to fight back even though they did their damnedest to destroy her.' Wajahat Habibullah says, 'Indira Gandhi was not the sort of woman who could accept defeat.'

In possession at last of the gaddi of Delhi, the Janata Party now set about their mission of Indira-Mukt Bharat. Yet rather than focusing on providing a radically different vision of governance or a different narrative of a Janata model, the Janata instead would soon turn Indira into a martyr. There was little substantively different about the Janata's conservative socialism from Indira Gandhi's secular socialism. They had relied on a united front to vanquish her and the trend of relying only on electoral arithmetic to defeat a dominant opponent continues to this day, reflecting the ideological convergence of parties rather than any genuine difference in manifestos. In the absence of any real ideological differences with Indira, with no radically different programme of action to implement, the Janata initiated a furious personality clash against her. To their rage against the manner in which she had jailed them was the added fury against a woman. The words 'impotent men' and 'mere woman' cropped up often in the diatribes of the senior citizens now holding power, as if her gender was as much an insult to them as her politics.

Morarji Desai, now eighty-one years old, who had battled Indira Gandhi for a decade, the Indira-hater who had never forgiven her for snatching away the prime ministership from him in 1966 and 1967, was sworn in as the prime minister of India's first non-Congress government. Desai had always thought of himself as Nehru's real heir. He had repeatedly staked his claim and each time been thwarted by the 'chit of a girl' who was 'not suitable' for office and whom he felt he had a 'duty' to oppose. Obsessed with humiliating his long-time competitor, he rushed to occupy Indira Gandhi's home, 1 Safdarjung Road, even ripping out her western-style toilets and replacing them with Indian toilets. It was a relatively small house and Morarji could have moved into a more stately dwelling but 1 Safdarjung Road was a symbol of power for the Janata. From Cleopatra to Catherine the

Great, women rulers have all been vain disasters, Morarji lectured the outgoing P.N. Dhar, holding forth at length on Indira's 'vanity' and expounding on the narcissism of Raziya Sultana which, according to him, compared with Indira Gandhi's. Aloof lone wolf in his younger days, Morarji was now a sour octogenarian fixated on the younger woman who had blighted his life.

The new political leadership was united only by its loathing of Indira Gandhi. Foreign Minister Atal Bihari Vajpayee vowed to throw her into the 'dustbin of history'. In May 1977, Charan Singh, Jat leader from Uttar Pradesh, strongman of the Janata and now the home minister, rose in Parliament to declare that Indira had thought of 'killing all opposition leaders in jail during the Emergency'. Disparate figures in the coalition such as Jagjivan Ram, Raj Narain, Charan Singh and Desai were bitterly competitive with each other. Charan Singh and Jagjivan Ram were both mortally disappointed that Morarji had been chosen as prime minister. But they were all united in their resolve to finish off Indira and her family.

The vituperation of the newly elected leaders was not universally popular though. One evening in early 1977, at a dinner in Delhi, Inder Malhotra records how the domestic help who was serving the meal suddenly interrupted the dinner table conversation and said, 'Vajpayeeji should not have used such bad language against Indiraji.' 'Why not,' asked Malhotra, 'hadn't Indira done bad things in the past?' 'Yes Indiraji did bad things and she did good things,' said the retainer, 'the people have dethroned her. Isn't that enough?'

The Janata failed to become a rational, democracy-restoring government that could systematically reverse the damage done by Indira to India's constitutional structure. Taking a leaf out of Indira Gandhi's own book and her imperiously dismissive treatment of state governments, the Janata now dismissed all Congress governments in the states on the grounds that the party had lost the moral right to rule. Some of the draconian amendments of the Emergency years were repealed and the civil liberties taken away by the Emergency were restored but there was no sustained attempt to rebuild the edifices whose foundations had cracked during the suspension of democracy.

In the Janata's disparate nature lay its ineffectiveness. A coalition that included the Jana Sangh and socialists was bound to be incoherent. JP's moral authority and persuasive powers had created the Janata Front. Yet JP, who had been a lifelong and staunch opponent of communal politics, now, in his determination to create the anti-Indira gathbandhan, became an instrument to give the Jana Sangh its share in political power in the new alliance. Such was the hatred they had for the younger woman that the older men became amnesiacs about ideology.

Initially, inner contradictions were kept at bay by keeping their eyes fixed on the common enemy. The Janata turned its ire on the Gandhis with almost as much fury as Indira had turned on democracy. Intelligence agencies tailed the Gandhi family. The CBI lurked around the house at all times and tapped their phones. They visited the Gandhis' unfinished Mehrauli home with metal detectors to search for hidden treasures. Their passports were impounded. Rajiv Gandhi was investigated for tax violations, although nothing was found. In May 1977, the Janata government set up the Shah Commission, a commission of enquiry under Justice J.C. Shah to investigate the 'misuse of power, excesses and malpractices' committed during the Emergency. Justice Jayantilal Chhotalal Shah was a former chief justice of India, described as 'the high priest of justice', a 'patrician' and a 'strict disciplinarian'.[5] Indira Gandhi distrusted him from the start, believing as she did that he was biased against her because of his strong views against bank nationalization.

However discomfited Indira may have been by it, outwardly she treated the Shah Commission with regal scorn, making it clear that it was illegitimate in her eyes[6] and saying, 'the commission was a vindictive action by the government . . . They set up this commission under a judge who had expressed himself very strongly against me and my policies before being appointed. He had made speeches against us. He opposed bank nationalization and had been speaking continuously against me and my government. Even in India there's seldom been a case where somebody known to be anti has been appointed to enquire against that person.'[7] How could such a judge, Indira accused, possibly conduct a fair probe?

She was fearful and friendless. Even her so-called diehard loyalists including the sycophantic Deb Kanta Barooah of 'Indira is India, India is Indira' fame abandoned her. She would write to Fori Nehru: 'Our own people are turning against me to save their own skins . . . because of surveillance people are hesitant to come, because of phone tapping the phone has become virtually useless . . . I am deeply worried though I realize that the warfare is psychological and I must keep my chin up.'[8] Above all she constantly worried about what the Janata would do to Sanjay. '[T]he wildest stories are being circulated about Sanjay, that he was a member of a dacoit gang is one of them,' Indira complained darkly.

Demonized in the media, she was convinced that the Hindu right was the foremost conspirator against her. 'We are the victims of a monstrous propaganda campaign opening in the Press in the shape of the most fantastic even vulgar rumours. Some group in the RSS or an outside agency is working very systematically and clothing us with every possible vice,' Indira Gandhi told B.K. Nehru. Months after Indira's defeat, in late May 1977, Maneka's father was found dead in an open field. Next to him was a pistol and note which read, 'Sanjay's worry unbearable'. He had committed suicide but his death led to more ugly rumours and speculation. The CBI had begun to interrogate Sanjay on Maruti and his financial dealings, and unable to find anything else, ended up filing criminal charges against him for destroying prints of the film *Kissa Kursi Ka* during the Emergency, a film critical of Indira Gandhi. The paranoid Emergency regime had gone to absurd lengths to shut down any possible criticism. Aiming to sanitize the media environment, the film *Aandhi* (starring Suchitra Sen and Sanjeev Kumar with a plot suggestively modelled on the Indira–Feroze story) was also banned in 1975. Ironically, when *Kissa Kursi Ka* was remade and released in 1978, the film bombed at the box office, although *Aandhi*, when released by the Janata government and premiered on Doordarshan, won much acclaim.

In their hate-filled vendetta campaign, Indira Gandhi sensed the frailty of the Janata gerontocrats. In their single, all-consuming desire to bring her down, she sensed her own power. 'She had a sixth sense as far as political opportunities were concerned,' recalls Moni Malhoutra. She had disingenuously written, 'I truly have no desire to remain in any sort of politics,' in a letter to Jayakar, hoping that her friend would convey this to the Janata leadership. She even met Morarji and Charan Singh in the hope of temperance, but sensed only their burning desire to get even. Their thirst for vendetta was understandable given the imprisonment, harassment and humiliation they had endured at Indira's hands, but in their short-sighted rage, the Janata lost an opportunity to create a genuine alternative to the object of their collective loathing. They practised and legitimized highly personalized politics, the eye-for-an-eye approach, only contributing to Indira's rebirth. In the end the Janata proved to be the handmaidens of Indira Gandhi's return.

When the sixth sense is active, the way forward is inevitably revealed. When a seasoned politician is attuned to the prevailing weather, even a brief burst of lightning illuminates the path ahead. When desperation begins to set in, the human will conjures up a ladder out of the quicksand. The year of humiliating defeat was also the year of unexpected resurrection.

Two opportunities of a return to the political centre stage presented themselves in rapid succession. A journey to Belchi in Bihar and, later, her arrest in Delhi. Both would bring Indira back to the front pages, both would show her political skills and survival instinct working sharply, both would swing public opinion, perhaps not yet fully but substantially, towards a recognition of the timbre of the woman who had been defeated at the polls compared to those who had won. Indira Gandhi would emerge as a specialist in political drama. Her instinctive awareness of the symbols that would resonate with the crowd would reawaken. With the shock of defeat, insight would return. Like a swimmer initially caught off guard by a change in current, she would now bend her technique to the altered direction of the waves.

Belchi is a tiny, remote village in Bihar, so remote that when the journalist Jug Suraiya went to report from Belchi, he discovered that no taxi driver at the Patna train station had even heard of it. Belchi, he wrote, is 'a village in empty terrain that lay beyond the land of half finished bridges, beyond the end of the dirt track'.[9]

In July 1977 news came in that several Dalits (then called Harijans) in Belchi had been savagely murdered by upper-caste landowners. While the ruling patriarchs twiddled their thumbs, the woman sensed a political moment. She had always known when to go to the people: during wars and language agitations, she had rushed to the spot while rulers failed to act. The people had rejected her, the Congress had been wiped out in Bihar just six months earlier, but once again Indira Gandhi journeyed to the people, with the first aid of her presence and the salve of her helping hand. She was too quick for the ruling party or others in the Opposition. Even as they made dilatory plans to travel, Indira Gandhi was already in Hermes mode, with wings on her sandals.[10] She set off for Belchi, deep in the heart of dacoit country, travelling first by train, then by jeep, then through pouring rain on a tractor and finally on an elephant. 'I have not come to make speeches, I have come to express sympathy with the bereaved,' she informed a crowd at Bihar Sharif.

The journalist Janardan Thakur evocatively describes her trip:

> 'No lunch, let us leave,' said Smt Gandhi firmly. Not to be deterred, when aides mumbled that the route was bad and no car could reach, she said: 'We shall go on walking. We shall go on walking even if it takes us all night.' Outside the town of Bihar Sharif, the road petered into a muddy track. When the jeep got stuck, a tractor was pressed into service but even that got stuck . . . Smt Gandhi was walking through the mud . . . Some Congressmen refused to go saying there was waist-deep water ahead but Smt Gandhi was

still marching on, her sari raised above her ankle. 'Of course I can wade through water,' she snapped at her frightened companions. A thoughtful local suggested an elephant. 'But how will you climb an elephant?' aides asked. 'Of course I will,' she said impatiently. 'This is not the first time I have ridden an elephant. Bahut dino baad haathi pe charh rahi hun [It's been some time since I climbed an elephant].'

As Moti the tusker heaved up with Indira Gandhi on its back and a terrified companion, Pratibha Singh clinging to her, an accompanying cameraman cried out in delight, 'Long live Indira Gandhi.' She smiled back at him.[11]

The skies were thunderous and the rivers were in spate. Light was failing and a thunderstorm gathered on the horizon. But on walked the doughty Moti, through dangerous currents and banks of mud carrying Indira Gandhi towards a political revival. The elephant had no howdah so sixty-year-old Indira lurched this way and that, finding it difficult to keep her balance. But then losing balance and yet holding on was the theme of her life these days; whatever happened, she would hang on and not let go. Sitting on the valiant elephant that carried her through the obstacles towards her goal, she knew that her people would be waiting. The bell around the elephant's neck rang out, as if keeping time for Indira Gandhi's political return.

'From where she got off the jeep, it was three and a half hours to Belchi. But she made it purely by her grit and determination and was hailed as a saviour of the harijans. Who could have imagined a Y.B. Chavan or a Brahmananda Reddy doing what she had done?'[12]

At Belchi, grieving families stared awestruck as Indira on Moti loomed into view. They lit torches and came running towards her. She had the elephant kneel, listened to them and offered words of comfort. Mother Indira was back, the 'saviour' of the Harijans had braved tempests and floods to bring comfort to her children. Belchi projected a larger-than-life Indira on to the political screen.

When the government and other politicians failed to provide help to the suffering, the lone Joan of Arc had rushed to the rescue. The symbolism was spectacular. She had captured an important political moment. Unfazed by her harrowing day, around midnight on the way back from Belchi, Indira Gandhi delivered a speech at a college. When the scent of a comeback sweetens the air, what price bad weather or fatigue?[13]

It was time for a fresh start, which meant wiping away unpleasant memories from public view. The day after her Belchi visit Indira Gandhi called on Jayaprakash Narayan, then in retirement in Patna. It was a political manoeuvre designed for the press cameras. A warm courtesy call to an implacable enemy who had unseated her, her visit wiped away the old bitterness and gave the people a chance to forgive. JP and she posed together for photographs and he wished her a 'bright future', brighter than the bright past she had already had. She readied for redemption.

After returning to Delhi she visited Raebareli. The visit was a risk because she had been defeated by over 50,000 votes only months earlier. But Raebareli's people welcomed her with open arms. Massive crowds turned out in enthusiastic reception. Indira's former constituents, reported the *Guardian*, 'forgave her in ten minutes flat'.

'Yes she had been defeated, but the people were never angry with her,' says Deen Dayal Shastri, her faithful pilot driver in Raebareli. 'She came here in an open jeep, like a heroine. Log unhe hara ke ro rahe the [People were weeping after having made her lose the election] . . . Even a victor would not have got the same reception.'

'Her wapsi [return] was amazing,' recalls O.P. Srivastava, remembering the journey she took by road from Raebareli to Kanpur on the same trip. 'All the way from Raebareli to Kanpur there were little fires burning alongside the road to welcome her all through the night. It's only a two-and-a-half-hour drive but because she had to make so many stops she reached Kanpur only at 4 a.m.'

In her public speeches she now kept repeating that a lone, frail woman was being persecuted by the powerful. Defenceless woman versus Delhi patriarchs became the theme of her fightback. 'Why is the Janata afraid of a frail woman like me?' she hectored a crowd in Hardwar some days later. 'What are they so afraid of?' As the crowd cried out in sympathy, in Delhi the blood of the Janata rulers ran cold.

Nervous at her tumultuous public forays, the Janata government stepped up its campaign against her. In August 1977, her personal aide R.K. Dhawan, campaign manager Yashpal Kapoor and Sanjay's benefactor and former defence minister Bansi Lal were arrested as were former ministers such as law minister H.R. Gokhale. 'I refused to depose against her in the Shah Commission,' says Dhawan. 'Charan Singh wanted me to depose and said I will face problems if I didn't. I said I am ready to face any problems but I will not depose against her.' 'Dhawan's loyalty to Indira Gandhi was indeed impeccable,' says Natwar Singh. Absolute personal loyalty was the quality Indira Gandhi liked best – it had been the ticket to her durbar.

In September 1977, the Shah Commission hearings began in Delhi's Patiala House. The courtroom was packed to capacity with a jeering crowd, and the proceedings were broadcast via loudspeaker to those waiting outside. A vengeful mob hooted and howled every time charges were made against Indira or Sanjay. Hundreds testified before the commission, including former diehard friends and camp followers like Siddhartha Shankar Ray and Jagmohan. Indira at first refused to appear before the commission saying she did not believe that the proceedings were being conducted in a lawful manner and she needed assurances that she would be allowed to provide evidence refuting the charges against her.

She won time. Soon the Janata handed her another opportunity to once again be the focus of attention. By this time the repeal of the Emergency's tough laws had brought India back to its normal state of lawlessness: crime rose, smugglers and profiteers were back in business and, among the conservative middle class, some even began to long for the order and discipline of the Emergency.

Sensing the slowly gathering momentum behind her, flailing around for ways to intimidate her, chafing at their own helplessness, startled by the people's reactions to Indira in Belchi and Raebareli, the Janata brought Indira Gandhi back to centre stage. In October 1977 Indira Gandhi was arrested. The case that was to be brought against her concerned her use of government jeeps during her elections.

Her arrest became excellent theatre. When the police arrived at her home, she made sure she looked the part. Keeping the police waiting for five hours, she took her time to change into a perfectly ironed stark white sari. Arrest and jail had been a family occupation and Indira Gandhi knew how important it was to do it right. In those five hours, calls were made from her home summoning her supporters and the press. Suitably attired in the dress of a martyr, she marched out of the door, insisting on being handcuffed. She was photographed by the press and garlanded by the crowd which had gathered by now. She then entered the police van with studied dignity and the police convoy took off to incarcerate her in the Badhkal Lake guest house in Haryana. Her family and lawyers followed in cars.

As the convoy approached the Haryana border, it was held up at a level crossing while a train rolled past. Indira Gandhi gracefully stepped out from the police van and took up position on a roadside culvert surrounded by a crowd of supporters. Her lawyers now got into an argument with the police, refusing to let them take her out of Delhi without a court warrant. An impassive Indira, head demurely covered, resignedly sat on the culvert, in no hurry to move. 'The government which fears [political opponents] cannot govern the country,' she declared dramatically to reporters, without the faintest hint of irony. '[They are trying to] wreck my nerves. My nerves are as strong as they had always been.'[14] When reporters asked what the charges against her were, she replied dismissively and with 'an air of disgust', 'some corruption charges in connection with jeeps, I think'.[15]

The police attempt to make a dash for Haryana with a captive Indira in their net had been laughably overeager. Faced with strong arguments from her lawyers, the police had to abandon their plan and had no option but to bring her back to Police Lines in Delhi where policemen dutifully saluted her and led her into her cell. She refused to eat anything and soon fell into deep sleep, waking up the next morning fresh and rested. She had reason to feel refreshed. Although the police thought they had a foolproof case, the magistrate tossed it out saying there were no grounds for the charges. Indira was immediately released, and she gained instant sympathy and publicity. 'Even Mummy could not have thought out a better scenario,' exulted Rajiv to a foreign correspondent. The bungled arrest and Indira's conduct through it showed how adept she was in creating political capital out of her enemies' helpless anger. While they flailed about, she manipulated them to perfection. Pranab Mukherjee quotes a joke from the time: 'Look at the competence of this government. A woman who had put a few hundred leaders in jail for nineteen months could not be put behind bars by them for nineteen hours.' Faced with the open show of hostility from the Janata government, she readied for battle.

She was back on the front pages, her arrest showing how pettily anxious the government was to get her; the flimsy charges only bolstered the impression that small-minded men had launched a dirty war against a woman who had once defeated them in elections. 'There is a distinction between justice and revenge,' noted the *Financial Times*.

~

Meanwhile, there was conflict in the Congress. Even loyalists like Y.B. Chavan and Siddhartha Shankar Ray lashed out against Sanjay and her. Ray had testified against Indira before the Shah Commission. But Indira's relationship with Ray had started to deteriorate during the Emergency itself. Bhaskar Ghose, then secretary to the chief minister, believes that Sanjay deeply disliked Ray for not enforcing sterilization in Bengal as forcefully as he wanted and succeeded in turning his mother against her old friend. In the last months of the Emergency, Ghose says, Sanjay's men tried to build a second power centre in Bengal around A.B.A. Ghani Khan Chowdhury, a prominent Congressman from West Bengal. Ray had become so isolated that Ghose says he once saw Ray crying in his room.

After Belchi, the crowds had once again started to gather at Indira Gandhi's home, but many Congress leaders were far too wary of Sanjay Gandhi and Indira herself to willingly accept her leadership again.

Many in the Congress now began to warn that Indira Gandhi wanted to once again force the Congress into becoming an instrument for her own personal ambitions and reduce Congressmen to enslaved retainers. While Indira acolytes like Vasant Sathe and Pranab Mukherjee insisted that she was the star attraction of the party, others could not stomach the fealty demanded to Sanjay Gandhi. 'We are not afraid of taking to the streets or going to jail . . . but should we agitate to support Sanjay Gandhi or Bansi Lal or Yashpal Kapoor?' asked party president Brahmananda Reddy.[16] The Congress headed for another parting of ways.

Although Sanjay had announced he would withdraw from the Youth Congress, he was the centre of his mother's world, her 'political adviser, son and hero'. Brahmananda Reddy, Swaran Singh, Y.B. Chavan, Vasantdada Patil and others formed the 'anti-Indira' camp. With many of Indira's own ministers appearing before the Shah Commission and testifying that they were forced to act wrongfully by her, the Congress was headed for a split. Pranab Mukherjee writes how Siddhartha Shankar Ray ran into Indira Gandhi while he was deposing before the Shah Commission in the Commission Hall. She was wearing a crimson sari and he remarked, 'You look pretty today.' She stared back coldly and retorted, 'Despite your efforts.'

On 1 January 1978, party president Brahmananda Reddy expelled Indira from the Congress and the party split again into Congress(S) and Congress(I), Indira becoming leader of the Congress(I) – I standing for Indira. The new party adopted the symbol of the open palm, many members quite relieved to be rid of the old symbol of cow and calf with its ill-fated parallels to mother and son. Her followers now included her steadfast loyalists Pranab Mukherjee, P.V. Narasimha Rao and Vasant Sathe.[17]

The journalist Rashid Kidwai writes about the 'comedy of errors' that led to the choice of the new party's symbol. Buta Singh, general secretary of Indira's new party, telephoned Indira Gandhi, then in Vijayawada, to ask for approval of the new party symbol of the hand, the other available options given by the Election Commission being the elephant and the bicycle. 'Haath, haath,' he shouted down the trunk call. The bad phone line and Buta Singh's thick Punjabi accent led to a comic exchange.[18] 'Haathi? Haathi?' asked Indira, 'No, no, no haathi.' Thankfully, Narasimha Rao, master of several languages, took the phone and advised, 'Buta Singhji, panja kahiye, panja.' Indira was relieved and said, 'Haan theek hai, panja theek rahega.' The new Congress(I) moved into 24 Akbar Road, which remains its party headquarters. This then is the Congress of today: not the party born of the Gandhi- and Nehru-led freedom movement, but a group that clustered around Indira both in 1969 and in 1978. Yet, as in 1969, this time too her gamble paid off. In state elections in 1978, the Congress(I) went on to win two-thirds majorities in the Karnataka and Andhra Pradesh assemblies, states which had stood by her even in 1977, and emerged as the single largest party in Maharashtra.

Charisma – part inborn, part cultivated, honed on the anvil of womanly suffering – family legacy and an eager, embracing oneness with what she called 'the great mass' shone through Indira Gandhi. What was that undefinable quality that brought multitudes to her side? That she talked to them like family members? That she spoke to a crowd as if it was to a single person? That she made no concession to class or region and took simple folk into confidence about high matters of politics and policy as if she were talking to close friends? However dictatorial, they saw a striving for India; however imperious, they saw patriotism; and however distant, they saw motherhood in all its flaws and vulnerability.

When it came to scripting a comeback, no Indian politician has so far managed it as spectacularly as Indira Gandhi did, just three years after a crushing defeat. 'She was a very effective if not a brilliant orator,' says Tully, 'and she was very good at getting sympathy. She always emphasized how people were attacking her, undermining her. She lived a life of austerity, there was nothing ostentatious about her. People liked that. No matter how much dishonesty went on in the Congress, no matter how undemocratic her behaviour was with Sanjay, for [a] large number she remained an example of honesty and austerity.' Her personality was marked by a simplicity of style and an economy of movement. When packing for travel her spartan minimalist needs were a source of amazement for her staff, as if lightness of foot and unencumbered freedom were more important to her than being weighed down by needless accessories and ostentation.

~

In January 1978, Indira appeared before the Shah Commission looking composed and disdainful. For the first two days she didn't say a word. On the third day as Shah thundered that she must make a statement, she coolly returned, 'I am bound by my oath of secrecy not to make any statement, I am not constitutionally bound either.' She then turned the tables on Shah by mentioning that when 'certain members of the judiciary' had opposed bank nationalization, because they reportedly had shares in banks, Parliament had even tried to launch impeachment proceedings against them. She had personally intervened to stall those proceedings. Shah rushed into a welter of defensive statements that he did not have any shares in any banks: 'I never was a shareholder of any bank . . . it's a false allegation,' he blustered.[19] 'I am not mentioning you at all,' said Indira unemotionally even as Shah gibbered helplessly. Her point was made. She had scored over Shah.

The Shah Commission appearance behind her, it was time to seek the blessings of a sage before setting off on her travels with the new Congress. Indira Gandhi received a message from Vinoba Bhave, the 'spiritual successor' to Mahatma Gandhi, the leader of the Bhoodan movement, asking her to visit him at his ashram in Paunar in Wardha, Maharashtra. The ageing savant was observing the vows of silence at the time but broke them to tell Nehru's daughter: 'Move forward, move forward.'

The Shah Commission closed its proceedings in February 1978, severely indicting Indira and Sanjay in its report. The Shah Commission report is a rambling, legalistic, pompously worded, over 500-page document which is particularly denunciatory about Indira, Sanjay, Pranab Mukherjee and Bansi Lal. It records how IAS officers 'collapsed at the slightest pressure', how beggars were rounded up and taken to sterilization clinics, and gives details of the Turkman Gate slum clearance, arbitrary arrests and press censorship. It states that during the Emergency, 'thousands were detained and a series of totally illegal and unwarranted actions followed involving untold human misery and suffering'.[20] However laboured its prose, the report remains a precious record of the months India spent as a dictatorship.

Indira refused to accept the report. 'We do not accept the Shah Commission's report and the people of India do not accept it, they have shown that he is quite irrelevant. How does Mr Shah know what's happening in the political world? What are the forces at work which want to destroy a developing economy? Is a judge competent to decide that? Then why have democracy, why have elections, why have political people in power? They did not want to inquire into any cases except those against me or those considered my supporters. They didn't record any evidence of those who said anything in my favour. In the courtroom itself they had a picked crowd which jeered us. If anybody cheered us that person was thrown out.'[21] How could a mere judge give a ruling on a people's heroine?

She set off determinedly on more public programmes. In April 1978, violent protests broke out in Pantnagar Agricultural University, then in Uttar Pradesh, with workers demanding higher wages. Police opened fire and sixteen were killed. Indira Gandhi was the first at the spot, telling the British journalist Bruce Chatwin, who was accompanying her, that 'physically she could outpace every other Indian politician'.[22] She was proud of her vigorous health, even at sixty as fit and active as her father wanted her to be. 'Indira was touchy about her health,' writes Khushwant Singh. 'To prove her doctors wrong, she rode on horseback, on elephants and walked vast distances, maintaining punishing schedules. Tiredness is a state of mind, not of the body,' she would say.[23]

Touring south India, she often encountered violent demonstrations. Stones were thrown at her car and she was shown black flags. Chatwin records how hard she worked at being a Madonna of all Indians. When it grew dark, she jammed a torch between her knees, directing the beam upwards to light her face, while saying to Chatwin, 'You have no idea how tiring it is to be a goddess.' In a democracy, even the divine need popular endorsement. As she continued her travels, she gained sympathy. She was the lone woman, head unbowed, bravely standing up to those intent on her destruction. Her speeches were an appeal to the nobler protective instincts of her voters, a plea for forgiveness by a display of wounds, an invitation to forget her sins because she was being so grievously sinned against.

'A person rejected the way Indira has been cannot stage a comeback,' Y.B. Chavan, now in the rival Congress, told Sathe. 'She is Jawaharlal's daughter but at present even to be seen in her shadow is destructive.' The grandees were out of touch. They felt tainted by her shadow, but the people flocked to that shadow as they would to the shade of a banyan. Her political skills were resurgent. In the summer of 1978, in the politically crucial Azamgarh by-election, the Congress(I) candidate Mohsina Kidwai won. Indira had campaigned energetically for the election, addressing scores of meetings, conscious of how crucial it was to win in Uttar Pradesh and to defeat the Janata candidate. Writes Sunil Sethi, 'Mrs Gandhi's astute politicking in Azamgarh paid off . . . The hallmark of her electioneering style was there again – the sheer stamina and drive; also her infinite capacity to shroud herself in mysterious martyrdom.'[24] To win in Azamgarh, in the heart of the Hindi belt, in Uttar Pradesh where the Congress had failed to win a single seat in 1977 was a morale booster and a strong signal of rejuvenation.

'It was fearfully hot,' recalls Sethi. 'She was travelling in an Ambassador without air conditioning. I asked her how she coped. She said she simply didn't eat and lived on a liquid diet. She also said she carried several sets of underwear which she regularly changed.'

Unnerved by Indira's political energy, an agitated Janata cancelled Sanjay's bail in the *Kissa Kursi Ka* case. He was arrested on charges of destroying prints of the film and sent to jail for a month. The net was closing in and Indira was racing to outrun the long arm of the Janata, a sprint that stopped at Chikmagalur from where Indira now decided to contest a by-election. Nestling in the beautiful foothills of Karnataka's Mullayanagiri range, dotted with coffee plantations and whispering, sparkling streams and rivers, the beauty of Chikmagalur or 'younger daughter's town' would soon smile on Nehru's daughter.

Meanwhile, as the Janata failed at governance, instability once again threatened India. Crime, extortion, smuggling and lawlessness began to make their presence felt. Crime in Delhi rose sharply. Violence against the poor and lower castes broke out regularly. There was growing discontent in the police: many of those who had obeyed orders during the Emergency were now persecuted by the Janata. Importantly, Indira's rivals were growing ever more bitter and divided. In June 1978, Charan Singh sent out a wrathful cry that the people considered the Janata government a 'collection of impotent men' for not being able to bring Indira Gandhi to justice. An angry Morarji dropped Singh from the cabinet, only to bring him back later. The Janata's jagged cracks were apparent to all even as Indira kept gathering strength.

Before taking the plunge back into an electoral contest, Indira gave a semblance of a public apology for the Emergency, saying in an interview 'muzzling the press was too strong a step' and admitted to things 'getting out of hand'.[25] She was to contest polls a year after a grinding defeat and the slate had to be wiped clean at least of some objectionable stains. In the same interview she said, 'I don't think there's anyone less authoritarian than I am.' Post-Emergency she would constantly try to live down the authoritarian tag. She would later also write to Dorothy Norman in 1980: 'You know me well enough to appreciate that I am neither authoritarian nor cold. But I am not effusive and perhaps this is misunderstood.'[26]

For now, a bow of regret, and Indira Gandhi was back on the road. Jayakar was struck by how easily she could switch off even in the midst of hectic campaigning. 'The moment she entered a plane, she put a cloth over her eyes and went to sleep. I was amazed at her capacity to relax and told her so. She said she rarely had difficulty in sleeping, she slept in cars, trains, planes and could wake up in an instant.' Her ability to sleep at will was commented on by others too. 'She did have this remarkable capacity to catch up on sleep very quickly,' confirms Wajahat Habibullah. 'She would tell us, right, I'm going to sleep and, irrespective of how much noise there was all around, would instantly fall into a deep sleep and wake up totally refreshed.' The battlefield was her natural habitat and the war front was her home. She lived in those zones with the ease of a soldier and fought the adversary as a reflex action in a never-ending contest of wills. In the Chikmagalur campaign, she travelled eighteen hours a day, lived on peanuts and fruit, addressed meetings, visited shrines, marched in processions, tireless, relentless, yet somehow fragile. 'Give your vote to your little daughter,' her posters proclaimed.

The Janata brought in her old adversary George Fernandes to campaign against her in Chikmagalur. Targeting Indira, the Janata put up posters saying 'Beware a powerful cobra is going to raise its hood'. The Janata, however, got its choice of wildlife wrong because in rural Karnataka the king cobra is worshipped as a protector and south of the Vindhyas the Emergency hadn't stained Indira's popularity: she was still Indiraamma. The image of Indira Gandhi as a solitary fighter against the full might of the ruling party was encapsulated in the colourful slogan heard at the time: 'Ek sherni, sau langur, Chikmagalur, Chikmagalur.' Trudging through driving rain in the luminously green countryside, she stopped to chat with coffee plantation workers as they huddled under a tree, as sparkling showers fell all around her. On 8 November 1978, Indira Gandhi won the Chikmagalur by-election by over 70,000 votes[27] and by the end of 1978 was back in Parliament. 'I said I would never contest elections again, but here I am,' she said. Could she imagine becoming prime minister again? 'I can certainly imagine the circumstances in which I could again be prime minister. The question is whether I want to be or agree to be or not.'[28]

~

Chikmagalur was a breakthrough. The Emergency had not just deprived her of the prime ministership but robbed her of the moral and intellectual credibility she claimed and yearned for. She had been scorned by the intelligentsia as well as by the people, from socialist darling she had gone to fascist dictator, from young, progressive leader she had become a symbol of regressive despotism. Karnataka's intellectuals and artists had actively campaigned against her in Chikmagalur. Now an emphatic win in the face of the prevailing government machinery gave her back a shadow of her popular heft, she regained some of her legitimacy and claims to being a woman of the people. Her relationship with the Indian cognoscenti would continue to be uneasy – in sharp contrast with the warmth with which she cultivated intellectuals abroad – although by now the aam janta (common public) had begun to return to her in droves.

Imploding under its own conflicts, the Janata struck at Indira again. When she took her seat in Parliament, Janata MPs hooted 'shame'. In December 1978, the Privileges Committee in Parliament declared that while she was prime minister she had wilfully tried to prevent an official investigation into Maruti Limited. It also held that she had harassed officials who were trying to carry out that investigation. A resolution was passed in Parliament that she had committed 'serious breach of privileges and contempt of the House'. She was expelled from Parliament, arrested and sent to Tihar jail. She had been expecting it. 'Never before in the history of any democratic country has a single individual who leads the principal political opposition, been subjected to so much calumny, character assassination and political vendetta of the ruling party . . . I am a small person but I have stood for certain values,' she said in Parliament. Her popularity was far higher now than during her first arrest. This time when she was taken away, thousands of Congress workers courted arrest with her, there were protests and strikes across India, and even an attempted hijacking of an Indian Airlines plane. Armed reportedly only with toy pistols and cricket balls, putative 'hijackers' Devendra and Bholanath Pandey boarded a flight from Lucknow to Delhi and forced the pilot to fly to Varanasi, demanding the immediate release of Indira Gandhi and withdrawal of all cases against Sanjay. *India Today* magazine humorously called it India's first Gandhian hijack. Two years later both hijackers were given Congress tickets; they won elections and became MLAs in Uttar Pradesh, showing that the Congress itself was hijacked by those who made a show of their loyalty. Indira called her jail term a 'rest cure' and while in prison ate frugally, read voraciously, practised yoga and was released a week later.

If Indira Gandhi started hollowing out the foundations of democratic institutions, all the Janata seemed to want to do was bury her in the rubble, rather than start the process of restoring those institutions. That the Janata Party hardly differed ideologically from Indira is seen in their legislative initiatives. Indira had legalized Emergency powers and inserted the words 'socialist' and 'secular' into the Preamble through the 42nd Amendment of the Constitution. The Janata revoked those Emergency powers through the 44th Amendment and personal freedoms were protected. But significantly, the 44th Amendment did not remove 'socialist' and 'secular' from the Preamble. Instead the 44th Amendment went an extra socialist mile and deleted the right to property as a fundamental right, so that it remained only as a constitutional right. This seemed to proclaim that the Janata's socialism was even more radical than the mere 'pseudo socialism' of Indira. As industries minister, George Fernandes led the Janata's socialist charge, forcing the exit of MNCs like IBM and Coca-Cola. Between the competitive socialisms of Indira and the Janata, there was only a battle against Indira the person. No wonder once the common enemy Indira had been defeated in elections, power and ambition drove the Janata partners apart.

Indira emerged from prison clear-eyed about the way ahead. From Tihar jail she had sent a bouquet of flowers to Charan Singh on his birthday. On her release she returned to Chikmagalur, the wronged queen among her adorers, enduring the slings and arrows of the Janata Party. The open desire for revenge and spitefulness in the powerful are anathema to voters. Just as the all-powerful Indira had invited their wrath by striking at innocents during the Emergency, now the fury emanating from Delhi evoked disgust.

For Indira, the blow of the 1977 loss had been somewhat lessened by the victories in Azamgarh and Chikmagalur. But now it was time to devise a strategy. Cases were piling up against Sanjay – by the end of the Janata's two and a half years, there would be as many as thirty-five criminal cases against him. There were twenty-eight cases against her. 'I only have two alternatives,' she confided to Jiddu Krishnamurti, 'to fight or let them destroy me like a sitting duck.' Deep inside, she remained fearful for her family. Her subcontinental brother-leader Sheikh Mujibur Rahman had been assassinated. Zulfikar Ali Bhutto had been sentenced to death and would be executed in 1979. In spite of their differences she publicly protested Bhutto's death sentence and wrote to Pakistan's military ruler General Zia-ul-Haq urging clemency for Bhutto, but the Janata government refused to take a stand.

Her ever-present worry was that her enemies were plotting to deal her a similar fate. 'She constantly feared for her life,' says Natwar Singh, 'but more than herself she was more concerned about what would happen to her family and her children. She used to say I don't care if anything happens to me but I couldn't bear it if anything happens to the grandchildren.'

By early 1979 the Janata looked as if it was already collapsing under the conflicting ambitions of its multiple power centres. Morarji Desai and Charan Singh were locked in a battle of attrition. Desai's son, Kantilal, was accused of corruption and murky business deals. Maneka Gandhi had set up the magazine *Surya* which 'vilified and undermined the squabbling Janata Party's khichhdi sarkar with gusto'.[29] Maneka Gandhi even published pictures of Jagjivan Ram's married, middle-aged son having sex with a young woman who allegedly had been drugged and forced to pose in the nude, much to Babuji's embarrassment.

Indira and Sanjay set about plotting the way out of the labyrinth. Sanjay, at thirty-two, had become an adept organizer of the Youth Congress and his cronies formed a ready phalanx of support for Indira whenever she needed it. Sanjay the impetuous youth was gone. In his place was a wily political calculator. Her dependence on him grew. She had written to him on his birthday: 'You have had to face a great deal from a very young age and I am proud of the dignified manner in which you have done so . . . What can I wish you? Only that these dreadful days slide away into the past and you emerge unscathed in your innocence, your honest intentions proved and that people recognize your worth and quality.'[30] She would advise: 'Learn to tolerate and to try and win over rather than reciprocating aggressiveness and dislike. This I can say from my own experience for I used to react as you do and have found it only increases one's troubles. A smile and a friendly word to one's enemy costs nothing . . . it makes one a better person. Never, never do anything mean.'

For her he was a misunderstood genius, the child who was a vindication of her expert mothering, the tough youth who understood an evolving India better than the old fogeys who surrounded her. He was her younger alter-ego.

The Sanjay phenomenon would lead to another revolt in the Congress when the Karnataka strongman and former Indira loyalist

Devaraj Urs began to chart an increasingly independent path. He had attacked Indira Gandhi in the AICC in April 1978, saying, 'Let people stop going surreptitiously to Mr Sanjay Gandhi . . . do not mistake me for a sycophant.' By 1979 Devaraj Urs was expelled from the Congress. Urs's revolt may have been outwardly directed at Sanjay Gandhi's dominance but it was also reflective of how the Congress under Indira was at this stage struggling to accommodate the new caste dynamics of politics. Urs had kick-started reforms aimed at uplifting Dalits and backward castes and had forged a coalition of Karnataka's poor and depressed communities. He was seen as a social reformer who created a 'silent social revolution' in Karnataka. Indira Gandhi, reared in the old-style patron–client Congress politics, never quite comprehended the nature of the aspirations of the newly assertive backward castes. In later years, this would cost the Congress its dominant position in north India and in the late 1970s deprived her of a powerful Karnataka stalwart. Unable to tolerate an opponent of Sanjay, Devaraj Urs's exit showed how badly Indira failed at building a team of competent and strong leaders in her constant preference for loyalty over talent.

Mother and son would now work towards an intricate plan. They focused their gaze on the future, working in the darkroom of their conspiracies, lifting out from the chemical bath negatives of photos yet only dimly visualized. It was a high-stakes battle. On 27 February 1979 Sanjay and V.C. Shukla were sentenced to two years in prison for destroying prints of *Kissa Kursi Ka*, although both were released on bail.

The battle would now have to be taken to the enemy's camp. The equivalent of the Trojan Horse would have to be activated to penetrate the enemy lines and deal the fatal blows. After receiving flowers from Indira on his birthday, Charan Singh invited her to bless his newborn grandson. She visited Charan Singh's home, sat on the living-room sofa next to Morarji Desai, took the child on her lap, ate the offered sweets and kept up a flow of courteous conversation. Swallowing past bitterness, Sanjay, through deft backdoor manoeuvres, had reached out to Raj Narain – yes, the same man who filed the Allahabad High Court case against his mother, defeated her in 1977 and coined the term Indira Hatao – and had begun to cultivate a friendship with him. Raj Narain was Charan Singh's loyal lieutenant and Indira and Sanjay realized that the best way to break the Janata was by pitting Charan Singh against Morarji Desai by igniting the former's ever-present prime ministerial ambitions. Already there was strong opposition to the Hindu right-wing Jana Sangh, an alliance partner in the Janata Party, among Charan Singh's supporters. Raj Narain and Sanjay began to plot the downfall of Morarji and the installation of Charan Singh in Morarji's place.

'The Janata members all disliked each other and disliked Indira the most. But in the quest for power they were willing to make friends with her to get the top job. Charan Singh did not hesitate to take even his enemy Indira Gandhi's support if he could become PM. Such was their hunger for office,' recalled Vasant Sathe.

Deep ideological fault lines began to take a toll on the Janata. Socialists in the coalition like Madhu Limaye who despised the Jana Sangh, believed that Jana Sangh members should not retain membership of the RSS while being in the Janata government. Limaye wanted the dismissal of Atal Bihari Vajpayee and L.K. Advani as well as Morarji Desai, seen to be close to the Jana Sangh, isolated. Eventually, the Jana Sangh would exit the Janata Party on the 'dual membership' issue and the Bharatiya Janata Party would be born on 6 April 1980.

In the summer of 1979, India teetered on the brink of widespread instability. Monsoons had failed, law and order was spiralling downwards and units of the CRPF mutinied for the first time. On 11 July 1979, Y.B. Chavan of the Congress(S) moved a vote of no confidence against the Morarji government. Charan Singh's supporters withdrew support from Morarji and socialists in the Janata, such as George Fernandes, and others such as the old Congressman H.N. Bahuguna resigned. Eighty-three-year-old Morarji was left isolated and had no option but to give up his prime ministership on 15 July 1979. As the Janata imploded, rumours began that burning pieces of Skylab, a now-defunct man-made satellite, were about to strike the earth, but instead it was the flaming debris of the dying Janata government which scattered in all directions. On 28 July Charan Singh was duly sworn in as prime minister, forming the government with outside support from the Indira faction of the Congress. Indira had made it clear that she would support Charan Singh's bid for prime ministership only if he withdrew the Special Courts Act – laws setting up special courts to try Sanjay and Indira Gandhi. When Charan Singh refused to deliver on this, Indira withdrew support and the twenty-four-day-old Charan Singh government also collapsed. On 22 August, Parliament was dissolved and fresh elections were ordered to be held in January 1980. 'The Janata which came in roaring like a lion, has gone away with the squeal of a mouse,' gloated Indira.

She hit the election trail. Carrying rations of milk and dry fruit, two pillows, an umbrella, and a suitcase of khadi saris, she set off on a sixty-two-day nationwide campaign, addressing twenty meetings a day, with Sanjay and the Youth Congress providing her organizational support, promising the people a government that worked. They believed her. Three years of chaotic Janata rule, of shortages, mutinies, strikes and shutdowns, had led to a hankering for a decisive leader who had built a reputation for providing order in the country. Four months before the polls, prices of essentials had registered the biggest spike in any comparable period since Independence. Prices of onions and potatoes pushed skyward. Oil prices soared as a result of the Iranian Revolution, the second 'oil shock', in 1979.[31]

Indira's weakness in 1977 was now her strength: then she was seen as authoritarian; now she was projected as firm and efficient. The collective amnesia of a nation meant that the excesses of the Emergency were set aside. Even if Indians never forgot the Emergency, Indira had been forgiven. She had not only suffered at the hands of the Janata but the election defeat of 1977 had cleansed her of her sins. Her suffering at the hands of the Janata and the suffering she caused to her opponents came to be equated. 'The two cancelled each other out.' According to the journalist Prabhas Joshi, the 1980 elections marked an 'end of ideology'.[32] While previous polls were fought on socialism, secularism, non-alignment, etc., this was just fought on the personality of Indira Gandhi. She could govern, the Janata could not was her simple campaign pitch. In January 1980 the *Times of India* announced in a banner headline 'It's Indira All the Way'.

In the general elections of 1980, the Congress(I) won 353 seats and Indira Gandhi herself won decisively from two seats, Raebareli and Medak in Andhra Pradesh. The Janata Party managed a paltry thirty-one seats. She was sworn in as prime minister for the fourth time on 14 January 1980 on a day decided on by astrologers. She was sixty-two years old. She took her oath in the name of God, much more sombre now than in 1971, when she had been filled with a 'wild euphoria'. Now her youthful arrogance was gone. In another break from Nehruvian agnosticism, this time before she moved back into her residence, 1 Safdarjung Road, the house was purified by pandits, who recited prayers and chanted for eight days, before she moved in. How does it feel to be India's leader again, a journalist asked her. 'I have always been India's leader,' Indira Gandhi countered.[33]

~

Dear Mrs Gandhi,

You emerged from desolation more vulnerable than ever before and even more wary and suspicious of people. Were you unable to forget the manner in which your close associates had abandoned you, the way friends had looked the other way, the way you had been shunned at social gatherings? In the wilderness of those thirty-four months were your worst suspicions about people confirmed?

You saw shades of your father's predicament in yours when after the 1962 war close colleagues had turned on him and had refused to support him. This life lesson conditioned your behaviour from now on as you embarked on government and politics with only Sanjay as your adviser, dispensing with the equivalents of Haksar, Dhar and others, trusting virtually no one. This trust deficit with almost everyone except your own family would play a crucial role in your politics from now onward.

Control and centralization would continue to be your methods of rule, an obsession with order, the desire to lay down the Pax Indira in states and throughout the government and party. Did this also stem from the familiar conviction that even though the people of India would occasionally stray from you, they would never go very far? You returned to power in 1980 with your belief in your own indispensability reinforced, once again convinced that the people would always end up coming back to you, that you were the sole repository of their trust and everyone else was not only wrong but simply illegitimate.

By 1980 you had become much more religious, ritual-bound than ever before. This religiosity was as much a personal belief as a device to garner votes in the absence of ideological convictions. You had visited several holy men and shrines in the time you were out of power: you had not only sought the counsel of Vinoba Bhave but also visited the Shankaracharya of Kamakoti Math, Anandamayi Ma in Hardwar and the ashram of Ramana Maharshi. Did you fall back on religious faith, which your mother had held so dear (and your father had rebuffed), as the only buffer between you and the world after your tryst with the wilderness? Did a new religiosity now creep into your political calculations as well? You had returned to power but by now you had slowly begun to abandon the Nehruvian secularism that defined your father's legacy. It was a political compromise that would darken your last days.

~

7

Twilight: 1980–84

Five months after Indira Gandhi's 1980 election victory, Sanjay Gandhi was killed in a plane crash. Indira was devastated. From this time on she seemed to lose her sharp instincts and tough resolve. The last years of her prime ministership were marked by violent conflict in many parts of the country. She gave orders for Operation Blue Star, the storming of the Golden Temple in Amritsar by the army to flush out pro-Khalistan terrorists hidden there. It was a decision that led to her assassination on 31 October 1984.

On the morning of 23 June 1980, in the blazing Delhi heat, a small aircraft leapt through the shimmering air above the sweltering city. It was a Pitts S-2A plane, somersaulting in the white-hot sky at high speed. Suddenly it steadied, paused, then plunged into a steep dive, but the pilot could not pull up in time. In seconds, the plane crashed. Its pilot – Sanjay Gandhi – and his flying instructor Captain Subhash Saxena (who had initially refused to go with him knowing Sanjay's inexperience at flying this particular plane) were instantly and gruesomely killed. The joy of the 1980 victory proved tragically short-lived.

Indira had repeatedly warned Sanjay against aerobatics on the Pitts S-2A. 'The evening before he died we went for a ride on the same plane,' recalled Maneka Gandhi. 'It was the first time he was going in it. In the plane I screamed and screamed for I think two hours and when we came down I ran home and told my mother-in-law: "Ma, I need you to tell Sanjay not to fly this plane. He can fly any plane he wants, but not this one." My mother-in-law said to him in front of me (and Dhirendra Brahmachari was also there),[1] "Maneka's never been so strong about something. If she's saying na jao [don't go], toh na jao tum [then don't go]." She said, "I'm afraid I have to put my foot down." Then Dhawan came in and started saying, "Arre yeh toh mardon ka jahaz hai. Manekaji aise bol rahi hai kyonki woh aurat hain. [This is a man's plane, Manekaji is saying this because she's a woman.]" My mother-in-law asked, "Sanjay, is it safe?" And I said, "No it isn't, it's a horrible plane." Then Sanjay said, "Do teen din mein theek ho jayega [It'll be fine in two or three days], she'll get used to it." The next morning he was dead.'

It was a massive, wrenching loss for his mother. One of the enduring images of Sanjay's death is of Indira visiting the site of the plane wreckage not once but twice on 23 June, inspecting bits of debris as if looking for remnants of her son and trying to relive his last moments. Unkind comments were made that she was looking to find keys to a safe deposit box or vault containing his wealth but instead it was Indira reverting to a primeval way of dealing with sudden and violent bereavement, returning to the site of death as if still searching for the disappeared loved one. 'Doctor, hamara dahina haath kat gaya [My right hand has been cut off],' she confided to Dr Mathur.

In 1980 Sanjay was at the very centre of Indira's political roadmap, the main organization man to whom Youth Congress cadres had remained tenaciously loyal even as the stalwarts fell away from Indira. With none of the heavyweights by her side it was Sanjay who had become the party's supremo-in-waiting, the kurta-clad karta of the new Congress family, by now the newly appointed general secretary of the Congress.[2] Sanjay's activities during the Emergency had cost his mother an election but three years later it was his organizational power and strategizing that had brought her victory, or so she believed. About 150 of the 353 Congress winning candidates in 1980 were Sanjay's recruits, impatient young bucks fiercely loyal to Sanjay, who scorned the old-fashioned niceties of their Congress seniors.

Motilal, Feroze and Sanjay were the alpha males in Indira's life. Brought up by a refined and intellectual father, Indira was paradoxically drawn towards darker versions of men, aggressive, dynamic men on the make who perhaps satisfied her own latent adventurous, defiant side. Perhaps hers was a subconscious revolt against the high bar set by Nehru, or perhaps insecure about wielding power without too much political conviction, she turned towards brash, power-wielding men rather than towards philosopher-idealists like her father with whom she had never been able to communicate easily and who might disapprove of her methods. Sanjay had been that more daredevil sort of man, so was Feroze and so was M.O. Mathai. Sanjay in a way was the last link with Feroze Gandhi and with Motilal Nehru, he was the last of the dominating men in her life to whom she warmed more intimately than she did with her cerebral father or the gentle Rajiv. If Jawaharlal was the saint-hero, these men were the anti-Jawaharlal, the opposite of saintly. She did not recognize that none of them could match Nehru's moral strength, telling Jayakar, 'No one can take Sanjay's place, he was my son but like an elder brother in his support . . . Rajiv lacks Sanjay's dynamism and his concerns.'

Nehru died at the age of seventy-four, a reigning prince almost to the end, for whom the cup of life had spilled over. When Sanjay died, short of his thirty-fourth birthday, Indira was consumed by frantic, helpless grief. 'She became very fragile, very bitter,' recalled Maneka Gandhi. 'She was never normal again. She was never Indira Gandhi again.'

With his death she also confronted the loss of her family's political future. Over the years Sanjay had grown from spoiled younger son to arrogant youth to dark prince of the Emergency but by the end he was a politician of guile and stealth, with the gift of outsmarting opponents and planning patient strategy. In crafting his mother's comeback, he had not stood on ego, and shrewdly let bygones be bygones in reaching out to once sworn enemies. He had built the Youth Congress into a loyal fighting force. In 1980, not only had Sanjay himself won from Amethi by a huge margin but many of his Youth Congress loyalists had also won. They were 'innocent of parliamentary proprieties, unencumbered by ideology or idealism', but not averse to using their lung and muscle power to demonstrate their strength. This 'shouting brigade' of youthful folk now took over Parliament insisting that the House function only on Sanjay's terms. Indira looked silently on, gazing at the new generation with awe.

The Sanjay style had begun to place its imprimatur on the government: independent-minded bureaucrats were summarily removed, humiliated and kept waiting for months for alternative postings, politicians suspected of being 'disloyal' were sidelined, and ministers and civil servants jostled with one another to carry out Sanjay's orders. Already all state governments under Janata Party rule had been dismissed and President's Rule had been imposed. These competitive cycles of dismissals of state governments by Indira, then the Janata and then again by Indira severely undermined federalism and regional politicians for more than a decade. The worst fallout of this would take place in Punjab where, after being dismissed, the Akalis were unable to return to power. Sikh rage would spiral into a deadly flame that would claim Indira's life.

The post-1980 Congress(I), its strategy and its complexion, was thus entirely left to Sanjay. Indira had begun to see herself as a presiding deity who would give an overall direction while Sanjay took care of the nitty-gritty of party and government. Now with him gone, that entire plan collapsed. The owner of the company lost her able, all-powerful CEO. 'If he hadn't died, Sanjay Gandhi would have been the No. 2 to Indira Gandhi and the entire work of the Congress and country would have come to him,' said V.C. Shukla.[3]

After Sanjay's death, Pupul Jayakar saw a 'wildness in her face, a dark despair . . . She held her stomach with both hands, crying out, "where should I go from here?"' Rajiv became worried about Indira's growing dependence on astrologers and rituals. Yet even as she consulted astrologers, she would throw up her hands at their uselessness and say, 'What use are they? Could they protect Sanjay? If I had died it would have been right. I am over 60, I have lived a full life, but Sanjay was so young.' Rocked by life's uncertainties, human beings had through the ages turned to the certainties offered by religion and so had she. Yet in the end, rituals and shamans could not keep turbulence at bay. The agnostic Nehru had been made of sterner stuff; he had trusted his political colleagues and supported them in building their strength on the ground. But she, unable to trust anybody else, now turned to her older son, Rajiv, the gentlemanly airline pilot, as a possible successor. By doing so, she dealt yet another blow to political democracy.

Rajiv had always been reluctant to join politics, but now said, 'the way I look at it is that Mummy has to be helped somehow'.[4] Natwar Singh recalls Rajiv being very apprehensive. 'He said, I am not Sanjay. My salary is very modest and I ride a motorbike. I know nothing about politics.' Falk quotes Feroze's friend Bhabani Sen Gupta: 'There is nothing on record to show that as a child and even as a young man, Rajiv got a great deal of his mother's love and care. But he was close to his father and developed a curiosity for technology.' Dr Mathur remembers Rajiv as a decent, well-meaning and kind-hearted person, but compared to Sanjay even the fond doctor was forced to describe him as a 'political novice'. On a Gandhi family trip to north Bengal, Bhaskar Ghose recalls how, when the Gandhis' flight landed and they disembarked, Sanjay was immediately surrounded on the tarmac by slogan-shouting Youth Congress supporters. As Ghose looked on, somebody tapped him gently on the shoulder. It was Rajiv, holding his wife, Sonia, and children in a close, protective circle saying, 'Excuse me, please can we have a car? My family and I want to get away from all this political stuff as fast as we can.'

~

After Sanjay's death, Indira Gandhi's relations with his widow, Maneka Gandhi, fell apart. The twenty-three-year-old and her three-month-old son were Sanjay's only remaining family, yet the bond between mother-in-law and daughter-in-law snapped. Why did it happen? 'I was too young and my mother-in-law was too old,' Maneka told Simi Garewal. She recalls the break with her mother-in-law thus: 'She lost everything in that crash and never picked herself up again. Her attitude to me was "Why didn't you die?" She was utterly destroyed. For her he was everything, political adviser, son, hero. So she found herself very vulnerable. She became very obsessive about dynasty.'

Maneka attributes the break to Rajiv and his family. 'She wanted another son. Rajiv then stepped in. And now she had to go back to him. He hadn't been talking to her for three years. She had to re-cultivate him, she had to bring him in, fill a vacuum for which she hadn't even trained him. And therefore she had to give in a lot to his demands and his family's demands. And one of their main demands was that Maneka has to go. They said we'll leave if she doesn't go . . . My mother-in-law had to listen to all sorts of demands and commands being put on her . . . Even then I understood that she was as weak and as helpless as I was, both of us were victimized.' Maneka believed the Gandhi family was not mature enough to give a young widow her due. 'Like in all traditional Indian homes, the widow is unnecessary.'

Jayakar describes Maneka as 'young, spirited and ambitious and someone not prepared to withdraw into anonymity after being close to the excitement of political life'. Bhagat recalls that during the Emergency, along with Sanjay, Maneka had also tasted power and after Sanjay's death in 1980, she may have thought that power was not reflected but belonged to her and she would be able to exercise it as before. Indira Gandhi's turning to Rajiv upset Maneka, because she saw herself as Sanjay's legatee. Khushwant Singh, then editor of the *Hindustan Times*, wrote a few days after Sanjay's death: 'The only possible inheritor of the Sanjay cult figure is Maneka . . . the very reincarnation of Durga astride a tiger.'[5] Durga astride a tiger was a slot already occupied by Indira herself and two Durgas in one home spelt cosmic conflict. After Sanjay's death, Maneka wanted to assert herself in the Gandhi household, as an equal. But she soon realized that her mother-in-law saw her as only her son's widow, outside the charmed circle of the 'chosen'. According to Khushwant Singh, Indira didn't think Maneka was of the same 'class' as the Gandhis and that she didn't behave as a widow should.[6]

Maneka would have to fade into the shadows and allow her brother-in-law to take her husband's place because, in Indira Gandhi's still-traditional brahminical worldview, the place of a son could be taken only by another son. Perhaps Maneka at the time failed to reflect on her formidable mother-in-law's history, how she had long and deliberately prepared herself for politics as Nehru's legatee since the late 1940s. Intensely and constantly conscious of family lineage, Indira wasn't about to hand over her life's work to someone outside the direct bloodline.

After 1980, Indira Gandhi played the politics of survival. The shock of 1977 had been so great that she was determined not to lose power again, whatever the cost. Staying in power had become an end in itself and even the remote possibility of her direct family losing out again on the levers of political supremacy alerted her to grave danger.

The death of Sanjay and the rise of Rajiv led to the marginalization of another figure in the prime ministerial household. Dhirendra Brahmachari – the tall, muscle-bound yoga teacher with a luxuriant mane and saturnine good looks, a bare-bodied, Rasputin-like figure – had had access to Indira and Nehru since the 1950s as their yoga teacher. During the Emergency the Swami's fortunes had bounced upwards, enabling him to set up yoga centres in Delhi and Kashmir. He set up his aircraft company and acquired a private plane, and there were whisperings on the Swami's ability to perform miracles in government, not on the basis of his spiritual powers but his very temporal access to the prime minister's house.

There were even rumours of a romantic liaison with Indira – there are insinuations of this in online versions of the unpublished 'She' chapter allegedly written by Mathai – which Frank refutes. 'Dheerendra Brahmachari used to visit PM quite often and guided her religious thinking and spiritual activities,' recalls Dr Mathur. However much Sanjay may have encouraged the Swami, the rationalist, technology-inclined Rajiv had always been suspicious of the hirsute yogi and one day at dinner, when the Swami was present, Indira gave vent to perhaps long-pent-up family emotions. When the Swami began to aggressively challenge Indira on the credentials of someone she had recently appointed in the education ministry, she told him he knew nothing about it and then made it furiously clear that she had had enough of his meddling. With Sanjay's death it was as if she had become emboldened to speak out against those who had misused their access to him. 'I know what was happening and how Sanjay's name was used by people to cover up,' she flared up in a rage, directing her remarks at the Swami. 'I will not permit corruption around me.' 'You have said a great deal,' Brahmachari responded angrily. 'I will say much more,' returned Indira Gandhi, thumping the table.[7] Soon the airborne Swami would find himself an unwelcome guest and from then on was rarely seen at 1 Safdarjung Road.

Indira's showdown with Maneka was much more volatile and heartbreaking for both. Matters came to an explosive head when Maneka attended a rally in March 1982 in Lucknow organized by the Sanjay loyalist Akbar 'Dumpy' Ahmed as a show of strength that she controlled the loyalties of a sizeable number of Uttar Pradesh MLAs who regarded Sanjay's widow and not Rajiv as their leader. Indira had already warned Maneka that if she attended the rally she need never again return to 1 Safdarjung Road. Maneka's presence at the function was seen as a direct threat to Rajiv's new role as Sanjay's heir. Shedding his blue jeans and T-shirts for khadi, thirty-eight-year-old Rajiv was now the Amethi MP, having won the by-election after his brother's death, by over two lakh votes.[8] As relations worsened, Maneka's mother, in a provocative snub to Indira, had sold her magazine *Surya* to two prominent BJP members. 'Selling the magazine to political opponents was designed to embarrass the prime minister,' an Indira aide told *India Today*.[9]

Indira heard about Maneka's plans to attend the Lucknow meeting when she was at the Festival of India in London, an Indian cultural extravaganza which was the brainchild of Pupul Jayakar. Amid the gala dinners with Prime Minister Margaret Thatcher and the Queen, operas and concerts, her rage gathered under the surface. On her return to Delhi, having learnt that Maneka had indeed gone for this meeting, Indira's iron calm deserted her and she completely lost her temper. In a saas versus bahu moment, she wrote a raging letter to her daughter-in-law shaming Maneka for her background and family and saying that she had never been in favour of Sanjay's marriage to her. It was never a good idea for anyone to cross swords with Goddess Durga in the power game. However weakened Indira Gandhi may have been, anyone who did so inevitably paid a price.

The country was in turmoil. Sikh separatist leader Jarnail Singh Bhindranwale's terrorist squads were on a murderous rampage in Punjab as demands for a separate Sikh state of Khalistan built to a shrill scream. There was upheaval in Assam as Hindu Assamese began to demand the deportation of Bengali-speaking Muslims from Bangladesh. Assam had already been declared a disturbed area. Amid upheaval and conflict, the prime minister's home too became a mirror image of the battleground that was India. Distraught at death and conflict in the family, Indira's grip on the national situation began to weaken.

On 29 March 1982 Maneka Gandhi packed her bags and moved out of the house she had come into as a bride. She took two-year-old Feroze Varun with her, breaking Indira's heart, as the little grandson she doted on now left his dadi's home. Hitting hard at her mother-in-law, Maneka wrote an open letter to Indira, which was published in the *Indian Express*, saying 'as soon as Sanjay died you started literally torturing me in every conceivable way . . . I fought so bitterly for you

. . . I spoke and will always speak for you . . . when the rest of your family was packed and ready to go abroad.'[10]

'This girl has taken Varun way from me . . . My grandson is being taken away,' a wounded Indira cried out helplessly to P.C. Alexander, then her principal secretary. 'You know my relationship to Sanjay's son. He is being taken away.' 'She adored him and she wanted very much to keep him,' Maneka recalled. 'Mrs Gandhi doted on Feroze Varun. Sometimes, she would have all three grandchildren sleep in her room and fussing over them gave her great joy . . . she had missed family togetherness as a child,' Bhagat remembers. With her grandchild gone, Indira burst out in grief, 'Why am I here? I have started to feel I have been here long enough.'

~

She had lost her son; now her daughter-in-law and grandson left her home. In these years, she 'seemed like a woman who had run out of steam', Marie Seton told Ian Jack. 'She seemed genuinely at a loss and more melancholic than I'd ever known her. She no longer knew whom to trust or what advice to rely on. And had begun to doubt her own judgement.'[11] 'If you ask me whether she lost her grip on India, I would tell you that she never really had a grip on India after she came back to power in 1980,' said Inder Malhotra. 'She couldn't understand what kind of energies were afoot, she was fumbling and faltering, virtually advertising her inability.' The A.R. Antulay corruption scandal in Maharashtra in 1981 was one example of her being increasingly at a loss. Then chief minister of Maharashtra, Antulay, one of Sanjay's chosen nominees as chief minister, was accused of an extortion racket in return for allocations of cement and other materials. The Bombay High Court would go on to convict Antulay, ruling that Antulay had forced Mumbai builders to make donations to a private trust in exchange for receiving more cement than the quotas allocated to them. Before Antulay was taken to court, the scandal broke in the press and caused an uproar in the assembly and in Parliament. The appropriate course would have been to accept Antulay's resignation once he had been publicly exposed. But instead Indira kept defending Antulay, saying he was the people's choice, and the 'people wanted him' clearly only because he had been close to Sanjay. After he was convicted, Antulay was forced to resign, leaving Indira shamefaced. Even Rajiv Gandhi, the future 'Mr Clean', was reportedly unhappy about the way Indira handled the Antulay affair.

However, Wajahat Habibullah believes it is unfair to say she had lost her political sense in these years. 'She wasn't at sea,' he says, 'she knew what she was doing. But she had softened a great deal, she was much quieter and mellower. She was no longer the sort of person who would impose the Emergency or move towards authoritarian rule.' On a trip to the United States to meet President Reagan in July 1982, she was the picture of elegance, posing for photos in a stunning fuchsia silk sari and chic sleeveless blouse. Yet there was a sadness in her eyes. The rich blossoming colour of the sari was in contrast to her rather melancholy and subdued manner. The meeting was not too fruitful. After the Soviet invasion of Afghanistan in 1979, America tilted strongly towards Pakistan and India was still perceived as a Soviet ally. 'Which way does India tilt?' she was asked on the trip. 'I think we stand upright,' she shot back. The trip brought a reunion with Dorothy Norman, to whom she would subsequently write, 'The world is becoming a nastier place . . . is it because of age that one thinks things everywhere are deteriorating?' As the past becomes more distant, the more glorious it seems. As shadows lengthen, the remembered sunshine of days gone by takes on a golden hue.

~

The affable and photogenic Rajiv Gandhi slowly began to take Sanjay's place as his mother's adviser. Rajiv's friends and advisers were clean-cut Doon School–educated professional young men like him, individuals like Arun Nehru and Arun Singh, very different from Sanjay's kurta-clad political cronies, drawing flattering comparisons between 'Sanjay's goons and Rajiv's Doons'. Rajiv had taken charge of the preparations for the Asian Games, which were held in Delhi in 1982. The Games were a race against time but they went off successfully. Asiad 1982 showcased India to the world and Rajiv gained a great deal of valuable experience organizing it.[12] The athlete P.T. Usha, the 'queen of Indian track and field', dazzled at the Games, becoming an instant favourite, crowning Asiad with India's first home-grown sporting heroine.

Organizing a mega sporting event was one thing, but organizing India was another. Rajiv was no Sanjay, and Indira, still the grieving mother and bereft grandmother, had lost the uncanny political instinct that had struck fear in her opponents for so many years. By asking Rajiv Gandhi and Arun Nehru to take charge of the upcoming assembly elections in Andhra Pradesh and Karnataka in 1983, Indira Gandhi showed her anxiety to create another Sanjay. She failed to realize that an apolitical former airline pilot would be hopelessly outwitted by the shrewd veterans barrelling around in the political arena. Wrote the journalist Prem Bhatia about Rajiv's coterie: 'They were political illiterates who imagined that power is mathematics, computers or word processors, qualities that counted little in the battle ahead.'[13]

India of the 1980s was not the India Indira Gandhi could easily recognize. The centralization of power, driven by her political insecurity and her incapacity to nurture local talent, had deprived Indian states of strong, locally rooted politicians who could command loyalty and maintain peace in their areas, as the Syndicate had been able to in the 1950s and 1960s. Local political leadership, crucial bulwarks in times of crisis and bridge-builders between communities, had been destroyed across the country. In a deserted landscape, the demons of conflict – religion, caste and community – roamed freely. Those leaders that emerged such as N.T. Rama Rao in Andhra Pradesh or the student politicians of the Assam movement increasingly came from outside the Congress system, harnessing regional or community passions to their cause. These local chieftains began to punch their way into a battlefield marked by the fraying dominance of the Congress, seizing the vacated space.

Malignant seeds planted in the 1960s grew into the weeds of decay. The Congress, once described as 'the largest and most formidable agency for the distribution of patronage and extraction of loyalty that the world has ever seen or is likely to see',[14] had, since the split of 1969, been systematically deinstitutionalized. Indira had captured all organs of the party like the working committee and the parliamentary board. Any state leader who could challenge the supreme authority was cut down. As a result the party became closed to new energies, unable to accommodate diverse aspirations. Federalism may not have been institutionalized even in Nehru's time but Nehru had a far lighter touch with regional governments. In Nehru's time, between 1950 and 1964, Article 356 dismissing state governments was invoked nine times, but from 1966 to 1977, in Indira's first tenure, President's Rule was slammed down as many as thirty-six times and Congress chief ministers too were repeatedly changed.[15] Pax Indira undermined democracy from within even as it created only an artificial short-term order.

The Congress's essentially federal character, with its once-strong party bosses, with the possibility of bargaining between states and the centre as long as the Congress remained in power in both,[16] was weakened once non-Congress parties came to power. Indira struck more body blows to federalism by her distrust of anyone who wasn't a loyalist. Haksar said of Indira that 'her will to power was not alas matched by her will to greatness'. Where she should have asserted the power of constitutional governance, she moved only to secure the fortunes of her party.

For example, in Assam and Punjab, the answer to boiling grievances was clearly to allow political space for regional forces like the Assam students union and the Akalis. In Jammu and Kashmir, she expected the regional party, the National Conference led by the Abdullahs, to defer to her and make no bid whatsoever for any independence in decision-making. Indira Gandhi's addiction to snuffing out local politicians grew into a disease that claimed the life of the system she presided over. Instead of recognizing the growing demand for representation across regions and communities, the clamping down of Pax Indira by a deinstitutionalized party meant that the Congress became an increasingly tottering palace in a seismically heaving landscape.

Rajiv Gandhi was good-hearted, earnest and well meaning, but he lacked the ruthless political edge of his younger brother. He hardly had any time to learn. His mother served an apprenticeship with her father for almost twenty years; Sanjay Gandhi was groomed by Indira for a decade. But Rajiv was thrown into the deep end with barely any notice. He struggled to come to terms with the complexities of Indian politics and did not quite know how to deal with the sycophantic culture that haunted the Congress. The best illustration of this is when he publicly humiliated the Andhra Pradesh Chief Minister T. Anjaiah, describing him as a buffoon, for giving him an over-the-top and rowdy welcome at the airport in 1982. The incident was enough to spark off a furious reaction that just months later would see the dramatic rise of Telugu film-star and local hero Nandamuri Taraka Rama Rao (NTR) on the plank of 'Telugu self-respect'.

Indira's induction of a hesitant and inexperienced Rajiv when domestic disturbances were raging from Assam to Punjab showed an astounding apathy and blindness to the current realities. With crises in the east and north, with the south slowly shaking off Congress dominance, was this the time to plump so squarely for a family member as successor, instead of moving to revitalize the party through a more worthy successor? The last thing a society crying out for change and power-sharing needed was more accumulation of power in the hands of not just a party but a family. But she simply did not see the imperative to cede control.

'There was a shift in her style of working in these years,' recalls Dhawan. 'After Sanjay's death, Rajiv and his coterie took over. He, Arun Singh, Arun Nehru, M.L. Fotedar functioned like an extraconstitutional authority, totally running the country in the second term. They wanted me out because they knew I would always tell her the truth. In the second term all these people [Rajiv and his advisers] were taking the big decisions,' says Dhawan. 'The death of Sanjay really shook her. She was never the same. That's why these cronies got together and, because her mind was weakened, they could easily feed her.'

~

Indira had come to power promising a government that worked, but the 1980s was India's violent decade, the decade of a million mutinies. Departing slightly from socialist dogma, she did take the first tentative steps towards economic liberalism. Suzuki was allowed entry to manufacture automobiles and the finance minister, R. Venkataraman, was sent to the IMF to negotiate a loan for which India agreed to conditionalities like fiscal restraint and bringing down inflation, even as the left howled 'sellout' and 'enormous heat and dust' was generated in the media. But given the political turmoil of these years, an 'opportunity to restructure the economy was neither a priority nor a compulsion'.[17]

The Congress suffered a series of election defeats in 1983. In state elections in Karnataka, where Indira Gandhi had started her political comeback after the Emergency, the Congress was defeated by the Janata Party and Ramakrishna Hegde, who had been a follower of Indira's Syndicate adversary S. Nijalingappa, became chief minister. It was the first non-Congress government in Karnataka. Andhra Pradesh too got its first non-Congress government, when the Telugu Desam Party stormed to power, with N.T. Rama Rao as chief minister. With M.G. Ramachandran and the All India Anna Dravida Munnetra Kazhagam (AIADMK) reigning supreme in Tamil Nadu, it looked as if south India, Indira's hope of an impregnable fortress, was deserting the Congress.

Bruised by the defeats in south India, Indira pushed forward with calamitous elections in Assam, in turmoil over the 'anti-foreigner' (or anti-Bangladeshi-Muslim) agitation. Ignoring warnings of violence, confident that the Muslim vote bank would carry the Congress to victory, polls were held in mid February. The decision to hold an election in the midst of the raging Assam movement was a horrible mistake. Leaders of the Assam movement, the All Assam Students Union and the All Assam Gana Sangram Parishad, backed by the Janata and BJP, asked people to boycott the polls and many polling stations were burnt down. But Muslim communities ignored the boycott call and voted in large numbers. The Congress won these bizarre elections where the voter turnout was only 2 per cent, and the polls resulted in a barbaric massacre.

On 18 February 1983, in the fields around the settlement of Nellie and other adjoining villages in central Assam, over a thousand Bengali-speaking Muslims, according to official figures, were killed, brutally hacked to death with machetes or burnt to death in their homes.[18] Unofficial figures of the butchery place the number of dead at over 3000.[19] Women and children suffered the most because they could not run away fast enough. Sixteen villages were destroyed. It was a bloody indictment of the decision to hold controversial elections. 'I cannot find words to describe the horrors,' Indira Gandhi stuttered three days later on a visit to Assam. Pictures of massacred children on the cover of *India Today* magazine welcomed delegates arriving at the seventh Non-Aligned Movement summit in Delhi the next week.

At the NAM summit, Indira would take over the chairmanship of NAM from Fidel Castro, President of Cuba. Later in the year she would host the Commonwealth Heads of Government Meeting in New Delhi with Queen Elizabeth in attendance. The events were planned to tasteful perfection in her usual style. For the NAM summit Fidel Castro arrived with his friend and Nobel laureate Gabriel García Márquez, and they and the other delegates were charmed by the folk music and classical dance concerts that had been organized. Yet the luminosity that normally surrounded Indira at international gatherings had begun to fade. Thoughts of dead young men echoed mournfully in a speech she gave in January 1984 at the 71st Indian Science Congress in Ranchi, where she quoted the war poet A.E. Housman: 'Life, to be sure, is nothing much to lose, but young men think it is, and we were young'.

In these years when things fell apart and the centre could not hold, Indira, and later Rajiv, took to cynically playing the Hindu card, the 1980s seeing Indira taking recourse to what is called 'soft Hindutva'. She had already begun displays of personal religiosity. After her election defeat of 1977, she had visited the temple of Tripura Sundari in Udaipur. She had performed yagnas and the Lakshachandi Path at the Kali temple in Jhansi. Her loss of power had pushed her towards religious rituals in a bid to alter her political fortunes. In the first thirty-eight days of her return to power in 1980 she had visited a dozen religious shrines from Jammu to Tamil Nadu. She now brought temple visits and trysts with religious sentiments into the political realm, attempting to strike a chord with Hindus by a subtle use of religious symbols.

In 1980 riots had erupted in Moradabad over simmering tensions between Hindus and Muslims after a Dalit girl was allegedly kidnapped by Muslims. Later a pig belonging to one of the Dalit families wandered into the Idgah, provoking outrage among the Muslims praying there. In the resulting violence, the police opened fire, an act the Muslim leader Syed Shahabuddin compared to the Jallianwala Bagh massacre.

Normally the first to dash to sites of communal violence, Indira Gandhi failed to arrive at the scene, blaming 'foreign forces' for the riots, giving rise to fears that she wanted to pander to Hindu sentiments by not being too closely identified with the Muslims. In 1981 when about a thousand Dalits converted to Islam in Meenakshipuram in Tamil Nadu, Hindu mobilization accelerated. When the Hindu right demanded a ban on conversions, Indira refused, saying India was a secular state, even though she could not fully resist the temptation to dabble in Hindu politics. By 1983 the movement to liberate Ram's birthplace at Ayodhya would begin and Indira's use of a 'lexicon borrowed from political Hinduism' would give respectability to the Hindu cause.[20] As Diego Maiorano points out, directly or indirectly, Indira Gandhi contributed to the rise of Hindu politics, by on occasion appealing to a national Hindu vote bank. She was accused of letting the agitation in Punjab boil to consolidate Hindu support for the Congress. In a bitter battle with Farooq Abdullah's National Conference in the Jammu and Kashmir assembly elections in the summer of 1983, she tried to rally the Hindu vote in Jammu by saying the National Conference government would be terrible for them, suggestively pointing to a Hindu–Muslim divide. She accused Farooq of being hand in glove with Islamist hardliners and of being a secessionist.

Habibullah, however, firmly denies she played any religious card in Kashmir. 'She expressed a concern for the sense of insecurity that the Kashmiri pandits were feeling, and said that unless we addressed it, our secular foundations would be under threat. At the same time she had often said "khuda hafiz" when campaigning earlier in Assam. She used to tell me, the press can say whatever they like but I don't play any religious card.'

In her first term, guided by the left-inspired secularism of Haksar, the 'secular sage' who could still 'match the scholiasts Sanskrit verse for Sanskrit verse', she had kept strictly out of religion's way. Haksar had always spoken out boldly against the intrusion of religion into politics and believed fanaticism was the greatest danger to India's unity. Now without wise advisers by her side Indira began to play precisely the kind of politics she outwardly inveighed against. When the party becomes entirely dependent on the supreme leader for votes, then the leader must try to co-opt all shades of opinion and persuasion as she remains the only agency to single-handedly mobilize support. Ideology becomes dispensable, only more and more numbers matter, wherever they may come from.

In Jammu and Kashmir, her campaign pitch did not work and Farooq Abdullah and the National Conference won the 1983 polls.

When Farooq Abdullah again became chief minister of Jammu and Kashmir, Indira Gandhi became determined to oust him.[21]

~

But the biggest challenge to Indira Gandhi in these years would come from Punjab, from the Sikhs who ironically were a 'community she regarded with great affection'.[22] The agitation in Punjab had simmered for decades. The demand for a Punjabi suba or a separate state for Sikhs, in its initial stages, was voiced as a demand for a Punjabi-speaking state. But essentially it was an openly communal demand camouflaged as a language campaign, a demand which had existed since Independence.

The Shiromani Akali Dal, the party of the Sikhs, had come into being in 1920 and functioned as the political wing of the Sikh religious order headed by the Shiromani Gurdwara Parbandhak Committee (SGPC). With the combination of the SGPC and the Akali Dal functioning as the ruling fountainhead of the Sikhs, political and religious power in the community was indivisible.

Nehru resisted the demand for a Sikh state with spirit and candour, refusing to create a state he believed was premised more on religion than language. As he told the communist leader Ajoy Ghosh, 'Sikhs are a fine people but they are led by separatists and fanatics. I cannot hand over a state to them on the border with Pakistan.'

Nehru determinedly opposed the Punjabi state until his death but the daughter did what the father had baulked at. She would say: '[When I became prime minister in 1966], I inherited this tricky problem [Punjab] from my predecessor . . . the demand [for a Punjabi suba or state] had grown too strong to ignore . . . When Sant Fateh Singh the leader of Akali Dal served notice of his fast unto death for a Punjabi suba, I reached the conclusion that only a linguistic reorganisation would solve the Punjab problem.' She did so in spite of her stated belief that the Akali Dal was the 'party of militant Sikh nationalism'.

She was Nehru's daughter but, lacking her father's stature or his far-sighted vision, was unable to articulate a resolute counterargument to aggressive statehood demands. Twenty years after Indira conceded the Punjabi suba, Indira's friend and Britain's prime minister Margaret Thatcher would remain unmoved as Irish republican hunger strikers such as Bobby Sands died in prison, amid agitations for an independent Ireland. But in the 1960s Indira Gandhi was no Thatcher-like iron lady.

Punjab was created in 1966. Within months Haryana was created and parts of the old Punjab state were merged with Himachal Pradesh. Chandigarh became a Union Territory and the capital of both Haryana and Punjab. The Akali Dal, however, was unable to establish political dominance in the state for which it had agitated for so long. They had managed to form coalition governments with the Jana Sangh in 1967 and 1969 but the marriages of convenience did not last. In the 1972 elections, as part of the Indira wave, the Congress routed the Akalis and Chief Minister Zail Singh tried to take away the Akali emotional plank of Sikh identity by ostentatiously pandering to Sikh sentiment in an attempt to snatch away the Akalis' emotive appeal. Indira Gandhi achieved her first objective of marginalizing the Akalis in the short term. But by allowing the entry of religion-based politics into public life through Zail Singh's methods, she encouraged a pattern that the Akalis then aggressively took forward. Politics in Punjab, already steeped in religion, would become further entangled with religious identity.

Misgovernance coupled with identity politics only opens a Pandora's box of ever-more extreme sectional demands. Playing competitive identity games with Zail Singh, the Akalis now pushed for an even more aggressive separatist campaign: the war cry of Khalistan. In the 1973 Anandpur Sahib Resolution, the Akalis demanded an area in India where the Union government's role would be limited to defence, foreign affairs, currency and communication and 'where the Khalsa can be pre-eminent', as the Sikh religion 'was not safe without sovereignty'.[23] The resolution demanded sole possession of the capital Chandigarh and control of the Ravi–Beas river waters. The resolution would be ignored while the Akalis hoped to gain power in Punjab. But it would be taken up as the pennant of war in 1980 when the Akali government was dismissed by Indira Gandhi.

In the 1977 post-Emergency elections in Punjab the Akalis won a comfortable majority and it looked as if political power may take the bite out of secessionist demands. But their rule was short-lived as the Akali government found itself out of power in 1980 when Indira Gandhi returned to being India's prime minister. She dismissed the Akalis and in fresh elections the Congress won.[24] Frustrated and bitter at their interrupted term, which they had expected would run until 1982, the Akalis became determined to pursue 'holy war'.

The Akalis had bounced back to power in 1977, with Parkash Singh Badal as chief minister, not only drawing on their religious base, but also aided by the abuses of the Emergency which helped consolidate anti-Congress votes in Punjab. Led by the Akali Dal, Sikhs had been in the vanguard of Emergency protests, and as many as 40,000 Sikhs were arrested during the crackdowns, accounting for one-third of all the Emergency arrests.[25]

In 1977, when the Akalis defeated the Congress, the reckless Sanjay Gandhi and the irresponsible Zail Singh tried to outdo the Akalis in playing Sikh identity politics. In their efforts to outwit the Akali Dal and deprive them of their Khalistan firepower, they searched for a rival Sikh identity warrior.

They found one in a tall, bearded, popular preacher in his thirties: Jarnail Singh Bhindranwale. He was, at this time, calling for Sikhs to return to the path of the Khalsa and shun drugs and alcohol that he believed were ravaging the Sikh way of life. Sanjay and Zail Singh plotted to create in Bhindranwale a counter to the Akalis, an even more passionate advocate of the Sikh cause who would split the Akalis and yet stay loyal to the Congress. That was their hope when they backed his candidates in the 1978 SGPC elections.

In April 1978, the Sikh sense of victimhood became further inflamed when clashes between Nirankaris, a reformist faction of Sikhism, and traditional Sikhs in Amritsar led to deaths on both sides. The acquittal of the main accused among the Nirankaris, on the grounds of self-defence, led to the widespread perception that the murderers of the Sikhs had not been brought to justice. When the head of the Nirankari sect, Baba Gurbachan Singh, was killed in Delhi in April 1980, Bhindranwale, reportedly the mastermind, became a hero in rural Punjab and was seen as the avenger of the Sikhs. It was thus a flawed Sikh hero that the Congress sought to co-opt and protect, clinging to the hope that he would help them divide and weaken the Akalis.

'Indira Gandhi had been long annoyed with the Akalis,' says Mark Tully. 'They had been vocal in their resistance to her during the Emergency. The truth was, she simply did not want any opposition party to gain strength in any state.' Through Bhindranwale, she thought she could tame the Akalis. Tully and fellow BBC journalist Satish Jacob show how Zail Singh even encouraged the establishment of the Dal Khalsa as a potential rival to the Akalis, the outfit which would later go on to become a spearhead of the militant demand for Khalistan.[26]

Bhindranwale was a 'bhayanak [fearsome] man' and encouraging him was a fatal misjudgement. Indira Gandhi failed to see Bhindranwale for what he was, a violent extremist who cared for nothing and no one but his own lust for power and the triumph of his mission of wresting a separate homeland for the Sikhs through armed conflict. He was a fundamentalist who was only playing a cat-and-mouse game with the Congress and soon became a force – hero and villain, messiah and nemesis – that no one from Delhi could control.

Indira Gandhi once showed Dr Mathur a limerick quoted in a newspaper with reference to herself: 'There was a young lady of Riga / who smiled as she rode on a tiger / they came from the ride / with the lady inside / and a smile on the face of the tiger.' Her actions in

Punjab were an apt illustration of the first instance in Indian politics when politicians who hoped to ride the 'identity' tiger only ended up being consumed by it.

By the 1980s a weak Indira was dwarfed by the looming spectre of fundamentalism in Punjab. Crises from the anti-foreigner movement in Assam to the killings of Tamils in Sri Lanka assailed her.[27] She was still grieving over Sanjay's death and the worsening relations with Maneka. Normally so insightful about people, she did not deploy her 'sixth sense' as she had done so often in the past.

In 1981 the Akali Dal, deeply bitter at being ousted from power, presented a list of forty-five demands, including on sharing of river waters and Chandigarh, and launched a 'virulent campaign'. In November 1982 the Akali leader Harchand Singh Longowal, in a new interpretation of the Anandpur Sahib Resolution, demanded a Sikh religious state. The slogan 'Raj karega Khalsa', the Khalsa will rule, was raised, although it was not clear yet whether the demand was for a separate Sikh state or autonomy within the Indian Union. Indira Gandhi attempted to negotiate, holding three rounds of talks, in October 1981, November 1981 and April 1982,[28] but each time the talks failed and extremists launched fresh rounds of agitations, until the Akalis surrendered leadership of the movement to the radicals.

Bhindranwale had actively campaigned for the Congress in the 1980 elections, but by 1981 the lethal weapon turned on his mentors, and unveiled his own independent and murderous agenda. On 9 September 1981 Lala Jagat Narain, owner of the Hind Samachar group, founder of *Punjab Kesari*, a Hindi daily, an outspoken critic of Bhindranwale and staunch opponent of Khalistan, was assassinated in a first show of the militant preacher's hand. Bhindranwale was arrested and then, on direct orders from the central government, in a move described as a 'Himalayan blunder', released. Punjab Chief Minister Darbara Singh told Inder Malhotra that Home Minister Zail Singh was 'still protecting Bhindranwale'. The lanky zealot acquired nationwide fame and travelled to Delhi and Bombay with hordes of supporters to show his support among Sikhs outside Punjab.

That he was allowed to move around so freely revealed how badly the centre misjudged him.

A deliberate campaign of provocation of Hindus in Punjab was started. Cows were killed and severed, bleeding cows' heads were hurled into temples. Hindu anger was matched by Sikh resentment. During the 1982 Asian Games many innocent Sikhs, travelling to see the Games, were humiliatingly searched and frisked, adding to the Sikh sense of grievance. The harassment of innocent, sports-loving Sikhs during the Asian Games led to widespread humiliation and a spreading acceptability for Bhindranwale's cause among urban middle-class Sikhs.

Indira was once again accused in 1981–82 of playing the Hindu card, of deliberately allowing the Punjab crisis to worsen to consolidate Hindu support behind the Congress, not just in Punjab but across the Hindi heartland. In fact, by the middle of 1982, the CPI general secretary C. Rajeshwara Rao publicly accused her of becoming a 'Hindu communalist'. 'Mrs Gandhi was attempting to consolidate the Hindu vote behind her for the next elections,' says Guha. 'This explains not only her visits to shrines and sadhus, but it also played into the decision to storm the Golden Temple. Bhindranwale had polarized Sikhs against Hindus, and Mrs Gandhi was taking him on at this game, albeit with an all India agenda. He would polarize Sikhs against Hindus to win Khalistan, she would polarize Hindus against Sikhs to win India.' 'Her handling of the Punjab crisis was shockingly inept,' pointed out Inder Malhotra.

By 1982 Bhindranwale had gathered a network of supporters spread across Canada, the United States and the United Kingdom. A steady flow of money and arms sponsored by these overseas supporters wound its way towards him. In 1982 he and his supporters moved into the Golden Temple. The strapping Sikh evangelist with the flowing beard and intense eyes, surrounded by heavily armed supporters, became a national and international media celebrity and started to give press interviews galore.

Waves of violence and killing began to rock Punjab. Gangs were sent out from the Golden Temple to loot, burn and kill. Bands of motorcycle-borne youths shot down Hindus and Sikhs like 'quails and partridges in open season'. Occupied with their own rivalries, the Akali leadership allowed Bhindranwale a free run, declaring that he was the 'danda [stick] with which to beat the government'.[29] Indira's negotiations with the Akalis carried on. The Akali leaders demanded the capital Chandigarh and insisted that all river waters for Rajasthan be stopped.

In 1982, an agreement with the Akalis was reached on Chandigarh and river waters but at the last minute Indira backed off. From his holy fortress in the Golden Temple, Bhindranwale rained curses on Indira Gandhi, calling her a 'pandit's daughter' and 'a Brahmin woman' for not giving Sikhs their rightful due.

On 25 April 1983, Avtar Singh Atwal, a devout Sikh openly critical of the Khalistan demand and a respected senior police officer, visited the Golden Temple to pray. As he emerged, he was brutally gunned down at the temple entrance. Atwal's killing shocked the entire state and appalled even believing Sikhs, infuriated that the sanctity of the Golden Temple was so badly violated. 'Atwal's killing was a turning point. From the moment Atwal was killed, [Indira] knew the situation was out of control and she would have to act,' says Tully. 'But she delayed for a year. When action should have been taken she didn't. She continued talks, messed around, she didn't seem to know what to do.'

Bomb blasts, killings and murders became almost everyday occurrences in Punjab. In a macabre discovery, drains at the Golden Temple were found crammed with mutilated dead bodies. Darbara Singh, then the Congress's Punjab chief minister, suggested a police raid on the Golden Temple to arrest Bhindranwale and his men but Indira Gandhi ignored this on the advice of Zail Singh, who by then was president and had his own rivalry with Darbara Singh. Stung by the 1983 election setbacks, petty electoral calculations to muster Hindu support ahead of the 1985 elections even in this hour of grave crisis intruded into Indira Gandhi's thinking.

In October 1983, in an incident that outraged the country, Hindu passengers on an Amritsar–Delhi bus were dragged out and killed. Indira Gandhi dismissed the Darbara Singh government but lawlessness only increased. The removal of Darbara Singh once again showed her disregard of regional leaders – in this case a local Sikh face – during a crisis. Through March and April 1984, Bhindranwale's terrorist gangs killed as many as eighty.[30] A military confrontation with Bhindranwale now became inevitable, some accounts saying that the decision for Operation Blue Star – an army operation in the Golden Temple against Bhindranwale's forces – was taken as early as January 1984 when Indira rose in Parliament accusing Pakistan of aiding Sikh militants in Punjab.

'She had grown up in the colonial era when the nation was an amorphous entity. There could be no compromise on the unity of India. That's why she finally agreed to Operation Blue Star,' says Wajahat Habibullah. But was Indira Gandhi thinking as sharply as she did in the 1970s? The departure of Maneka and Varun had severed a link with her dead son, and her soul howled in Lear-like agony. First Sanjay's then Feroze Varun's absence from her house filled her with an anguish that she was only barely able to hide. Nursing an inner wound, at the mercy of advisers – among them, her surviving son – her resilient calm deserted her and she lashed out impatiently towards a final solution. A younger, stronger Indira may have opted for the waiting game, playing on the nerves of terrorists, holding on till the army had complete intelligence on the capacity of the guerrillas in the shrine, may perhaps even have chosen to act earlier, immediately after the killing of Atwal when the sympathy factor would have been very high. But it was a bereft grandmother, sole embattled leader of a party which by now had been hit by severe electoral defeats in state elections, who first delayed and then gave orders for a military strike against the nation's own citizens in their holiest place of prayer. 'Throughout 1983, she was under a lot of pressure to do something, political leaders would say kuch kijiye [do something],' says Habibullah, 'but right until the end she was in two minds.' Lieutenant-General S.K. Sinha, in line to be army chief, had counselled against army action in the Golden Temple. In a decision that was widely criticized, he was superseded by General Arun Shridhar Vaidya, showing that the prime minister had made up her mind on an armed confrontation.

Under pressure from Bhindranwale, Harchand Singh Longowal announced that by 3 June – the martyrdom anniversary of Guru Arjan Dev, the fifth Sikh Guru, who built the Golden Temple – no grain would be allowed to leave Punjab and electricity lines would be cut. This meant north India would be paralysed, deprived of wheat and power supply.

On 2 June Indira Gandhi made a broadcast to the nation in her characteristic tough, no-nonsense style: '[I will not allow] violence and terrorism in the settlement of issues. Those who indulge in anti-social and anti-national activities should make no mistake about this.'[31] She went on to make an appeal for harmony, desperately trying to inject a tone of normalcy into what was by now a perilous situation. 'A systematic campaign is spreading bitterness and hatred between Hindus and Sikhs . . . This is not the time for anger. Too much blood has been shed . . . Don't shed blood, shed hatred.'

Orders had already been given for Operation Blue Star. The tide of blood from Amritsar would course its way to the prime minister's home and break over her head in a wave of gory retribution.

~

The night of 5 June 1984 was moonlit. At exactly 10.30 p.m. soldiers of the 9th Infantry Division, under the command of Major General Kuldip Singh Brar, a clean-shaven Sikh, entered the Golden Temple. Ahead of them the white marble of the temple's parikrama (walkway) gleamed stark and quiet. First went the commandos, moving swiftly and silently, clad in black dungarees, each a sharpshooter. Other army units, among them 26 Madras, 9 Garhwal, 10 Guards, followed. 'We had to complete the operation overnight, because we knew that at dawn hundreds and thousands of armed villagers would converge on the shrine once they heard the army had entered,' says Brar, the last surviving member of the army leadership of Blue Star.[32] Two days earlier, all foreign journalists had been ordered out of Punjab, all transport in and out of the state had been blocked, villages had been evacuated and telephone lines cut. Mark Tully recalls leaving Punjab and seeing, while driving down the GT Road, deserted villages on either side, with no traffic and not a soul in sight. 'There was total chup [silence] everywhere.' On the afternoon of 5 June the army sent out requests on loudspeakers that pilgrims be allowed to exit as their lives could be in danger. 'But Bhindranwale and his lieutenants did not let most of them come out,' recounts Brar.[33] None of the extremists came out but 126 pilgrims did manage to exit the temple.

On the night of 5 June, the army was under strict instructions to use 'minimum force' and not to fire at the Harmandir Sahib. But as soon as the army entered the Golden Temple, gunfire rained down. The troops were caught off guard by a fierce counter-attack. 'We encountered extreme opposition,' says Brar.[34] 'The entire temple was a fortress. We found weapons with Chinese and Pakistani markings, we found Pakistani passports. The methods they used were brutal, ones which no human being or sane person would use.' There were bunkers and gun emplacements in windows, doors and rooftops. 'The intelligence we had received led us to believe the resistance would be much less than it was,' says Brar.

Brar tells a moving story about the army's entry. 'I can never forget the early morning prior to the launch of the operation. I went from one battalion to the next and to each I said, "If there is anyone among you who doesn't want to go in for religious reasons please stand up and step aside. No action will be taken against you." Not one soldier stood up except one Sikh officer. I assured him that no action will be taken against him, but instead he said, "Sir, I want to be the first to enter the temple and get to the Akal Takht."[35] I was so proud of his spirit. I told his commanding officer, Col. Israr Khan, that this officer, Captain Raina, and his platoon should be tasked to be the spearhead during the entry.' And so it was that Captain[36] Jasbir Singh Raina, a Sikh, led the army into the Golden Temple. On his entry Raina was met with a massive volley of bullets which instantly destroyed both his legs. Brar ordered his immediate evacuation. But Captain Raina refused to retreat. Instead he kept advancing, crawling on lacerated legs towards Bhindranwale's command post, determined to liberate his holy shrine from terrorists. Captain Raina was finally forcibly lifted and taken to hospital and had to have both legs amputated. He was later awarded the Ashok Chakra for bravery of the highest order. 'I get tears in my eyes when I think of this young boy standing up to say, "I want to be the first to enter,"' says Brar.

As soldiers crept along the temple paths, they came under brutally heavy fire. Machine guns cut them down when they attempted to crawl. Casualties mounted immediately. The soldiers, many of them barefoot as a mark of respect for the shrine, were sitting ducks for Bhindranwale's do-or-die force. The Akal Takht was impregnable, ringed around with machine guns, making it impossible for soldiers to enter. At one point it even looked as if the Indian army would have to retreat. 'The quantity of weapons and ammunition with the militants was huge,' recalls Brar. 'And they were fighting like lions.'

Desperate at the loss of life, taken by surprise by the formidable enemy, General K. Sundarji, then head of the army's Western Command who planned and coordinated the operation, frantically made a direct personal call to Indira Gandhi. 'Very few know about Sundarji's panicked phone call,' says Habibullah, 'but he told Mrs Gandhi that unless armoured vehicles were brought into the temple the Indian army would have to retreat. And that would have terrifying consequences for the country and would also dishonour the army. Indira Gandhi had no choice but to agree to tanks entering the Golden Temple, something she had expressly forbidden,' Habibullah recalls. So, on the early morning of 6 June, Vijayanta tanks rolled in and took aim at the Akal Takht. After twenty-four hours of fighting, the Golden Temple was declared 'cleansed'. Indira's first reaction when she was told that the operation had been a 'success' was: 'Oh my God, they told me there would be no casualties.'

Operation Blue Star was criticized as being typical of Sundarji's flamboyant, rushing-in-where-angels-fear-to-tread approach, an operation launched in a hurry with not enough intelligence preparedness.[37] It has been argued that a police, paramilitary and commando action would possibly have done far less damage than a military one, as Operation Black Thunder, a smaller commando operation against Sikh terrorists sheltering in the Golden Temple, was to prove two years later.

'Sundarji refused to take the help of the civilian administration in Punjab. He concentrated all power to himself,' says Habibullah. However, Brar steadfastly defends Sundarji and maintains that there was no alternative to army action. 'General Sundarji was a highly experienced strategist with a sharp mind and exemplary professional acumen,' says Brar. He believes the operation was beyond the capability of the police which had washed their hands of the situation, leaving the army to go it alone without sharing any information with them. 'The police knew exactly what was going on, they knew arms were being brought into the temple in kar seva trucks, but they did nothing,' says Brar.[38] 'The police was defunct in Punjab.'

The reason why the army faced such a severe challenge from the militants in the Golden Temple is that Bhindranwale's forces were organized by the military brain of Major General Shabeg Singh, a former officer of the Indian army who had been a hero during the Bangladesh war. Piquantly, he had been Brar's instructor during training at the Indian Military Academy, and they had fought in the 1971 war together.[39] Court-martialled on corruption charges before he was due to retire, an embittered Shabeg Singh had joined Bhindranwale and become the commander of his militia.

'Shabeg Singh was a very clever general,' points out Tully. 'So when the army entered the Golden Temple, they found a full-scale military defence awaiting them.' Tully says the BBC had even filmed the way Shabeg's fighters had sandbagged and fortified the temple complex.

Militants made clever use of underground tunnels. Manholes were converted into gun positions, from which terrorists emerged to lob grenades or fire machine guns. 'One of the great mysteries of the operation,' says Tully, 'was how did the army fall into the trap of General Shabeg Singh? When we as journalists had gathered so much information, how did the army walk into the trap?' 'There was no question of being led into a trap,' counters Brar. 'Yes, we didn't expect the type of resistance that we encountered. We would have liked more time. But there were reasons why the operation had to be carried out quickly because there were fears that Bhindranwale was on the verge of declaring "Khalistan". If Khalistan had been declared, if Pakistan had recognized it, if they had come across the border, the army feared India would go the Bangladesh way.'[40]

It took ferociously heavy fighting for the army to gain control of the temple. By the time the operation was over the Akal Takht was in ruins and 300 bullet holes had been blasted into the Harmandir Sahib. Bhindranwale was killed. Shabeg Singh's body was discovered still clutching his weapons.[41] Operation Blue Star was an act of horrendous sacrilege and created rage and revulsion among Sikhs, just as an armed invasion of Mecca or a gun battle in the Tirupati temple would do among Muslims and Hindus. Khushwant Singh returned his Padma Bhushan, a reflection of the anger the operation created even among moderate Sikhs. In an absurd blunder, Operation Blue Star's launch coincided with the martyrdom anniversary of Guru Arjan Dev and the temple was crowded with pilgrims. Along with the hundreds of troops and commandos killed, well over a thousand pilgrims died, according to unofficial estimates. But the fountain of militancy was only temporarily quenched. The riots and killings of Sikhs after Indira's death would fuel another decade of insurgency in Punjab and the anger still hasn't died. General Vaidya paid for Operation Blue Star with his life. He was killed by Sikh militants in 1986 in Pune, shot in the head while driving his car by a motorcycle-borne shooter. Three decades later, Brar still remains a marked man, recently surviving being knifed in the throat in London by Khalistan activists.

Indira's old Oxford friend and journalist Nikhil Chakravartty was to say that Operation Blue Star was a testimony to Indira's courage and commitment to India's unity. But Operation Blue Star turned out to be a monumental mistake, a disaster. The battle at the Golden Temple stoked fury among Sikhs. Sikh soldiers mutinied in several regiments and many were later court-martialled. In some army posts, peace was maintained by indomitable Gurkha forces holding their mutinous Sikh brothers in custody at gunpoint. At the Binnaguri Cantonment in Jalpaiguri district, district officers saw poker-faced Gurkhas standing in a circle pointing their guns at Sikh brother soldiers who huddled in a group in the middle. Operation Woodrose would soon begin in Punjab with thousands of Sikh youth detained, interrogated and tortured.

Indira Gandhi's first visit out of Delhi after Operation Blue Star was to Ladakh to rally the Sikh forces there. Habibullah accompanied her on the trip. 'She told the soldiers that she was like their mother,' Habibullah recalls, 'that she felt their pain, but sometimes some things had to be done for the security of the country.' But it was too late. Her words of explanation went in vain. On a trip to London that year Habibullah's mother, Hamida Habibullah, noticed posters all over the Sikh quarter in Southall calling for death to Indira Gandhi. She was now on death row but remained typically blasé and no-nonsense. A few weeks before her assassination, she told the BBC: 'I've lived with danger all my life and I think I've had a pretty full life. It makes no difference whether you die in bed or die standing up.'

~

'Indira Gandhi did not want to send in the army into the Golden Temple,' reveals R.K. Dhawan. 'Operation Blue Star was forced on her by the then army chief, A.S. Vaidya. Arun Singh [Rajiv Gandhi's Doon School and Cambridge classmate and adviser who would become minister of state for defence in Rajiv's government] and Arun Nehru also pushed for it. They were the ones who kept using language like we should finish the buggers off once and for all. They assured her that no damage would be done to the Akal Takht. In fact, she gave the orders only on condition that the Akal Takht was not to be touched. When she saw a video of the damage that had been done she was very upset, upset beyond words.'

Habibullah agrees. Indira was 'dragged into Blue Star by the self-promoting General Sundarji', he says. Inderjit Badhwar and Dilip Bobb write in *India Today* that General Sundarji had told Indira Gandhi that the operation would be completed in a day. 'Her strict instructions were flouted,' says Natwar Singh. Echoing the words of R.K. Dhawan, he adds, 'She said the Golden Temple was not to be touched. All these gung-hos like Sundarji were responsible for what happened. She herself was stunned when she heard about the extent of what they had done.'

'I don't think the decision was forced on her,' says Tully. 'The army had given her two alternatives. One was Operation Blue Star, which the army favoured, and the other was starving or gheraoing the Golden Temple and cutting off its water, electricity and food supply. With the second alternative, the army feared the Sikh peasantry would march on the forces for starving the Golden Temple and the army would be hemmed in between Bhindranwale on one side and the *sardar log* [Sikh people] on the other. But it's true that she was misled by the army into believing it would be a quick and surgical operation,' says Tully.

~

Wrong-footed and blundering in Punjab, an agitated Indira acted impetuously in Kashmir, striking out blindly to impose Pax Indira when the situation there demanded caution and reconciliation. On 2 July 1984, a month after Operation Blue Star, Indira Gandhi dramatically threw out Farooq Abdullah from the chief ministership of Jammu and Kashmir. Farooq had rubbed her the wrong way. After becoming chief minister, he had attended an Opposition conclave at Vijayawada in Andhra Pradesh hosted by N.T. Rama Rao in May 1983. Farooq had also hosted another Opposition conclave in Srinagar in October, with N.T. Rama Rao and West Bengal Chief Minister Jyoti Basu and others present. The Opposition was trying to forge an anti-Indira coalition for the forthcoming polls of 1985. 'The only way to defeat Mrs Gandhi,' said NTR, 'is by confronting her in each contest on a one to one basis. Otherwise we doom ourselves . . . In 36 years of independent history, we've never had an Opposition. We've simply been the non-Nehru, non-Gandhi forces, quarrelling among ourselves.'[42] These words intriguingly echo the predicament of India's present opposition, which is pinning its hopes on a grand coalition against a dominant ruling party. With polls due in 1985, an anti-Indira alliance was taking shape, once again relying on poll arithmetic rather than any properly articulated charter of alternative ideas.

In an effort to demonstrate his autonomy, Farooq had not only met Indira's opponents like N.T Rama Rao, he had also met the Akali leaders in 1982 in Punjab and even met Bhindranwale in the Golden Temple. Such defiance made Indira Gandhi deeply uncomfortable about Farooq. B.K. Nehru, then governor of Jammu and Kashmir, believes Indira had a personal vendetta against Farooq because, at an election rally in Iqbal Park in Srinagar, people in the crowd lifted their phirans and exposed their private parts to Indira. She flew into a rage, her face red with anger, and blamed Farooq for the incident. The process of dismissing Farooq involved a serious face-off with B.K. Nehru, who flatly refused to dismiss an elected government. For his pains Nehru would be summarily removed as governor and sent to Gujarat. 'In my talks with her she did not really have any logical answer to my objections. All she wanted was that Farooq should be out . . . she never explained what the urgency was,' writes Nehru. Not only was Indira in a hurry to remove Farooq, she was equally impatient to transfer Nehru. 'My refusal to be hustled caused even greater annoyance to Indira Gandhi,' and while Indira's government tried to turn him out from Srinagar almost overnight, Nehru refused to go in a hurry, saying he wasn't a 'bloody chaprasi'. Jagmohan, whom Nehru describes as a 'faithful servant of 1, Safdarjung Road', would replace him and on 2 July 1984 Farooq would be sent packing. Just two months later, in another brazen demonstration of Pax Indira, Andhra Pradesh governor Ram Lal dismissed Andhra Pradesh Chief Minister N.T. Rama Rao on 16 August 1984, resulting in a national uproar about a return of the dictatorship. Once again newspapers ran headlines like 'Rape of Democracy'. 'Like the warrior Goddess Kali, she set out to smite all centres of Opposition power, from Punjab, to Kashmir, to Andhra Pradesh,' wrote *The Economist*.[43]

However hostile she had become to Farooq, the Abdullahs and Nehrus had been old family friends, despite the political differences that often separated them. Farooq was a boyhood friend of Rajiv's and even called Indira 'Mummy'. Indira originally wanted to have an alliance with the National Conference for the 1983 elections but Farooq rejected this, much to the outrage of Kashmiri Congressmen such as Mufti Mohammad Sayeed as well as Rajiv's adviser Arun Nehru. 'Farooq even invited Rajiv for dinner at Kashmir House to discuss a possible alliance and then didn't even show up for the dinner!' Habibullah recalls. Indira Gandhi had never quite trusted Farooq and once asked Habibullah, 'Is there a genetic defect in the Sheikh Abdullah family? One brother is mad, and Farooq seems quite mad too.'[44]

Clearly Farooq's attendance at the Opposition conclave, where he had directly spoken against Indira, was enough to seal his fate. The mercurial Jammu and Kashmir leader was not a chief minister Indira Gandhi could easily stomach. 'How am I to deal with Farooq?' she asked Habibullah. 'He has discussions with me, tells me he will do this and that and then goes and does the complete opposite.' According to Habibullah, Indira dismissed Farooq right after Operation Blue Star because the security of India was her uppermost concern. 'I don't approve of what she did in toppling Farooq but we have to understand that it happened a month after

Blue Star when her fears about the unity of India were very high,' he says. 'If Indira hadn't done what she did, we may well have had a Khalistan, an independent Tamil Nadu, or a separate state of Assam. All the things that were regarded as her failings in fact made India strong and ensured its survival.'

Amid the darkness in India in 1984, the only hope seemed to come from the distant stars. Death and conflict took a back seat when, in April 1984, Squadron Leader Rakesh Sharma became the first Indian in space. Aboard the Soviet Salyut 7 orbital station, the Soviet–Indian crew held a press conference. When Indira Gandhi asked Rakesh Sharma, 'Upar se Bharat kaisa dikhta hai aapko [How does India look from up there]?' his response, 'Saare jahan se achcha [The best in the world],' pulled the heartstrings of every Indian. The sight of the beaming, maternally proud prime minister on earth talking via satellite to a handsome young Indian cosmonaut in space created a momentary whoop of delight and starry dreams of greatness coursed through the strife-torn land. Yet the beautiful calm Sharma saw was deceptive. In those troubled days the beauty of India seemed visible only from outer space. That exhilarating space flight would not be needed to deliver votes for the Congress in the coming polls. Another much uglier event would carry the Congress to victory. The harsh truth was that the Indira Gandhi model of politics was nearing the end of its shelf life: the more she sought to dominate, the more things spiralled out of control. When she gave the order for Operation Blue Star, it was almost as if she was admitting she was no longer equal to the challenges of a violent new India.

~

Indira had cut her political teeth in the age of Nehru, when the Congress was the near-invincible dominant force, a legacy of its role in the freedom struggle. But by the late 1960s, when she became prime minister, Congress hegemony was slowly unravelling as the 1967 election showed. Indira's response to this was a leftward lurch and the drive to populism to capture the greatest possible numbers. The growing demand for representation across the board paradoxically led not to an opening up of the Congress system or the democratization of the party but instead to a clamping down of a centralizing system.[45] It has been argued that the urge to centralization existed in Nehru's time when the Planning Commission and a planned economy had created a dominance of the centre vis-à-vis the states. Since the centre and states all had Congress governments, federal aspirations were worked out 'informally' within the Congress system as opposed to being institutionalized between governments.[46]

Indira Gandhi's preferred mode was riding roughshod over regional politicians, and as non-Congress heavyweights like NTR and MGR entered the scene, Nehru's 'informal federalism' by which centre–state relations were worked out within the Congress fold began to crack. In the 1980s, caste, religious and regional movements were reaching a fever pitch. But the Congress clung to the delusion of one-party rule like an ageing, delusional monarch, calling unruly subjects to order in vain. It was only because of the historical accident of her assassination that Indira Gandhi left behind a parting gift of over 400 seats to her party in the preponed general elections of December 1984. Without the bloodstained benefaction of the great sympathy wave, the general elections in the normal course due in 1985 may well have seen the Congress limping towards the position of a single largest party, largely on the strength of the vestiges of Indira's fraying personality cult. By now its party structures, regional stalwarts, inner-party debate and dissent had all but disappeared and its only hope would have been the disarray in the Opposition and the TINA factor. After Indira's death, a semblance of a will was discovered among her papers, in which she had written: 'If I die a violent death as some fear and a few are plotting, I know the violence will be in the thought and the action of the assassin, not in my dying . . . for no hate is dark enough to overshadow the extent of my love for my people.' Like Othello, she had loved too well if not wisely; she had sought to gather an entire country under the pallu of her khadi sari in an act of confident matriarchy, believing that 'a country is an extended family'. But in the end that all-encompassing sari was shredded because she smothered her 'family' with an excess of controlling 'love'.

~

Dear Mrs Gandhi,

If you had not been assassinated, would you have declared a second Emergency and again postponed the general elections of 1985? It seemed as if you had not learnt any lessons from the Emergency, and Pax Indira was to the fore yet again. You still did not recognize the damage you were doing when you dismissed the Farooq Abdullah government, dismissed the NTR government and built up a zealot like Bhindranwale. You were pushed to the wall by Bhindranwale's war and the violence in Assam. Hindu groups were setting the stage for the demolition of the Babri Masjid a decade later. You were far too weakened by now to mount a bold new counter-narrative of unity by reinventing federalism and allowing space for the new regional chieftains. The situation once again called for a grand reconciliation but as we have seen in the run-up to the 1975 declaration of Emergency, you were no reconciler. With the manner in which crises were spiralling out of your control, would you once again have been tempted to take away citizens' rights? Was your politics in general based on a regular negation of democracy? You said, 'Personally, I would like to die like Gandhiji – suddenly, not after a prolonged illness – for I know how my father suffered during his life-and-death struggle.' You did die like the Mahatma, in a death that conferred on you a heroic mien. It was an end that sublimated your life to a realm far higher than the petty intrigues that occupied you in your last years.

~

8

The Woman: Seeking the Real Indira Gandhi

'Life has given of its fullness to me, in happiness and in pain. How can one know one without the other?'

~

Dear Mrs Gandhi,

Is the quest to find the 'real' Indira Gandhi futile? You were a collection of contradictions, one dominant motivation balanced by an opposite one. You evoked hate and love, you alienated and you charmed, you frustrated some and delighted others.[1] You regularly interacted with intellectuals and thinkers, yet were unable to give India a new intellectual direction. You thought of yourself as an agent of transformation yet remained firmly wedded to the status quo of your father's legacy. You claimed India as your family yet brought your own family to the centre of politics. You imposed the Emergency and you also revoked it. You stripped the hereditary princes of their privileges but instituted the principle of hereditary privilege in a democracy. You went to war to uphold democracy in Bangladesh yet you snatched away democracy from

India. You claimed not to be a feminist yet created a template of a modern Indian woman for scores to emulate. You loved beauty and encouraged traditional arts yet created a persisting ugliness in politics. You refused to dismiss your Sikh bodyguards after Operation Blue Star showing how hard you clung to the idea of secular India, but that idea went up in flames in the riots after your death. You would describe yourself as an 'ordinary person except for the accident of my birth' but you were an extraordinary woman who left a diverse legacy.

Could you have foreseen, for example, that your championing of Indian handicrafts would grow into a fashionable revival of Indian crafts? As prime minister, you regarded Indian arts and design as outward manifestations of the struggle for national renewal and identity. You promoted saris, crafts, new design concepts combining east and west, encouraged the Festivals of India abroad, built on the handicraft and handloom movements pioneered in the 1950s by Kamaladevi Chattopadhyay and others. You encouraged initiatives to bring age-old arts into new conceptions of a modern Indian aesthetic identity.

Your romance with the preservation of Indian wisdom and the Indian genius extended into the natural world as well. Your concerns for protection of the environment, encouragement of animal sanctuaries and wildlife conservation were part of your robust defence of the entire spectrum of India's inheritance, the source of her 'soul-force' and distinctiveness in the world.

What did you leave behind for India's women? Did you strongly deny being a feminist because you feared being trapped in a peripheral ladies' compartment when your ambitions were decidedly mainstream? You left a model of modern womanly achievement that inspired thousands, many imbibed your example perhaps without even being aware that they were doing so. The Idea of Indira shapes modern women in India to date. You said, 'Mahatma Gandhi was the first person who thought of women as political beings,' and you were the first woman to show a national and international audience what an Indian woman could achieve and how proudly and formidably she could hold her head up among accomplished, experienced men, both at home and abroad. The short-haired, sari-clad, publicly active woman whose glimpses we see today in so many teachers, scientists, doctors, social workers and politicians draw some inspiration from the idea of Indira. Violent oppressions on women remain widespread, but the patchy freedom that an active woman enjoys, the fact that she is, in certain enclaves of Indian society at least, accepted as a dignified professional is in no small part due to the symbol you continue to be.

The idea of Indira gave Indian women a sense of pride. In an unequal society where you were both the victim and vanquisher of powerful phallocrats, you continue to be, in village and small town, Shakti who came to life.

You destroyed the Congress party by splitting it in 1969, but awakened democratic energies on an unprecedented scale. You awakened the Indian masses as no other politician had done before yet you became a victim of this same awakening because it ultimately led to a rejection of your politics.[2]

How did you become so very different from your father, breaking almost completely from his politics even as you saw yourself as his staunch defender? You had much refinement and delicacy when it came to managing a household or holding charming receptions and state dinners but where did the sophistication go when it came to the rough politics you played? Was it because you had a secret contempt for all the 'men of small stature' who surrounded you? Did you not consider them worthy of even a modicum of respect? Were you the populist still trapped in an old-fashioned elitism where those outside your charmed circle were to be manipulated and outmanoeuvred but never treated as equal?

You were intensely conscious of family relationships and revelled in your home, sons, daughters-in-law and grandchildren. You would say, 'My life has been so full of excitement and incidents. But I would say that the most wonderful moment was when I held my first child in my arms.' But did you ever stop to think what the role of family should be in politics? Unlike your father were you unable to separate your role as mother from your role as politician and leader? Dynastic succession was ingrained in your thinking. You never questioned dynasty in politics as your father did. In your defence it could be said that you were up against massive odds and did not have the advantages of Nehru's unequalled authority. Perhaps there was no one you could trust outside your own family.

You ruled in fraught, bloodstained times, conflicts rearing up in every corner of India. Did you therefore take joy in the little pleasures of life? Doing the *Times* crossword, dressing playfully in kimonos and Bengali-style saris on holidays, playing with dogs and teaching your grandchildren about plants and flowers? Those were your most carefree moments when the real Indira Gandhi could come out of hiding.

~

'Spirituality means the strengthening of one's inner resources and the stretching of one's range of experience; the ability to accept joy and sorrow with the same equanimity.' Indira Gandhi's words sound like a new-age guru's exhortations on achieving peace in daily life but the truth is she was deeply and instinctively religious. According to Sonia Gandhi, 'From her mother she imbibed a profound spirituality that enabled her to face grief with immense fortitude.'[3] 'Indira Gandhi is seen as someone who was always secular, but she was very attached to religious beliefs,' says Jagdish Shukla, whose father, G.P. Shukla, was part of her office in Raebareli. Shukla recalls that every time she visited Raebareli she made it a point to visit the Baleshwar Mandir as well as the Devi Ka Mandir nearby.[4]

The two-storeyed Congress karyalay in Raebareli is moss-covered and deserted but a little puja room overlooking the courtyard is crowded with colourful deities and sacred depictions. A sandalwood Ganapati sits on a shelf from Indira Gandhi's time. 'She would always do a little puja here,' says Shukla. 'She would light diyas and put flowers at the idol's feet, she knew exactly what to do, what rituals to follow.'

On her last visit to Srinagar, she climbed the holy mountain Shankaracharya to visit the temple at its summit. All through her life she would keep returning to Kashmir, as if drinking in its very air was an escape from grim reality and imparted stability and comfort. On this visit, she visited a Sufi dargah and the temple of Sharika Devi, where her Kashmiri Pandit ancestors had worshipped. She made it a point to visit the sage Lakshmanjoo in his ashram. She gazed on her beloved chinars, disappointed that their leaves had not turned autumnal red. 'My mother-in-law was very deeply religious, but embarrassed about it,' recalled Maneka Gandhi.

Religion was the bull in the china shop of Nehruvian rationalist secularism. Nehru was an agnostic and his daughter had been a student in 1930s England, when radical youth turned fervently to revolutionary socialism. She was the revolutionary whose life's mission had been laid down as one that would build a forward-looking, progressive India. Secularism's soldier could never accept or openly admit how central religious faith and superstition were to her. In 1971 she was admired when she told a television interviewer that she didn't believe in God. When she first took oath as prime minister in 1966 she refused to swear in the name of God. Yet she was also the daughter of Kamala Nehru, who as she battled mortality embraced the Ramakrishna Mission, Anandamayi Ma and in her last days turned to striving for a nun-like purity. For Indira, sharing her mother's faith was an act of love, the filling of a void, a link to the woman she had loved with passion and fierce protectiveness. Kamala Nehru had taken diksha from a swamiji at the Ramakrishna Mission and it was to those swamijis that Indira turned in sorrow after Feroze Gandhi died. She had seen the horrors that religious conflict had wrought, lived through Partition and the assassination of the Mahatma, but in spite of witnessing religion's power to destroy, she was no agnostic like her father.

In the years after her defeat in the elections of 1977 Indira participated in rituals at the Kashi Vishwanath temple in Varanasi. She also visited the Annapurna and Sankatmochan temples there. In Satna district in Madhya Pradesh, she visited the Kamla Nath shrine as well as temples of Rama, Sita, Hanuman and Sati Anusuya. In Satna she also went to the Jankikund pond, which according to mythology was the bathing place of Sita. She made a 'flying pilgrimage' to Vaishno Devi, where she 'covered the 2 kilometre distance from the helipad on foot'.[5] She offered chaddar at the tomb of Khwaja Moinuddin Chisti in Ajmer and 'prayed for the welfare of the country'. She sat 'engrossed in prayer' at the temple town of Ambaji and also 'lay prostrate in pranam for a minute'.[6] As troubles crowded in on her in the 1980s she took to rituals and superstition at home, refusing to let the pregnant Maneka view the solar eclipse and on her birthday performing a puja in front of a lithograph of Rama after Sanjay's death. 'It was astonishing to see the hold orthodox religion had gained on her,' Jayakar recalled.

Hers was not just a personal veering towards faith to seek protection for herself and her family. She wanted to claim the 'wisdom of India' because the words of sages, the teachings of the epics were part of her civilizational inheritance and the distinctive markers of Indian identity. They were also a link to the people. She said: 'The stories of the Ramayana and the Mahabharata have been a kind of open university, quickening our people's sense of right and wrong, and endowing them with examples with whom they can identify and which enlarge their moral sense.'

'PM was religious minded and a traditionalist and always wore the rudraksha beads which Anand Mayi Ma had given her,' writes Dr Mathur. 'She was guided in her yoga exercises by Swami Dhirendra Brahmachari although she didn't like it when he drank milk and then burped loudly.' Visiting the Golden Temple after Operation Blue Star, Indira ordered two dozen caps for her companions so that everyone had the proper headgear and didn't just put handkerchiefs on their heads.

Her puja room at home was a tumult of varied divinities. There was Christ, the Buddha, Ramakrishna Paramahamsa, the Mother of Pondicherry, a conch shell and a brass plate with diyas. India's wisdom and religiosity sprang from a common sacred source and was encapsulated in the arts and crafts she patronized and showcased internationally. She recognized that India's artistic and craft traditions had developed from within the realm of the sacred. She promoted the Festivals of India, a celebration of India's culture, in the west, where inevitably the spiritual moorings of Indian arts were on display at the world's best and most prestigious museums and galleries. So much of the creative exploration of the artisan, the musician and the painter was an exploration of paths towards the divine and she saw the links between the sacred and the aesthetic. Vedic chants were as much art as they were religion, the rescue and preservation of India's genius from the annihilating tread of imperialism was both religious instinct and aesthetic inclination. The arts were her own rediscovery of India, a rediscovery she wanted to share with the world.

'What does one seek from art?' she would ask. 'A few hours of pleasure or an experience which has the seed of timelessness that touches one's innermost self?' She could say about art what she couldn't say openly about religion. Art was heritage and heritage was also religion and hers was the proud defence of a modern nation with an ancient heritage. Intensely religious as she was, not above using religion and religious platforms in political campaigns as in Kashmir and Punjab, Indira Gandhi's religiosity was cultural and ritualistic rather than any spiritual, other-worldly yearning. She turned to religion as a superstitious enabler of good luck in politics. However inspired she may have been by her mother, hers was no Kamala Nehru–type attachment to a pious life. For her, religion was an extension of culture, expressed through art and decorations. On Basant Panchami she would wear yellow saris and instruct her mali to arrange yellow flowers around the house. At Nehru's funeral, she took special care that the most melodious kirtans were sung. In 1948, when she insisted that they move into Teen Murti House very early in the morning, Nehru explained in a letter to Vijayalakshmi Pandit: '[the timing was] a sudden urge of Indu to come at an auspicious moment. A holy gentleman in Uttar Kashi, who apparently takes an interest in my career, sent word about the auspicious moment. Indu felt it would be unwise to challenge fate.'[7] Did she fall short here of the paternal ideals of the scientific temper? Nehru's tone is indulgent yet gently mocking.

Indira's secularism was flawed, not because she didn't believe in it, but because she was unable to reconcile or balance her public and private lives. A private life of religiosity contrasted with a constitutional distancing from religion in public was a balancing act she did not quite pull off. She was unable to reconcile this duality into a personal philosophy on the one hand and the needs of practical governance on the other. She went out of her way to show she embraced all India's faiths, yet used one religion against another as a tactical political ploy without realizing the massive cost this would impose.

Embarrassed about, yet drawn to, religion and not quite clear how to uphold a real secularism except in appointing Muslims to high office, Indira Gandhi consigned the Congress to a future of confused secularism, of alternative uses of the 'Hindu card' and 'Muslim card'. The Congress remains a party that failed to develop a modern blueprint for how a secular state should function in a religious land. She said in an interview, 'religion has an important place in our culture and society. It has no place in our politics . . . our secularism doesn't mean opposition to religion, it means all religions will receive equal recognition. The idea of an established religion or a government authorized by religion is abhorrent.'[8] But a truly secular politician would eschew public displays of religiosity.

Her failure to properly define this duality had resulted in the Congress still struggling to find its way out of the 'secular' cul-de-sac. The party has failed to emerge as a modernizing, progressive force for all religions. She constantly pointed to the dangers of the

RSS, yet dabbled in Hindu politics herself, as we have seen, during the communal riots in the 1980s and in her handling of the crisis in Punjab. This showed a helplessness, a lack of inner conviction against the ideological challenge posed by rising Hindu political mobilization throughout her political life.

~

'She was deeply Indian but she was also more westernized than her father,' says Moni Malhoutra. She was only eight when she navigated her way around the Swiss town of Geneva. She skied in Switzerland, romanced in Paris, spoke fluent French, studied Latin, trudged through London during the Blitz, was schooled in England; one of her closest friends was the American Dorothy Norman; and her relationship with her Italian daughter-in-law was much closer than that with her Indian one. Her diplomacy was centred on a rejection of western bullying, standing up to the great powers, and positioning India at the forefront in the struggle against neo-imperialism. Yet much of her intellectual inspiration was drawn from the western world.

Visiting the opera and theatre in the United States and the United Kingdom was a kind of pilgrimage too. On a visit to Paris in 1981 she made sure to meet architects and thinkers at the George Pompidou centre. On the same trip, she swept into a Paris restaurant, bowed and smiled generously at the other guests and ordered her meal in faultless French. In London during the Festival of India, she watched the newly created production of the opera *Cats*. She attended performances of the New York Philharmonic Orchestra, watched Rudolf Nureyev dance at the Royal Ballet and visited the Metropolitan Opera in New York to listen to Puccini's *La Boheme*. *Doctor Zhivago* and *Black Beauty* were her favourite films.

Style was an integral part of the Indira persona. On a visit to the Soviet Union in 1953 with her father she cut a dashing figure in an expensive mink coat, pulling off a signature combination of fur coat and sari. She loved Madhubani paintings and classic tanchoi saris, celebrated Basant Panchami and Christmas and lived and fashioned her personal culture as rooted in Indian art yet also redolent with the flair of the European sophisticate. As Sethi says, 'her home's interiors were very European, lots of books, Indian handicrafts but western-style minimalist furniture.'

She liked to think of herself as a connoisseur of high culture in food, arts and thought. She took pride in connections and conversations with western thought leaders and she was very interested in keeping up with cultural innovations and new ideas, inviting the architect and thinker Buckminster Fuller to lecture in India, making sure to hold 'meetings with intellectuals' every time she visited cities abroad. 'I have always found my visits to the USA very stimulating. There is so much dynamism there, a lot of new ideas, innovations, in every sphere: architecture, dance, music and so on,' she said.

'She was a young person when the revival of Indian crafts began, but as prime minister she promoted Indian crafts to the world,' says Laila Tyabji, crafts revivalist and founder of Dastakar. 'At a time when houses would be decorated with velvet and chandeliers, her home would always be decorated with beautiful handicrafts.'[9]

Festivals of India abroad were an important legacy of Indira Gandhi; they demonstrated her pride in communicating India's soft power. Showcasing India's arts to the world was her way of ensuring that India's genius was kept alive, reinforced and rejuvenated. She was determined that the beauty created in the subcontinent over generations be displayed to the world as a mighty high tradition not just as native folksy baubles.

Pride in being Indian was the family heirloom, so however much she may have revelled in the music, theatre and cuisine of Europe and America, her personal statement of identity both at home and abroad was the handloom sari. The sari in all its varieties and colours was not just a personal statement of style but a garment of India's history, both political symbol and aesthetic flourish. Since east and west coexisted in her persona with ease, she popularized the modern handloom-wearing look of the short-haired woman, with the elegant bouffant hairstyle, usually no jewellery or accessories except the man's wristwatch and the occasional pair of high-heeled shoes. Fashionable, chic handloom was her preferred look and she was drawn to the vibrant colours of the earth, orange, red, brown and shades of green. It was no-fuss elegance, yet always created an impact. 'I dislike frills, whether in clothes or anywhere else. I am always for the simple line,' she would say. Nayantara Sahgal recalls the two of them exclaiming over fashions in *Vogue* magazine, yet also recalls how severely Indira disliked ostentation and opulence. Her personal style was minimalist and modest but with a firm statement of elite lineage. East and West fused seamlessly at home too. While she sent one daughter-in-law, Maneka, to learn Cordon Bleu cooking from Bhicoo Manekshaw, the other daughter-in-law, Sonia, was instructed to learn Hindustani and referred to as 'bahurani' by household staff.

Hers was no Gandhian rejection of western civilization and she refused to don the metaphorical Indian loincloth or the dress of the poor. She had always scorned the hypocrisies of the Mahatma's devotees: 'I am sick of the vague goodness of the so-called Gandhians,' she would write to her father.[10] 'Many in my age group found it difficult to understand Gandhi . . . we were impatient with his fads . . . and quarrelled with him for bringing mysticism into politics.' She was not about to, in an emulation of the Mahatma, embrace the penniless fakir image. Indira Gandhi's East–West fusion was instead a marriage of high cultures.

Incarcerated by the Janata government in 1978, her thoughts flew to Beethoven. Counting the bars on her prison window, she had quoted the composer's words to herself: 'I shall seize fate by the throat. It shall never wholly overcome me.' Asked by a German student to quote her favourite song, she had gravitated towards Tagore and painstakingly translated 'Ekla Chalo Re' herself.

'She didn't believe in being dowdy either while campaigning or abroad. No crumpled clothes for her,' recalls Ambika Soni. 'She would say just because you are in politics doesn't mean you can't be who you are.' 'Her saris and accessories were decided upon with great care and entered into a chart in different columns,' Usha Bhagat recalled. There was nothing sloppy about Indira and she was always well dressed and freshly groomed. She took painstaking care of herself and used light make-up and transparent nail polish. 'She used a lot of creams and lotions for her skin and took very good care of her hands and feet, she was proud of how beautiful they were,' recalls Habibullah. 'I remember seeing her barefoot, the skin on her feet was almost translucent.'

She loved wearing her sari in the Bengali style on days she wasn't working. She was an expert skier who spoke fluent Hindustani and recited the Gayatri Mantra when worried and the sophisticate who slept under open skies in Azamgarh. Beethoven and Tagore, skiing and the Gayatri Mantra, handloom and caviar, Raga Darbari and the Fifth Symphony, she laid claim to the best of both worlds. Her Indianness reflected in her dress and personal culture and her westernness in her ease abroad. When asked about which books and authors had most affected her, she listed the Ramayana, Mahabharata, Oscar Wilde, Victor Hugo, Tagore, *Alice's Adventures in Wonderland* and *Through the Looking-Glass, and What Alice Found There* and *Fabre's Book of Insects*. One of her close friends believes she discovered the Ramayana and Mahabharata only late in life, and in many ways was a 'denationalized' person.

In March 1982 the Festival of India was held with great fanfare in London. At the Royal Festival Hall, M.S. Subbulakshmi sang and Ravi Shankar played the sitar. At the end the London Philharmonic Orchestra, conducted by Zubin Mehta, struck up India's national anthem for the high-powered international audience. As the orchestra played 'Jana Gana Mana' while the Prince of Wales stood to attention, Pupul Jayakar glanced at Indira Gandhi to find her eyes shining with tears. 'Young people don't remember this but the worst part of foreign rule was the constant humiliation . . . the really galling part was that you were constantly being humiliated in your own country,' Indira once recalled. An Indian maestro in orchestral tribute to his motherland in the presence of England's prince was for Indira Gandhi a coming of age of her precious country, the fierce patriot's reaffirmation to her ancestors that she had steered the ship safely so far. From the vantage point of the Festival of India in London that March, the troubles at home must have briefly seemed negligible and forgettable. Festivals of India reflected the persona she wanted to project: a fusion of unabashed patriotism and artistic efflorescence.

~

Indira was an avid, constant reader. Led into police lockup in 1977 during her botched arrest, she remained immersed in a novel in her jail cell. Natwar Singh tells an interesting story. On a flight to Lusaka in 1970, information came in that there was a bomb on the plane. When Indira Gandhi was informed, she retorted that it was a hoax and they should just carry on. Haksar intervened and pointed out that it was best to err on the side of caution. The plane returned to Bombay airport, where they had to wait for three hours while the baggage was searched. While waiting, Indira headed straight for the bookshop, where the shop attendant was shocked to find the prime minister nonchalantly browsing through books. And the book she bought? Arthur Hailey's *Airport*.

She was not as cerebral a reader as her father was. She was not fascinated with history and the history of ideas like Nehru. The life of the mind was not her central pursuit; she was of the pragmatic, this-worldly realm. 'A homely person,' says Dhawan, 'not a great intellectual like Panditji.' Her left leanings were a result of her environment, the influence of her father's Fabian socialism and her husband's ideas, her socialism and her commitment to democracy always subject to the vagaries of politics. Perhaps it was this relative lack of the long-term vision that led her to the Emergency in the first place. Still, she was admiring of ideas, a lover of books but not a writer of them. 'Few heads of government were so free of pomposity, so nimble and so sensitive to pain and beauty,' recalled Sharada Prasad.

She may have lacked Nehru's grasp of world history but her intellectual pretensions were not entirely skin-deep. She always wanted to meet 'interesting people' and once made a list of people she wanted to meet. The list read: 1. Bright young people – mixed-artists, students, 2. Social workers, 3. Lawyers, senior citizens, and 4. Architects. Tycoons, maharajas and the aggressive newly rich made her uncomfortable and she fled from flashiness towards the earthiness of those she considered authentic and real. She frequently interacted with many Indian writers, among them Amrita Pritam and Mohan Rakesh. While abroad she conversed with the political theorist Hannah Arendt, the playwright Edward Albee and the writer Victoria Ocampo, among many others. Meeting western and Indian intellectuals was always on her itinerary and she revered and sometimes even mocked them by turn. When Buckminster Fuller delivered a lecture in India, Moni Malhoutra confessed to her that he hadn't understood a word. She laughed so loud and so heartily that it was clear she enjoyed sending up the great minds a little. The intellectualism of her father led her to mount a little rebellion of her own. She moved towards a direct contract with the people, learning from the Mahatma that 'an approach to the people could not be an intellectual one, logic and rational arguments had limited place'. Yet while the Mahatma's relationship with the people was a moral project, a lift-off into a struggle for high personal standards like truth and self-mastery, hers was an emotional and populist bond with her voters, a turbulent relationship of love and hate.

She cultivated intellectuals yet was impatient with too much theory. She listened attentively to great minds but, unlike her father's, her politics was not about ideas. In fact, her politics was the antithesis of her father's, and she attracted not the thoughtful or the enlightened but the cynical camp follower. Her relations with the intelligentsia, for whose approval she yearned, were based on politics and a need for legitimacy, not open debates on policy or a genuine search for answers.

Yet she inherited from her father the commitment to India's scientific forward march, and once a close friend of the brilliant Cambridge-educated scientist Homi Bhabha, she can be credited with beginning India's space programme in earnest. The Indian Space Research Organisation (ISRO), today a proud nationalist showpiece, was set up when she was prime minister in 1969 by Vikram Sarabhai, father of Indian space research, growing out of the Indian National Committee for Space Research (INCOSPAR) set up in Nehru's time. Like her father, she remained an unfailingly enthusiastic guardian of India's initiatives in space. U.R. Rao, project director on the Aryabhata, India's first indigenously made unmanned satellite launched in 1975 from Kapustin Yar, a rocket launch site in the Soviet Union, recalls her bubbling joy and enthusiasm at the prospect of an entirely Indian satellite and of space exploration in general. When scientists on the Aryabhata project went to her for approvals she burst out, 'Fantastic!' and agreed immediately to their proposal.[11] For Indira the space programme was not only about scientific exploration but also about India's self-reliance and security, giving her support to the missile development programme in the 1980s. Explorations in space and securing Indian defence were part of her overall drive for a country that would hold its head up high, that would not be defined simply by poverty and illiteracy, that would make great strides towards the future on the strength of its formidable achievements of the past. She would delve into Indian tradition to name India's first satellite: she named it Aryabhata, after the sixth-century mathematician and astronomer. For Indira, India needed to only harness the power of its great inheritance to achieve an even greater future – the artisan, the architect, the builder and the space explorer would create anew, but remain legatees of their grand forebears.

~

She played politics with inbuilt expertise. The 1969 split in the Congress which she engineered must have been for her a dive into the unknown with only her own instinct and inborn skill to guide her through uncharted waters. To break the party of her father and the freedom movement required not just an ability to play for high stakes but self-confidence and strength of will. She was able to do it because 'politics had been her entire upbringing'. She was, since childhood, growing up in a revolutionary family, used to days where taking risks, death, imprisonment, emotional and physical strain were the daily diet. Political understanding came quickly and naturally to her. Power was her stock-in-trade and the drive for power was her second nature. She held no truck with too much ideology; ideology mattered only if it was a shortcut to power. Once when she was asked about the one quality needed for leadership, she replied, 'Liking people is the most important quality. Only if you truly like them can you have the patience to deal with all kinds.'

After her return to office in 1980, she was anxious to recoup her credentials with the intelligentsia, to show off a new, thoughtful persona. Her image abroad had taken a battering, so it was important to strike a high note re-establishing her place as a world leader of the front rank. When she was conferred an honorary Doctor of Letters by the Sorbonne, she drafted and redrafted many times the speech she would deliver at the university. In the land of liberty, equality and fraternity, she attempted to banish all perceptions of her as a Third World despot. During the speech, she emphasized the cosmic totality of the Indian vision and how the 'wholeness of the earth can only come from the wholeness of human beings'. She said 'goodness is not assumed as a state that is untainted. Instead every human being is a tiny element in the cosmos'. She struck the cerebral notes as if to erase the ignominy of the Emergency which had cost her the friendship of many international friends and admirers. She was anxious that India be once again presented as the repository of millennia-old wisdom, her identity far grander than any momentary anti-democratic blip. She was heard in pin-drop silence in a packed hall and received a rapturous ovation. That the speech was mainly designed as her own image makeover is evident from the fact that there is hardly any evidence to suggest that a new wisdom had dawned on her post-Emergency in the way she practised her politics.

~

To the officers in her secretariat 'Mrs G' was two different people. 'There were two sides to her,' recalls Natwar Singh, 'one was the warm, friendly, completely informal side when we were not discussing politics. When discussing politics, however, she was a different person altogether. But when she got angry, she could be waspish. Indira Gandhi getting angry with you was a terrifying experience, but in the next instant she would say, [I] am sorry, forget it.'

Her officers remember her as someone for whom leisure and work were never strictly divided, but flowed into each other; she was a multi-tasker who arranged flowers, listened to music and disposed of files, held meetings and seemed to work and relax at the same time. 'She would say "sit down, sit down" like an elderly aunt every time one of us entered the room,' recalls Habibullah. 'She was very sharp but always affable, of course [she] could fly into a rage as well.' He recalls how she came storming out of a meeting in Madras, holding a sheaf of papers. As she stomped out, she found Dr Mathur lurking nearby and dumped all the papers in his hands, raging, 'Here, you keep these!' 'She was a very lovable personality,' recalls Habibullah.

'The Nehrus were courteous to a fault,' says Natwar Singh. 'So bitter rival Morarji was still "Morarjibhai"; even after he deserted her Jagjivan Ram was always "Babuji". Her manners, like her father's, were impeccable.'

Her personal touch is well remembered. He may have authored a highly critical first-hand account of Indira's baser motives in declaring the Emergency, but B.N. Tandon recalls Indira as a 'very human person' who would ring up her own doctor and ensure Tandon was well attended to when he fell ill. She remembered to bring cigarettes for the then chain-smoking R.K. Dhawan from an overseas trip. Once when a band of monkeys entered Moni Malhoutra's office room in South Block and broke a bottle of perfume he had got for his wife, Mrs Gandhi came up the steps yelling, 'This place smells like a brothel!'

Catching sight of Dr Mathur chatting up an attractive lady at a function, she commented, 'I notice you were getting along with her rather well.' She had an easy, intimate warmth with those around her, although this could snap easily. 'She could become very angry at one moment, but in the next moment forget about it completely,' says Dhawan.

Indira was a compulsive letter writer and apart from her official letters wrote hundreds of letters to her family and friends. Letters, notes, jottings, doodles flowed from her pen. One of her closest relationships – with her father – had been expressed in large part through letters. The simply penned, personal written word was often an easier communication tool than speech. If Indira Gandhi had lived in our times, she would probably have been a whiz with SMSs and WhatsApp messages.

She wrote scores of little notes to Usha Bhagat over the three decades that Bhagat was her aide. These notes, missives and sometimes longer messages were written in a simple, direct, unfussy style, quick words here and there, as if writing them helped her release her tensions and overcome emotions that could not be spoken about. The notes were often accompanied by artistic doodles, of several Indian faces in different headgear and jewellery, a Bankura horse, Bengali-style alpona, a conch shell, or a wreath of flowers. On some occasions, while being spoken to, she doodled compulsively, often causing consternation to the person addressing her. 'I come to talk to her on important matters and she just sits and doodles,' fumed an annoyed Krishna Menon once. Her letters, some signed off with a doodle, were written at all hours, from trains, planes and even helicopters, as if she found it easier to say in writing what she couldn't face-to-face. There are notes to keep the right type of 'Kum Kum' in a little silver 'dibia' for the Sanjay–Maneka engagement ceremony, notes to get the roof cleaned, blouses dyed, suitable Hindi tutors for Sonia, instructions to buy the right type of Kwality's toffees for Sanjay, breathless descriptions of Kashmir's beauty and meticulous notes on Rajiv and Sonia's wedding arrangements, from choices of plants and flowers to creating jasmine screens and alpana to choosing the wedding march music from Mendelsohn and Wagner's bridal chorus from the opera *Lohengrin*. On choosing saris, she would ask Bhagat, 'Please give a connoisseur's point of view.' Schoolgirlish jokes would be exchanged: 'For your information, I'm not biting my nails but eating the small Ladakhi almonds!' or 'Nobody even noticed my hairdo!' Another note about her measurements for her wax model at Madame Tussauds reads: 'The latest! 35.27.35½. The entire figure must be reduced by 1 and a half inches at least.' Another accompanied with a gift says: 'Since you have plenty of Chanel No.6, I thought some Chanel No.5 might be more welcome.'

The letters show a tasteful, meticulous, fastidious personality for whom creating the right ambience for a wedding or even a funeral was a demonstration of a subdued yet artistic style, a quiet flourish of a fine and refined sensibility. She would specify: 'For foreign mail, let's use the nice stamps – Beethoven for example or the miniatures.'

She planned official menus with great care, naming dishes according to the guest. When the Russian cosmonaut Yuri Gagarin, the first human to journey into outer space, came for tea, she produced a menu comprising Flying Saucer Samosas, Meteorite Sweets and Laddoo Lunar. Bhagat points out that lunches and dinners always had to have a personal touch. When Jacqueline Kennedy came to stay at Teen Murti, Indira decorated her room with objets d'art and books on Indian culture, even putting up a Gujarati-style jhoola in the garden for her to swing on. She travelled hard during campaigns and was known to spend nights under the open sky during elections, but life's luxuries were not unwelcome. Nehru's bedroom in Teen Murti did not have an air conditioner but once on a trip to Bombay

Indira refused to stay at a bungalow in the Raj Bhavan because it did not have air conditioning.

Indira's was a life of upper-middle-class 1970s India with its spartan pleasures and its low-key family-centred celebrations. Her methods of relaxation are on display at her memorial museum: knitting needles, crochet work, binoculars for birdwatching and a set of playing cards. On holidays, she would shed her formal saris and lounge at home in kaftans and kimonos, play with the dogs, or sometimes organize family trips to the Dachigam hunting lodge in Kashmir. In Dachigam everybody in Indira's travelling party would make their own beds, clean their own bathrooms and share cars. In the evenings, there would be card games and dumb charades. Dr Mathur recalls laughter-filled evenings when during dumb charade games Yashpal Kapoor, Indira's PA, attempted to imitate a *sapera* (snake charmer) playing a *been* (snake charmer's flute) by swaying this way and that or when Dr Mathur essayed the role of an Arab Sheikh with his head wrapped in a massive towel. 'When I retire from active politics I will start a theatre company and you can be the lead actor,' Indira told Dr Mathur. The mountains rather than the beach were her preferred holiday option. 'The sea is relaxing but the mountains stimulating,' she would say. These were the pre-liberalization days when there were no malls, multiplexes, TV entertainment or five-star hotels. Instead there were family outings, badminton in the garden and playing with dogs. Picnics would be had of samosas and garam chai and lazy winter afternoons would be spent on chatais in the sun playing with grandchildren. Relaxation meant going for long walks in the mountains or solving the challenging *Times* crossword puzzle, which she did almost every day. On her return from her last trip to Kashmir, just a few months after Operation Blue Star when fears for her life were very high, grandmother Indira and granddaughter Priyanka still spent a peaceful and contented evening together watching Jane Austen's *Pride and Prejudice* on TV.

Those were days when there was joy in eating simple kurkuri bhindi, a dish often prepared at her home, when fresh south Indian coffee was a special treat and the aroma of a nice soap was treasured for days. The Indian consumerist economy was decades away; gifts from abroad were excitedly exclaimed over, the arrival of a sarda (melon) from Afghanistan would be shared with the entire household as an unusual delicacy.

Her days followed an old-fashioned discipline. Up at 6 a.m., yoga exercises, a cold bath, ready by 8 a.m., simple breakfast of slightly burnt toast, one half-boiled egg, fruit and milky coffee. Then off to work, to return for lunch. Lunch was always simple Indian fare, usually a thali, and always only in the company of her family. Then a short rest and back to work again, with a light dinner at night. Dinner was mostly western but never anything very rich or extravagant. Did she ever go out? 'Never,' says Dhawan. 'Only to official functions. Never to any restaurants or parties at anyone's house.' Her food habits were an eclectic mix of Indian and European. While lunch was always Indian, dinner was invariably continental.

'The food at her home was always simple but delicious,' recalls Moni Malhoutra. She was fond of fish. I remember smoked pomfret often on her menus.' Malhoutra remembers her taste for culinary adventure, such as insisting on trying Moreton Bay Bugs (a type of lobster) on a trip to Australia. Roast veal, steamed fish and soufflés were some of her favourite European foods.

When Malhoutra's wife, Leela, created an elegant European-style dinner in a small Uttar Pradesh town, even writing out menus on bhojpatra and serving hot lemon soufflé for dessert, Indira was most impressed. 'She relished good food but generally was a simple, frugal eater,' recalls Dr Mathur, 'as she was very conscious of not putting on weight. She was very regular with her yoga exercises and didn't touch a drop of alcohol all her life.' Mathur, however, says she was a gourmet, herself an excellent cook, and always keen to try local flavours. 'Once in south India, she complained, why have they given me this instant coffee when they have such good local freshly ground coffee here.'

Friends remember her as keenly alert to what was going on around her. Sarwar Lateef, former World Bank economist, and a friend of Rajiv Gandhi's, recalls how sharp her hearing was. 'I visited the family after Priyanka's birth. I was sitting with Rajiv at one end of the room, and Mrs Gandhi was at the other end sitting on a sofa with Sonia. I mentioned to Rajiv that naming his baby "Priyanka" may mean people will start to mistakenly call her "Priya". I had been speaking in a low voice, but still from across the room Mrs Gandhi called out, "No, I don't think anyone will call her Priya"!'

At another function, Lateef recalls Mrs Gandhi circulating among the guests while at the entrance a small group debated whether Uttar Pradesh should be broken into three states for better governance. After a few minutes, as she was leaving, Mrs Gandhi stopped at the door and addressed the group: 'Over my dead body!'

'She could be intimate, leisurely and provocatively intelligent . . . the other side was businesslike, cool in appearance with a swift withdrawal to irritability,' wrote Marie Seton.[12] She found it difficult to forgive and could never let go of a grudge, memories of hurt always fresh in her mind as the long history of tense relations with her aunt Vijayalakshmi Pandit showed. Even when she became the exalted prime minister and could afford to be large-hearted, she was not able to transcend her feelings of anger towards her aunt.

Jacqueline Kennedy described her as a 'real prune – bitter, kind of pushy horrible woman . . . it always looks like she's been sucking a lemon'.[13] But Dr Mathur remembers a sunny, ever-present sense of humour. 'Once when President Zia of Pakistan complained to her about getting bad press, she advised, "Don't worry about these pressmen, they know nothing; look, they call you a democrat and me a dictator!" The President was not amused.'

In spite of her informality, she had the great gift of silence, of political reticence, says Natwar Singh. 'If you, as prime minister, talk about something you can always be misquoted or be gossiped about. That's why she often just said nothing. She liked to keep her views close to her chest and not argue too much. It was impossible to get anything out of her.'

She could recognize the spark of political talent however much she could also be threatened by it. 'She was particularly impressed with Jayalalithaa,' recalls Dr Mathur. Once at an official banquet, when Jayalalithaa [then a member of the AIADMK] had been seated far down the main table, Indira Gandhi changed the seating order and brought her to the centre. She was very impressed with Jayalalithaa's combination of brains and beauty and knew she would be a rising star in politics which of course she went on to become.

~

To be involved in engrossing work for the country was a duty and a joy, her idea of a fulfilling life revealed in this New Year wish she sent Bhagat: 'With every good wish for a year of good health, good humour, good friends and good work!' 'Politics is not a career for me, it's something that is essential to do,' she said. Politics was the family trade, something the family did and would always do. She rebelled against her father's modest ambitions for her and vowed never to short sell her own children – with unfortunate results for Indian democracy. She remained convinced all her life that it was her family which was entrusted with the care and guardianship of India. There was never any doubt in her mind about this.

Writes Marie Seton, 'No matter how retiring or malleable she might appear at moments, when it came to protecting her father's interests she could become as impenetrable as obsidian.'[14] Her engagement abroad, her desire that India be taken seriously on the world stage and that India's moral purpose be recognized grew from her determined protection of Nehru's internationalist legacy. 'She was always very concerned about how she and India would be judged internationally, that was very important for her,' says Dhawan. Whether in the leadership of the Non-Aligned Movement or in her closeness with the Soviet leadership, Indira Gandhi believed she stood for India's unique place in the world. The ideological moorings of her foreign policy were clear: she would keep the Nehruvian presence alive on the world stage. The Non-Aligned Movement remained an article of faith. Initiated into it by her father, its early idealism stayed with her. She would always stoutly defend India's right to chart its own course, apparently independent of the two warring blocs. Today NAM is ridiculed as a pro-Soviet club, yet for Indira it was a symbol of sovereign agency, a natural outcome of seizing political freedom from imperialist rulers.

In the eyes of the world she was India's empress, a byword for power. To many foreign observers, she was an exotic bird of paradise, surpassing in style her contemporaries Sri Lankan Prime Minister Sirimavo Bandaranaike and Israeli Prime Minister Golda Meir, a woman leader of elegance and authority leading a nation that had given the world the moral weapon of Gandhian non-violence. On her travels abroad she spoke fluent French, or slightly Oxford-accented English, determined to show that India was about high style and dignified presence even if grinding poverty was its dominant face.

She insisted on a foreign service officer in her secretariat, as she was intensely involved with international affairs at all times. Diplomacy was vital to her leadership and self-image. Even in the midst of the upheavals in the early 1980s in Assam and Punjab, the NAM summit was held in Delhi in grand style. Indira Gandhi took over as chairman of NAM and the world saw the famous photo of her bear hug with Fidel Castro, who called her his 'sister'. She gave the call her father had of solidarity with liberation movements worldwide. At the Commonwealth Heads of Government Meeting in Delhi in 1983, with Queen Elizabeth and Margaret Thatcher in attendance, Indira Gandhi betrayed not the slightest hint of the dark clouds closing in on her from every direction. She continued her campaign against nuclear weapons, missing the irony that it was the 1974 'peaceful nuclear explosion' that had contributed to conferring on her the nationalist credentials of which she was so proud.

The belief in the rightness of India, the conviction that India's wisdom held many important answers led her to try to convince the world of India's natural thought leadership in framing international debates. At the 1972 UN Environment Conference in Stockholm she emphasized in her speech how Emperor Ashoka had made it a king's duty to protect animal life and forest trees and how the *Atharva Veda* had advised against destroying the vitals of the earth. She said 'one earth' meant one environment and one humanity, not a world divided into 'those who condition' and 'those who are conditioned'. For the earth can best be protected with individual transformation so that each inhabitant of earth is a 'thinking person' 'imbued with compassion'. In a spirited attack on the West, she said: 'On the one hand the rich look askance at our poverty, on the other they warn us against using their methods. We do not wish to impoverish the environment any further and yet we cannot for a moment forget the grim poverty of large numbers of people . . . the environmental problems of developing countries are not side-effects of excessive industrialisation but reflect the inadequacy of development. Are not poverty and need the greatest polluters?'

It was a seminal, intelligent and hard-hitting speech, asserting the need for an equal world order to save the environment, for the first time linking the fight against poverty to the protection of the planet. It laid the foundations for the key debates on ending poverty and protecting the environment that have developed around climate change, and echoes till today in global conferences. 'The Stockholm address was a landmark speech,' says Moni Malhoutra. 'She was passionate about the environment and wildlife and was ahead of her times in ecological issues.' Environmental legislation, Project Tiger, establishment of nature reserves and animal sanctuaries are some of the major environmental achievements of Indira Gandhi's prime ministership, although many of these have been subsequently criticized as, once again, overly centralizing, creating agencies and institutions ill-equipped to deal with future challenges.[15]

She stopped work on the Silent Valley dam project in Kerala, and wrote to chief ministers suggesting a drive to plant 'a tree for every child'. She was extremely worried that the beloved trees of her childhood – those green cathedrals of solace and tranquillity –

were disappearing and often visited forests to check that the trees she remembered were still there. She adored dogs and always had more than one dog, a crowd of dogs, a permanent feature of the Gandhi home. In Nehru's home in Teen Murti there was a panda, tiger cubs, ducks, parrots and fish. Thanks to wildlife legislation keeping many of those animals at home would be unlawful today!

'She was a very teaching mother to all of us,' recalls Maneka. 'The first book I ever wrote was on plants and trees. And all of it was started by her. She would always say do you know which plant this is and what it does?' She would never throw away any flowers that were presented to her, making sure they were put in vases or given to others. She would write on the Kulu Valley: 'Let the Kulu Valley attract those who can appreciate the beauty of nature and draw from it spiritual, mental and physical vigour . . . humanity is losing itself in the unnatural because it no longer takes its strength direct from nature.' The preservation of nature, wildlife and the arts were all of a piece: she supported Project Tiger as much as the Delhi Urban Arts Commission as part of her determination to uphold India's heritage, civilizational and environmental.

~

Family remained Indira's haven. 'When she went home for lunch she was very particular, she wanted nobody there but her family,' recalls Dhawan. She lived with the same sense of duty that she had first shown with her mother, in her determined care and protection of Kamala against her in-laws. She was used to taking charge, like a male head of family would. Widowed at forty-three, did she miss an intimate male presence? In 1966 there were rumours that Dinesh Singh, the handsome raja of Kalakankar and minister in her first cabinet, was her lover and even functioned as the power behind the throne. There were rumours of her closeness to Dhirendra Brahmachari in his younger days, in addition to rumours about M.O. Mathai. 'It was just not possible for her to have an affair,' says Natwar Singh. 'There were security men under the bed! Dinesh Singh only spread rumours about his so-called closeness to her to advance his own cause and was soon turfed out. Of course you're not made of wood but this is the price you pay – you don't have a private life.'

She loved being admired and being the centre of attention of good-looking, witty and intelligent men, but the 'sexual side of her was underdeveloped'.[16] 'I do not behave like a woman,' she confessed. 'The "lack of sex" in me partly accounts for this. When I think of how other women behave, I realize that it is the lack of sex and with it a lack of woman's wiles, on which most men base their views on me.' The lack of sex, the reluctance to play a subordinate, seductive role was a subconscious resistance to male authority. She may have submitted to her father, husband and son but rebelled against them as well, entering full-time politics with gusto against her father's wishes, refusing to be a Lucknow wife to a parliamentarian husband, lifting the Emergency in defiance of her son.

When dominating principal secretaries like Haksar asserted their wisdom too much she removed them. When American presidents thought they could take 'the girl' for granted, she thumbed her nose at them. 'I'm not a feminist. Till I was 12 years old I hardly knew the difference between being a boy or a girl. I was brought up amongst boy cousins climbing trees, flying kites and playing marbles. But that is not the normal experience. Women in India . . . are so dominated and discriminated against. There is so much unnecessary cruelty and humiliation.' She felt the pain of womanhood but did not admit it for herself. At home an old family retainer from Allahabad always called her 'bhaiyaji', because the firstborn, according to tradition, was always treated as a boy. She signed off Indu-boy in her letters to her father. She was the firstborn child who was treated as a male, the daughter who was brought up by a father to be a little 'soldier-boy'. Her self-image as a child and in adulthood was more male than female, the man inside the woman often dominant in her personality. Likening herself to her grandfather Motilal, she once said, 'He was a biform human being, both man and woman.'[17]

She refused to call herself a feminist but she would not allow herself to be subordinate in any relationship. The relationships she was most comfortable in were the ones in which she was the dominant maternal force, such as with her sons and their wives. Grooming Sonia, initiating her into Indian ways, teaching her Hindustani may have been a labour of love but was also a guardianship of a novice, a relationship that fitted easily into the power equation of saas and bahu. She never forgot who she was, that she was Indira Nehru Gandhi and hers was the bloodline that was joined to India's. When you are the 'chosen', you don't submit easily to the bondage of romance or to being the lesser partner. 'She was the head of the family, no doubt about that,' recalled Maneka Gandhi. 'At home she was the boss,' says Priyanka Gandhi.

The woman trapped in preconceived roles bothered her. She would quote from Tagore's *Chitrangada*: 'I am Chitra. I am no goddess to be worshipped nor yet object of common pity to be brushed aside like a moth with indifference . . . allow me to share the great duties of your life, then you will know my true self . . .' 'I believe in the liberation of women in the same way as I believe in the liberation of men, liberation from the narrow confines of outdated thoughts and habits,' she said. She believed 'A woman who is involved in larger issues and is interested in many things usually makes a better wife and mother.'

She was worried that her sons were brought up with too much privilege and entitlement and wanted them to travel by third-class train as she had done in her childhood. Yet in the end, the mother's love overcame her ideals and she not only gave them a highly privileged upbringing in prime ministerial homes but even smoothed the way for them to take over her prime ministership. She remained convinced all her life that she and her family were India's foremost change agents, that it was her lineage that would give India its shape and future. The centrality of her family in the destiny of India remained her lifelong conviction and goal. Her natural inclination was artistic, tuned towards nature and culture, but at the same time as if in an unspoken promise to her father and grandfather, she felt it was her duty to lead India and work for India in the way her family had always done and always would.

She was very observant about people and relationships. 'She once hinted that she had seen only two happy marriages in her life, B.K. and Fori Nehru and Rajiv and Sonia,' recalls Dr Mathur. She prided herself on her powers of observation. 'We in India are taught not to observe, but I learnt it from my schooling in Switzerland.' Her penetrating gaze could see ahead of others in immediate situations. Yet she failed at visualizing the horizon, at the line where the present ends and the future takes over, as she remained watchful over, alas, only her daily realities.

'Her most important quality was courage,' says Priyanka Gandhi. 'She was incredibly brave. And unhesitating about using power. She saw power as her birthright and used it. Unlike Sonia Gandhi, who feels she is only a trustee of power and hesitates to use it.' On her death anniversary in 2016, Rahul Gandhi wrote in a Facebook post: 'My grandmother was the bravest woman I know.' Without exception, all her biographers point to her 'fabled courage', 'remarkable bravery' and 'tremendous heroism'. Even her cousin and bitter critic Nayantara Sahgal admits, 'The Bangladesh intervention was her finest hour . . . it was the most successful military intervention in history, but India also dealt heroically with a humanitarian crisis on a scale the world had never seen.'

Taking on the Syndicate, achieving a military victory over Pakistan, facing the storms of the Emergency and in the end striking the deadliest blow for the unity of India, Indira Gandhi was indeed the stout-hearted risk-taker, however malign their consequences. Raw, daring courage was her hallmark and even when she sinned, she did so stoutly and with audacity. In grief she was efficient and philosophical and she was fired by a fierce sense of duty and responsibility. She was the poised society lady and street-fighting politician, beautifully dressed, charming hostess, suspiciously paranoid backroom manipulator, a steadfast patriot and a deeply flawed democrat.

'When she came into the room it was as if she was surrounded by electricity, bijli!' says Natwar Singh. 'All eyes turned to look at her. She was always the centre of attention, even among world leaders. Yet there was too much jealousy, there was immense jealousy of her.' 'I don't see her as an iron lady,' says Tully. 'I see her as an indecisive woman who kept dilly-dallying around until things got so bad that she had to overcompensate and take drastic measures. Each of her periods in power thus ended in disaster, whether it was splitting the Congress, the Emergency or Operation Blue Star or the dismissal of Farooq.'

She 'failed to realize that India could be best governed if it was governed as a democracy with fully functioning democratic institutions', continues Tully. 'She seemed not to understand her own power and rise to it. If she had realized her own power she could have risen to the level of a great stateswoman. But she didn't realize her power to do good. She only realized her power to stay in power.'

'She was the greatest prime minister India had,' says Wajahat Habibullah. 'She was prime minister at a critical time when the unity of India was threatened. That she was at the helm ensured the country stayed together, and stayed relatively stable.' She was not a democrat as her father and husband were, often regarding democracy as an obstacle to her mission. Yet she was India's unflagging guardian, a protector unto death of the country's borders and sovereignty.

~

Indira Gandhi's public life can be divided into two distinct phases. The first, from 1967 to 1974, saw the emergence of a kind of people's leader India had never seen before, a confident young woman pushing the country towards robust self-reliance and assertion of sovereignty. Then from 1975 to 1984, the ruthless power politician, betraying her father's ideals and desperately trying to impose a centralizing order in a country restless for decentralization. But then she had a family obligation to uphold, she had a mission to accomplish. Nehru's daughter had to ski down the high mountain and expertly ride a horse, be a powerful swimmer, be a graceful runner, study at Oxford, be constantly fit and active, stand on her head and read the best books. She was the country and the country was her, its journey mirroring her own turbulent life. She wanted to be able to say: Look, Papu, your work wasn't in vain. India had made it, India had grown up, and so had Indira: Indira–India could conquer adversity, fend for herself, assert her presence in the world and look her enemies in the eye. She had sought her father's approval all her life, however robustly she may have scorned his innocence and betrayed his ideals. In the end, she sought his and the country's benediction that at least she had brought India this far, as if to say: Look, Papu, I've done it. Indira–India has done it.

~

Dear Mrs Gandhi,

Why these letters? Why all these questions? Why this interrogation of your life and legacy? You were simple but complicated, tough but fragile, aloof, queenly and haughty but also warm, familiar and capable of great intimacy; you were a solitary soul who was convivial, a loner who nurtured relationships with a huge network of friends, relatives and contacts; sensitive but not generous, champion of the underdog but not large-hearted like Motilal; in public you were more man than woman, hardly a nurturing 'feminine' force, even though at home you were a decidedly caring mother and grandmother; you were a man in politics and a woman at home, the abrasive political warrior who loved interior design, the commander-in-chief who took joy in hospitality; you had a core of inner steel that protected you in your life of turmoil, you were unfailingly courteous, yet always kept a distance from most. You had a great love of adventure and a rugged spirit that refused to accept defeat yet you could retreat into a shell and become timorous and fearful. 'Are most people not just a split personality but several personalities? I feel I am . . . But I still don't know how to present them to the world, different people see different me-s!' you wrote to Dorothy Norman.[18]

The only time I saw you was when I was a schoolgirl in the late seventies. We were in the then austere Calcutta airport, a bare hall, neon lights staring down on stained plastic chairs. You had lost power and were no longer prime minister. I remember a slight, solitary, short-haired woman in a sari in the distance with a companion walking in and taking a seat away from the other passengers.

A whisper went around: 'Isn't that Indira Gandhi?' You were quite alone, no one came up to greet you, most pretended not to recognize you, or perhaps they were too fearful, some even turned away. I was struck by the stark contrast between this ordinary-looking woman and the grand prime minister I had seen in photographs. I wanted desperately to reach out and scurried up to you for an autograph – for those were the days of autographs and not selfies – which you refused, holding up a bandaged finger and gravely saying that you were sorry but you couldn't write because of a finger injury.

As I turned to go, I vividly recall the long, searching stare that you gave me as if to say, yes, I am Indira Gandhi, I am the prime minister you once saw in newspapers. Don't forget me. Remember me. A school poem popped into my head, 'My name is Ozymandias, King of Kings, look on my works ye Mighty and despair!' The mighty monarch suddenly reduced to bare stumps lying face down in an endless desert, alone in an airport unescorted and unrecognized.

Letters were your constant companions. Your father had kept his presence alive in your life through intellectually stimulating teaching letters. You had poured out your heart in letters to your father, to Dorothy Norman and to Fori and B.K. Nehru. You had written regularly to your sons, not in your father's brainy style but with the intimacy and directness of a devoted mother. Letters were your means of self-expression. Letters after all are not emails, or text messages. They are considered, thoughtful, with salutations and a sign-off which are deliberated on with care. In the letter-writing times, the addressee was treated with courtesy and the correct form of address was given thought.

Your letters often spoke about subjects difficult to mention verbally even between old friends. You didn't seem to have the capacity or desire to use letters for a public purpose as Nehru did with the chief ministers nor for open self-exploration, being as reserved and restrained as you were, but nonetheless your letters were documents of self-analysis, glimpses of self-awareness, communications to friends with an unstated plea for understanding.

And so you too will remain the woman in the letter, from an era when politics was competitive but not cut-throat, when there was time for courtesy even between political adversaries, when enemies respected each other, when even an Emergency was transparently declared rather than surreptitiously unleashed.

You could not build the India of your father's dreams. You consigned the Indian economy to the doldrums for a decade, left behind a political culture that rode roughshod over democratic institutions and destroyed your party's roots among the people. Yet you left behind for Indian citizens an embodiment of leadership, both at home and abroad an example of a remarkable politician and a leader of astounding courage, impeccable style and crackling charisma. Power was your quest, power that would compensate for your own griefs, power that would enable you to realize your father's dream, power that would stun your detractors and mesmerize your voters.

On your first visit to the United States as prime minister, *Life* magazine published an interview with you saying you did not like to be addressed as Madame Prime Minister. When President Lyndon Johnson, having read the interview, sent a message to the Indian ambassador asking how you would like to be addressed, your answer was typical Indira Gandhi.

'You can tell the president,' you said to the ambassador, 'that my cabinet colleagues call me "sir". He can too.'

So perhaps that is what I should have called you when I asked for your autograph in that neon-lit Calcutta airport, all those years ago.

Indira Gandhi: Prime Minister sir.

Notes

1. Death of Indira, Birth of a Legend

1. This and all subsequent quotes by Habibullah are from an interview with the author.
2. Dr Mathur, in interview with the author; and K.P. Mathur, *The Unseen Indira Gandhi* (Delhi: Konark Publishers, 2016), p. 159.
3. *The Guardian*, 1 November 1984.
4. This and all subsequent quotes by Dhawan are from an interview with the author.
5. Rahul Gandhi, speech in Churu, Rajasthan, 2013.
6. Sonia Gandhi, in interview with Rajdeep Sardesai, India Today TV, 21 November 2016.
7. Sikhs were also attacked in other cities like Kanpur (Uttar Pradesh), Jabalpur (Madhya Pradesh) and Rourkela (Orissa). More than 200 Sikhs died in incidents in Uttar Pradesh. Twenty were killed in Indore and sixty in Bokaro.
8. Amitav Ghosh essay, 'The Ghosts of Mrs Gandhi' (*The New Yorker*, 17 July 1995), quoted in *When a Tree Shook Delhi*, Manoj Mitta and H.S. Phoolka (Delhi: Roli Books, 2007).
9. Ibid., p. 15.
10. Ibid.
11. Mitta and Phoolka, p. 34.
12. Ibid., p. 49.
13. Mitta, in interview with the author, on the CNNIBN show.

2. Revolution's Child

1. H.Y. Sharada Prasad, *The Book I Won't Be Writing and Other Essays* (New Delhi: DC Publishers, 2003), p. 14.

2. Krishna Hutheesing, *We Nehrus* (New York: Holt, Rinehart and Winston, 1967), p. 7.
3. Jawaharlal Nehru, *An Autobiography* (New Delhi: Penguin Books, 2004).
4. Sunil Khilnani, *The Idea of India* (New Delhi: Penguin Books, 1997), p. 168.
5. Nehru began working on *The Discovery of India* in 1944 in Ahmadnagar Fort prison. It was published in 1946.
6. Krishna Hutheesing, *Dear to Behold: An Intimate Portrait of Indira Gandhi* (New York: Macmillan, 1969), p. 18.
7. Ibid., p. 10.
8. Mushirul Hasan, *The Nehrus: Personal Histories* (Delhi: Roli Books, 2006), p. 124.
9. Pandit, in interview with Rajiv Mehrotra, on the Doordarshan show *In Conversation*, https://www.youtube.com/watch?v=LmFZoGSPi6o
10. The Hunter Commission of Enquiry said 379 were shot and 1200 were wounded but unofficial figures say many more died.
11. Emmanuel Pouchpadass, *My Truth: Indira Gandhi* (New Delhi: Vision Books, 1981), p. 13. In 1976, beginning on the tenth anniversary of Indira Gandhi's installation as prime minister, she gave a series of interviews to the writer and diplomat Emmanuel Pouchpadass. This lengthy, exclusive and candid interview has been compiled into a book, *My Truth*, by Pouchpadass, which is now out of print. Many of the quotes of Indira Gandhi which appear here, unless otherwise specified, are taken from that interview as her words have been reproduced verbatim by Pouchpadass without any editing. The book is almost an autobiography and was first published in French in Paris in 1980.
12. Indira Gandhi, quoted in Promilla Kalhan, *Kamala Nehru: An Intimate Biography* (Delhi: Vikas Publishing House, 1973), p. 143.
13. Priyanka Gandhi, in an informal conversation with the author.
14. Vijayalakshmi Pandit's letter to Nayantara Sahgal, 1979, Quoted in Nayantara Sahgal, *Indira Gandhi: Her Road to Power* (New York: Frederick Ungar Publishing Co., 1982), p. 39.
15. Vijayalakshmi Pandit's daughters Nayantara Sahgal and Chandralekha Mehta have said their mother never made the 'ugly and stupid' remark, and only used the word 'sickly' as Indira was often ill.
16. Sonia Gandhi (Ed.), *Freedom's Daughter: Letters Between Indira Gandhi and Jawaharlal Nehru, 1922–39* (London: Hodder & Stoughton, 1989), pp. 124–25.
17. Quoted in Kalhan, p. 141.
18. Hutheesing, *We Nehrus*, p. 57.
19. Quoted in Coomi Kapoor, *The Emergency: A Personal History* (New Delhi: Penguin Books, 2015), p. 10.

20. Sonia Gandhi (Ed.), *Freedom's Daughter*, p. 45.
21. Jawaharlal Nehru, *Glimpses of World History* (New York: John Day, 1960), p. 3.
22. Pupul Jayakar, *Indira Gandhi: A Biography* (New Delhi: Penguin Books, 1997), p. 39.
23. Sonia Gandhi (Ed.), *Freedom's Daughter*, pp. 124–25.
24. B.N. Pandey, *Nehru* (London: Macmillan, 1976), p. 182.
25. Jawaharlal Nehru, *Selected Works of Jawaharlal Nehru*, Vol. 1, edited by Sarvepalli Gopal (Delhi: Orient Longman, Nehru Memorial Museum and Library, 1972), p. 267.
26. Sonia Gandhi (Ed.), *Freedom's Daughter*, pp. 158-60.
27. Jawaharlal Nehru, *Selected Works*, Vol. 1, p. 377.
28. Nehru to Vijayalakshmi Pandit, quoted in Sahgal, p. 31.
29. Sonia Gandhi (Ed.), *Freedom's Daughter*, p. 404.
30. Kamala Nehru to Syed Mahmud, in Syed Mahmud, *A Nationalist Muslim and Indian Politics, Being the Selected Correspondence of Syed Mahmud*, edited by V.N. Datta and B.E. Cleghorn (Delhi: Macmillan, 1974). Kamala's letters to Syed Mahmud are very revealing of her suffering and show they shared a close friendship.
31. Katherine Frank, *Indira: The Life of Indira Nehru Gandhi* (New Delhi: HarperCollins, 2007), p. 33.
32. Motilal Nehru, *Selected Works of Motilal Nehru*, Vol. 5, edited by Ravinder Kumar and D.N. Panigrahi (Delhi: Nehru Memorial Museum and Library, 1982), p. 64.
33. Indians were outraged that there was not a single Indian member on the commission.
34. This happened when as prime minister she attended a Congress session in Calcutta.
35. Ray to Bhaskar Ghose, in a conversation.
36. Stanley Wolpert, *Nehru: A Tryst with Destiny* (New York: Oxford University Press, 1996), p. 107.
37. Jawaharlal Nehru, *Selected Works*, Vol. 8, edited by Sarvepalli Gopal, pp. 519–25.
38. Bertil Falk, *Feroze Gandhi: The Forgotten Gandhi* (New Delhi: Lotus, 2016), p. 22.
39. Feroze's biographer reports rumours that Feroze may even have been her child, born out of wedlock, and that his biological father may have been Hindu, named Raj Bahadur Kamala Prasad Kakkar (Falk, p. 10).
40. Krishna Hutheesing, *With No Regrets* (Bombay: Padma Publishing, 1943), pp. 133–34.

41. Kalhan, p. 69.
42. Indira Gandhi, *What I Am* (Delhi: Indira Gandhi Memorial Trust, 1986), p. 10.
43. Sonia Gandhi (Ed.), *Freedom's Daughter*, p. 56.
44. Nehru Papers, Nehru Memorial Museum and Library, quoted in Frank, p. 87.
45. Quoted in Anand Mohan, *Indira Gandhi: A Personal and Political Biography* (New York: Hawthorn Books, 1967), p. 120.
46. Indira Gandhi, in a letter to Frank Oberdorf in 1936, quoted in Jayakar, p. 88.
47. Jayakar (p. 84) writes how important it was for Jawaharlal that his daughter graduate from Oxford.
48. G. Parthasarathi and H.Y. Sharada Prasad (Eds), *Indira Gandhi: Statesmen, Scholars, Scientists and Friends Remember* (New Delhi: Indira Gandhi Memorial Trust, 1985), p. 308.
49. Sonia Gandhi, in interview with Rajdeep Sardesai, India Today TV.
50. Dorothy Norman (Ed.), *Indira Gandhi: Letters to an American Friend, 1950–1984* (New York: Harcourt Brace Johanovich, 1985), p. 78.
51. Falk (p. 52) writes that Feroze's family disapproved of his proximity to the Nehrus as the Parsi community preferred to maintain a distance from the freedom struggle.
52. Quoted in Zareer Masani, *Indira Gandhi: A Biography* (London: TY Crowell, 1976), p. 52.
53. Welles Hangen, *After Nehru, Who?* (London: Harcourt, Brace & World, 1963), pp. 166–67.
54. Frank, p. 514.
55. Ibid., p. 135.
56. Jawaharlal Nehru, *Selected Works*, Vol. 1, edited by Sarvepalli Gopal, p. 88.
57. Indira Gandhi's convocation address at Viswa Bharati, quoted in Mohan, p. 120.
58. Sonia Gandhi (Ed.), *Freedom's Daughter*, p. 342.
59. Ibid., p. 471.

3. From Woman-in-Waiting to Nehru's Heir

1. Shanta Gandhi, quoted in Pupul Jayakar, *Indira Gandhi: A Biography* (New Delhi: Penguin Books, 1997), p. 85.
2. Bertil Falk, *Feroze Gandhi: The Forgotten Gandhi* (New Delhi: Lotus, 2016), p. 26.
3. Ibid., p. 27.

4. Haksar, quoted in Katherine Frank, *Indira: The Life of Indira Nehru Gandhi* (New Delhi: HarperCollins, 2007), p. 161.
5. Sonia Gandhi (Ed.), *Freedom's Daughter: Letters Between Indira Gandhi and Jawaharlal Nehru, 1922–39.* (London: Hodder & Stoughton, 1989), pp. 392–95.
6. In a letter to Pupul Jayakar, Indira would speak of Jayaprakash Narayan as an example of Gandhian hypocrisy. Jayakar, p. 391.
7. Ibid., p. 111.
8. M.K. Gandhi, *Collected Works of Mahatma Gandhi*, Vol. 75 (Ahmedabad: Navajivan Trust, 1975), pp. 375–76.
9. Indira to Jayakar, p. 100.
10. The Congress passed a resolution that the British must 'Quit India' and British rule must end immediately.
11. Dorothy Norman (Ed.), *Indira Gandhi: Letters to an American Friend 1950–1984* (New York: Harcourt Brace Johanovich, 1985), p. 29.
12. Dom Moraes, *Mrs Gandhi* (London: Little, Brown, 1980), p. 83.
13. Pranay Gupte, *Mother India: A Political Biography of Indira Gandhi* (New Delhi: Penguin Books, 2009), p. 219.
14. Jawaharlal Nehru, *Selected Works of Jawaharlal Nehru*, Vol. 1, edited by Sarvepalli Gopal (Delhi: Orient Longman, Nehru Memorial Museum and Library, 1972), p. 501.
15. Ibid., pp. 588–89.
16. Shashi Tharoor, *Era of Darkness: The British Empire in India* (Delhi: Aleph Book Co., 2016), p. 157.
17. Jawaharlal Nehru, *Selected Works*, Vol. 2, edited by Sarvepalli Gopal, p. 331.
18. Sonia Gandhi (Ed.), *Two Alone, Two Together: Letters Between Indira Gandhi and Jawaharlal Nehru, 1940–64* (Delhi: Penguin Books, 2004), pp. 547–59.
19. Frank, p. 230. Dorothy Norman was invited to India when India became a republic on 26 January 1950.
20. Falk, p. 173.
21. Frank, p. 202.
22. Falk, p. 170.
23. Jayakar, p. 161.
24. Jawaharlal Nehru, *Selected Works*, Vol. 2, edited by Sarvepalli Gopal, p. 335.
25. Frank, pp. 210–12.
26. Jawaharlal Nehru, *Selected Works*, Vol. 2, edited by Sarvepalli Gopal, pp. 83–84.
27. Ibid., pp. 107–09.
28. Exactly when Hari Singh signed the Instrument of Accession remains a subject of intense debate. Some accounts say Indian troops landed even

before Hari Singh signed. The official Indian version is that troops landed after the accession was signed. Pakistan believes that the Kashmir accession was fraudulent as the maharaja signed under duress.

29. Sagarika Ghose, 'Jinnah's Two Nation Theory Looks Dominant in Kashmir', *Sunday Times of India*, 23 April 2017.
30. Aijaz Ashraf interview of D.L. Sheth in *Outlook*. It was the anti-Emergency movement that converted the RSS from a fringe group to the storm troopers of the Jana Sangh to eventually the parent of the BJP.
31. Falk, p. 137.
32. Indira Gandhi, *Selected Speeches and Writings of Indira Gandhi* (Delhi: Publications Division, Ministry of Information and Broadcasting, Government of India, 1971), p. 300.
33. Nehru to Nayantara Sahgal, telling her when she was separating, 'don't be like Indu. She is neither married nor separated.' Quoted in Nayantara Sahgal and E.N. Mangat Rai (Eds), *Relationship: Extracts from a Correspondence* (Delhi: Kali for Women, 1994), p. 163.
34. Nayantara Sahgal, *Indira Gandhi: Her Road to Power* (New York: Frederick Ungar Publishing Co., 1982), p. 377.
35. Inder Malhotra, *Indira Gandhi: A Personal and Political Biography* (New Delhi: Hay House India, 2014), p. 68.
36. Zareer Masani, *Indira Gandhi: A Biography* (London: TY Crowell, 1976), p. 83.
37. This and all subsequent quotes by Bhaskar Ghose are from an interview with the author.
38. Bhaskar Ghose was driving the jeep that Indira Gandhi was travelling in.
39. Jawaharlal Nehru, *Selected Works*, Vol. 2, edited by Sarvepalli Gopal, p. 36.
40. Sahgal, pp. 1–2.
41. This and all subsequent quotes by Srivastava are from an interview with the author.
42. Falk, p. 33.
43. Anand Mohan, *Indira Gandhi: A Personal and Political Biography* (New York: Hawthorn Books, 1967), p. 202.
44. Frank, p. 242.
45. Quoted in Falk, p. 173.
46. Sarvepalli Gopal, *Jawaharlal Nehru: A Biography*, Vol. 2 (Delhi: Oxford University Press, 1975), pp. 311–12.
47. This and all subsequent quotes by Natwar Singh are from an interview with the author.
48. Jayakar, p. 154.

49. Marie Seton, *Panditji: A Portrait of Jawaharlal Nehru* (New York: Taplinger Publishing Co., 1967), p. 198.
50. Norman, p. 27.
51. Hangen, quoted in Malhotra, p. 81.
52. Mohan, pp. 203–05.
53. Sahgal, p. 378.
54. Falk, p. 243.
55. Norman, p. 48. In a letter Indira writes of the extremely 'good looking yogi' with the 'magnificent body'.
56. Quoted in Frank, p. 241.
57. Ibid., p. 249.
58. Nehru, quoted in *Times of India*, 8 February 1959.
59. Betty Friedan, 'How Mrs Gandhi Shattered the Feminine Mystique', *Ladies Home Journal*, May 1966.
60. Dom Moraes, *Mrs Gandhi* (London: Little, Brown, 1980).
61. Falk, p. 210.
62. Sarvepalli Gopal, *Jawaharlal Nehru*, Vol. 3, p. 68.
63. Ramachandra Guha, *India After Gandhi: The History of the World's Largest Democracy* (New Delhi: Pan Macmillan, 2011), p. 296.
64. Falk, p. 212.
65. Falk, p. 213.
66. Norman, p. 57.
67. Sonia Gandhi (Ed.), *Two Alone, Two Together*, p. 627.
68. Uma Vasudev, *Indira Gandhi: Revolution in Restraint* (Delhi: Vikas, 1974), p. 293.
69. Moraes, p. 146.
70. Oriana Fallaci, *Interview with History* (New York: Houghton Mifflin, 1977), p. 107.
71. Mohan, p. 241.
72. K.P. Mathur, *The Unseen Indira Gandhi: Through Her Physician's Eyes* (Delhi: Konark Publishers, 2016), p. 42; and in interview with the author.
73. B.N. Mullick, *My Years with Nehru* (Delhi: Allied Publishers, 1972), pp. 442–43.
74. Sonia Gandhi (Ed.), *Two Alone, Two Together*, p. 619.
75. Frank, p. 267.
76. Ibid., p. 273.
77. Norman, p. 103.
78. Usha Bhagat, *Indiraji through My Eyes* (New Delhi: Penguin Books, 2005), p. 98.

4. From Goongi Gudiya to Goddess

1. K.P. Mathur, *The Unseen Indira Gandhi: Through Her Physician's Eyes* (Delhi: Konark Publishers, 2016), p. 26. When asked where she got her energy from, Indira said I have atomic energy.
2. Jawaharlal Nehru, *Selected Works of Jawaharlal Nehru*, Second Series, Vol. 30, edited by H.Y. Sharada Prasad and A.K. Damodaran (New Delhi: Nehru Memorial Museum and Library, 2001). Nehru is quoted as saying: 'There must be definite checks and balances to see that a communal majority does not abuse its power in the garb of a linguistic state.'
3. Ramachandra Guha, *India After Gandhi: The History of the World's Largest Democracy* (New Delhi: Pan Macmillan, 2011), p. 189.
4. Ibid., p. 231.
5. Telangana revolts from 1946 to 1951 in Andhra Pradesh.
6. Jawaharlal Nehru, *Letters to Chief Ministers, 1947–1964*, Vol. 111, general editor, G. Parthasarathi (New Delhi: Government of India, 1989), p. 439.
7. Nehru, quoted in Uma Vasudev, *Indira Gandhi: Revolution in Restraint* (Delhi: Vikas, 1974), p. 302.
8. Nehru, in a letter to Vijayalakshmi Pandit, quoted in Nayantara Sahgal, *Indira Gandhi: Her Road to Power* (New York: Frederick Ungar Publishing Co., 1982), p. 52.
9. Coomi Kapoor, *The Emergency: A Personal History* (New Delhi: Penguin Books, 2015), p. 166.
10. Sarvepalli Gopal, *Jawaharlal Nehru: A Biography*, Vol. 3 (Delhi: Oxford University Press, 1975), p. 245.
11. Quoted in P.N. Dhar, *Indira Gandhi, the 'Emergency', and Indian Democracy* (Delhi: Oxford University Press, 2000), p. 142.
12. Rajni Kothari, 'The Congress System in India', *Asian Survey*, 1(12): 1161–73.
13. Joel Samuel Migdal, Atul Kohli, and Vivienne Shue (Eds), *State Power and Social Forces: Domination and Transformation in the Third World* (Cambridge, UK: Cambridge University Press, 1994), p. 94.
14. H.Y. Sharada Prasad, *The Book I Won't Be Writing and Other Essays* (New Delhi: Chronicle Books, 2003), p. 65.
15. Her national standing had made Shastri insecure about her, according to both Inder Malhotra and Natwar Singh.
16. C.P. Srivastava, *Lal Bahadur Shastri, Prime Minister of India, 1964–66: A Life of Truth in Politics* (Delhi: Oxford University Press, 1996), p. 85.
17. Indira Gandhi, in interview with Chris Panos for *TV Eye*, Thames Television, 1978.
18. Inder Malhotra, *Indira Gandhi: A Personal and Political Biography* (New Delhi: Hay House India, 2014), p. 84.

19. Ibid. Indira related this story to Malhotra to show how much Shastri disliked her.
20. Quoted in Kapoor, p. 164.
21. Sahgal, p. 5.
22. Bhaskar Ghose witnessed this when she was information and broadcasting minister.
23. Arnold Michaelis, 'An Interview with Indira Gandhi', *McCall's*, 93 (April 1966), p. 105.
24. P.V. Narasimha Rao, *The Insider* (New Delhi: Penguin Books, 1998), p. 493.
25. This and all subsequent quotes by Tully are from an interview with the author.
26. Rajinder Puri, *India: The Wasted Years* (New Delhi: Chetana, 1975).
27. This and all subsequent quotes by Malhoutra are from an interview with the author.
28. Sujay Gupta, 'Forgotten Legacy of 6/6/66', *Times of India*, 6 June 2016.
29. Ibid.
30. Ashok Mitra, *Telegraph*, 6 August 2004.
31. She said this to Inder Malhotra, p. 95.
32. Guha, p. 409.
33. Sujay Gupta, 'Forgotten Legacy of 6/6/66', *Times of India*, 6 June 2016.
34. Guha, p. 414.
35. Indira Gandhi, *Selected Speeches and Writings of Indira Gandhi*, Vol. 1 (Delhi: Publications Division, Ministry of Information and Broadcasting, Government of India, 1971), p. 93.
36. Reported in *Times of India*, 13 June 1966.
37. C. Subramaniam would be honoured too; he would be awarded the Bharat Ratna for being the 'Indian' father of the Green Revolution in 1998. His key aides in bringing about the Green Revolution were the eminent scientist M.S. Swaminathan and the bureaucrat B. Sivaraman.
38. *Times of India*, 20 January 1967.
39. This and all subsequent quotes by Deen Dayal Shastri are from an interview with the author.
40. Malhotra, p. 107.
41. Sharada Prasad, p. 84.
42. Haksar's huge collection of personal papers contains many details of this period.
43. Malhoutra, in interview with the author.
44. Sarvepalli Gopal, *Radhakrishnan: A Biography* (Delhi: Oxford University Press, 1989), p. 345.
45. Indira Gandhi, in interview with Chris Panos for *TV Eye*, Thames Television, 1978.

46. Bhaskar Ghose, in interview with the author, about the Green Revolution in Bengal.
47. Sathe, in interview to IBN, for the documentary *Indira of India*, scripted and anchored by the author in 2009. Sathe has since passed away.
48. Pupul Jayakar, *Indira Gandhi: A Biography* (New Delhi: Penguin Books, 1997), p. 207.
49. Guha, p. 436.
50. 'Swaminomics', *Sunday Times of India*, 10 April 2016.
51. Forty years later, in 2008, Sonia Gandhi would applaud her mother-in-law's politics when she stated that the 'much reviled' bank nationalization had kept the country afloat and spurred the good of society without surrendering to corporate interests (HT Leadership Summit, 21 November 2008). Given that general elections were only a year away, this reiteration of the Congress's default mode of the socialist pro-poor line for votes upheld the supremacy of politics over economics.
52. Pranab Mukherjee, *The Turbulent Years: 1980–96* (Delhi: Rupa, 2016), p. 57.
53. Malhotra, in interview to CNNIBN, for the documentary *Indira of India*, scripted and anchored by the author in 2009.
54. Malhotra, p. 122.
55. Quoted in Kuldip Nayar, *India: The Critical Years* (Delhi: Vikas, 1971), pp. 2–3.
56. Gandhi was born on 2 October 1869.
57. Mary Carras, *Indira Gandhi in the Crucible of Leadership: A Political Biography* (Boston: Beacon Press, 1979), p. 59.
58. Katherine Frank, *Indira: The Life of Indira Nehru Gandhi* (New Delhi: HarperCollins, 2007), p. 323.
59. The 'Modi revolution' of today, the chaiwallah's son who leads the charge against the entitled sons of the Congress, paradoxically borrows from the same lexicon as Indira's campaign against feudal rulers and hereditary privileges.
60. Quoted in Malhotra, p. 128.
61. 'The colour red suffused me through the war', Indira Gandhi to Pupul Jayakar, in Jayakar, p. 245.
62. Mohammad Ali Jinnah, founder of Pakistan, claimed that Hindus and Muslims were 'two nations' that could not occupy the same country and that Muslims needed a separate homeland.
63. The Awami League won 160 out of 162 seats from East Bengal and got the majority to form the government at the centre.
64. Quoted in Dhar, p. 152.
65. *Sunday Times*, 13 June 1971.

66. Yahya Khan, quoted in http://www.genocidebangladesh.org/
67. Gary J. Bass, *The Blood Telegram: Nixon, Kissinger and a Forgotten Genocide* (Delhi: Random House India, 2013).
68. Quoted in Surjit Mansingh, *Indira Gandhi's Foreign Policy, 1966–1982* (Delhi: Sage Publications, 1984), p. 213.
69. JP to Ganga Saran Sinha, quoted in Jayakar, p. 227.
70. Dhar, p. 156.
71. Indira Gandhi, *Selected Speeches and Writings of Indira Gandhi*, Vol. 2 (Delhi: Publications Division, Ministry of Information and Broadcasting, Government of India, 1971), pp. 611–13.
72. *The Times*, London, 30 December 1971. Report by Peter Hazelhurst.
73. Vajpayee subsequently denied it was he who had called her Durga. That he called her Abhinav Chandi Durga is mentioned in the *Telegraph*, 27 February 2016, quoting an article by Prem Kumar Mani written in 2001. Guha says it is possible she was called Durga by the socialist leader S.N. Mishra.
74. Srinath Raghavan, *1971: A Global History of the Creation of Bangladesh* (Cambridge, Massachusetts: Harvard University Press, 2013).
75. Dhar, p. 210.
76. Inderjit Badhwar, in 'Introduction' to *Indira Gandhi: A Living Legacy* by Raghu Rai (Delhi: Timeless, 2004).

5. The Great Dictator: Downhill towards the Emergency, 1972–77

1. Jawaharlal Nehru, *Letters for a Nation: From Jawaharlal Nehru to His Chief Ministers, 1947–1963*, edited by Madhav Khosla (Delhi: Penguin Books, 2015).
2. Dom Moraes, *Mrs Gandhi* (London: Little, Brown, 1980), p. 220.
3. Pupul Jayakar, *Indira Gandhi: A Biography* (New Delhi: Penguin Books, 1997), p. 274.
4. Coomi Kapoor, 'Inside Track', *Indian Express*, 3 April 2016. In a diary item Kapoor reports that a friend of the BJP president Amit Shah found that he is an admirer of Indira Gandhi. Shah is reported to have also said that in reality a good leader cannot be democratic.
5. Krishna Hutheesing, *We Nehrus* (New York: Holt, Rinehart and Winston, 1967), p. 54.
6. Kirti Narain, *Participation of Women in the Uprising of 1857—Redefinition of Social Status: Then and Now* (Delhi: Himalaya Publishing House, 2016).
7. Jayakar, pp. 252, 254.

8. *Statesman*, 10 March 1971.
9. In 1953, on suspicion of harbouring secessionist tendencies, Sheikh Adbullah, leader of Jammu and Kashmir, was dismissed and arrested.
10. Nayantara Sahgal, *Indira Gandhi: Her Road to Power* (New York: Frederick Ungar Publishing Co., 1982), p. 156.
11. Swami, in interview to IBN, for the documentary *Indira of India*, scripted and anchored by the author in 2009.
12. Katherine Frank, *Indira: The Life of Indira Nehru Gandhi* (New Delhi: HarperCollins, 2007), p. 321.
13. This and all subsequent quotes by Maneka Gandhi are from her interview with Simi Garewal, *Rendezvous with Simi Garewal*, 2000. https://www.youtube.com/watch?v=4ZJ9PVLWkG4
14. Vinod Mehta, *The Sanjay Story* (Bombay: Jaico Publishing Company, 1978), p. 56.
15. *Free Press Journal*, 28 June 2015; also in Malhotra, p. 356.
16. Sahgal, p. 248, quoting Ram Jethmalani in Parliament in 1976.
17. Karan Tripathi, 'Maruti and Sanjay Gandhi: The History of an Illicit Extraordinary Love Affair', www.motoroids.com.
18. Kuldip Nayar, *The Judgement: Inside Story of the Emergency in India* (Delhi: Vikas, 1977), p. 197; Raj Thapar, *All These Years* (Delhi: Penguin Books, 1991), pp. 397–98.
19. *Free Press Journal*, 28 June 2015; and Coomi Kapoor, *The Emergency: A Personal History* (New Delhi: Penguin Books, 2015), p. 209.
20. Vasudev, in interview with the *Telegraph*, June 2015.
21. Uma Vasudev, *Two Faces of Indira Gandhi* (Delhi: Vikas, 1977), pp. 106–07.
22. The author's article on the Dhritarashtra syndrome, *Times of India*, 24 November 2014.
23. Indira Gandhi speech in Ahmedabad, quoted in *Free Press Journal*, 28 June 2015.
24. Sunil Sethi, 'If Sanjay Gandhi Had Lived', *India Today*, 9 December 2016.
25. The A.C. Gupta Commission, set up by the Janata government to probe Maruti and Sanjay's dealings, produced its report by September 1979. It contains details of the manner in which the Indira government went the extra mile for Maruti.
26. Karan Tripathi, http://www.motoroids.com/features/maruti-and-sanjay-gandhi-the-history-of-an-illicit-extraordinary-love-affair/
27. In February 2012 the company sold its ten millionth vehicle in India (Kapoor, p. 330).
28. Haksar to Frank, p. 353.
29. Josy Joseph, 'The Aide Effect', *Caravan*, 1 August 2016.

30. Frank, p. 437.
31. Quoted in Mark Tully's review of Ian Jack's book in *India Today*, 12 April 2013.
32. The Congress got 44 per cent vote share in 1971, and the others in the range of 1 to 10 per cent.
33. After the 1972 elections Indira eased out Mohan Lal Sukhadia of Rajasthan, Brahmananda Reddy of Andhra Pradesh, M.M. Chaudhary of Assam and S.C. Shukla of Madhya Pradesh (Inder Malhotra, *Indira Gandhi: A Personal and Political Biography*, New Delhi: Hay House India, 2014, p. 147).
34. Indira Gandhi, in interview with Pran Chopra, *The Citizen* and *The Weekend Review* magazines, January 1970.
35. Indira Gandhi, in interview with Chris Panos for *TV Eye*, Thames Television, 1978.
36. Arvind Datar, 'The Case that Saved Indian Democracy', http://www.thehindu.com/opinion/op-ed/the-case-that-saved-indian-democracy/article4647800.ece
37. The Golak Nath judgement held that Parliament could not amend fundamental rights. The Kesavananda Bharati judgement held that Parliament could not change the 'basic structure or essential features of constitution'.
38. Ray was also the lone dissenter among the eleven Supreme Court judges who examined the constitutionality of the Bank Nationalisation Act 1969.
39. 'The power shortage and scarcity of essential commodities had already created considerable difficulties for the general public and the state government was trying to grapple with these problems as well as growing student unrest when it had to face a serious situation caused by some sections of the civil police and PAC . . . subordinate ranks in some companies in the PAC had to be dealt with firmly, and the assistance of the armed forces had to be requisitioned to meet this unprecedented situation' (12 June 1973 letter of Uttar Pradesh Governor to the President).
40. 1973 article, quoted in Sahgal, p. 137.
41. RAW was set up in 1968 by the Indira government as a separate agency to gather foreign intelligence, hived off from the original Intelligence Bureau.
42. *Hindustan Times*, 12 November 1986.
43. Malhotra, p. 144.
44. *Times of India*, editorial, 10 February 1975.
45. *The Hindu*, 11 June 1974.
46. *Times of India*, January 1974.
47. Indira Gandhi, in interview with Jonathan Dimbleby for *TV Eye*, Thames Television, 1978.
48. Indira Gandhi, in interview with Chris Panos for *TV Eye*, Thames Television, 1978.

49. *Pioneer*, 25 June 2010.
50. Indira Gandhi to Fori Nehru, 9 October 1979.
51. Cartoon by Abu Abraham, 10 December 1975. The cartoon shows the President naked in a bathtub signing the Emergency proclamation and saying, 'If there are any more ordinances, ask them to wait.'
52. L.N. Mishra's son Vijay Mishra said the CBI had manipulated the case and he had no reason to believe that Anand Margis were behind his father's murder (interview to rediff.com, 9 December 2014).
53. Morarji Desai, in interview with Oriana Fallaci, *The New Republic*, 25 June 1975.
54. H.Y. Sharada Prasad, *The Book I Won't Be Writing and Other Essays* (New Delhi: Chronicle Books, 2003, p. 113) writes: 'there is a question on whether Justice Sinha had a sense of proportion when he equated a couple of days delay in the notification of a minor functionary's resignation with a corrupt practice.'
55. Dr Mathur, in interview with the author.
56. Prashant Bhushan, *The Case that Shook India* (New Delhi: Vikas, 1978).
57. This and all subsequent quotes by Prashant Bhushan are from an interview with the author except if otherwise mentioned.
58. Jayakar (p. 271) writes how the then minister Uma Shankar Dikshit had been contacted by an official in the Income Tax Department who had told him, even before the judgement, that 'Mrs Gandhi's election will be declared invalid'. When Dikshit asked him who he was, the official had replied, 'We are religious people and we are running this country.'
59. Letter accessed by Kapoor, p. 5.
60. B.N. Tandon, *PMO Diary: Prelude to the Emergency* (Delhi: Konark Publishers, 2003), p. 218.
61. Indira Gandhi, in interview with Jonathan Dimbleby for *TV Eye*, Thames Television, 1978.
62. Tandon, p. 221.
63. Morarji Desai, in interview with Oriana Fallaci, *The New Republic*, 25 July 1975.
64. Tandon, p. 214.
65. Kapoor, p. 4.
66. Ray, in an interview with *Outlook* (2009).
67. Indira Gandhi, in interview with Chris Panos for *TV Eye*, Thames Television, 1978.
68. Sharada Prasad, p. 113.
69. Letter to Jayakar, p. 268.
70. Ibid., p. 286.

71. Indira Gandhi, in interview with Chris Panos for *TV Eye*, Thames Television, 1978.
72. Ibid.
73. Philip Ziegler, *Mountbatten: The Official Biography* (London: Fontana/Collins, 1985), p. 654.
74. Madhukar Dattatraya Deoras was RSS sarsanghchalak from 1973 to 1994.
75. T.V. Rajeswar, *India: The Crucial Years* (Noida: HarperCollins, 2015).
76. Jayakar, p. 278.
77. Nayar, in interview with *Daily O*.
78. Indira Gandhi, in interview with Jonathan Dimbleby for *TV Eye*, Thames Television, 1978.
79. K.P. Mathur, *The Unseen Indira Gandhi: Through Her Physician's Eyes* (Delhi: Konark Publishers, 2016), p. 96.
80. Frank, p. 399.
81. Sahgal, p. 295.
82. Mehta, p. 67.
83. This and all subsequent quotes by Soni are from an interview with the author.
84. Mary Carras, *Indira Gandhi in the Crucible of Leadership: A Political Biography* (Boston: Beacon Press, 1979), p. 250.
85. P.N. Dhar (*Indira Gandhi, the 'Emergency', and Indian Democracy*, Delhi: Oxford University Press, 2000, p. 318) says Indira's ears were poisoned against B.N. Tandon.
86. John Dayal and Ajoy Bose, *Delhi Under Emergency: For Reasons of State* (Delhi: Orient Paperbacks, 1977).
87. Kapoor, p. 252.
88. *Times of India*, 28 April 1976.
89. Emma Tarlo, *Unsettling Memories: Narratives of the Emergency in India* (London: Hurst Publisher, 2014).
90. Siddhartha Shankar Ray, in interview with *Outlook* magazine, 2009.
91. B.K. Nehru, *Nice Guys Finish Second: An Autobiography* (Delhi: Penguin Books, 1997), p. 629.
92. *Illustrated Weekly of India*, August 1976.
93. Swami, in interview to IBN, for the documentary *Indira of India*, scripted and anchored by the author in 2009.
94. Jayakar, p. 312.
95. Indira Gandhi, in interview with Chris Panos for *TV Eye*, Thames Television, 1978.
96. Indira Gandhi, in interview with Jonathan Dimbleby for *TV Eye*, Thames Television, 1978.
97. Dorothy Norman (Ed.), *Indira Gandhi: Letters to an American Friend,*

1950–1984 (New York: Harcourt Brace Johanovich, 1985), p. 149.

98. Indira Gandhi, in interview with Chris Panos for *TV Eye*, Thames Television, 1978.
99. Indira Gandhi, in interview with Jonathan Dimbleby for *TV Eye*, Thames Television, 1978.
100. In 1977, the Congress got 34.5 per cent of the vote share, more than the 31 per cent that swept the Narendra Modi–led BJP to power in 2014.
101. In 1988 the Rajiv Gandhi government had tried to bring in an anti-defamation bill which was condemned as an attempt to gag the media. The bill was subsequently withdrawn.

6. Resurrection: 1977–80

1. *Guardian*, 21 September 1977. Interview with James Cameron.
2. Aruna Asaf Ali, *Public Face of a Public Person: A Study of Jawaharlal Nehru* (Delhi: Radiant Publishers, 1989), p. 281.
3. Pupul Jayakar, *Indira Gandhi: A Biography* (New Delhi: Penguin Books, 1997), p. 326.
4. Katherine Frank, *Indira: The Life of Indira Nehru Gandhi* (New Delhi: HarperCollins, 2007), p. 434.
5. Sunil Sethi, 'High Priest of Justice', *India Today*, 22 August 2015.
6. Judicial enquiry commissions in India can be set up by law on the basis of a felt public demand for an independent and impartial authority to probe an individual or an event. They have the powers of a civil court.
7. Indira Gandhi, in interview with Jonathan Dimbleby for *TV Eye*, Thames Television, 1978.
8. Indira Gandhi to Fori Nehru in April 1977, quoted in Jayakar, p. 330.
9. Jug Suraiya, 'Belchi Revisited', *Times of India*, 24 May 2010.
10. Dom Moraes, *Mrs Gandhi* (London: Little, Brown, 1980), p. 296. He writes how she sped around like Hermes.
11. Janardan Thakur, *Indira Gandhi and Her Power Game* (Delhi: Vikas, 1979), pp. 33–34.
12. Ibid., p. 34.
13. The Belchi killings would lead to more caste violence in Bihar, but Dalit anger and rebellion would see a new political upsurge in the rise of the Bahujan Samaj Party (BSP) which would be founded by Kanshi Ram in 1984.
14. *Patriot*, 4 October 1977.
15. Ibid.
16. Pranab Mukherjee, *The Turbulent Years: 1980–96* (Delhi: Rupa, 2016), p. 158.

17. The Congress headed by Y.B. Chavan now had 131 MPs (Lok Sabha and Rajya Sabha) while Indira's Congress(I) was reduced to 148 MPs (Lok Sabha and Rajya Sabha) (V. Krishna Ananth, *India Since Independence: Making Sense of Indian Politics*, Delhi: Dorling Kindersley, 2011, p. 209).
18. Rashid Kidwai, *24 Akbar Road* (Gurgaon: Hachette, 2013).
19. Frank, pp. 426–27.
20. Era Sezhiyan (Ed.), *Shah Commission Report: Lost, and Regained* (Chennai: Aazhi Publishers, 2011).
21. Indira Gandhi, in interview with Jonathan Dimbleby for *TV Eye*, Thames Television, 1978.
22. Bruce Chatwin, 'On the Road with Mrs G', in *What Am I Doing Here?* (London: Picador, 1990).
23. Khushwant Singh, *Absolute Khushwant: The Low-Down on Life, Death and Most Things In-Between* (Delhi: Penguin Books, 2010).
24. Sunil Sethi, 'Azamgarh Byelection: Beginning of the End', *India Today*, 1978.
25. Indira Gandhi, in interview with Mary C. Carras, July 1978.
26. Dorothy Norman (Ed.), *Indira Gandhi: Letters to an American Friend, 1950–1984* (New York: Harcourt Brace Johanovich, 1985), p. 154.
27. She defeated the Janata's Veerendra Patil.
28. Indira Gandhi, in interview with Jonathan Dimbleby for *TV Eye*, Thames Television, 1978.
29. Sunil Sethi, 'If Sanjay Gandhi Had Lived', *India Today*, 9 December 2016.
30. Jayakar, p. 372.
31. The 1979 (or second) oil crisis or oil shock occurred due to decreased oil output in the wake of the Iranian Revolution. Though global oil supply decreased by only 4 per cent, widespread panic resulted, driving the price far higher than justified by supply.
32. Quoted in Ramachandra Guha, *India After Gandhi: The History of the World's Largest Democracy* (New Delhi: Pan Macmillan, 2011), p. 547.
33. Quoted in James Manor (Ed.), *Nehru to the Nineties: The Changing Office of Prime Minister in India* (London: Penguin, 1994), p. 8.

7. Twilight: 1980–84

1. The aircraft had reportedly been a gift to Brahmachari from one of his foreign 'disciples'. The Swami had been allowed to import the plane without paying import duty. Some reports say the Swami paid $40,585 in cash on a visit to the United States. Brahmachari shared Sanjay's passion for planes and in

1973 had set up a company, Aparna Agro Private Limited, to buy and sell aircraft. Sanjay was one of the company directors.
2. Sanjay was appointed general secretary of the AICC in May 1980.
3. Vidya Charan Shukla, in interview to ABP TV, *The Day Sanjay Died*, ABP News, 23 June 2012.
4. Suman Dubey, quoting Rajiv Gandhi, in *India Today*, 26 December 2005.
5. *Hindustan Times*, 28 June 1980.
6. http://indiatoday.intoday.in/story/exclusive-extract-from-khushwant-singhs-autobiography/1/289506.html
7. Incident quoted in Pupul Jayakar, *Indira Gandhi: A Biography* (New Delhi: Penguin Books, 1997), p. 404.
8. Rajiv won the Amethi seat in February 1981.
9. Chaitanya Kalbag, 'Surya: Sun Changes Its Spots', *India Today*, 17 October 2013.
10. *Indian Express*, 31 March 1982.
11. Marie Seton to Ian Jack, quoted in Pranay Gupte, *Mother India: A Political Biography of Indira Gandhi* (New Delhi: Penguin Books, 2009), p. 110.
12. Krishan Datta, 'How the 1982 Asian Games Changed Delhi', *Business and Economy*, 16 February 2012.
13. Quoted in Jayakar, p. 446.
14. James Manor, 'Anomie in Indian Politics: Origins and Potential Wider Impact', *Economic and Political Weekly*, Annual Number, 1983, pp. 725–34.
15. Diego Maiorano, *Autumn of the Matriarch: Indira Gandhi's Final Term in Office* (Noida: HarperCollins India, 2015), p. 183.
16. Robert L. Hardgrave and Stanley A. Kochanek, *India: Government and Politics in a Developing Nation* (Boston: Thomson Wadsworth, 2008).
17. Shankkar Aiyar, *Accidental India: A History of the Nation's Passage through Crisis and Change* (Delhi: Aleph, 2012).
18. Nilim Dutta, 'Remembering the Nellie Massacre', twocircles.net
19. Nitin A. Gokhale, 'Who Is Responsible for Nellie Massacre 1983?', *Tehelka*, 21 September 2011.
20. Maiorano, p. 214.
21. When his father, Sheikh Abdullah, passed away on 8 September 1982, Farooq had inherited the chief ministership of Jammu and Kashmir.
22. Mark Tully and Satish Jacob, *Amritsar: Mrs Gandhi's Last Battle* (Delhi: Rupa, 1985), p. viii.
23. Text of Anandpur Sahib Resolution.
24. When Indira Gandhi came back to power in 1980, she dismissed nine state governments ruled by non-Congress parties in Rajasthan, Bihar, Gujarat,

Maharashtra, Odisha, Punjab, Tamil Nadu, Uttar Pradesh and Madhya Pradesh.

25. Jeff Kingston, *Nationalism in Asia: A History Since 1945* (London: Wiley Blackwell, 2016).
26. Tully and Jacob, pp. 57–58.
27. Thousands of Tamils fled to India after the massacre by Sinhala soldiers, and the Indian government began to provide the Tamil Tigers, the militant secessionist Tamil movement, with money, arms and training. Indira was in the piquant situation of fighting secessionism at home in the shape of Bhindranwale and encouraging it abroad in the shape of the Tamil Tigers (Katherine Frank, *Indira: The Life of Indira Nehru Gandhi*, New Delhi: HarperCollins, 2007, p. 470).
28. Pranab Mukherjee, *The Turbulent Years: 1980–96* (Delhi: Rupa, 2016), p. 275.
29. Harchand Singh Longowal, quoted in the South Asian Terrorism Portal, satp.org http://www.satp.org/satporgtp/publication/nightsoffalsehood/falsehood4.htm
30. The warriors of faith had turned against their own flock. In the entire period of militancy in Punjab between 1981 and 1993, more than 60 per cent of the dead were Sikhs (satp.org, 'Knights of Falsehood').
31. Tully and Jacob, p. 143.
32. Then army chief A.S. Vaidya was assassinated in 1986. The two other generals who planned and led the operation, K. Sundarji (COAS 1986–88) and Lt Gen. Ranjit Singh Dyal, died in 1999 and 2012, respectively.
33. This and all subsequent quotes by Brar are from an interview with the author.
34. Brar, in interview to Associated Press, 1984.
35. The Akal Takht is the holiest shrine within the Golden Temple complex.
36. Some accounts give his rank as second lieutenant.
37. Dilip Bobb and Inderjit Badhwar, 'General K. Sundarji: Disputed Legacy', *India Today*, 15 May 1988.
38. Brar, in interview with Kanwar Sandhu, https://www.youtube.com/watch?v=JLiBFUQexoc
39. Brar to Shekhar Gupta, in *Walk the Talk*, NDTV.
40. Ibid.
41. Lt Gen. Brar, *Operation Blue Star: The True Story* (Delhi: UBSPD, 1993).
42. N.T. Rama Rao, quoted in *Christian Science Monitor*, October 1983.
43. *The Economist*, 25 August 1984.
44. Wajahat Habibullah belonged to the Jammu and Kashmir cadre of the IAS and served in the state for many years.

45. Maiorano, p. 24.
46. Ibid.

8. The Woman: Seeking the Real Indira Gandhi

1. Mary Carras, *Indira Gandhi in the Crucible of Leadership: A Political Biography* (Boston: Beacon Press, 1979), pp. 1–2.
2. Diego Maiorano, *Autumn of the Matriarch: Indira Gandhi's Final Term in Office* (Noida: HarperCollins India, 2015), p. 217.
3. Sonia Gandhi, Foreword to Indira Gandhi, *Selected Sayings* (Delhi: Penguin, 2007).
4. This and all subsequent quotes by Shukla are from an interview with the author.
5. UNI, 4 March 1980.
6. *Statesman*, PTI, *Times of India*, 11 March–6 April 1980.
7. Jawaharlal Nehru, *Selected Works of Jawaharlal Nehru*, Vol. 2, edited by Sarvepalli Gopal (Delhi: Orient Longman, Nehru Memorial Museum and Library, 1972), p. 684.
8. Pranay Gupte, *Mother India: A Political Biography of Indira Gandhi* (New Delhi: Penguin Books, 2009), p. 341.
9. Tyabji, in interview with the author.
10. Sonia Gandhi (Ed.), *Two Alone, Two Together: Letters Between Indira Gandhi and Jawaharlal Nehru, 1940–64* (Delhi: Penguin Books, 2004), p. 598.
11. U.R. Rao to Livemint, 20 April 2015.
12. Marie Seton, *Panditji: A Portrait of Jawaharlal Nehru* (New York: Taplinger Publishing Co., 1967), p. 189.
13. Quoted in Nayantara Sahgal, *Indira Gandhi: Her Road to Power* (New York: Frederick Ungar Publishing Co., 1982), p. 374.
14. Seton, p. 273.
15. In *The Last Tiger: Struggling for Survival* (Delhi: Oxford University Press, 2012), Valmik Thapar has strongly criticized the apparatus created by Project Tiger and the forest bureaucracy.
16. Pupul Jayakar, *Indira Gandhi: A Biography* (New Delhi: Penguin Books, 1997), p. 479.
17. Indira Gandhi, in interview to BBC Television, 26 October 1971.
18. Dorothy Norman (Ed.), *Indira Gandhi: Letters to an American Friend, 1950–1984* (New York: Harcourt Brace Johanovich, 1985), p. 59.

References

Aiyar, Shankkar. *Accidental India: A History of the Nation's Passage through Crisis and Change*. Delhi: Aleph, 2012.

Ali, Aruna Asaf. *Private Face of a Public Person: A Study of Jawaharlal Nehru*. Delhi: Radiant Publishers, 1989.

Ananth, V. Krishna. *India Since Independence: Making Sense of Indian Politics*. Delhi: Dorling Kindersley, 2011.

Bass, Gary J. *The Blood Telegram: Nixon, Kissinger and a Forgotten Genocide*. Delhi: Random House India, 2013.

Bhagat, Usha. *Indiraji through My Eyes*. New Delhi: Penguin Books, 2005.

Bhushan, Prashant. *The Case that Shook India*. New Delhi: Vikas, 1978.

Brar, K.S. *Operation Blue Star: The True Story*. Delhi: UBSPD, 1993.

Carras, Mary. *Indira Gandhi in the Crucible of Leadership: A Political Biography*. Boston: Beacon Press, 1979.

Chatwin, Bruce. *What Am I Doing Here?* London: Picador, 1990.

Datta, Krishan. 'How the 1982 Asian Games Changed Delhi', *Business and Economy*, 16 February 2012.

Dayal, John; and Ajoy Bose. *Delhi under Emergency: For Reasons of State*. Delhi: Orient Paperbacks, 1977.

Dhar, P.N. *Indira Gandhi, the 'Emergency', and Indian Democracy*. Delhi: Oxford University Press, 2000.

Falk, Bertil. *Feroze Gandhi: The Forgotten Gandhi*. New Delhi: Lotus, 2016.

Fallaci, Oriana. *Interview with History*. New York: Houghton Mifflin, 1977.

Frank, Katherine. *Indira: The Life of Indira Nehru Gandhi*. New Delhi: HarperCollins, 2007.

Gandhi, Indira. *Selected Speeches and Writings of Indira Gandhi*, Volumes 1–5. Delhi: Publications Division, Ministry of Information and Broadcasting, Government of India, 1971.

———. *What I Am*. Delhi: Indira Gandhi Memorial Trust, 1986.

———. *Selected Sayings*. Delhi: Penguin, 2007.

Gandhi, M.K. *Collected Works of Mahatma Gandhi*. Ahmedabad: Navajivan Trust, 1975.

Gandhi, Sonia (Ed.). *Freedom's Daughter: Letters Between Indira Gandhi and Jawaharlal Nehru, 1922–39*. London: Hodder & Stoughton, 1989.

———. *Two Alone, Two Together: Letters Between Indira Gandhi and Jawaharlal Nehru, 1940–64*. Delhi: Penguin Books, 2004.

Gopal, Sarvepalli. *Radhakrishnan: A Biography*. Delhi: Oxford University Press, 1989.

———. *Jawaharlal Nehru: A Biography*. Delhi: Oxford University Press, 1975.

Guha, Ramachandra. *India After Gandhi: The History of the World's Largest Democracy*. New Delhi: Pan Macmillan, 2011.

Gupte, Pranay. *Mother India: A Political Biography of Indira Gandhi*. New Delhi: Penguin Books, 2009.

Hangen, Welles. *After Nehru, Who?* London: Harcourt, Brace & World, 1963.

Hardgrave, Robert L., and Stanley A. Kochanek, *India: Government and Politics in a Developing Nation*. Boston: Thomson Wadsworth, 2008.

Hasan, Mushirul. *The Nehrus: Personal Histories*. Delhi: Roli Books, 2006.

Hutheesing, Krishna. *With No Regrets*. Bombay: Padma Publishing, 1943.

———. *We Nehrus*. New York: Holt, Rinehart and Winston, 1967.

———. *Dear to Behold: An Intimate Portrait of Indira Gandhi*. New York: Macmillan, 1969.

Jayakar, Pupul. *Indira Gandhi: A Biography*. New Delhi: Penguin Books, 1997.

Kalhan, Promilla. *Kamala Nehru: An Intimate Biography*. Delhi: Vikas Publishing House, 1973.

Kapoor, Coomi. *The Emergency: A Personal History*. New Delhi: Penguin Books, 2015.

Khilnani, Sunil. *The Idea of India*. New Delhi: Penguin Books, 1997.

Kidwai, Rashid. *24 Akbar Road*. Gurgaon: Hachette, 2013.

Kingston, Jeff. *Nationalism in Asia: A History Since 1945*. London: Wiley Blackwell, 2016.

Mahmud, Syed. *A Nationalist Muslim and Indian Politics, Being the Selected Correspondence of the Late Dr. Syed Mahmud*, edited by V.N. Datta and B.E. Cleghorn. Delhi: Macmillan, 1974.

Maiorano, Diego. *Autumn of the Matriarch: Indira Gandhi's Final Term in Office*. Noida: HarperCollins India, 2015.

Malhotra, Inder. *Indira Gandhi: A Personal and Political Biography*. New Delhi: Hay House India, 2014.

Manor, James (Ed.). *Nehru to the Nineties: The Changing Office of Prime Minister in India*. London: Penguin, 1994.

Mansingh, Surjit. *India's Search for Power: Indira Gandhi's Foreign Policy, 1966–1982*. Delhi: Sage Publications, 1984.

Masani, Zareer. *Indira Gandhi: A Biography*. London: TY Crowell, 1976.

Mathur, K.P. *The Unseen Indira Gandhi: Through Her Physician's Eyes*. Delhi: Konark Publishers, 2016.

Mehta, Vinod. *The Sanjay Story*. Bombay: Jaico Publishing Company, 1978.

Migdal, Joel Samuel; Atul Kohli; and Vivienne Shue (Eds). *State Power and Social Forces: Domination and Transformation in the Third World*. Cambridge, UK: Cambridge University Press, 1994.

Mitta, Manoj; and H.S. Phoolka. *When a Tree Shook Delhi*. Delhi: Roli Books, 2007.

Mohan, Anand. *Indira Gandhi: A Personal and Political Biography*. New York: Hawthorn Books, 1967.

Moraes, Dom. *Mrs Gandhi*. London: Little, Brown, 1980.

Mukherjee, Pranab. *The Turbulent Years: 1980–96*. Delhi: Rupa, 2016.

Mullick, B.N. *My Years with Nehru*. Delhi: Allied Publishers, 1972.

Narain, Kirti. *Participation and Position of Women in the Uprising of 1857—Redefinition of Social Status: Then and Now*. Delhi: Himalaya Publishing House, 2016.

Nayar, Kuldip. *India: The Critical Years*. Delhi: Vikas, 1971.

———. *The Judgement: Inside Story of the Emergency in India*. Delhi: Vikas, 1977.

Nehru, B.K. *Nice Guys Finish Second: An Autobiography*. Delhi: Penguin Books, 1997.

Nehru, Jawaharlal. *Glimpses of World History*. New York: John Day, 1960.

———. *Selected Works of Jawaharlal Nehru*, Volumes 1–15, edited by Sarvepalli Gopal. Delhi: Orient Longman, Nehru Memorial Museum and Library, 1972.

———. *Letters to Chief Ministers, 1947–1964*, Vol. 111, general editor, G. Parthasarathi. New Delhi: Government of India, 1989.

———. *Selected Works of Jawaharlal Nehru*. Second Series. Volumes 29–32, edited by H.Y. Sharada Prasad and A.K. Damodaran. New Delhi: Nehru Memorial Museum and Library, 2001.

———. *An Autobiography*. Delhi: Penguin, 2004.

———. *Letters for a Nation: From Jawaharlal Nehru to His Chief Ministers, 1947–1963*, edited by Madhav Khosla. Delhi: Penguin Books, 2015.

Nehru, Motilal. *Selected Works of Motilal Nehru*. Vol. 5. Edited by Ravinder Kumar and D.N. Panigrahi. Delhi: Vikas, 1982.

Norman, Dorothy (Ed.). *Indira Gandhi: Letters to an American Friend, 1950–1984*. New York: Harcourt Brace Johanovich, 1985.

Pandey, B.N. *Nehru*. London: Macmillan, 1976.

Parthasarathi, G.; and H.Y. Sharada Prasad (Eds). *Indira Gandhi: Statesmen, Scholars, Scientists and Friends Remember*. New Delhi: Indira Gandhi Memorial Trust, 1985.

Pouchpadass, Emmanuel. *My Truth: Indira Gandhi*. Delhi: Vision Books, 1981.

Prasad, H.Y. Sharada. *The Book I Won't Be Writing and Other Essays*. New Delhi: Chronicle Books, 2003.

Puri, Rajinder. *India: The Wasted Years*. New Delhi: Chetana, 1975.

Raghavan, Srinath. *1971: A Global History of the Creation of Bangladesh*. Harvard University Press, 2013.

Rai, Raghu. *Indira Gandhi. A Living Legacy*, Introduction by Inderjit Badhwar. Delhi: Timeless, 2004.

Rajeswar, T.V. *India: The Crucial Years*. Noida: HarperCollins, 2015.

Rao, P.V. Narasimha. *The Insider*. New Delhi: Penguin Books, 1998.

Sahgal, Nayantara. *Indira Gandhi: Her Road to Power*. New York: Frederick Ungar Publishing Co., 1982.

Sahgal, Nayantara; and E.N. Mangat Rai (Eds). *Relationship: Extracts from a Correspondence*. Delhi: Kali for Women, 1994.

Sarkar, Sumit. *Modern India*. Delhi: Macmillan, 1983.

Seton, Marie. *Panditji: A Portrait of Jawaharlal Nehru*. New York: Taplinger Publishing Co., 1967.

Sezhiyan, Era (Ed.). *Shah Commission Report: Lost, and Regained*. Chennai: Aazhi Publishers, 2011.

Singh, Khushwant. *Absolute Khushwant: The Low-Down on Life, Death and Most Things In-Between*. Delhi: Penguin Books, 2010.

Singh, Tavleen. *Kashmir: A Tragedy of Errors*. Delhi: Penguin, 1995.

Srivastava, C.P. *Lal Bahadur Shastri: A Life of Truth in Politics*. Delhi: Oxford University Press, 1996.

Tandon, B.N. *PMO Diary: Prelude to the Emergency*. Delhi: Konark Publishers, 2003.

Tarlo, Emma. *Unsettling Memories: Narratives of the Emergency in India*. London: Hurst Publisher, 2014.

Thakur, Janardan. *Indira Gandhi and Her Power Game*. Delhi: Vikas, 1979.

Thapar, Raj. *All These Years: A Memoir*. Delhi: Penguin Books, 1991.

Thapar, Valmik. *The Last Tiger: Struggling for Survival*. Delhi: Oxford University Press, 2012.

Tharoor, Shashi. *An Era of Darkness: The British Empire in India*. Delhi: Aleph Book Co., 2016.

Tully, Mark; and Satish Jacob. *Amritsar: Mrs Gandhi's Last Battle*. Delhi: Rupa, 1985.

Vasudev, Uma. *Indira Gandhi: Revolution in Restraint*. Delhi: Vikas, 1974.
Vasudev, Uma. *Two Faces of Indira Gandhi*. Delhi: Vikas, 1977.
Wolpert, Stanley. *Nehru: A Tryst with Destiny*. New York: Oxford University Press, 1996.
Ziegler, Philip. *Mountbatten: The Official Biography*. London: Fontana/Collins, 1985.

Acknowledgements

Indira Gandhi had a long and varied public life and a tumultuous personal one and understanding her would not have been possible without the help and guidance of several people who saw her in close proximity, and worked and interacted with her. Natwar Singh and Moni Malhoutra, long-time associates of the Gandhis, who were in Indira Gandhi's secretariat in her first term, were incredibly generous with their time, providing me with their rich memories and personal insights. Meeting them both was a true delight. R.K. Dhawan, Lt. Gen. K.S. Brar, Wajahat Habibullah and Mark Tully were equally generous, sharing their memories and observations of those years and providing many unknown anecdotes and details. It was particularly heartwarming to converse with Dr K.P. Mathur, who has written his own book on Indira Gandhi and readily shared his many memories as her personal physician for two decades, someone who saw her every day of her life from 1966 onward. My father, Bhaskar Ghose, who was in her secretariat when she was information and broadcasting minister and a district officer when she later visited West Bengal as prime minister, shared with me his observations and recollections of her, as did his senior colleague B.N. Tandon, who was in the prime minister's office from 1969 to 1976 and whose book, *PMO Diary*, chronicling the events that led up to the Emergency in 1975, remains a detailed account of historical value. Rajiv Gandhi's boyhood friend, economist Sarwar Lateef; the irrepressible Sunil Sethi, senior journalist with *India Today*, who tracked the Indira years closely; Ambika Soni, Youth Congress leader in the Sanjay years; Laila Tyabji, doyenne of crafts; Prashant Bhushan, who has written a book on his father Shanti Bhushan's prosecution of Indira Gandhi in the Allahabad High Court case; and Vandana Haksar, a member of P.N. Haksar's family, also shared their views and I am indebted to them. My gratitude to Priyanka Gandhi, who gave me the benefit of a wonderfully long conversation about her grandmother and who gracefully never once asked what kind of book I was writing. She kindly leant me her copy of Emmanuel Pouchpadass's long interview with Indira Gandhi, *My Truth*, a book now out of print, which is a goldmine of Indira's thoughts in her own words. Pouchpadass's book is an unedited recording of Indira's words about her life and political career.

I was very fortunate to be able to spend time with my senior colleague Inder Malhotra, Indira's biographer, who had known Indira and Feroze Gandhi closely. When I met him in April 2016 at his Press Enclave apartment I was shocked to see that he was not his old self. However, once we started talking about Indira Gandhi, almost miraculously an eloquence flooded in and we spent some happy time talking about the woman whom he described as India's 'second-best PM after Nehru'. I was dreadfully saddened to hear of his death just two months after we had had such a candid conversation.

My tryst with Indira began even before this book. In 2009 I had scripted and anchored a documentary on Indira Gandhi twenty-five years after her death. The documentary was called *Indira of India*, and parts of it are available on YouTube. In the course of interviews for that documentary, I had met and talked to the veteran Congressman Vasant Sathe who had told me that, instead of a TV show, I should write a book on Indira. I am sorry that Mr Sathe is not here to see that I took his advice.

Ramachandra Guha, doyen of the history of modern India, mentor and friend, was kind enough to read through the book and offer me his extremely invaluable inputs. Am very thankful to Ram.

My gratitude is due to the Honourable President of India, Shri Pranab Mukherjee, who spared his valuable time for a conversation with me on his former boss and mentor. I have taken the liberty of quoting from his detailed memoirs of the Indira Gandhi years.

It was also a pleasure to spend time in Raebareli and Allahabad to meet many old-timers and veteran associates of the Nehrus and Gandhis. I am thankful to all who spoke to me and shared photographs, letters, memorabilia and personal recollections.

All of Indira Gandhi's letters and personal writings are still not available although two volumes of her correspondence with Nehru have been published in the Sonia Gandhi edited selections: *Freedom's Daughter* and *Two Alone, Two Together.* I found these volumes invaluable. Katherine Frank's biography of Indira Gandhi is packed with details, and I have particularly drawn on Frank for Indira's years overseas.

Through the book, readers will notice that I have used the reminiscences of Pupul Jayakar, Usha Bhagat, B.K. Nehru and Dr K.P. Mathur a great deal. This is because they were closely and personally associated with Indira Gandhi over the years and vital witnesses to many events in her life. In that sense I have treated them as interviewees, like Moni Malhoutra and Natwar Singh, and drawn heavily upon their memories of a woman most of whose contemporaries are no longer with us.

Thanks are due to my friends Mahesh Rangarajan, Suraj Kumar and Barun Mitra who read through drafts of the book and gave me the huge benefit of their insights. After almost three decades in journalism, there are many colleagues and fellow reporters, both seniors as well as peers, who through the years have been supportive and stimulating friends. Dileep Padgaonkar and Vinod Mehta were dream bosses who gave me the space and guidance to chronicle the excitement of a changing India.

My thanks to my editors at Juggernaut Books: the luminous Chiki Sarkar whose deep perception and enthusiasm enhance every book she commissions. The wise Nandini Mehta and the brilliant Parth Mehrotra were engaged, and inspiring.

The most important person to thank as always is my best friend and the kindest human being I know: my husband Rajdeep. To him and to my beloved children Ishan and Tarini I will always be indebted for their constant love and unfailing encouragement.

Index

Click the QR Code with a QR scanner app
or type the link into the Internet browser
on your phone to download the app.

SCAN TO READ THIS BOOK ON YOUR PHONE

www.juggernaut.in

DOWNLOAD THE APP

www.juggernaut.in